Radical Egalitarianism

I0085579

Radical Egalitarianism

LOCAL REALITIES, GLOBAL RELATIONS

Edited by

FELICITY AULINO, MIRIAM GOHEEN, AND
STANLEY J. TAMBIAH

FORDHAM UNIVERSITY PRESS

New York 2013

Copyright © 2013 Fordham University Press

All rights reserved. No part of this publication may be reproduced, stored in a retrieval system, or transmitted in any form or by any means—electronic, mechanical, photocopy, recording, or any other—except for brief quotations in printed reviews, without the prior permission of the publisher.

Fordham University Press has no responsibility for the persistence or accuracy of URLs for external or third-party Internet websites referred to in this publication and does not guarantee that any content on such websites is, or will remain, accurate or appropriate.

Fordham University Press also publishes its books in a variety of electronic formats. Some content that appears in print may not be available in electronic books.

Library of Congress Cataloging-in-Publication Data

Radical egalitarianism : local realities, global relations / edited by Felicity Aulino, Miriam Goheen, and Stanley J. Tambiah.
    pages cm
    Includes bibliographical references.
    ISBN 978-0-8232-4189-7 cloth
    ISBN 978-0-8232-4190-3 pbk.
    1. Ethnology.   2. Ethnology—Sociological aspects.
3. Sociology.   4. Social sciences   5. Culture and globalization.   6. Equality—Philosophy.   I. Aulino, Felicity.
    GN320.R28 2013
    305—dc23

                                                    2012041921

15 14 13   5 4 3 2 1
First edition

CONTENTS

Introduction: Engaging Radical Egalitarianism

Felicity Aulino and Miriam Goheen

This book represents a form of historically grounded, ethnographically driven anthropology that seeks to understand social phenomena by dialogically engaging global and local perspectives. As a whole,
it promotes an approach to scholarship that actively avoids privileg-
ing any one conceptual framework or cultural form at the expense
of recognizing another—a style of engagement that we are calling
radical egalitarianism. The papers collected here provide examples
of such an approach through original ethnographic and theoretical
contributions that stem from research in Africa, Europe, Asia, and the
Americas. Assembled into a single volume, these chapters allow for
a comparative examination of contemporary societies along several
avenues of inquiry.

All of the contributors to this volume are in conversation with some
aspect of the work of Stanley J. Tambiah.[1] From his earliest research
on village agriculture and land tenure in Sri Lanka to his recent engagement with issues of reproductive technologies and perceptions
of the self among Sri Lankan immigrants, Tambiah's work has demonstrated remarkable breadth and depth in both topic and theoretical

approach. Ethnographically focused primarily in South and South-east Asia, his work includes studies of religious syncretism, kinship and marriage systems, the relationships between religion and politics, ethnonationalist politics, multiple forms of rationality, theories of ritual, meaning in non-Western thought systems, and communal violence. A cosmopolitan figure in the larger worlds of the social sciences and humanities, Tambiah has produced a corpus of work that is drawn on by scholars in a wide range of disciplines.

Throughout this variegated field are two overarching concerns: (1) respect for creative human differences, what Tambiah has called "multiple orientations to the world"; and (2) the political potentialities of difference (both positive and negative) as historically constituted. From this standpoint, Tambiah has offered related insights into the historical development of social scientific categories and socio-political categories, and has raised vital questions regarding the possibilities of achieving equality and justice in the presence of competing realities. These matters lie at the heart of radical egalitarianism and form the backbone of the concerns of this volume.

Interlocking Themes

This introduction is intended as a brief guide to key themes in Tambiah's work, themes that are not only at the root of the articles presented here, but are also critical for the future of the social sciences and area studies alike.

First and foremost, Tambiah's anthropology insists on historical analysis. *World Conquerer and World Renouncer* (1976) is a prime example. In that monograph, Thai religion and society come into clearer focus as Tambiah traces the history and logic of Thai kingship and corresponding political structures. Drawing on historical data in this way counters would-be scholastic presumptions. For instance, Tambiah deploys the phrase *galactic polity* to depict a decentralized constellation of influence that typifies administrative realities in the past without relying on contemporary presumptions regarding bureaucratic hierarchy. This is but one of many examples; history figures large in many of Tambiah's writings, including *Bridewealth and Dowry* (co-authored with Jack Goody, 1973), *The Buddhist Saints of the Forest and the Cult of Amulets* (1984), *Buddhism Betrayed? Religion, Politics, and Violence in Sri Lanka* (1992), and *Leveling Crowds: Ethnonationalist Conflicts and Collective Violence in South Asia* (1996).

Such a method goes beyond the comparative tradition of Boas and his students and adds a dimension of movement, of trajectory, to historical accounts, without losing sight of primary contradictions and meanings as they are negotiated through time.[2] Due to the dialogical nature of Tambiah's work, he is able to describe the complex realities of global discourse, composed simultaneously of flows and structures, with its relentless interplay among various social formations and ceaseless negotiations between internal and external meanings and forms of power. In cinematic metaphor, this is akin to seeing the moving picture when all you have at any given point is a snapshot. Tambiah conceptualizes continuity and change acting simultaneously, necessary as they both are to any description of the social totality or formation in question.[3] He recognizes some continuities as more potent than others, forming ongoing dialectics of necessary contradictions that are not negated or transformed but are seldom resolved and continue to inform the history of the totality through time.[4] Neither structure nor system disappears, nor are they moribund or stagnant. Thus we find an insistence on history and context as a prerequisite to understanding the present meanings and overarching cosmologies in any given society.

This dual emphasis on history and context also leads to an insistence on the rationality of all societies. Tambiah's *Magic, Science, Religion, and the Scope of Rationality* (1990) is a significant contribution to the history of ideas in this regard, as he traces the antecedents of the debates on magic and science in the humanities and the social sciences. Tambiah understands there to be multiple rationalities in the world. But whereas standard notions of cultural relativism can leave one without a basis for taking an ethical stance, Tambiah's resolve to assess social totalities provides grounds for understanding the local roots of social oppression and the means by which adequately to judge moral worth, both from within the local context and from the outside. *Leveling Crowds* (1996) provides a compelling example of this theory in practice, as Tambiah traces the specific origins of ethnonationalist conflict in South Asia as someone quite troubled by the violence it entails.

Finally, appreciating how context and history inform Tambiah's discernment of social totalities, all rational in their own right, leads us to the importance of meaning in Tambiah's work. Of course the emphasis is on meaning within the logic of context, more than on meaning in the psychological sense. Tambiah's "A Performative Approach to Ritual" ([1979] 1981) demonstrates this well. In it Tambiah draws on Austin's speech-act theory to elucidate rituals as constitutive acts—like marriage vows, baptism, the naming of a ship—and on Peirce's three-part classification of signs to infer the communication of understanding in ritual performance. In that article as elsewhere, Tambiah integrates formal analysis into a cultural account to elucidate meaning and its structure. Such analyses then open out to the exploration of political power and can make comprehensible the motivations for and particular maneuvers of political action, for instance, in terms of the larger framework in which they occur.

These four interlocking themes of history, context, rationality, and meaning all inform the engagement with radical egalitarianism in this volume. This then is not a simple stance that emphasizes individual rights and extends liberal largess toward those "less fortunate." It is a deep and abiding appreciation of the value of difference and a commitment to the kind of careful scholarship that can adequately bring the contours of a given society or situation to light. Such scholarship cannot and does not adhere to any one particular lens of theorizing. As Tambiah would say, "You use what works!"[5]

As proponents of this sort of radical egalitarianism, the authors in this volume use "what works." Rather than exemplifying a particular school of thought or promoting a single theoretical vantage point, the authors here follow Tambiah's lead, focusing on the significance of context, the importance of ethnography and historical analyses, and the need to see societies as totalities. They argue the urgency of constructing inclusive ways of knowing in the twenty-first century. They promote a diversity of knowledge that does not privilege Western discourse but draws on it for understanding. And they share a commitment to humanitarianism alongside a demand for global solutions rooted in local meanings and understanding.

The Essays

This volume is divided thematically into three sections: "Religion, Trade, and Transnational Networks via Thailand"; "Cosmologies, Ideologies, and Localities"; and "Violence, Political Conflict, and Humanitarian Intervention." Like the loose description of key elements of Tambiah's scholarship above, however, the thematic division suggested by these section titles is loose: many of the papers here demonstrate elements from all three themes, reflecting the rich complexity of thought and analysis promoted throughout the collection.

Stanley Tambiah provides the first selection of the volume. In "The Charisma of Saints and the Cult of Relics, Amulets, and Tomb Shrines" he offers a sample of a comparative project that identifies the "organic affinity" among saints and related objects across religious traditions. He draws largely from Buddhist and Christian examples, with additional reference to Sufi and other Islamic sources, to argue that saints are in fact "creators of community and conduits to the divine or to the supramundane." Tambiah revisits important pieces of earlier scholarship to make vital differentiations in the classifications of holy objects and religious followers. He shows that saints have commonalities across religions, but more than that, he contends that saints in fact *constitute* communities as much as they serve as a religious model for them. Tambiah demonstrates how saints, through social engagements and "objectified" charisma—both when they are alive and after death—can help us to trace political and economic lineages; moreover, they provide the links that allow and indeed constitute the power passed therein. Harking back to his extensive work on commensurability, ritual, semiotics, and center-periphery relations, Tambiah offers here a glimpse of an enormous scholastic project with great future potential.

The second article, James Taylor's "Understanding Social Totalities: Stanley Tambiah's Early Contribution to Sociology of Thai Religion," first provides a synopsis of Tambiah's work in Thailand, particularly his use of Weber and the notion of "totalization" relevant to this section's themes of religion and transnational networks. Taylor goes on to offer a "Tambiahan analysis" of Thai forest monks, or the *dhutanga Kammaṭṭhāna* tradition. Here he uses historical and linguistic tools to discuss the *vinaya*, or monastic disciplinary charter, and its connection to affiliation lines distinct from—and often hidden by—nationally recognized sects. He concludes that "Tambiah was correct in his early analysis of Thai Buddhism as he emphasized a need to see the religion as a dialectical relationship between doctrinal, textual perspectives on the world, and action within the world as a consequence of historical transformation"—and his own ethnographic contribution supports this agreement in important detail. Ingrid Jordt in turn offers a "view from Burma" in her "Transnational Buddhism and the Transformations of Local Power in Thailand." She focuses on a key figure from

Tambiah's research, Phra Phimolatham, and his Burmese counterpart, Mahasi Sayadaw, as a means of delineating the political landscape of Thai monastic reform and exploring the transnational ties between the Thai and Burmese sanghas during key years of national development. Jordt connects the lay meditation movement following Mahasi's teachings to the colonial landscape in Burma, revealing another angle of the viniya reforms and sectarian divisions brought out in Taylor's piece. She argues that the visits between Phra Phimolatham and Mahasi Sayadaw can be seen "as a form of Buddhist diplomacy." Despite the ultimate political ramifications (namely, Phimolatham's forced disrobing and six-year imprisonment), she traces "cultural models by which Buddhism travels in the region and beyond" and the "possibilities [that] existed for Phimolatham (and for us today) for a nonsectarian and indeed a nonnationalist Buddhism."

Drawing on the same period of nationalization in Thailand discussed by Taylor and Jordt, Irving Johnson concludes the first section with a discussion of Kelantan Buddhist monks and their communities along the Thai/Malay border—communities that have increasingly drawn upon a "system of Thai Buddhist cultural patronage emanating from Bangkok" while strategically maintaining political and social ties to the Malay sultan. In "A Muslim King and his Buddhist Subjects: Religion, Power, and Identity at the Periphery of the Thai State," we are asked to consider notions of the galactic polity, with an ethnographic case study from the periphery of the Thai state. In this short piece, Johnson considers the role of the Muslim Malay sultan as he in some ways stands in for the Buddhist monarch as protector of the Dharma in this small, distinctly non-Buddhist region. Johnson paints a picture of a people positioned between two polities, of "Kelantanese Thais living on the frontiers of two colonially imagined states" and how they "continue to define themselves based on the way powerful centers of power impact on their lives."

Michael Puett and Prista Ratanapruck open Part II of the volume, "Comparing Cosmologies, Ideologies, and Localities," with pieces that bring to bear Part I's themes of religion, trade, and transnational networks in an expanded arena. In "Economies of Ghosts, Gods, and Goods: The History and Anthropology of Chinese Temple Networks," Puett follows a trail of Chinese ghost stories to vast temple networks that he claims are again on the rise in China and beyond. To understand these networks, which have significant religious and economic implications, Puett also describes an ontology of discontinuity fundamental to the creation and continuation of these networks' connections. He recounts Tambiah's assertions about such ontologies—in which the world is fragmented and humans must impose order and harmony—and their distinction from ontologies of continuity, upon which so many Western cosmologies and contemporary theories are based. With historical acumen and vital ethnographic data, Puett is thus able to challenge popular readings of what is taking place in contemporary China. As he asserts, any perspective that lacks the insight offered by a more totalizing analysis such as this "misconstrues the economy and society of so-called premodern China" and "misses a very significant aspect of the resurgence of these older economic patterns." Ratanapruck too promotes such an alternative appreciation of economic and religious patterns in "Trade, Religion, and Civic Relations in the Manangi Long-Distance Trade Community." Here she discusses the cosmological underpinnings of Manangi trade, with accounts of religious tributes and wealth redistribution. Both Puett and Ratanapruck take up Tambiah's ideas to promote reconceptualization of unexamined assumptions. Puett thus captures a core intention of this collection as he writes: "An anthropology worthy of its name is one that will take non-Western theories of the self, ritual, statecraft, and economy seriously and allow them to help us question the Western narratives and frameworks that are still too often taken for granted."

James Ferguson obliquely heeds this call in his "Cosmologies of Welfare: Two Conceptions of Social Assistance in Contemporary South Africa" by putting economic issues squarely in the realm of cosmological inquiry. In his examination of the Basic Income Grant (BIG) proposed for South Africa, Ferguson succeeds in making the familiar unfamiliar as he uncovers the cosmological frameworks implicit in this new welfare scheme, marking a shift from a social democratic standpoint to what he calls a neoliberal frame.

Moving north from South Africa to Nigeria, Victor Manfredi's "'A Recurrence of Structures' in Collapsing Nigeria" next turns on Tambiah's Southeast Asian "galactic polity" to probe parallel "Asiatic" social formations in Atlantic Africa. Manfredi details the history of an Ágbọ̀ land dispute, which he argues can be seen as "an instance of galactic 'pulsation between modalities.'" He thereby uses Tambiah's theoretical lens to prompt a careful reconstruction and reconsideration of past events in Nigeria. Manfredi locally recasts events otherwise too easily rendered in a colonial tone (anthropological or

otherwise), with particular attention to language and the ramifications of the United States' current global presence.

Where Manfredi implicitly critiques the anthropological trend of
"othering," Mariza Peirano takes it on directly, drawing attention to
another key aspect of the volume as a whole, namely the importance
of a tight connection between ethnography and theory. In her article
"People and Ideas Travel Together: Tambiah's Approach to Ritual and
Cosmology in Brazil," Peirano traces the influence Tambiah has had
on anthropology in Brazil, providing an informative bibliography that
follows a number of theoretical threads from Tambiah's research—
with welcome attention to "Tambiah's transformation of ritual from
a classical empirical subject to an analytical tool" and his characteristic "combining [of] microethnography and macrosociology." In this
piece, as throughout the section, we see Tambiah's influence on the
field of anthropology in the use of close historical and ethnographic
context in service of totalizing analyses that lead to rich theoretical
openings. Peirano ends with a call for a closer look at Tambiah's *Leveling Crowds*, as does Sahlins in Part III, as a means of understanding
how microevents turn into larger social issues, and vice versa.

Michael Herzfeld concludes Part II with a piece entitled "Paradoxes of Order in Thai Community Politics." Reflecting on political
negotiations in his field site of Pom Mahakan—a small, contested
community in Bangkok's Rattanakosin Island—Herzfeld once again
returns us to Thailand. His analysis demonstrates the continued util-
ity of Tambiah's ideas of the galactic polity, ritual, and performance
for elucidating political subtleties in a country where cryptocolonial
surface structures belie the ambiguities of social practices that are
themselves a "more identifiably indigenous strain in the political
thought of the residents and their leaders." Herzfeld unpacks the uses
of national symbolism and the "global hierarchy of value" in this Thai
community's struggle for survival. He documents the formality of
group meetings and other tactical engagements in which, he claims,
the "highly ritualistic performance does not in the least undermine
its performative force." In concluding this section on cosmologies,
ideologies, and localities, Herzfeld does not attempt to analyze contemporary communities in terms of sacred geometry or the reproduction of traditional configurations. He does, however, show how
"ethnographic observation opens up some of the intimate spaces of
social life that official ideology deliberately occludes." Here he draws
on the rich frames of Tambiah's work to assess the historical links and

present-day implications of his observations on political conflict, providing a natural segue to the book's next set of themes.

The third section of the volume focuses on violence, political conflict, and humanitarian intervention. Marshall Sahlins introduces these topics with his article "Structural Work: How Microhistories Become Macrohistories and Vice Versa," in which he brings Tambiah's notions of transvaluation and parochialization to bear on a vital discussion of "how small issues are turned into Big Events." Sahlins draws on the three examples of Elián Gonzalez, seventeenth- through nineteenth-century Catalan peasants, and Greek city-states during the Peloponnesian War to understand structural patterns. Whereas in this collection's first article Tambiah uses the concepts of *transvaluation* and *focalization* to elucidate a general phenomenon of saints and amulets across religions, Sahlins takes on these concepts to uncover "the dynamics of structural amplification"—drawing out the section's themes with formal significance.

Mary-Jo DelVecchio Good and Byron Good next take up issues of ethnonational conflict in "Perspectives on the Politics of Peace in Aceh, Indonesia." Building on Tambiah's 1996 avowal that "something has gone awry in center-periphery relations throughout the world," their paper examines how "crises, such as natural disasters or conflicts, and a society's accommodation to humanitarian responses, reveal larger social and political forces usually hidden from view." Drawing on their rich ethnographic experience in the region since the devastating 2004 tsunami, the Goods suggest that Aceh is now a "kind of laboratory for new forms of governance," an experimental case study in decentralization in the midst of delicate peace negotiations brokering the end of a gruesome, decades-long struggle. In the end, the situation in Aceh is brought into clearer relief through comparison with parallel events in Sri Lanka. One country sustains peace while another tumbles back into violent clashes in the face of an enormous natural disaster. This underscores for the authors the continued importance of Tambiah's call for "sustained comparative examination of ethnonational conflicts," with ramifications for understanding varied forms of governance, reconciliation, and humanitarian aid.

Liisa Malkki approaches the ethics and politics of humanitarian practices from another angle in her discussion of the International Committee of the Red Cross. Her "Tale of Two Affects" presents a depiction of two contradictory yet interdependent sensibilities present

in international aid—the humanitarian sensibility on one hand, and
the professional sensibility on the other. Malkki employs the compelling example of "aid bunnies," handmade stuffed animals donated by
thousands of well-intentioned knitters. This example draws attention
to a "shared, universalizing social imagination of human need and
suffering 'out in the world'" as well as to the international professionals who at times rely on the "humanitarian affect" for funds and a certain degree of protection. She calls for an appreciation of professionalism as a kind of affect, and in the end proposes that occupational
categories can help us see beyond "states of exception" even in zones
of brutal devastation.

Emiko Ohnuki-Tierney closes the section with her piece "At the
Base of Local and Transnational Conflicts: The Political Uses of Inferiorization." Again emphasizing the importance of extensive historical
and ethnographic data for incisive theoretical perspectives, Ohnuki-
Tierney illuminates the causes of violent clashes with their concomitant ideological underpinnings with an analysis of the United States'
"master narrative" for the attacks of September 11, 2001, in comparison to the discourse it created concerning the attack on Pearl Harbor
during World War II. Here she points out noteworthy, unnerving parallels between these two storylines, particularly in terms of their use
of stereotyping, as she advocates "us-ing" rather than "other-ing" and
demonstrates the power of scholarship for deconstructing the means
by which war is propagated.

Michael Fischer's afterword brings the collection full circle, returning once more to Tambiah and our conversations with him in this
volume. Fisher offers an extended introduction to Tambiah's work for
those who are unfamiliar with it, and a biographically rich review for
those to whom Tambiah's opus is already well known. Entitled "Galactic Polities, Radical Egalitarianism, and the Practice of Anthropology:
Tambiah on Logical Paradoxes, Social Contradictions, and Cultural
Oscillations," this piece revisits the theme of radical egalitarianism,
drawing out the paradoxical and fraught nature of the term and the
multiple meanings it assumes in varying contexts. Beyond the style
of anthropological engagement we claim for it here, Fischer traces six
iterations of the theme of radical egalitarianism in Tambiah's work,
moving from Buddhist monks renouncing the world yet maintaining
a claim to guide it, to forms of colonialist "egalitarian nostalgia" and
socialist and fundamentalist utopianism; from wealth redistribution
schemes and social welfare politics, to the "juggernaut of mass par-

ticipatory politics." He reweaves the themes of the volume, stitching in ideas of cosmic rituals, charismatic circuits, and collective violence to complement the existing organization of the book by drawing additional connections between pieces. With unusual insight, Fischer highlights some of the most exciting elements of Tambiah's eclectic and rich contribution to knowledge; he provides a lens for understanding why these intellectual contributions have been the source of inspiration for several generations of scholars, and gives a sense of how they will continue to inspire many more to follow.

This volume would not have been possible without generous contributions from many friends and colleagues. Special thanks are due to everyone who contributed here, as well as to those who attended the overflowing panels that in part gave rise to this volume. Much gratitude goes to the organizers of the 2007 American Anthropological Association panel—Saipin Suputtamongkol, Prista Ratanapruck, Deborah Tooker, and Felicity Aulino. Thanks also to Saipin Suputtamongkol and Michael Herzfeld, organizers of the panel at the 2008 International Thai Studies Conference in Bangkok. We thank Engseng Ho, Deborah Tooker, John Kelley, Thongchai Winichikul, and Paritta Chalermpow Koanantakool, who were key discussants in those sessions. We are indebted to James Boon and Elizabeth Traube for their insightful comments on the collection. And very special thanks go to Michael Puett, Michael Herzfeld, and especially Mary-Jo Delvecchio Good, who were particularly key to the production of this volume and have provided immeasurable support in the process.

Decades after the utterance, the wisdom of Tambiah's intellectual call to arms cannot be overestimated:

> Now, then, might be the proper time for anthropologists—for whom a "totalized" account of how the various levels and domains of man's life intersect and hang together is a necessary entailment of their disciplinary perspective—to infiltrate health care, the legal system, and other domains, and to maintain strenuously that the physical and the mental in man, his sense of person and self and of his rights and obligations, are embedded in his social relations, and these again in the collectivities of family, occupation, class, community, and nation. The times are appropriate to reiterate and demonstrate that the pursuit of social sanity and prosperity requires the broadening of the frontiers of knowledge into areas

which, because they are difficult to quantify or to atomize and reduce to the models of molecular biology and genetics, should not therefore be abandoned as worthless or subversive to orthodoxy. (Tambiah 1985a, 355)

Tambiah remains a leader for anthropologists, who perhaps are now more than ever ready to heed his call.

PART I

Religion, Trade, and Transnational Networks via Thailand

.

The Charisma of Saints and the Cult of Relics, Amulets, and Tomb Shrines

Stanley Jeyaraja Tambiah

As a sequel to my third monograph on Thailand—*The Buddhist Saints of the Forest and the Cult of Amulets* (Tambiah 1984)—I have begun a comparative study that aspires to span *some* Christian, Islamic, Buddhist, and Hindu traditions with regard to their characterization of saints and the cults of relics, amulets, and shrine worship associated with them. In this essay I cannot realistically cover all the dimensions of the comparative project I have embarked on and which I hope others will consider. The main question I wish to probe is why ordinary worldlings are elevated and edified by, and draw energies from, the labors of the "athletes of God," as early Christianity hailed its saintly martyrs, of "the canker-waned *arahants*" (perfected saints), as classical Buddhism venerated them, and of the *auliya' Allah,* or "the friends or protégés of God," as the Qur'an celebrated them.

Lest you think that I have chosen a topic too remote in time and experience from contemporary sensibilities and modern concerns, let me cite a few paragraphs from an article by Alan Riding that appeared in the *New York Times* of April 15, 1989, under the title "Vatican 'Saint Factory': Is It Working Too Hard?":

> Despite a Roman Catholic calendar already so crowded that some days are shared by several saints, Pope John Paul II has sharply increased the number of saints honored by the church, apparently in the hope that devout role models can help reinforce the Christian faith.
>
> Complementing his frequent trips abroad, he has also made a point of reaching out to the third world to find examples of long-forgotten martyrs and 'heroically virtuous' Christians worthy of canonization or beatification, which is the first step toward sainthood.
>
> As a result, in his first 10 years in office, John Paul has already carried out 254 canonizations and 305 beatifications, far more than all previous Popes together in this century. Furthermore, the number of candidates for beatification has swollen to more than 2,000....
>
> ... Pope John Paul has been able to step up canonizations and beatifications thanks to a simplification of the procedure over the last 20 years. For example, while giving local bishops responsibility for initiating cases of canonization, the Pope ruled in 1983 that only one miracle—instead of the traditional two—would be needed in each case. (Riding 1989)

John Paul II's penchant for making pious visits to both great and remote shrines has elicited the remark that he had an "apparently insatiable appetite for visiting sanctuaries" (Sox 1985).[1] He was particularly attached to Marian shrines: "There have been the widely publicized papal visits to Lourdes, Fatima, Czechtokowa and Knock, but lesser known are his visits to venerate the Turin Shroud, the Eucharistic Miracle of Lanciano, the Holy House of Loretto, Our Lady of the Miracle at the Church of St. Andrea della Fratte in Rome, among many others" (ibid., 6).[2]

The purpose of my citation of the *New York Times* article is not to poke fun at the former Pope's sponsorship and extension of the cult of saints, but to underscore the point that the phenomenon is not simply archaic—that it also massively appeals to contemporary sensibilities.

The question then arises: why does the cult of saints have such a general appeal both in space and time?

The Saint as a Cultural Type and Social Person

The veneration of saints, and the literary genre of biographies and hagiographies of saints—however stereotyped and ritualized they may be—raise the general question of why societies and cultures committed to diverse religious traditions, including Christian, Islamic, Hindu and Buddhist, have at all times, but more intensely at certain times, responded to the lives of the saints—that is, to the attributes, virtues, and acts of saints as celebrated and outstanding individual persons. Is there a "spontaneous" inclination in human life to think and experience power and influence in personal terms? Are there special times and circumstances when these person-focused phenomena have a special appeal? It looks as if the stories of saints, as stories of individual lives, are an effective way of focusing religiosity. It seems as if religiosity in turn finds an effective representation, embodiment, and enactment in the charismatic virtuoso, and in some ways attains a greater potency and persuasiveness in his or her person than through the medium of abstract dogma and intellectual doctrines.

A Methodological Note

There are, I readily recognize, important methodological and substantive issues that need to be recognized and clarified in this comparative enterprise.

For example, each religion may have its own cluster and configuration of thematic concerns which have to be appreciated in relation to that religion's cosmological contours and moral concerns. If we recognize ascetic and contemplative regimes as central to the conception of sainthood as a general category, we have nevertheless to bear in mind that those regimes may have different positional values and weight in different religious complexes.

Thus Ernest Troeltsch makes it quite clear that in the "organic" whole of Christianity a variety of tendencies already present in the early Gospels—ascetic, secular, and theocratic—existed side by side in a cosmos of mutual recognition, but that asceticism never occupied a position of supremacy in the medieval Christian Church. In the Buddhist cosmos of callings, however, contemplative meditation and ascetic renunciation are prime constituents of the apical and exemplary calling for monks and are recognized as such by the laity. (The same may be said of the Jain expectations of their saints—the *tirthankars* and *jinas*; see, for example, Babb 1993). Sufi mysticism has its own configuration of emphases; aside from love of God and the practice of asceticism, it emphasizes the mystery of initiation and spiritual progress through a well-established hierarchy within the brotherhood (*tariqa*).

I can think of at least two problems of translation and glossing which have to be faced in an extended comparative treatment. One is the question of the extent to which the word *saint*, which derives from a Christian context, overlaps with the term *wali* in Islam, *arahant* in Buddhism, and so on. The other relates to the possibility that within each tradition, the term in question—*saint* in Christianity, *wali* in Islam, *arahant* in Buddhism—may encompass a continuum of characteristics, and a range of attributes or a spectrum of persons, which at best portray a family of resemblance rather than a single unambiguous exemplary type. The literature of experts shows variant responses to these two issues. But by and large there is support for my supposition that there is a family resemblance between the conceptions of "saint" and "sainthood" in the religious traditions I am discussing, and that within each tradition one can make a case for a "focal" characterization, although the whole category may not be clearly bounded and may overlap with other categories or personae at the edges.[3]

My comparative enterprise will not I think be ruled out of court by those who are sympathetic to the proposals of William Brede Kristensen, the Egyptologist and scholar of the religions of the Mediterranean basin, who saw the phenomena of one tradition illuminated by their comparison with similar phenomena in historically and geographically proximate traditions. Kristensen went so far as to say that the study of religion on these lines "takes out of their historical setting the similar facts and phenomena which it encounters in different religions, brings them together, and studies them in groups. The corresponding data, which are sometimes nearly identical, bring us automatically to comparative study. The purpose of such study is to become acquainted with the religious thought, idea or need which underlies the group of corresponding data" (Kristensen 1971, 1–2).

While I by no means devalue historical, contextual, and circumstantial particulars, and while I am fully aware that as totalities as well as in their internal differentiations and emphases, there are distinct differences in the religious complexes I am examining,[4] I wish to pursue in this study the entailments of the possibility that differences between traditions do not rule out some interesting convergences.[5]

So my beginning question is whether in some selected major religious traditions, where sainthood is recognized and institutionalized, there exists a set of shared conceptions about the profiles of their highest achievers, namely: the *saint* in Christianity, the *wali* or *siyid* in Islam, the *arahant* in Theravada Buddhism, the *siddha* in Hinduism, the great *lama* of Tibetan Buddhism, the *tsaddik* in Hasidism, the *guru sahib* in Sikhism, and so on.

William James, in *The Varieties of Religious Experience,* made a general assertion that at first blush sounds odd in these days of postmodern deconstruction with its relativist implications and questioning of consensual knowledge and of authorial objectivity. James wrote:

> The collective name for the ripe fruits of religion in a character is Saintliness. The saintly character is the character for which spiritual emotions are the habitual center of the personal energy; and there is a certain composite photograph of universal saintliness, the same in all religions, of which the features can easily be traced. (1904, 271)

James thus suggested that the essential features of saintliness as conceived in many religions formed a coherent set that constituted the profile of the saint. He also seemed to postulate that this profile of religious sensibilities, forming an "organic unity," was discoverable in the major religious traditions whatever their substantive differences (280). As I describe James's composite photograph I shall cross-reference some of its features to well-known Buddhist concepts.

James distinguished "inner conditions" of the following kinds as having practical consequences in the lives of saints. Saints practice asceticism, and their "self surrender may become so passionate as to turn into self-immolation." They have a "strength of soul," because "as personal motives and inhibitions become insignificant, blissful equanimity takes their place" (273). (We are reminded here of the threefold Buddhist concepts of *karuna* [compassion], *metta* [loving kindness], and *upekha* [detachment].) "The cleansing of existence from brutal and sensual elements becomes imperative" in their life, thereby leading to a state of purity. (The famous text of Buddhaghosa, *Visuddhimagga* [Path of Purity], comes to mind here.) In some temperaments "this need of purity of spirit takes on an ascetic turn, and weaknesses of the flesh are treated with relentless severity" (273). The saints' tenderness toward fellow-creatures comes to be labeled as charity. "Like love or fear, the faith-state is a natural psychic complex, and carries charity with it by organic consequence" (279). The saint manifests "brotherly love" and he "loves his enemies, and treats loathsome beggars as his brothers." As in the cases of Francis of Assisi and Ignatius Loyola, who exchanged their garments with those of filthy beggars, it can be said that "the inhibition of instinctive repugnance is proved not only by the showing of love to enemies, but also by the showing of it to anyone who is personally loathsome" (284).[6]

The appropriateness of my cross-referencing some of James's essential features of universal saintliness, primarily drawn from Christian notions, to some well-known Buddhist concepts, is partially sustained by reference to the writings of Evagrius of Pontus, one of the most important of the Desert Fathers of fourth-century Egypt, who "established himself as a master practitioner of the ascetic discipline of these Christian solitaries," and became a famous teacher of the "emerging discipline of contemplative prayer" (Linge 2000, 538). While of course Evagrius's thought has deep Christian theological and Platonic philosophical underpinnings, what impresses me is his exposition, based on disciplinary practice, of the stages of ascetic purification and the experiential path of purification by which the ascetic ascends to union with the divine. Expressions such as "purity of heart," "singleness of mind," the state of tranquility leading to *apatheia* (dispassion), appear in the ascetic teaching (ibid., 553 and 557). Linge opines that Evagrius's discussion of "a reflective dimension of ascetic practice" marks a "fruitful area of convergence with Buddhism," especially Theravada Buddhist "doctrinal truths such as 'impermanence, unsatisfactoriness, and impersonalness of all things' as set forth in the *Abhidhamma* literature, and the monk's understanding of them as subjects of *vipassana* meditation" (560).

The Impact of Saints on the World

Let me now introduce the proposition that saints are not so much models of virtue to be actually imitated by their lay followers as they are creators of community and conduits to the divine or to the supramundane. This assertion poses for us the problem of how to describe and account for the saints, who are devoted to a transcendental quest but seem to have an impact on the world that they wish to transcend. This very detachment from the world, and its transcendence, appears to give them, especially in the eyes of the ordinary laity, extraordinary capacities to influence it. This attribution and interaction is a central problem, or paradox if you will, that we have to construe. One suggestion might be that saints as renouncers, after achieving detachment from and transcendence of this world, are seen as returning to the world and being effective in it, dispensing loving kindness and advice, without being caught up in the chains of reciprocity and therefore escaping the "impurity" and obligations of the gift. Another suggestion is that the ascetic regime is a form of "self-sacrifice" or "violence" imposed on oneself, and this act of abnegation has a kind of redeeming value; the regime is tantamount to achieving a living death that is not touched by causality and the terminality of mortal death. At this point we can only wonder at these possibilities.

The Holy Men of Roman Antiquity

Using William James as a point of departure for our journey, let us make as our first stop two essays by Peter Brown that self-consciously juxtapose two characterizations of the saint in Late Roman Antiquity. The first is "The Rise and Function of the Holy Man in Late Antiquity" (1971), and its successor, some twelve years later, is "The Saint as Exemplar in Late Antiquity" (1983). Although Brown views his second essay as a passage to a new paradigm, I feel that this sense of contrast is of his own making, in that, having in his first essay missed dimensions that he did not perceive in Late Antiquity, he later fills in the blank spaces in the light of new knowledge and new perspectives. In fact, as those of us who have studied and written with ampler information about the cult of saints in other places and contexts know, both perspectives should be combined to construct a composite mural.

Peter Brown's first classic essay, "The Rise and Function of the Holy Man," is centrally concerned with the issue of the basis of the ascetical saint's impact on the world, which Brown expounds in a thoroughgoing anthropological mode. The context is the Late Roman society on the fringes of the Mediterranean.

Brown asks a precise historical question: "Why did the holy man come to play such an important role in the Late Roman society of the fifth and sixth centuries, especially in Syria and later in Asia Minor and Palestine?" His answer is that the village communities of the time in which the holy man came to play so vital a role were passing through a crisis of leadership, owing to the withdrawal from rural society of their traditional patrons, the substantial landowners who had mediated relations within rural communities and between them and the outside world of cities and the imperial government.

Brown asserts that the holy men of Syria, "ascetic stars" who figured so importantly in village society, were in fact unattached strangers on the edge of villages. The hermit deliberately placed himself on the mountaintop and looked down on the prosperous villages and the farmers working on the slopes. In this sense "he belonged to a world that was not so much antithetical to village life as marginal." Prominent among his clientele, who comprised the crowd which followed him and made his reputation, were the fluid components of rural life in Syria, the seasonal laborers, the gangs of skilled craftsmen who roamed the mountain villages, and above all, the mobile soldiers of the inland garrisons.

What were the elements in the holy man's position that were most valued by his contemporaries in Syria and elsewhere? Why, when it came to arbitrators and leaders, did the villagers and, to a lesser extent, the townspeople, pick on the unlikely figure of the lone hermit? Because he was the "stranger" *par excellence.* In an illuminating paragraph, Brown writes:

> The life of the holy man (and especially in Syria) is marked by so many histrionic feats of self-mortification that it is easy, at first sight, to miss the deep social significance of asceticism as a long drawn out, solemn ritual of disassociation—of becoming the total stranger. For the society around him, the holy man is the one man who can stand outside the ties of family, and of economic interest; whose attitude to food itself rejected all the ties of solidarity to kin and village that, in the peasant societies of the Near East, had always been expressed by the gesture of eating. He was thought of as a man who owed nothing to society.... His very powers ... were entirely self-created.... [T]he holy man drew his powers from outside the human race: by going to live in the desert, in close identification with an animal kingdom that stood, in the imagination of contemporaries, for the opposite pole of all human society. (Brown 1971, 92)

Thus did the holy man of this time rise to become the quintessential bearer of objectivity in society.

Though Brown did not recognize the connection, his description resonates compellingly and graphically with Buddhist writings that describe the *bhikkhu,* the mendicant monk, as going forth from home into homelessness, and that prescribe for the forest-dwelling monk not only the ascetic practice of eating just one meal a day, but also of accepting food from everyone rich or poor regardless of their social status, and of receiving all foods in the same bowl. What could be better prescriptions for the detached renouncer than these, which adjure him to disregard the social distinctions of the laity and to transcend their culinary tastes and food categories?

Brown further remarks that the holy man of Roman antiquity had in an important sense "achieved" his status. The comparativist sees Buddhist meditation as involving a rigorous and long regime of techniques of dissociation and detachment by which salvation is achieved by individual effort. "Men entrusted themselves to him [the holy man] because he was thought to have won his way to intimacy with God;" he was an "athlete" who had engaged in spectacular labors and won his victories by an enviable mobility. The objective of closeness to a high deity in Christianity is paralleled by the Sufi conception of the saint becoming a friend and protégé of Allah, and by the Hindu siddha's objective of achieving union with God. The strong urge to be peripatetic and avoid rootedness in one place is evident in the careers of the saints in all religious traditions.

Let me now more briefly dwell on the second of Brown's essays mentioned above, "The Saint as Exemplar," which he eccentrically represents as "a [perspectival] move from a largely British tradition of social anthropology to a largely American tradition of cultural anthropology" (1983, 14). He asserts that the single feature of his former description of the holy man in greatest need of revision would be the holy man's "splendid isolation" and his role as ombudsman; in place of that "basically clinical image" of "'removed' decision-maker," Brown would now substitute the portrait of the holy man as "an accessible exemplar," as "a Christ-carrying man" and a representative of "the central value system" who is a part of a "*longue durée* of Jewish and Christian imaginative structures in the Near East ... coming to rest, in the daily life of the Church in the villages, in a tantalising humus of Early Christian liturgy, ritual and prophylaxis" (1983, 14). The chain of associations runs thus: God as exemplar in Jesus; Jesus as exemplar in the saint; the saint as exemplar reflected in the life of ordinary Christian. Asceticism was thus "a way of passing on, in a manner appropriate to the times, the mighty image of the presence of Christ among men" (16). Thus Brown moves the spotlight from the holy man as a distanced solitary to one loved and admired in terms of teacher-pupil relations among an "intimate circle" of persons. The intensity of the master-pupil relationship in the early phases of the ascetic movement of the fourth century ensured the continuity and characteristics of the "Civilization of *Paideia*." Direct force of example was what mattered most.

In his usual evocative language, Brown describes his revelatory task as the study of "the abiding mental structures of the Mediterranean villagers" and of the religious expectations that led "villagers to recognize in a holy man, however spasmodically, imperfectly, and in however self-interested a manner, a figure who distilled in a concrete and accessible form values and expectations that had a lifetime, a viscosity and a resilience that outlived the day-to-day strategies of patronage, 'objectification' and arbitration, whose spoor I had learned to trace, in the sources, with such relish, in individual incidents in the lives of holy men" (14).

Was Brown's shift of paradigms as dramatic, as oppositional and mutually exclusive, as he makes it out to be? Let me in riposte polemically advance here a composite picture based on my own study of Buddhist saints of the forest in Thailand and thereby suggest its plausible wider relevance for comparative study. The holy man as saint has usually three sides simultaneously operative. He is virtually always associated with a circle of disciples who are in a sustained way focused on him and for whom he is an exemplar and teacher of the religious quest, and whom they are motivated to imitate and replicate. He is also surrounded by a larger penumbra of lay supporters and devotees who venerate him and who throng to see him and receive his blessings—this larger penumbra of laity "participate" tenuously and sporadically in the saint's charismatic gifts, but they scarcely think of "imitating" him or her, though they are edified by visits and by being in the presence of the saint. Brown does not differentiate between these two quite different circles of persons, and his formulation of the "accessible exemplar" is too homogeneous and conflated.

Another dimension is that the meditative and contemplative quest, especially for the virtuoso, is a singular individual quest; the adept, while being among a circle of disciples, necessarily periodically "distances" himself and conducts his own isolated vigils and mystical journeys, and thereby attains to higher and higher spiritual states and his "miraculous" charismatic capacities. The Buddhist arahant for instance, may go through quite different phases in his annual calendar—in the rainy season (*vassa*) he may reside in a *wat* and teach his disciples and preach to audiences; in the dry season he may retreat to mountain or remote meditation sites to conduct intensive meditation (he may be accompanied by a few disciples who do their own meditative exercises at their own separate locations). I would suggest that the reclusive life of the early Christian desert saints and the holy men of Late Roman Antiquity might have followed such distinctive phases.

A laudable feature of Brown's second essay is his intent empathetically to delineate the mental structures of the Mediterranean peasants, but his imaginative reconstruction might be a shade too romantic about the saint as exemplar in the ordinary man. The Buddhist evidence in modern Thailand is that the laity are "aired" by the holy man's loving kindness, blessings, powers of *iddhi*, and transference of his objectified charisma through the amulet cult. This phenomenon, which Brown inadvertently dismisses, is a fact that cannot be realistically predicated on the general public's "intimate" knowledge or experience of the exemplar. The saint may be a "replica" of Jesus, but the ordinary layman is not a "replica" of the saint.

To sum up: significant formulations of sainthood in different religious traditions seem to postulate certain core features as distinctive of the quintessential saint as a cultural type and a social conception. Those features that seem to constitute an "organic affinity" are as follows: celibacy and sexual continence; the contemplative life, including the practice of meditation; asceticism, the nonindulgence of the senses, and minimal physical comfort; the vow of poverty and nonpossession of goods; a sense of distance, of detachment, of being a stranger, ensuing from the elimination of the self, and the ethic of detached action; altruistic cosmic love for all beings, and charity as well as neutrality towards all; nonviolence and pacifism; the reclusive life, preferably lived among a community of fellow seekers (exemplified in monasticism); the ability to concentrate on and follow the moment at hand and to realize the nature of process and ephemerality; and the receptivity to and the pursuit of mystical experience, whether it be "union with God" as the supreme being, or reaching a "state of ultimate voidness." Finally, an essential part of this organic unity of constitutive features is that the highest forms of sainthood are achieved and/or sustained through effort and conduct, by following "paths" that are usually specified in terms of regimes, phases, stations, and levels of mystical consciousness.[7] Finally, let me sketch another axis of saintship that combines two notions: in respect of his own religious regime, the saint is an exemplar and a model for imitation among the core community of his disciples following the path; at an extended reach, the saint is a focus of veneration for a larger following of lay devotees who expect to receive gifts of grace, blessings, and other charismatic benefits from him. In this latter aspect, his radiance and cosmic love suffuses the world.

The Saints of Sufism

I have time here only to mention, without developing in detail, some examples from some branches of a different religious tradition, namely Sufi Islam.

Annemarie Schimmel's *Mystical Dimensions of Islam* (1975) is a marvelous account of the tenets of Sufism, and of the central importance of saints (*wilaya*) in that tradition. Hujwiri, the author of one of the oldest Persian treatises, stated that "the principle and foundation of Sufism and knowledge of God rest on saintship" (Schimmel 1975, 199). The saints who are referred to as *auliya' Allah*, the "friends of God," are described as manifesting a combination of traits and attributes that are familiar to us: their gift of divine grace, their love for the Absolute, their asceticism (they possess nothing and are possessed by nothing), their attaining purification by following the path of contemplation and piety, their knowledge gained from God and so different from the legalistic knowledge of the *ulamas*, their love for and taming of wild animals, and finally, critical to popular religiosity, the saints' capacity to perform miracles. I may add that the Sufi saints' miracles (*karamat*) are in many respects similar to the feats of saints described in other religious traditions.

It seems to me that a text such as Spencer Trimingham's *The Sufi Orders in Islam* (1971) might serve as a bridge and a transition from Schimmel's elevated and magisterial exegesis to the practices and concerns of the plethora of Sufi orders that developed and branched through time, and which in their last stage from the fifteenth century onwards attained their final forms of organization and spiritual exercises such as the "veneration for the *shaikh* of the *ta'ifa* [Sufi order] as inheritor of the *baraka* of *wilaya* [saintship]," the practice of a collective *dhikr* (invocation of God's names) "as pivot of the assembly" and of "a cult related to the tombs of holy men," and "the association of *walis*, dead or alive, with the properties embraced by the terms *baraka* and *karamat*" (Trimingham 1971, 103–04).[8]

Let me on this occasion, however, refer to an anthropological study which describes Sufi saintship in a modern context. Michael Gilsenan's *Saint and Sufi in Modern Egypt* (1973) affirms certain basic features about sainthood in a comparative context.[9] Gilsenan's portrait of a modern saint, Salama ibn Hassan Salama, who founded the Sufi Order of Hamidiya Shadhiliya in the poorer quarters of Cairo in the 1920s, carries these features: that Salama led an ascetic life and observed a strict spiritual discipline; that he and his followers were linked by bonds of love, altruism, and compassion, which he showed in abundance; that besides being an eloquent preacher, he was above all a performer of miracles or "acts of grace" (*karamat*); and that he was an effective founder and head of a brotherhood (*tariqa*) of religious practitioners. In short, in Saint Salama we have an eloquent expression, enactment, and realization of the Islamic concept of *baraka*.

Saintly Charisma and the Creation of Community

Let me pursue further the question of the impact of saints on the world they wish to transcend. I previously remarked that saints are in their special ways creators of community and conduits to the divine or the supramundane.

Comparative study suggests that there are two foci around which these attributions cohere. The *world renouncer*, to use a term that has coinage in Buddhist and Hindu contemplative asceticism, has in the past and present exerted a special kind of influence on life in the world, precisely because—having emancipated himself from worldly involvements and having gained a priority in relation to it by burning away all defilements, and by virtue of his detached and impartial yet compassionate love for all beings—he can, as Heesterman (1985) puts it in his explication of the renunciatory ideology, "reenter into relation with the world, where he now enjoys unequalled prestige.... He is no longer a party to the affairs of the world because he is independent from it" (38).[10] Much the same logic seems to inform the manner in which many Christian and Islamic saints are seen as radiating their virtues to their lay devotees, without losing their world-transcending sanctity.

Another focus, closely related to that adumbrated above, directs our attention to a distinctive patterned relation between a saint and his or her followers which we may call, borrowing from Troeltsch (1949), the "circulation of grace" in regard to Christianity, and for Buddhism the "circulation of merit." Troeltsch characterized the way in which the medieval Christian Church redistributed the supernumerary good works of its ascetics and saints as a process of "vicarious oblation" and "circulation of grace." These terms aptly illuminate how certain religious traditions see the manner in which the saint's virtues are radiated to his devotees. Writes Troeltsch:

> The idea of vicarious repentance and achievement is really a living category of religious thought; the vicarious offering of Christ both as a punishment and as a source of merit is only a special instance of a general conception.... Thus the duty of those who live "in the world" towards the whole is that of preserving and procreating the race—a task in which ascetics cannot share, while they for their part have the duty of showing forth the ideal in an intensified form, and of rendering service through intercession, penitence and the acquisition of merit. This is the reason for the enormous gifts and endowments to monasteries; men wanted to make certain of their own part in the oblation offered by monasticism. (239-40)

Troeltsch's notion of the circulation of grace can be compared with the Buddhist idiom without excessive distortion. While there is of course no sense of a vicarious offering of the Buddha, there is a strong sense in which the members of the *sangha* (order of monks), by leading exemplary lives, and thereby occupying an elevated position in relation to the laity that surrounds them, keep the universe in moral balance. Thus the purity of the sangha and its adherence to the discipline is of concern to the laity. The circulation of merit is as follows: the exemplary monk is the receiver of *dana* (material gifts) from lay householders. He in turn provides the field and context in which the layman makes merit (*punnak khetta* in Pali). The monk in return, not only by virtue of his disciplined conduct but also through preaching the *dhamma* (doctrine) and through ritual recitations, makes a return in the form of *dhamma dana*, a return which does not compromise his journey in search of liberation.

Though many saints during their lives were situated outside the establishment and were marginal to the ecclesiastical and government centers of their societies, they were by another mode of counting, according to the doctrinal traditions of their religions, their societies' greatest achievers. Typically the Thai forest monk saints—like the Hasidic tsaddiqim and the Christian ascetic saints referred to by

Troeltsch, and the Islamic *sufi* saints—are "illuminates." Rather than creating doctrine, they bring doctrine to life, especially for their lay communities, and are capable of circulating their grace and radiating their charisma as quintessential achievers of the highest values of their faith. In the end, the personal, interiorized, mystical illumination of the saints is seen in these religious traditions as flooding the vast spaces of the world with their cosmic love. Religion is embodied in and proceeds from them, just as they, as individuals, interiorize the whole religion. Frequently the saint as holy man devoted to practice is differentiated from the bookish legists—the *ulama* of Islam, the *ganthdhura* (those dedicated to the vocation of books) in Buddhism, and the hierarchs, such as bishops, of the Christian church. But after their death these saints, in the form of their relics and other material traces such as talismans and amulets, *are incorporated* by an *established* religion and placed at its heart.

There are two modalities or dimensions present in the saint's circulation of grace and/or merit and creation of a community, which I shall call *objectification of charisma* and *participation in charisma*. Objectification of charisma relates first to the process of transferring or transmitting charismatic energy or virtue from the living saint to an object (an amulet, talisman, clothing, image, etc.), and second, to the object in turn subsequently embodying and radiating that energy and potency to its possessors. By *participation* I mean the interaction and fusion between the community of devotees and their radiant saint or guru at the center: they are first of all in a relation of contiguity, and then they translate that relation into one of existential immediacy, contact, and shared affinities. There is an "indexical" transference, to use the jargon of Peircean semiotics, of energies and grace from leader to follower.

In the language of Hinduism, the same two modalities are conceptualized by the terms *prasad* and *darshan*, and both are contained within the larger conception of *bhakti* worship, and the even more general phenomenon of miracles.

The Objectification of and Participation in Charisma: The Forest Monks of Thailand

Let me now explicate processes of the objectification of charisma and participation in charisma by ethnographic reference to the cultic aspects surrounding the forest monks of contemporary Thailand. This ethnography is still another account of how the saints in a particular tradition and context articulate with the society at large.

In my book *Buddhist Saints of the Forest and the Cult of Amulets* (1984), I described how a wave of popular religiosity has become focused on a number of reclusive, ascetic, and meditative monks residing in forest hermitages in the interior provinces at the periphery of Thailand. These monks, acclaimed as arahants (saints) by the public at large, are to a varying degree followers of the path of purification as set out in the *Visuddhimagga,* a classical text composed by Buddhaghosa in the fifth century C.E.

Somewhat unexpectedly in our modern times, which give prominence to politicians, generals, and captains of industry and to the acquisition and expenditure of power and wealth, it is the very holiness, saintliness, and detachment of the virtuoso forest monks that have raised them into national prominence. First acclaimed by the common people at the grassroots level in the rural hinterland and small provincial towns, more recently they have been lionized and patronized by the ruling and commercial elites in the capital of Bangkok, including the royalty. The King and Queen, the Crown Prince, the ruling generals and ministers, and the managers of the largest banking and business houses have all sought these arahants in their remote habitations and have bowed before them, hoping to be edified and strengthened by their visits to them. The center of the polity and economy goes to the periphery to be reinvigorated, because it is in the periphery that the heart of the religion beats.

The amulet, the object imbued with the saint's charismatic energy or virtue, itself represents a conjunction of two parties: the lay sponsor who organizes and finances the manufacture of the amulet-medallion and has his or her insignia imprinted on one side of it, and the holy man, the famous monk, whose image (head or bust) is imprinted on the other side, and who through chanting sacred words of protection and through meditation sacralizes the amulet-medallion and transfers his virtuous energies to it. Thus the amulet-medallion is physically, iconically, and indexically a meeting and a linking of the lay sponsor and the monk adept, and in itself becomes an "animated" object of great anthropological interest.

The cult of saints and amulets, which on the face of it is a religious phenomenon, soon becomes implicated in the world of politics, commerce, and influence, in a number of ways:

1. The cult brings meditation masters in forest hermitages, their monk disciples and coresidents, and the outer circles of lay society in the rural periphery as well as in urban centers, capped by the metropolitan capital—all of these—into one religio-political space. All these distributions of persons and their networks define and participate in a field of power and merit.

2. A complementary and symbiotic dialectic operates in this field. The sponsorship of the amulet cult—their manufacture, their sacralization by the saints, and their distribution to the lay devotees and consumers at large—is largely in the hands of the powerful and affluent lay patrons such as royalty, generals, bankers, and higher bureaucrats. These powerful laity "legitimate" and mark the religious achievements and charisma of the saintly monks at a societywide or national level, just as they in turn are also indirectly empowered and legitimated by the saints.

3. The Thai attribution of charisma to their saints, and the ability of these saints to transfer their radiant presence and energies to amulets, which become concrete repositories of power, is a form of fetishism constituted of two social cycles or loops in which saint and lay public are implicated. One cycle is the ideologically developed and transparent one; the other is more hidden and manipulative and rides on the former. The first cycle is to be understood in terms of the Buddhist path of salvation: according to its cosmography, the ascetic meditator attains progressively higher spiritual levels of consciousness, leaving the grosser material excrescences behind, and through the control of his sense doors and sensory states attains understanding, wisdom, and universal compassion. This, then, is a state of transcendence, which also generates supranormal powers with which to affect the phenomenal world through detached action. The specifically Buddhist formulation, then, is that detached action can also become effective pragmatic action, because by being removed from the immediacy of desires and entanglements, it is all the more encompassing and creative. Now it is in the space of this first cycle that these virtuoso saints are approached by merit-making laymen, to whom the amulets are distributed as part of the saints' dispensation of blessings. At this level of exchange, the conventional Buddhist exegesis has some explanatory value: amulets (like relics) act as "reminders" of the virtues of the saint and the Buddha, and the saints act as "fields of merit," in which laymen plough, sow, and harvest their donations.

Moreover, in this frame the pious intentionality of the layperson's merit-making is stressed.

At the next remove, we have the cycle of transactions by which laypersons possess, accumulate, and secrete on their persons or otherwise employ these amulets to influence, control, seduce, dominate, and exploit fellow laymen for worldly purposes—in the corridors of politics, the stratagems of commerce, the intrigues of love, and the sycophancy of clientage. In this arena we perceive two developments: first, the iconic and indexical properties of the amulets are recognized not as mere reminders but as pragmatically efficacious. The emblems of the saints, the Buddha, and other sacred beings come to embody the beings' virtue and power by existential contact with them and by virtue of their impregnating them with sacred words, purifying them with sacral water, and other similar acts of transference. This objectification of the virtue of the sacred being also implies the descent of his spiritual and transcendental powers from the higher realms of spirituality and universality to the lower realms of material desires and limitations of space and time.

It is inevitable in the Thai case that this process of materialization, this process of gravitation, should have further consequences. One is that the amulet moves in time from a context of donation and love (*metta*) to a context of trade and profit: it is converted into a highly salable good and enters the bazaar and marketplace. When it does so, it also stimulates the production of fakes and becomes a pawn in the usual media of advertisements, collectors' catalogues, magazine articles, books, and the mythology of miracles. A second consequence is that the more amulets are produced, the more they are faked, and the more they are purchasable for money, the more they deteriorate in their mystical powers (despite the inflationary spiral of prices for those amulets regarded as rare antiques). This in turn ensures that new amulets come into fashion, and that many others already in circulation are condemned to be forgotten or less desired; moreover, the propensity for collectors to accumulate amulets increases, in the simple arithmetic calculation that the more you possess, the more clout you have. Thus the comparison of the relative virtues of amulets leads to mystical power itself, which at its source in the form of the saints' cosmic love was both limitless and rare, becoming graduated, differentiated, and quantified by the play of market forces: in short, commoditized.

J. L. Taylor's *Forest Monks and the Nation State* (1993) takes my account of the forest monk saints of Thailand further along in time
and in elaboration, especially in terms of the cult of stupas built to
commemorate famous forest saints and the associated cult of relics
generated by their remains (188; see also Taylor's contribution to this
collection).

Taylor's book gives valuable new information about how many of
the monks associated with the blessing and distribution of amulets
during their lives became after their death and cremation the source
of sacred relics, and the posthumous focal points of monumental
building activities such as stupas (*jedii*) and other structures (the
equivalent of the Thai word *jedii* is *cetiya* in Pali).[11]

It is a well-established practice in Thailand that the ashes and bone
fragments collected from the sites in which famous monks were
cremated become sacred relics (*phrathaat* in Thai; *saririka-dhatu* in
Pali) preserved in urns and pots. In *Buddhist Saints of the Forest* I cited
from the hagiography of Acharn Man how after the cremation of
his body in 1950, his ashes were distributed to "the bhikku delegates
from various towns . . . so that they could be enshrined in places to
be specially built," and to his various lay disciples and devotees also
attending from various towns (Tambiah 1984, 109-10). On the very
place where the cremation pyre stood was later built the convocation
hall of Wat Suddhavas. The master's ashes were reported by some collectors to have, in due course, crystallized into jewel-like relics. In the
words of the hagiography, they turned into "smooth and glossy grains,
sand-like in appearance, resembling relics of the Buddha and some
other arahant in ancient times" (quoted in ibid., 109). Taylor provides
ampler information about similar formations of relics from the collected ashes of many other forest saints, contemporaries as well as
disciples of Acharn Man (examples are Acharns Orn, Fan, and Jan
Khemapatto). One notable feature of this process of relic formation
is that the crystallized bone fragments are alleged under certain conditions to be capable of "miraculous multiplication." Moreover, just
as amulets blessed by forest monks find their way into the marketplace, so do the minute, partially or fully crystallized bone fragments
of forest saints. The building of stupas or *jediis* in which to store and
enshrine "relics" of famous arahants constitutes a kind of final phase
in the careers of forest saints, and arguably also, the inevitable waning
of the "presence of the saint" with the passage of time, as the stupas

and their relic chambers become less and less frequented as places of pilgrimage. This is a gradual process, and some stupas and the temple complexes in which they are located are more durable than others, depending on the continuing faith in the miraculous power (*ithirit*) of the dead saint combined with the organizational energies and the maintenance of disciplinary practices, especially meditation and ascetic practices, by the dead saint's successors and "lineage."

The Cult of Relics, Stupas, and Shrines

What I have labeled the *objectification of charisma* of great men (in Pali Buddhist terminology, *mahapurisa*) and the capacity of these exemplary persons to perform miracles and marvels provide the links between living saints and the cult of relics, stupas, and shrines as a posthumous celebration and manipulation of their continuing presence (in Latin, *praesentia*) after their death. Parallel to miracles in Christianity are *karamat* in Islam, and acts of *iddhi* in Buddhism and *siddhi* in Hinduism.

In Christian traditions of Late Antiquity and the Middle Ages, and in Sufi Islamic traditions, the saint's distinctive capacity to perform miracles while alive finds its posthumous extension and continuation in the veneration of the saint's relics and/or his or her tomb as the repositories and conductors of miracle-making powers. In Buddhism the cult of relics, embedded in stupas, relates first and foremost to the bodily remains of the Buddha himself, though various Buddhist saints throughout the centuries have also been the foci of relic cults.

Richard Southern remarks on the centrality of the cult of relics in *Western Society and the Church in the Middle Ages* as follows:

> Relics were the main channel through which supernatural power
> was available for the needs of ordinary life. Ordinary men could
> see and handle them, yet they belonged not to this transitory world
> but to eternity. On the Last Day they would be claimed by the saints
> and become an integral part of the kingdom of heaven.[12] Among
> all the objects of the visible, malign, unintelligible world, relics
> alone were both visible and full of beneficent intelligence. (South
> ern 1970, 31)

Two articles published in the *Journal of Early Christian Studies* (1999), an introduction and translation by Gillian Clark of a sermon by the fourth-century bishop Victricius and an essay about Victricius by David Hunter, illuminate the cult of relics, especially as it was elaborated theologically in tandem with the translation and wide distribution of relics in the late fourth century in Roman Gaul. These works extend seminal themes introduced by Peter Brown in his *The Cult of Saints* (1981).

The following are points from these articles that are germane to the themes dealt with in this essay. A major reference point is found in the Roman tradition in which entombed bodies should not be disturbed; they were not to be moved or dissected. This tradition was reaffirmed by two imperial rulings of 386 issued at Constantinople, but it was disregarded a few months later by Bishop Ambrose of Milan when he found the bodies of the martyrs Gervasius and Protasius and moved them from the cemetery to the high altar of his new church.[13]

Ambrose was a patron who lavishly distributed relics, and one of the recipients of his generosity was Victricius, bishop of Rouen, who probably in 396 delivered in thanks the famous sermon entitled "De laude sanctorum," translated as "Praising the Saints," to welcome a gift of relics from Ambrose. Clark makes this general comment on a nexus of interrelated phenomena: in late twentieth-century scholarship, "*de laude* has, quite rightly, been used as evidence for the cult of patron saints, the power of relics and the beginnings of asceticism in the western church, and the networks of ecclesial patronage that are revealed by gifts of relics" (Clark 1999, 366-67). There is no space here to describe and discuss in detail the commentary on Victricius's sermon by Clark and Hunter or to quote from Clark's translation of the sermon itself. As I see it, Victricius's theology of relics justifies, and lends validity to, the fragmentation and divisibility of relics, and their translation, distribution, and redistribution; it attributes sacred power to these relic fragments, which continue to participate in the unity and wholeness of the deceased saint. The saint in turn participates in the indivisibility and divinity of the Trinity. In short, by means of these steps Victricius asserted that in relics of saints' bodies, God's divine presence was manifest.

I find this novel theological validation of the cult of relics functional for the spread and transmission of Christianity as a "universal" and universalizing religion. Contemplate the double power of this formulation: ordinary Christians, by virtue of baptism, are "adopted" by God and participate in His spirit; and the fragments of the relics of saints as treasured possessions also relate ordinary Christians to living divinity. The saint's unity and union with God is not dissipated by the fragmentation of his or her body. The healing power of the relics is evidence that the martyrs are present therein.[14]

In a review of two books dealing with the relics and shrines associated with the "cult of saints" in Christianity, John McManners remarked that the rules concerning the cult of relics in the Christian church were laid down by St. Augustine himself:

> "The clothing or ring of a saint ought to be dearer to us than those of our parents." ... From Ambrose's annexation of newly discovered bones of martyrs for the altar of his new basilica in Milan in AD 385 to the ruling of the Second Council of Nicaea in AD 787 that no church was to be consecrated without relics to sanctify it, we trace the way in which the cult became universal. ... Mementoes of the saints became psychological weapons flourished by churchmen to outface tyrants; they were used as solemn guarantors of oaths, and as creators of wealth and status for ecclesiastical institutions. (McManners 1986)

In fact a series of Church councils vigorously propagated and protected the relic cult. The Council of Gangra in Asia Minor (circa C.E. 345) excommunicated those who questioned its practices; the Second Council of Nicaea anathematized those who despised it and laid down that no church should be consecrated without relics. Going one step further, the councils held in Carthage in 801 and in 813 directed that all altars lacking relics should be destroyed. It is worth remembering that "[t]o this day the technical definition of an altar in Roman Catholic canon law is 'a tomb containing the relics of saints' (*sepulchrum continens reliquas sanctorum*). The real altar [is] the altar stone with its relics, and until fairly recently when liturgical regulations have become rather lax in some parts of the Catholic world, no priest would celebrate mass without this altar stone with its relic" (Sox 1985, 8).

The treasures and secrets of the Vatican will never cease to surprise and edify us. There is a large room in the Apostolic Palace in the Vatican which is "lined from floor to ceiling with cabinets and shelves loaded with containers of every conceivable size encasing bone ashes, clothing and what not" (ibid., 7). They are the relics waiting to be dispatched to consecrate the altars of new churches. Overseeing the transfer and authentication of these relics occupies much of the time of the Pope's Vicar-General.

The Multiple Dimensions of the Cult of Relics

Many major religious traditions, such as Christianity, Islam, and Buddhism, have explicitly developed formulations, doctrines, and interpretations regarding the characteristics, powers, and genealogies of the relics and other objects associated with their saints. The following is an enumeration of some five major interrelated themes I have identified:

1. Relics and other sacra are classified and ranked into systems of signs invested with semiotic properties, and recourse is made to the doctrines of "presence" and "reminders" to explain their relation to the saint when he or she was alive.

2. Powers and *potentia* are attributed to these objects, such as their ability to perform or serve as conduits for miracles, marvels and wonders, to enliven or "animate" monuments and shrines in which they are embedded, and to radiate energies to the spaces around them and make them sacred sites.

3. The travels and "translations" of some of these sacred objects from place to place are related in various written chronicles as well as through oral traditions. The dispersion and transmission of these objects through time and space are matched and complemented by the opposite process of their aggregation, installation, and deposition at monumental sites in political and religious capitals. The sites in which they repose become the foci of pilgrimages and ritual veneration, eventually leading to chains and networks of pilgrimage sites and elaborate calendars of festivals.

4. The travels, translations, installations, and aggregations of relics and sacred objects constitute the processes and activities by which they enter the stream of history and become involved with and implicated in political and economic manipulations and in worldly games of power, conquest, domination, and affluence.

5. Finally, the animated presence and immanence of relics and sacred objects are also central components of utopian prophecies and millennial hopes. A potent futuristic expectation concerns the final coming together of relics and their reconstitution at the Last Judgment or at the end of cosmic cycles.[15] As such, they comprise an ideological component in the generation of revivalist movements, millennial rebellions, and mystical cults.

Ideally, if I had the luxury of time, I would want to illustrate these five features by recourse to four examples, relating to saints and relics in medieval Western European Christianity; the cult of the stupa in early and medieval Buddhism in South Asia; Sufi tomb shrines in Pakistan and India; and Moroccan Maraboutism in recent times as it relates to the tombs of Berber saints. For lack of time I shall have to leave out Sufi tomb shrines and the Moroccan case altogether, and discuss aspects of only the first and second of the themes listed above.[16]

The Doctrines of "Presence" and "Reminders"

The continued presence of the saint in his relics is reiterated in Christian and Buddhist writings. Peter Brown gives this explication of *praesentia* in *The Cult of the Saints*: "The devotees who flocked out of Rome to the shrine of Saint Lawrence, to ask his favor or to place their dead near his grave, were not merely going to a place; they were going to a place to meet a person—*ad dominium Laurentium*" (Brown 1981, 88).[17]

The *Mahavamsa*, the Great Chronicle composed in Sri Lanka around the sixth century C.E., relates this eloquent story: Mahinda, Emperor Asoka's son who brought the Buddha's teachings to Sri Lanka, tells the Sinhala king that he and his company desire to return to India because "Long is the time . . . we have lived without a master. There is nothing here for us to worship." Mahinda is referring to the relics of the Buddha, which the island still lacked. Explains Mahinda: "If we behold the relics, we behold the Conqueror" (Geiger 1986 [1950], 116; ch. 17, verses 1–4). In popular Sinhalese conception, the seeing of relics is equated with the viewing (*dassana*) of the Buddha, which gives serene joy (*pasada*) to the devotee (Trainor 1997). In both early and medieval Buddhist and Christian writings, there are assertions that the physical viewing of relics induces a vision of the presence of the Buddha and of Christ, respectively. This theory of visualization and of presence is also extended to seeing holy places in pilgrimage.

The doctrine of "reminders" can be explicated by reference to Buddhist linguistic usage. The words *cetiya* (Pali) and *caitya* (Sanskrit) are said to be derived from the Sanskrit root *ci*, which means to arrange or to heap up; *cita* thus means funeral pile. It has also been associated with *cit*, which carries the meaning to remind, to fix the mind on something, to instruct.

Similarly the dual associations of mental reminding and recollection on the one hand, and of heaping up into a mound, is said to cohere around the word *stupa* (relic mound). Scholars have suggested multiple derivations from Sanskrit: examples are the root *stup*, which means to heap up or pile, the root *stu*, which means to be clotted or conglomerated, and the root *stu* again, meaning to praise, laud, extol (Snodgrass 1985, 156–57; see also Trainor 1997, 26–27).

From a comparative point of view it is suggestive that the English word *tomb* has been associated with the Greek word *tumbos* (sepulchral mound, barrow) and with the Latin word *tumulus*, derived from the verb *tumeo*, to become inflated or to swell. The English word *monument*, on the other hand, can be linked to the Latin word *monere*, to advise, to remind.

Christian and Buddhist Classifications of Relics

Elaborate classifications of relics and other sacra associated with saints can be illustrated from both Buddhist and Christian traditions.[18]

In Christianity we have to start with the relics associated with Christ's Passion. Christ left no corporeal remains because he rose on the third day after his crucifixion and ascended to heaven forty days later. The foremost relic is the Holy Cross,[19] and high value is attached to other crucificion-related items such as the nails, the crown of thorns, linen that touched the body of Christ (the most spectacular example of which is the Shroud of Turin), reeds, sponges, and so forth.

The term *reliquaie* (Latin), meaning "remains" or "leftovers," became associated with the remains of a saint from early Christian times. In the *New Catholic Encyclopedia* (1967; s.v. "Relics") Francesco Chiovaro defines a relic as "the material remains of a saint or holy person after his death, as well as objects sanctified by contact with his body."

By Late Antiquity and the early Middle Ages, within Western Christianity a well-known classification and rank order distinguished between (1) corporeal relics, the bodily remains of a holy person; (2) instrumental relics, objects used by a holy person either in his or her daily regime or during penance, captivity, and supplication; and (3) contact relics, that is, objects that came into contact with a saint's corpse, his bones, or his tomb. The most common type of contact relic was *brandeum*, a piece of cloth or linen that was placed in a box and then put in contact with the body of the saint. The authenticity of this relic was demonstrated if the cloth, when cut, exuded the dead saint's blood from the incision. Other examples of contact relics are dust and dew from the saint's tomb, metal filings from the chains that bound him, and oil from the lamps placed before his tomb (McCulloh 1976, 145–84; see also Benard 1988). Synonyms for these contact relics were *beneficia, benedicto,* and *sanctuaria.* All these contact relics originating at the tombs of saints were used in the dedication of churches, and were frequently embedded in altars.[20]

It would seem that the Council of Trent (1534–49 C.E.) further differentiated and ranked corporeal relics into *reliquiae insignes* (distinguished relics), which pertained to the entire body or to such chief parts as the head, arm, or leg, and *reliquiae non insignes* (undistinguished relics), which category was again divided between *notabiles* (notable relics) such as hand or foot, and *exiguae,* small pieces such as teeth and fingers (MacCulloch 1961; Benard 1988).

Let us now review some Buddhist classifications. I have previously glossed the meanings associated with the words *cetiya* and *stupa.* Relics in Theravada tradition are also referred to as *dhatu,* a word that carries other meanings as well, including "constituent elements" and "seeds."[21] To the array of terms *stupa* and *cetiya,* meaning burial mound containing relics, we can add *dhatu garbha,* which connotes the pregnant meanings, among others, of "the container of the elements constituting the world," "the world egg," and a "womb" containing seeds, thereby conveying the potency of relics (as corporeal remains) to be fertile and their capacities to inseminate the masonry, to generate, and to radiate outwards (Snodgrass 1985, 189, 200, 354, 360). The term *dagaba* (relic chamber) derives from *dhatu garbha* and is another equivalent term in the set. Equally suggestive in the study of the fan of meanings of these terms is the idea that there is a homology between the stupa and the body of the Buddha, with a cross-referencing of their respective parts, especially in Mahayana Buddhist traditions.[22]

In early Indian art, say before the first century C.E., the Buddha was never represented in human forms but only by certain symbols (although this convention or interdiction did not apply to human beings in attendance on the Buddha). The use of symbols (Coomaraswamy calls it an "aniconic" method) was so elaborate that it constituted by itself "a complete artistic vocabulary and an iconography without icons" (Coomaraswamy 1927).

In this early Buddhist art, the Buddha was represented by symbols that were reminders of the great events in his career: a Bodhi tree represents his attaining enlightenment under a tree, protected by the serpent Muchalinda; a wheel (*cakra*), his preaching the first sermon, which "set the wheel of the Doctrine" in motion; a stupa, his cremation and the enshrining of his relics; footprints (*paduka*), his sojourn in the wilderness, and so on. Some of the symbols taken as a set designate the Four Great Events (later increased to eight) of the Buddha's life.

The *Kalingabodhi Jataka*, while giving an early Buddhist view against the representation of the Buddha in human form, also attributes the origins of relic veneration to the time of the Buddha and provides a discriminating classification of cetiya as cult objects, sacred symbols, and reminders (Cowell 1904, 4:142-43). In the introductory part of the story, the Buddha's favorite disciple Ananda desires to set up in the Jetavana monastery a substitute for the Buddha, so that people may be able to make their offerings of flowers not only when the Buddha is in residence, but also when he is away preaching elsewhere. To the Buddha's question as to how many kinds of cetiya there are, Ananda replies that there are three—those of the body (*saririka*), those of association (*paribhogika*), and those prescribed (*uddesika*). The Buddha rejects bodily relics on the grounds that they can be venerated only after his passing away, and he rejects the prescribed, "personalized" symbols because such are "groundless and merely fanciful"—that is, they are only artificially, arbitrarily, and by convention referable to the absent being. So he concludes that only a great wisdom tree that has been "associated" with a Buddha is fit to be a cetiya, whether the Buddha is still living or is extinguished. Thus, according to this precedent, the associated symbols, such as the Bodhi tree, the cakra (wheel), the footprints and such entities are declared the most appropriate.

The formulation found in the *Kalingabodhi Jataka*, or some variant of it, may well have served as the precedent for the transformed valuation of "reminders" later given by a Thai monk, probably Bodhiransi. He wrote around C.E. 1417 a chronicle about the origins and travels of a famous Buddha image, called the Buddha Sihing, which served as a palladium of Thai kingdoms and principalities, particularly in the fourteenth century (see *P'ra Buddha Sihinga* [Notton 1933b], as well as Tambiah 1984, ch. 14). The chronicle was written to celebrate the powers of the image and the eminence of its royal possessors, especially the kings of Lan Na, in whose possession it was at the time the monk wrote the chronicle.

In the chronicle, it is reported that the Buddha had once told Ananda that there were three kinds of cetiya, or reminders, namely *paribhogacetiya, udisacetiya,* and *saririkacetiya.* (Translator Camille Notton [1933b] glosses the first of these terms as all that had been used by the Buddha, the second as "all that which has been determined by him," and the third as all that has been left by him.) The Buddha image would be a merit included in the category *udisacetiya.*

The foregoing serves as a useful introduction for understanding a classification of "reminders" into four types provided by A. B. Griswold, a scholar of Thai art forms: (1) *sariradhatu* or *dhatucetiya,* bodily relics; (2) *dhammacetiya,* doctrinal reminders, as contained in the canon, originally referring to the Dhamma transmitted orally and later including the written canonical texts as well; (3) *paribhogacetiya,* reminders by association, which include objects with which the Buddha has had physical contact, such as his alms bowl and robes, the footprints he has left, the Bodhi tree under which he reached enlightenment, and more generally, all the sites associated with his peripatetic career (in the terminology of Charles Peirce, these are *indexes*); and (4) *uddesikacetiya,* indicative reminders, which Griswold (1968, 3) glosses as "reminders by convention," that is, manmade substitutes, replicas of paribhogacetiya. They are all copies of originals, so to say, and in Peirce's language constitute *icons.* Examples are trees grown from the seeds or cuttings taken from the original Bodhi tree; replicas of stupas containing the Buddha's bodily relics or footprints; representations of historic sites or great events associated with the Buddha in painting, sculpture, and architecture, and so on.[23]

We know that from early times these objects were not regarded as merely reminders and fields of merit, but also as repositories of power. This power on close scrutiny is seen to stem from many bases, such as, first of all, the powers possessed and radiated by the Buddha himself by virtue of his "presence"; second, the powers of the makers and sacralizers of these objects, who had either been in contact with the Buddha or had attained heroic proportions themselves as heirs of his doctrine; third, the efficacy attributed to the rituals of sacralization themselves; and lastly, the power of the substance—the metal, gem, wood, or stone—out of which the object was created.

Travels and Translations of Christian Relics

In a book entitled *Furta Sacra: Thefts of Relics in the Central Middle Ages* (1991), covering the later Carolingian period,[24] Patrick Geary recounts the remarkable story of the thefts, real or alleged, of the relics of saints from poorly guarded or decaying churches, their transport and translation to new church sites, and their ceremonial re-entombment in the presence of the pious community who would benefit from the saint's radiant presence in his bones and relics. Writes Geary:

> From the reign of Charles the Great until the age of the crusades, we have nearly one hundred relic theft accounts.... These stories are, at first reading, bizarre: monks creeping into a neighboring church to force open a tomb and flee with the body of a long dead saint; merchants landing on distant shores fully armed to capture a church and force its guardians to divulge the resting place of its patron; professional relic-mongers systematically despoiling the Roman catacombs for the benefit of Frankish ecclesiastics. But even more bizarre for modern readers is the almost universal approval of contemporaries who heard of these thefts. Far from condemning them as aberrations or as sins against the fellow Christians from whom the saints were stolen, most people apparently praised them as true works of Christian virtue, and communities such as Bèze boasted of their successful thefts. (1991, xii)

Geary suggests that thefts were perpetrated (or, more frequently, alleged) at particular moments of crisis by members of religious or secular communities as calculated means of crisis intervention. Relics were perceived as the living saint, and that the account of a translation is really an account of a ritual kidnapping by which the saint passed from one community to another.

Geary links the flourishing of the cult of saints and the preoccupation with their bodily remains in the later Carolingian period to the uncertainties of a fragmented post-Carolingian world, when central authorities had ceased to give adequate protection to religious institutions, which were now prone to plunder. He considers this a major reason for the latter to seek supernatural protection; they looked to saints as their defenders.

Translations of saints' relics were made with a specific purpose:

> Through the latter part of the ninth century, as the over-extended, centralized system of Carolingian government receded before the rising power of local and regional aristocracies, ecclesiastical institutions were forced to look elsewhere for support and protection. Far-thinking churchmen looked beyond mortal efforts to supernatural defenders, and in importing saints hoped to find a solution to their society's ills.... Across Europe, saints [that is, their relics]

were responding to the crisis and assuming those tasks so eagerly pressed upon them by a disintegrating social and political system. (Geary 1991, 20–21)

Moreover, the saints as foci of devotion were excellent fundraisers—they inspired generous donations from the faithful in return for the saints' favors. These offerings were largest at pilgrimage sites, which supported numerous monastic communities.

From the tenth century onwards a decline of this particular form of the cult of saints' relics was brought about by numerous developments. One chain of developments was signaled by the rise of the new monastic orders of Cluny and Citeaux, which catered to the need for integration of monastic communities into a wider world. The local saints who were patrons of small local families and communities were superseded by "universal" saints of the Christian Church—for example, the patron of Cluny was Saint Peter, and the Cistercian churches were uniformly dedicated to the Virgin. Increased communication and mobility resulted in the widespread diffusion and expansion of the worship of the universal saints throughout Christendom. The cult of the Virgin in particular expanded enormously across Europe in the course of the eleventh and twelfth centuries. Papal insistence on the dignity of the successor of Peter enhanced the apostle's reputation throughout Europe.

Not only did the importance of relics diminish in the face of competition from universal saints, but they were particularly affected by the growing importance of the cult of Christ. "The process moved from the cult of a physical relic of Christ, the host, which was to be treated rather like other relics ... to the final popular recognition that the eucharist enjoyed a unique position in Christian worship.... This evolution of the role of the eucharist from one among many other relics to sacred object distinct from relics, parallels the evolution of medieval religious devotion from an essentially hagiocentric practice to a christocentric one" (Geary 1991, 28–29). These changes in the structure and organization of Christian worship and devotion were themselves intertwined with important political and economic changes from the eleventh century onwards that reduced the need to rely on the multicentric small-scale reach of local saints. The significance of the emergence of the modern state and an expanding economic base is summed up by Geary as follows:

Protection and peace, too, were increasingly provided more thoroughly and effectively by the reemerging political institutions that would in time develop into the modern state. As protectors, central authorities were more effective than local saints; and as antagonists, counts, kings, and emperors had to be met by more powerful defensive weapons than humiliation of relics or curses. By the thirteenth century such practices had therefore almost entirely disappeared.

The economic revival of the eleventh and twelfth centuries brought new possibilities of economic planning and growth that reduced but did not eliminate the importance of saints' financial contributions. The first phase of this development was the regularization of monastic incomes and the reorganization of the budget, a process which began at Cluny under the abbacy of Peter the Venerable. Also significant were the effects of agricultural improvements, particularly evident in Cistercian houses which gave monasteries a degree of fiscal independence never before seen. (ibid., 23)

Travels and Translations of the Buddha's Relics

While Christ left no corporeal remains, the Buddha's remains became a focal point of Buddhist cultic worship and monumental construction in the form of stupas. Relic veneration began early in the development of Buddhism. It is clear in the excavations conducted in Anuradhapura in Sri Lanka that the spread of Buddhism entailed the widespread replication of an architectural complex, namely the monastic residence, together with the stupa, side by side. The monks preached the word; the stupa provided the focus for cultic worship. Together they sacralized and elevated the spreading agrarian settlements. The spread of Buddhism was seen as a colonizing project as well as a civilizing process. Royal as well as local lay support in the building and provisioning of these monastic-cum-cultic complexes seems to have been critical in the legitimation, continuation, and reproduction of both small-scale polities and local communities in the early Anuradhapura period.[25]

Thus Buddhist practices regarding the veneration of relics and the construction of stupas, which are the nodes of pilgrimages, are movingly, triumphantly, and fulsomely recorded in the canonical *Mahaparinibbana Sutta*, which in variant forms is a central text for all

Buddhist schools.[26] This *sutta* (discourse), after tracing the Buddha's last peripatetic journey and his passing away, describes the cremation of his remains in the royal style accorded to a universal ruler (*cakka-vatti*), and the subsequent distribution of his relics.

The discourse delineates a dual transmission of the Buddha's legacy. To the brethren of the *sangha*, the *bhikkhus*, the Buddha allocated the practice and preaching of the Dhamma and the pursuit of the path of conquest of the body, but he allotted the care of and worship of his bones to the laity, nobles, and householders, who were enjoined to build *dagabas* (relic chambers) over them.[27] This dual transmission would be subsequently formalized in certain doctrinal traditions in terms of the two bodies of the Buddha: *dhamma-kaya* (the doctrinal body), and *rupa-kaya* (the material body).[28]

The *Mahaparinibbana Sutta* records the first distribution after cremation of the bones; they were divided into eight parts, and given to eight kings and tribal chiefs, who built eight dagabas over them. (The vessels used to measure the bones and the embers became two additional relics, which the recipients also deposited in mounds.) The Buddha's relics are alleged to have been distributed, reaggregated, and then redistributed and relocated through time and space in an ever-expanding circle of territorial space, occupied by polities and empires that had espoused or patronized Buddhism.

An array of subsequently composed chronicles record the later travels and translations of the original eight portions of bone relics. I want to focus here on the redistributive acts and spectacular monument-building attributed to Emperor Asoka, as told in variant forms in a string of famous chronicles such as the *Asokavadana*, a Sanskrit text compiled probably in the second century C.E. in Northwest India; the Sri Lankan Pali chronicles such as the *Dipavamsa*, composed probably between the fourth and the beginning of the fifth century C.E.; the *Mahavamsa*, attributed to the sixth century C.E. and the *Thupavamsa*, written in the twelfth century C.E.[29]

Let me briefly recount here the *Thupavamsa*'s rendition of Asoka's monumental piety. King Ajattasattu, advised by the elder Mahakassapa, who foresaw danger to the relics, managed to aggregate those that had been buried in seven of the eight original sites (leaving behind only small portions) and to deposit them at one site.[30] Ajattasattu's aggregation was in line with the prophecy made by the Buddha that Emperor Asoka would find this relic trove and distribute its contents far and wide throughout his empire, in 84,000 places.

All of the chronicle accounts make the interpretive move of ho-mologizing, even equating, the Buddha's doctrine, conventionally di-vided into 84,000 sections, with the 84,000 monasteries or stupas.[31] Asoka builds over the relics in or near 84,000 cities. For instance, the *Dipavamsa* reports Asoka as proclaiming, "'Full and complete eighty-four thousand most precious sections of the Truth have been taught by the most excellent Buddha; I will build eighty-four thousand mon-asteries, honouring each single section of the Truth by one monas-tery.'" The text then relates, "At that time there were in Jambudipa eighty-four (thousand) towns; near each town he built one monas-tery" (Oldenberg 1982, 154). In even more dramatic and poetic terms the *Asokavadana* says:

> Now when King Asoka had completed the eighty-four thousand dharmarajikas, he became a righteous dharmaraja, and thenceforth known as "Dharmasoka." As it is said:
>
> For the benefit of beings throughout the world
>
> the noble Maurya built stupas.
>
> He had been known as "Asoka the Fierce";
>
> by this act he became "Asoka the Righteous."
>
> (Strong 1983, 221)

John Strong acknowledges that Paul Mus was clearly right in suggest-ing that the 84,000 minute relics constitute the Buddha's physical body, and that the stupas themselves are realizations of the Dhamma in stone; and in turn in building them, Asoka is pictured as recon-structing the body of Buddha's teachings, his *Dharmakaya* (ibid., 117). Surely our awareness has been deepened by this Buddhist intellectual and aesthetic feat of juxtaposing and homologizing doctrinal catego-ries with the elements of the body, and realizing that union of mind and body in the architectural medium of stone, thereby achieving a passage between intellect and sense, between verbal constructs, cultic actions, and aesthetic productions, and effecting a simultaneous en-gagement of multiple sensory modalities—visual, auditory, tactile.

The mythology surrounding the Indian emperor Asoka (274–232 B.C.E.) has a parallel in the Christian mythology concerning the Roman emperor Constantine the Great (280–327 C.E.), who is cred-ited with presiding over church councils, building a great number of churches, and attempting to reconcile contending forces inside and outside the Church. In Greek Orthodox tradition, Constantine is considered the founder of the Byzantine Empire and the savior of the Christian religion.

There is a luxuriant mythology and mythohistory celebrating the deeds of Emperor Constantine and his mother Helena. Constantine in 312 C.E. allegedly saw a shining cross that bore the inscription, "By this, conquer," which he took to signify that adopting the cross as his standard would ensure his winning the battle against Maxentius, his chief rival for the throne of Rome. Constantine entered Rome in 312 after the battle of the Malvian Bridge. Helena apparently became a Christian in 313 C.E., the year her son officially recognized Christianity. The story is that in 326 C.E., Helena, now much aged, went to Jerusalem in search of the Cross and engaged the aid of a man named Judas, who dug twenty fathoms deep in Golgotha, where a delightful aroma of spices pervaded the air, and found the three crosses.[32] The Holy Cross itself was identified by Bishop Mararios by the miracle it performed: it restored a dead youth to life. Helena brought the Cross and three nails to Constantine, who distributed pieces of the Cross throughout the Empire. One nail he placed in his war bridle, another he embedded in his statue that overlooked Rome, and the third he threw into the Adriatic, which changed from being a perilous and turbulent body of water into a calm sea.[33] Another version has it that among the relics found at the same time as the True Cross were the nails used in Christ's crucifixion, the spear with which a Roman soldier pierced his side, and the title from the top of the Cross. These relics were divided and distributed over the Christian world, and Constantine was said to have decorated his armor, his helmet, his sword, and his horse's bit with some of the nails (see Sox 1985). It is claimed that the Basilica di Santa Croce in Gerusalemme in Rome, built near a palace of Helena, still preserves a piece of the Cross, one of the nails, and the title from the Cross. Helena is credited with the building of churches in the Holy Land on the sites of the Nativity and the Ascension.

These two mythic traditions, one Buddhist and the other Christian, unite two themes: the evangelical spread and the missionary propagation of Buddhism and Christianity through the diffusion of the cult of relics, and the use of the relics to legitimate and extend the empire-making of famous kings. This combined religious and political project of extending religion and polity to the widest territorial limits was in fact aided by the fact that relics were divisible and easily transportable. Their translations and installations in multiple centers marked by large-scale festivities also laid the grid for a plethora of sacred sites and for ever-flowing pilgrimages to them. As Kenneth Clark (1969) has remarked, "From our point of view nearly all the relics in the world depend on unhistorical assertions; and yet they, as much as any factor, led to that movement and diffusion of ideas from which Western civilization derives part of its momentum."

It seems to be no personal oddity, then, that Pope John Paul II, in his drive in the last decade of the twentieth century to reclaim a universal Catholic Church from Poland to Brazil to the Philippines, should want to canonize a new crop of saints and to revitalize the cult of saints as an essential spearhead of his imperial project on behalf of Christendom.

Let me conclude with a reference to the travels, changing possession, and successive installations of sacra such as the Buddha's tooth relic in Sri Lanka and famous Buddha images such as the Emerald Buddha, the Buddha Sihing, and Mahamuni Buddha in the Southeast Asian polities of Burma, Thailand, and Laos. The journeys and powers of these sacra, which have served as the palladia of Buddhist kingdoms, legitimators of their kingly possessors, and foci of collective worship, have been richly celebrated in numerous chronicles, and deserve an extended treatment in their own right.[34] Their religio-political significance may be briefly stated as follows: the mobility of these sacra is a pointer to many features of the traditional polities in question. The polities were what I have elsewhere called "galactic" in organization: that is, they were a loose formation composed of a central domain surrounded by vassal states, and at the outer rim by tributary states, which are all reproductions on a smaller scale of the dominant center.[35] These galactic polities were fluid, and the center-satellite relations and patterns changed constantly. One corollary of such instability is that there were no stable dynasties of rulers who succeeded one another according to defined and predictable rules of heredity.

Individuals of personal charisma who assumed kingship found two more or less enduring bases for claiming legitimacy and, through it, stability of power. One was the claim to being a *cakkavatti* or a *dharmaraja* on the basis of personal achievement and commitment to Buddhist norms of kingship. These positions, according to Buddhists, are not so much inherited as proven by individual *karma* and meritorious conduct. Though they cannot be inherited, those attaining them can claim to be incarnations and avatars of archetypal heroes.

A second basis, linked to the first, is the possession of palladia and regalia that are enduring sedimentations or objectifications of power and virtue. Possession of them is a guarantee of legitimacy, and these embodiments of virtue and power will remain with the possessor for as long as he is deserving. They cannot be removed from their locations against their consent; their travels are evidence of their passage from one deserving ruler to another.

For anthropologists and historians, the travels of Buddha statues, such as those of the Sinhala Buddha or the Emerald Buddha Jewel, provide a chain or genealogy of kingdoms and polities that these statues have legitimated. They also provide a map of a vast political arena in Southeast Asia, made up of a number of principalities, changing boundaries, and affiliations, and possessing an identity by virtue of commitment to a religio-political ideology, on the one hand, and the sharing of similar economic, demographic, and logistical features, on the other.

In the traditional galactic polities, divine kingship was accompanied by perennial rebellions, and shallow dynasties are evidence of such instability. In such a context we can also appreciate how important sacred objects such as Buddha images, recognized as permanent embodiments of virtue and power, helped provide their temporary possessors with legitimation, and at the same time embodied a genealogy of kingship by serving as the common thread that joined a succession of kings and polities with separate identities.

Understanding Social Totalities:
Stanley Tambiah's Early Contribution
to Sociology of Thai Buddhism

James Taylor

Stanley Tambiah's legacy to Thai scholarship has been in his eluci-
dation of underlying structures and dialectic within Theravada Buddhism and his explication of a Weberian paradox: namely, the way
that social actors make the religion meaningful to their worlds, and,
likewise, the way that the Buddhist laity creates meaning in a religion which espouses in a normative frame the concept of mundane
worldly abandonment. This apparent paradox can be appreciated most
clearly in the notion of the reclusive forest-dwelling Buddhist saint
(*arahant*), the exemplary renunciant figure so highly esteemed in
Thailand. In this essay, which relates to the renunciation question in
Thai Buddhism, I wish to show, first, something of Tambiah's method,
especially as articulated in his monograph on Thailand entitled *The
Buddhist Saints of the Forest and the Cult of Amulets* (1984), and how he
elucidates critical historical forces and social practices based on Max
Weber's early ruminations. Second, I will also show briefly, using an
example from my own fieldwork on reform forest monks and the
monks' primitive charter (*vinaya*), how Tambiah's research method
gave me a sense of intellectual direction and was, in his own words,

a "primary point of reference" (Tambiah 1996) as I followed on from his final and, in my view, most significant monograph on Thai Buddhism, the abovementioned *Buddhist Saints*.

Indeed, much of my own work, carried out a decade after Tambiah's *Buddhist Saints* was published, attests to many of his early "interdisciplinary" (Tambiah 1987, 188) observations, though it further elaborates on the use of biographical sources and includes a sustained ethnography, over fourteen months and seventy-two forest monasteries, of wandering monks. Tambiah tended to lean more toward the center than to work outward, while I started in the periphery, in the forests, and then worked toward the center. I was concerned with two mutually reinforcing tendencies: a conscious attempt by actors to reproduce the past from memory work, and the lived experience of the monks ritually ascribing meaning to practices in the present.

In my view, Tambiah's enduring gift to contemporary Thai scholarship, specifically on Buddhism—aside from his more general insightful anthropological contributions to knowledge and the theory of myth, ritual, and performance—lies in his well-known Thai trilogy, *Buddhism and the Spirit Cults in North-east Thailand* (1970), *World Conqueror and World Renouncer* (1976), and the aforementioned *Buddhist Saints* (1984). Tambiah started in the village, moved to the city/nation-state, then to the forests. Nor must we forget his numerous papers over a highly productive twenty-plus years of research on Thailand, which was largely put aside with his renewed interest in ethnic issues in his native Sri Lanka in 1983. Indeed, I know of few, if any, courses on the anthropology and history of mainland Southeast Asia that have not cited his work on Thailand.

Weber, Charisma, and the Dialectics of History: Tambiah's Contribution to Knowledge on Thai Buddhism

Before looking at Tambiah's methodology, his contribution to knowledge, and his relevance to my own work, in this section I present a brief synopsis of some critical moments in his research on Thai Buddhism.

When Tambiah initially undertook fieldwork in Thailand in 1960, he was mainly concerned with education, but within the context of the many interrelated aspects of village life. As I will discuss in more detail later, in looking at the totality of everyday life in a northeastern Thai village he noted that Buddhism/folk religion had center stage, providing an all-embracing, coherent (if sometimes contested) ritual system. He also saw in village life a smaller social unit of the macrocosm, the village giving insights into the larger civilization, while Buddhism acted as a culturally sophisticated force impacting through time on local animistic worlds.[1] In turn, within this differential space, Buddhism became interwoven into the seasonal/agricultural ritual cycle of village life. This study coincided with Tambiah's ongoing theoretical interests in an interpretation of the structural interaction between cosmology and ritual as a dialectical, semantic, and pragmatic process,[2] and, in the case of myth, the way that this interaction relates to everyday practices.

Perhaps less widely known is the fact that although Tambiah's first monograph was on a village in northeastern Thailand, he also undertook initial fieldwork in the north and central regions of Thailand. In the latter case Tambiah seemingly still has an unpublished manuscript—written, he has said, "in a different mode anticipating some of Bourdieu's writings about strategic choices and practices as outcomes"[3]—which may even surface one day. Similarly, he has unfinished research material on Bangkok from the early 1980s, concerning five urban monasteries. Interestingly, a study of practice would have been a marked shift in emphasis from his more traditional focus on social structures and normative systems.

Tambiah's first monograph, *Buddhism and the Spirit Cults*, gave rise to an extended interest, namely, how to understand Buddhism in a wider national perspective. Hence his second monograph, *World Conqueror and World Renouncer*, which took him more firmly to the intersection of history and anthropology. Here he looked at the religio-political dimensions of Buddhism and monks' involvement in national rituals. It was of course in this work that Tambiah introduced his well-known notion of a "galactic polity" to describe the precolonial regional polity, and discussed the critical changes in the nineteenth century involving the Thai *sangha* (monastic order) in what he termed a "radial polity." It was while looking at establishment religion and its links to monarchy, polity, and related political structures that he identified another religious orientation, that of the forest monks.

It is clear—to rebut some of Tambiah's critics, such as Oxford Sanskritist Richard Gombrich and his "disciples"[4] Steven Collins and Michael Carrithers and, across the Atlantic, Charles Keyes[5]—that Tambiah's attention to history, language, and culture, while looking from the center-polity outward, encapsulated social actors located in both the center and the periphery of the Buddhist state. Tambiah refers to this as the *center-periphery* dialectic. In the forests he noted the periphery's articulation with the economic, religio-political, and ritual center through famous forest monks. He noted that these monks, in the doctrinal traditions of Buddhism, are its "greatest achievers" and the "true world renouncers," as they have entered the direct "arahant path to salvation" (Tambiah 1984, 333). They are in a sense both outside and above society, a seemingly ambivalent position emphatically rooted in Indian asceticism. In Louis Dumont's terms (cited in Taylor 1993, 11), they are an idealization of the "individual-outside-the-world," though defined by their own condition and individuality in the world. Since the 1960s, forest monks have been a source of much-needed charisma and sacred power, accrued through their distance from the center and their asceticism and meditation.

Importantly, Tambiah's engagement with Weber's interactive view of religion, society, and economics, and especially his notion of charisma, was intensified while he worked on *Buddhist Saints of the Forest*. At this time he extended Weber's thinking on charisma as objectified in certain ritual objects, and its importance in the religio-political domain.[6] Tambiah's research on amulets notes the way in which these are produced, and how ascetic monks are able to transfer to them their "untamed," "free-floating" charisma. Such charisma is very unstable, while at the same time potentially creative. He also notes how certain ritual objects link well-known forest monks to lay supporters, and how these objects are used and manipulated in economic, political, and historical processes.

It was Tambiah's use of Weber's ideal-typologies, especially in relation to charisma among acclaimed saints and sacred objects, that first influenced the direction of my own research in the late 1980s.[7] I also revisited Weber and saw that his social formulation was a useful basis for understanding the successive institutional transformation, in four distinct development phases,[8] of forest monasteries in the lineage of the famous Thai Buddhist saint Phra Ajaan Man Phuuritthato (1870–1949). I suggested a correspondence between these phases and Weber's categories of charisma, from individuated to routinized, and saw, along with Tambiah, an "objectified" charisma attributed to certain sacred objects, which accounts for the final "Terminal Phase" of forest monasteries and the construction of reliquaries (in Thai, *Jedii-phiphithaphan*). These mark the local landscape while at the same time imputing universal religiosity to the modern Buddhist nation-state.

In my view, Tambiah explores well the popular religiosity around the charisma of religious objects. He recognizes that an object's meanings, functions, and values are constituted not just in relation to form, but also in relation to social imperatives, as we see in the circulation and commodification of amulet-medallions.[9]

In all three of his monographs on Thailand, methodologically Tambiah enumerates a distinctive use of the concept of "totalization," whereby he articulates the underlying structures and meanings attributed to social, political, and historical aspects of Thai Buddhism. He refers to "different kinds and scale" of totalities (Tambiah 1987, 192). This shows the multifaceted and dynamic relationship in religion between stasis and change, "where certain kinds of persistence *coexist* with certain kinds of changes of state" in relation to the "complexity and pervasiveness of a historical condition" (ibid., 194). It is to Tambiah's not uncontroversial use of the term *totalization* in relation to Thai Buddhism that I now turn.[10]

From the Center Outward: Tambiah's Dialectical Approach

As I understand Tambiah, "totalization" implies a compelling dialectical set of relations that indicate open rather than closed systems. He views Buddhism from the center of power outward, as encompassing both an enduring, universal textual base and a synchronic, parochial, ritual action in the world. Indeed, he made this position clear in his first monograph, based on work undertaken in the 1960s in the now-modern village of Baan Phran Muan situated outside the northeast regional city of Udornthani, though he would refine his method over the next two monographs.

Tambiah believes that Thai Buddhism is best seen as a single system rather than subdivided into separate cultural categories of action.[11] He also recognizes that both text and practice have at times undergone transformation. All Buddhist practice, he would also argue, is linked in some way to a primitive literary or cosmological tradition. This is understood as a "total social phenomenon," or later, "totalization"—a concept that Tambiah initially credited to Marcel Mauss's early sociology in the context of the structuralism of Edmund Leach.[12] Using this method Tambiah has been able to encompass both structure and history in understanding current interrelated social arrangements. In his view these cannot be readily compartmentalized into distinct religious, political, and economic domains (Tambiah 1984, 7).

Although Tambiah has linked certain contemporary practices to early modulations, he is ready to acknowledge various social facts. He makes clear consistencies as ritually enacted in villages, towns, courts, and forests. These are connected, in turn, to a traditional vocational polarity found in early Buddhist monasticism (Keyes 1987, 130–31); namely, between religious study, or *pariyattidhura/kantha-thura*, and meditation practice, or *patipattidhura/vipassana-thura* (Tambiah 1970, 66–67; Taylor 1993, 15–16). This polarity presented a dilemma which, as I show later, confronted Mongkut (the monk reformer who became the Fourth Reign monarch), and it especially confronted Fifth Reign sangha reformers. As these modalities relate to the locus of practice, such that town = study and forest = meditation/asceticism, we could include a third, namely, vernacular/village monasticism (*Phrasong-baan*), a domain of interest in Tambiah's early work. In fact, a Fifth Reign document also mentions a tripartite vocational division in the sangha, one that includes "chanting monks" (*Phra Suat-mon*),[13] regarded by reform elites as engaging in a less reputable mode of monastic practice.[14] As Tambiah (1984, 53) mentions, the Pali texts clearly refer to specific dwelling orientations, including forest (*āraññavāsī*), village (*gāmavāsī*), and town (*nagaravāsī*). This distinction is also implicit in Dumont (1970) between the "renouncer" and the "man-in-the-world," which can be extended to include distinctions within the sangha itself, for example between forest and village/town monks, according to their degrees of increasing worldliness.

Tambiah looks at "totalizing" politico-religious relations in reference to the *Aggañña Sutta*,[15] which he sees as a charter text, showing the development and hierarchical ordering of human societies.[16] In relation to Tambiah's thinking on the Weberian question of "this-worldliness" or "other-worldliness" is the social construction of the world as an imagined and real space, an active cosmology showing the "ideal" social interaction under a benevolent monarch (Maha Sammata) of the Buddha's Khattiya caste. This cosmology in turn implies governance according to the principles of Buddhist morality. The arahant/saint is the most important figure in this cosmology. Tambiah sees living Buddhism in this text in its entirety, involving multiple relationships between monk and king, between the Buddha and the Cakkavatti (ideal world ruler) as the two wheels of the Dhamma, between "this-" and "other-worldly" pursuits. He notes (1976, 15–16) that this multiplicity also makes Buddhism a lived world religion, and not just a religion for the select few practitioners or religious virtuosi.[17]

But, as Tambiah later added (1984,7), as a doctrinal basis of social action Pali Buddhism needs to be read as an "interwoven tapestry" of elements—biographical, philosophical, mythological, and cosmological. These elements relate to particular ritual practices as a *total system*, as he showed in his first monograph, integrating contemporary normative Buddhist and pre-Buddhist traditions (insofar as we can discern a boundary between these, in syncretic readings). Here, the peasantry is incorporated into a total cultural system through their participation in an active Buddhist cosmology (Tambiah 1970, 35).[18]

In his early formulation Tambiah was concerned mainly with relations between sangha and polity, though he would elaborate this formulation in later work to include the following dualities: on the one side, king and establishment sangha; on a second side, relations between king and reform forest monks; and on a third side, the internal engagement within the sangha itself between town-dwellers and forest-dwellers. The relations that exist between political authority and the internally segmented sangha could, as Tambiah notes in a classic statement, "be profitably regarded as a centre-periphery dialectic exhibiting a variety of pulsations and oscillations" (1984, 2-3). In his *Buddhist Saints of the Forest* (1984) he engages with a more sustained discussion on the role of the Buddhist laity, aside from "ruler and polity."[19] In my view it is certain that had Tambiah not shifted his focus to ethnic conflict, ethnonationalism, and political violence in Sri Lanka, he may well have taken this analysis and research further. But on this matter we can only speculate.

I now turn to the final section of my article and a "Tambiahan analysis" in respect to my own work on the forest monks' vinaya as ritual performance and primary paradigmatic charter.

Paradigms in Theravada Buddhist Tradition: The Primitive Monks' Charter, Reform, and the Modern Kammaṭṭhāna Monks

In this section I extend Tambiah's recent methodology and his Weber-inspired analysis on charisma by way of a short case study from my own work on the *dhutanga Kammaṭṭhāna* tradition.[20] In one of his more recent papers, in which he starts to extend his thinking across multiple religious traditions, Tambiah has generously acknowledged my research as following his in time, noting that my "documentation is worthy of recognition" (Tambiah 1997, 538-61). He further notes generously how my work has elaborated on the "forest monk narrative" where he left off, contributing what he calls valuable new information in relation to the cult of relics, amulets, and relic-museums as embodied memory of famous northeastern-born forest monks.

In *Forest Monks and the Nation-state* (1993) I show a persisting dialectics and tension among forest monks, which has brought about compromise in more recent times with the need for increasing distance between the world-renouncer and wider society. This spatial separation accounts for the luminosity and purity of forest monks. Being at the potent mystical center of the cosmic order, the *kammathaan* (ascetic meditation) monks are sought out for their merit. The further their distance from society and the greater their purity (and thus the greater their acclaimed spiritual attainments), the more merit there is to be gained by the laity from contact with them, and hence the classic dilemma: the more sought-after the recluse becomes. As Weber (1970, 327) suggested, in renouncing the world and gaining higher spirituality, the recluse may also accrue special magical powers that permit mastery over the mundane world.

The quandary for kammathaan monks, given Thailand's disappearing frontier, seems to be one of trying to outdistance a fervent laity wishing to connect through merit-making with the powers the monks are assumed to have (Taylor 1993, 315-16). This is where Tambiah focused particular interest in his last extensive research in Thailand (1978-1979), exposing for the first time these dilemmas and the social, politico-religious, and historical significance of famous forest monks. Tambiah was absolutely correct in his early comments on Ajaan Man's religio-political and historical significance in the nation-state as embracing both continuities and transformations; this significance is best understood by means of Tambiah's approach, which he has summarized as "retrospective and prospective, textual and contextual, semantic and pragmatic, referential and indexical—in short, the tracking of persistences and transformations" (1987, 205). He states that to understand the significance of Ajaan Man we need to both go back to an early monastic charter and regional heritage, and at the same time situate the saint in the context of contemporaneous late-nineteenth/early-twentieth-century religious and political reforms (ibid., 209).

The modern kammathaan tradition, as I also show later in this essay in relation to the vinaya, may be understood in spatial terms as both localized and Buddhalogical, or universal, in scale. Indeed, in the forest tradition, interpretations relevant to the reform forest tradition of Ajaan Man ritually cross-cut the binary politico-religious divisions of the Thai Nikaya (Pali: literally, "assemblage," or "grouping"; used here to refer to the two main monastic "sects" in Thailand).

The normative ritual and historical reference pertains to particular understandings of the early vinaya and the thirteen allowable ascetic practices (*dhuṭangas*). These practices were reassessed in accordance with doctrinal bases understood in the late-nineteenth-century reforms. They were selectively followed by Ajaan Man and his first meditation teacher, Ajaan Sao Kantasilo (1859–1942). They subsequently became routinized monastic practices for contemporary ascetic forest monks (*paṭipatti*) (Taylor 1993, 303).

The myth created around Ajaan Man's life and the disciplinary practices he established among his disciples became a social charter for the modern forest tradition; it was an assertion of the continuity and importance of the moral and social practices of forest monastic tradition and its primitive vinaya established far back in time.

In his last monograph on Thai Buddhism, then, Tambiah essentially shows how a particular modern forest monk lineage emerges from the nineteenth-century sangha reforms. At the same time he identifies common textual sources of the forest-dwelling arahant, lived out on the contemporary Thai frontier. An ancient tradition has been reworked; or, to use a normative simile, the "path has been cleared" through intuitive understanding of the Dhamma. Although antischolastic (but not antitextual), the modern kammathaan tradition was clearly fashioned by the reforms. The original textual sources of influence were to be found in Pali materials brought back from Sri Lanka and reconsidered largely under the auspices of Mongkut while he was still a monk. This body of material was compared with existing Theravada knowledge and practice and with the politico-religious context during the reign of Phra Nang Klao (Rama III, r. 1824–1851). The sangha at this time was loosely organized, and, lacking a systematic centralized administration, consisted of four groups (*khana*), the Northern, Central, Southern, and the less clearly delineated "Forest-Dwellers." Mongkut's new reform Thammayut Nikai (sect),[21] established in 1833 initially with a small number of Bangkok followers, was in the Central Group.[22]

The Pali works from Sri Lanka were translated into Thai. These works included the Indian-born monk Buddhaghosa's fifth-century translations from Sinhalese to Pali of a commentary on the Vinaya Pitaka, the *Samanta-Pāsādikā*, based on ancient commentaries brought to Sri Lanka from India; sections from Buddhaghosa's classic exegesis, the

Visuddhimagga, dealing with the thirteen ascetic practices; and an introspective discourse on "mindfulness of the body," the *Kāyagatā-sati Sutta*.[23] Buddhaghosa, resident at Sri Lanka's conservative Mahavihara Monastery, also translated a commentary on the code of monastic discipline (*Pāṭimokkha*).[24] Perhaps it is not surprising, then, that there are similarities between the practices of reform kammathaan monks in Thailand and the nineteenth-century reforms of a forest tradition in Sri Lanka conducted under the forest monk Paññananda (1817-1887), studied by Michael Carrithers of Durham University (Carrithers 1983, ch. 4).[25] In 1862 Paññananda, seeking ordination purity, went to the Mon or Ramañña country in southern Burma to receive a second, higher ordination under a Mon lineage. This same lineage had earlier had important implications for Mongkut's doctrinal reforms. Both reforms, then, were clearly inspired by orthodox Mon monasticism, with its doctrinal antecedents in the fifteenth century under the sangha reforms of ethnic-Mon King Dhammazedi.[26]

In Thailand, kammathaan monks were able to maintain certain aspects of Mongkut's vision of doctrinal asceticism, as observed in the practices of these Mon monks, by their distance from the center (Tambiah 1984, 165), at least until the effective modern domestication of the frontier by the center and its disciplinary apparatuses.

An interesting feature of Thai Buddhism that Tambiah discussed in his *Buddhist Saints* is the centrality of the acclaimed arahant, which has a dual dimension, both vernacular (as an incorporated oral tradition) and textual/inscribed. This duality relies on the dialectic between the modes of transmission through clearly defined monastic pupilages. In such contexts it is not surprising that the charisma of the monastic teacher, or *krubaa-ajaan,* is so critical and that "routinization" of the teacher is similarly extended to direct pupilages (Taylor 1993, 6).

The important characteristic in the identity and sustainability of formal monastic lineages (*paramparā*) and segmented pupilages (in Thai, *saai*) is the monks' disciplinary charter, or vinaya.[27] The vinaya was initially deployed as a mnemonic device to be used by small face-to-face groups of wandering monks, who were encouraged to review it internally first and then rehearse it in groups each fortnight. However, the vinaya (such as it was) was bitterly contested in the early sangha, leading to dissent within the greater monastic community and to the various vinayas as we have them, passed down today in living traditions. The vinaya therefore is closely connected to the identification and development of monastic lineages, and subsequently to the proliferation of subtexts and various pupilages. In the Theravadin tradition the vinaya has central place and is at the core of many disagreements, such as the more recent debate involving the sanction of full ordination rights for women. In the case of forest monks in Thailand, while they may be affiliated through a formal ordination lineage with the Thammayut Nikaya, in a kind of primordial identification based on early vocational divisions in the sangha, they consider affiliation with their monastic pupilage through their teacher as more important. As found among Sinhalese forest monks, pupillary succession (at least that based on the charisma of the founding teacher) does not usually survive the death of the teacher (Carrithers 1983, 140).

In the case of the reform kammathaan tradition of Ajaan Man, a small pupilage of dedicated monks with a distinct characteristic appeared who shared in common the new reform nikaya's vinaya. In the second phase of Ajaan Man's monastic career, from 1916 to 1928, he started to attract a dedicated group of monks and lay followers.[28] These monks, as a corporate entity, agreed to follow the same "forest vinaya"; they collaborated in collective sangha rituals (Sanghakamma); and importantly, they participated in the fortnightly Patimokkha recitation by virtue of their new re-ordination, while accompanying the Master on his wanderings.

My own experience as a kammathaan monk in the Ajaan Man tradition during a rains-residence in 2007 suggests that it is not uncommon for a krubaa-ajaan to emphasize consistently the correct observance of the forest vinaya and its solidarity rituals. At the same time he may refer to the now deceased head of the tradition, Ajaan Maha Bua (Bhikkhu Ñanasampanno, 1913–2011), whom I have discussed elsewhere (Taylor 2001), as a disciplinary knowledge source. The paradigmatic primitive forest vinaya is undoubtedly the core frame of reference among kammathaan monks. In a mythic context it provides a basis for a social charter. But to understand the nineteenth-century version of the vinaya, monks had to have a foundation in the Pali language. This was not a problem in many *reform* monasteries in the northeast region, where Pali and Thai were for the first time programmatically taught to novices.

The forest saint Ajaan Man gained a basis of Pali learning in the Dhamma-Vinaya in at least two ways: first, through early sangha reformers sent by Mongkut to establish the Thammayut Nikaya in Ubon, the regional center for the reforms; and second, from later,

Bangkok-based Northeastern Region administrative scholar-monks during Ajaan Man's occasional rains residence at one of Mongkut's royal monasteries, Wat Pathumwan, from 1914 onward. At the time this was a monastery intended for the residence of northeastern monks (Maha Bua 2005, 143). By around 1915, after having become an *anagami*—a "non-returner," one who has reached the third of the four stages of enlightenment—the Master started actively teaching. He was especially close to a number of influential monks, although given the tensions among Bangkok-based Thammayut elites at the time, not all new reformers regarded him well (see Thanissaro 2005). But his concern with orthopraxy he shared with many reformers, even if he was evasive when it came to extending state hegemony in the periphery. In 1893, in the new nikaya at Wat Liap in Ubon, Man was re-ordained under Mongkut's personally chosen missionary, Preceptor Phra Ariyakawii "Orn" (1845–1903).[29] This was the monastery, then situated on the outskirts of the town, where Ajaan Sao was abbot for a while. Formerly the monastery had belonged to the more diverse majority Thai sect, the Maha Nikaya, and, like many, was resanctified around the turn of the century (Wiphaakphojanakhit 1970, 632). It is certain that the new monastic movement created considerable resistance in the region, essentially taking "wat away from locals," as Richard O'Connor (1993, 330) aptly put it.[30] But there was also resistance within the court, as Mongkut was well aware, and later he had to moderate his strong line, before his accession to the throne (Reynolds 1976, 212 n. 50). By the time he ascended the throne as Rama IV, he had around him one hundred and thirty close disciples (Eoseewong 1982, 282).

The first Thammayut regional monastery in fact was Wat Supat'an'aaraam, established in 1851–53, some forty years before Ajaan Man's re-ordination (Taylor 1993, 46–48, 75). The establishment of the Thammayut in the northeast region, as indeed elsewhere, would be best understood as both a political and religious movement, given its importance in the centralization and unification of the nation-state (Eoseewong 1982, 282). Alongside state-funded technological development, especially in printing, it was the educated, literate elite, both secular and religious, sharing the same vernacular language, who created the conditions that enabled the new movement to extend itself so effectively in the countryside (Anderson 1983, 37–46). It was around this time that Ajaan Man went wandering with Ajaan Sao; from 1892, for the next few years, he shared with Ajaan Sao the kammathaan way of life (Maha Bua 2005, 469 n. 18). Although the

1902 Sangha Act brought monasteries and monks under stricter state controls, it seems to have been a merger of convenience between new kammathaan monks and sangha reformers. Both seemed to take what was useful from the other. As time went by, many of Ajaan Man's forest disciples became de facto reform "frontiersmen" and thereby consolidated the state in hard-to-reach places, whatever the personal reservations some state functionaries may have had about these monks (Taylor 1993, 41).

Mongkut, and later one of his sons, prince-monk Wachirayan (who in 1913 produced a three-volume treatise on the vinaya still used today, the *Vinaya-Mukha*), considered wandering forest monks without a credible ordination tradition to be idiosyncratic and aberrant. Throughout Theravada history, however, forest monks with a reputable vinaya heritage were in fact always sought after by kings and elites during times of instability and change. Chulalongkorn (Rama V) also believed there were no longer any monks capable of attainments, and could find little inspiration in peri-urban forest monks, seeing them as influenced by Tantric and Brahmanical practices. This in turn convinced the reformers to look instead to Pali textual sources. It was clear eventually that reform kammathaan monks were able to act out the normative ideals and maintain the Dhamma-Vinaya to the inspiring level expected by elites. The eventual "routinization" of Ajaan Man and his incorporation into the institutions of the state neutralized his potentially worrisome individuated charisma. This was a time when the state was clearly concerned about activities on its boundaries, about emergent definitions of nationhood, and about the need to invent nationalist doctrine (Kedourie 1993).

The need for reconciliation and normalization, aided by a universal education program, was foremost in the minds of sangha reformers during the Fifth and Sixth Reigns. This explains the increased hostility of Wachirayan, during the latter part of his life when he had become Supreme Patriarch, toward the nonparticipating, nonscholastic kammathaan monks. Political concerns affected changes in the Thammayut as in the wider secular and religious domains, as Chulalongkorn, looking westward, saw possibilities of reorganizing the country as a modern nation-state. According to Thanissaro (2005), the king even noted the example of Meiji Japan, where Buddhist monks played what he considered a useful role in modernization.

Although Wachirayan's sangha reforms were far-reaching, rooted in the understanding of the vinaya as universal tradition, at the same

time they were historically particularistic (Taylor 1993, 134). The interaction between local and universal forces can be appreciated in relation to the monastic disciplinary charter. The most important source
used by kammathaan monks from at least 1906 was the *Pubbasikkhā-
viṇṇanā* (literally "to study from the beginning"), a comprehensive
vinaya code for use initially in the new nikaya (Taylor 1993, 134-36,
303-05). But it was also used by kammathaan monks ordained in the
greater Maha Nikaya, notably the well-known teacher Ajaan Chaa
Subhato (1918-1992), who was not re-ordained. For instance, as Ajaan
Chaa noted:

> So, when it comes to the *Vinaya*, I've studied a lot. Some days dur-
> ing the rains retreat I would study from six o'clock in the evening
> through till dawn. I understand it sufficiently. All the factors of
> *āpatti* (offences) that are covered in the *Pubbasikkhā* I wrote down
> in a notebook and kept in my bag. I really put effort into it ... when
> I teach the monks here I still take the *Pubbasikkhā* as my standard.

> (Chaa 2002, 84)

The *Pubbasikkha* was completed around 1860, toward the latter years
of Mongkut's reign, by a notable scholar-monk named Phra Amarā
Bhirakkhit (Amaro Koet); he was the second abbot of Wat Boromni-
wat. He was a friend of Mongkut when the latter was a monk, and was
re-ordained with him, along with forty-eight monks, at Wat Samorai in 1829. The group spent the first rains' residence discussing a
shared vision of orthodoxy in a new Dhamma-Vinaya. Mongkut also
learned meditation at Wat Samorai, which already had a reputation
as a locale for ascetic monks. Until the first decade of the twentieth
century, when reformers started to question the "purity and principles" of the original Pali sources on hand, much doctrinal learning
had been passed along by oral transmission.[31] In fact we know little of
the mechanics of how monks actually remembered normative texts
(Gombrich 1990, 25), other than the traditional mnemonic system of
repetition, formulae, meter, and numbered lists.[32] Transmitting this
learning may have been the responsibility of specialist monks, as in
the ancient tradition of *bhāṇakas* (monastic reciters).

The *Pubbasikkha* gives a detailed explanation of vinaya points and
arguments organized according to topic. Wachirayan used the text as
a sub-commentary (*tikā*) for his work. The text is still used as a source
by kammathaan monks, as we saw above in the case of Ajaan Chaa, as
it is considered "purer" and more detailed than existing texts dealing

with Dhamma-Vinaya. Ajaan Sao apparently once carried a copy of an early edition with him (Taylor 1993, 135). But it was the 1906, Fifth Reign version, still extant, that was mainly used by these monks, as it contained the thirteen ascetic practices, which had been omitted from earlier versions. There are many references to forest-dwelling in this edition, which is still current, including minutiae and duties when staying in forest areas (*Araññikavatta*). We should keep in mind that during the early Chakri reigns many monasteries favored by kings were situated in forests on the outskirts of the capital, with charnel grounds, or crematoria—places considered useful for insight (*vipassana*) meditation (O'Connor 1978, 1980), or for contemplation on loathsome (*asubha*) aspects of the body (from the Pali source work *Kāyagatā-sati Sutta*). Mural paintings at the royal temples Wat Bowonniwet and Wat Somanat, for instance, commissioned by Mongkut, graphically show *asubha kammatthana atthika* body meditations (Listopad 2001).

The reforms alone, as Tambiah has recognized, do not explain the thriving of forest monasticism (cf. O'Connor 1980, 36) which, as noted, has had a resurgence from time to time throughout Thai history. However, the reforms clearly raised popular consciousness (Keyes 1987, 141), especially in relation to vinaya and orthopraxy. Here were monks enacting the religious heritage of the Buddha in the present time, through the direct arahant path of discipline and practice (*arahattamagga*).

As a reference point, the *Pubbasikkha* consists of canonical and post-canonical material from the two missions to Sri Lanka (1842 and 1844) that were requested by Mongkut, missions that were similar to earlier revitalization initiatives by his grandfather, Rama I (r. 1782–1806).[33] The central issues here are the perceived purity of monks associated with their disciplinary charter and as a much-sought-after field of merit; establishing, accordingly, a basis for the moral legitimation and right of Buddhist kings to rule. Mongkut clearly had "faith in the lineage of the sāsana in Ceylon" (Sasanasobhon 1968, 55). Phra Amarā was one of five or six monks sent on both missions to bring back Pali texts, especially vinaya texts, for copying in Thailand. He also accompanied back home Sri Lankan monks who had been staying at Wat Bowonniwet, which shows the extent of early religious exchanges between the two countries—a tradition, intersecting with reform Mon-Buddhism in southern Burma, that also goes back to the First Reign. Although the *Pubbasikkha* has integrated consid-

erable Sinhalese Pali sources, Thanissaro (2007, 1:9) notes that there
is still textual detail that is particular to the Thai experience and the
reform mix that cannot be traced directly to Buddhaghosa's earlier-
mentioned *Samanta-Pāsādikā*.

The extant version of the *Pubbasikkha* was originally found in a
bookshelf belonging to the prince-monk Wachirayan at the Thammayut's monastic center in Bangkok, Wat Bowonniwet. The text was
written in an early, limited romanized Pali version that Mongkut
called *Ariyaka*, a term etymologically taken from *Ariya* (Noble One) in
reference to the purity of the Buddha's heritage; it was meant for an
elite group of reformers. Perhaps influenced by medical missionary
Dan Beach Bradley's innovations in the 1830s, Mongkut used an early
printing press which he established at Wat Bowonniwet for the mass
production and circulation of new monastic and teaching materials,
including the *Pāṭimokkha* in the Ariyaka script. This was claimed to be
the first Thai-owned and controlled printing press. At that time, Pali
was ordinarily written using the Khmer or old Khom alphabet, which
Mongkut considered too complicated.[34]

In general the *Pubbasikkha* was an important text in the forest
tradition, as it not only provided a normative reference, but facili-
tated a vital link between the elusive kammathaan monks and the
early sangha reformers (Taylor 1993, 136). The text was sponsored in
a number of printings by royalty until after 1900; the current king
of Thailand, Bhumibol Adulyadej, also sponsored a new printing in
1955.[35] Tambiah may have been intrigued, given his interest since the
1960s in semantics, linguistic structural-functional theories, and in
particular in the importance of ritual words as ritual acts,[36] by the inclusive use of the power and ritual function of language in the elite
Ariyaka method.[37] Here the Ariyaka script had the exclusive power
to influence a certain kind of reality marked by its difference from
ordinary language, being generally perceived as having mystical ritual power (Tambiah 1968, 184).[38] In the Ariyaka script, the sacred text
and its articulation, or the uttering of words, constitute in themselves
an exclusive ritual (Leach 1966, 407). For instance, it would be interesting to know how Ariyaka was used as a "performative" by sangha
reformers and among elites residing at the palace to delineate pure
groups from vernacular groups considered to be impure or ritually
polluting (in the sense outlined in Dumont 1970). In devising this
limited language, one Bangkok-based scholar-monk noted, Mongkut
clearly wanted to communicate in simplified romanized Pali to elite

Sri Lankan monks and reformers in neighboring countries. He also wanted to show a connection to the normative doctrinal bases and establish a ritual distance from local (Thai and Khmer) traditions, in order to affirm universal Theravadin values (Anil 2008). Finally, it was the associational thought of this language, though short-lived, that was to have a lasting impact on the configuration of contemporary Thai Buddhism.

Conclusion

In my view, Tambiah was correct in his early analysis of Thai Buddhism in emphasizing the need to see the religion as a dialectical relationship between doctrinal, textual perspectives on the world and action within the world as a consequence of historical transformation. Actors clearly imprint meaning in a variety of modalities of the religious in a dialectical intermediacy of the present. The world-renunciation quest, as Tambiah has shown, is not a contradiction or paradox to those who live the religion. My own work in Thailand in the late 1980s, concerned with the charismatic social field of forest-dwelling Buddhist saints, the political ecology of elite patronage, and the culture of popular devotion, owes a debt of intellectual gratitude to Tambiah's anthropology of Theravada Buddhism. Methodologically Tambiah may have leaned toward the center more than he worked outward, while I started on the outside and worked toward the center. However, it is more than gratifying to note that, while we may not have always agreed on some detail in relation to matters of ethnography and history, we share a convergence of intellectual perspectives.

Transnational Buddhism and the Transformations of Local Power in Thailand

Ingrid Jordt

In his autobiographical introduction to *World Conqueror and World Renouncer,* Stanley Tambiah reconstructs for his readers the intellectual journey that led him to his path-breaking work on the Thai polity in religious and historical perspective. It is at least in part for this work that we honor him in this collection, and it bears profitable recounting to repeat his words on how he saw himself located as an ethnographer and analyst:

> I was conscious then, and even more so later on subsequent visits and especially when I was writing the book *Buddhism and the Spirit Cults in North-east Thailand,* that my view of the Thai world was a projection outward from the village. Such a perspective, though partial, was rewarding, for my intensive close-to-ground labors gave me some idea of how religious conceptions and rites were interwoven with village institutional life and some inkling of how the great tradition of Buddhism, in both its doctrinal and cosmo-logical aspects, may be refracted in the microcosm of village life.
>
>   I promised myself that some day I would attempt a macro-scopic view of religion's connection with society as a whole, espe-

cially in society's aspect as a polity.... I realized that if I wanted to
study how kinship and Buddhism interrelated, how religion and
politics informed and interpenetrated each other, I would have
to manage a panoramic and telescopic view of the society, from a
vantage point located high above the bustling metropolis of Bangkok. So, in 1971 I began wide-ranging fieldwork in Bangkok, studying closely four urban monasteries and visiting others (including
some in provincial towns); inquiring into the organization of
the monks' universities, particularly Mahachulalongkorn, and
the careers and views of their administrator-monks and monk-
students; interviewing officials at the Department of Religious
Affairs and collecting whatever official documents I could; and
doing many other things such as visiting shrines and meditation
centers, attending ceremonies and curing sessions, and so on.
(1976, 3)

As I have periodically returned to Tambiah's writings, I have been
struck by his capacity for binding together complex and wide-ranging
strands of data and theory under a single paradigm. It is not hyper-
bole to refer to Tambiah's accomplishment in synthesizing Thai Buddhist cosmology with the historical and regional power principle as
"world conquering." In writing this paper, my goal initially was to use
several interviews I had conducted in 1988 with Phra Phimolatham
(1903-1989), the prominent monk whose position in the Thai *sangha*
(Buddhist community) drew Tambiah's attention in the 1970s, and
to combine my interview material with what I knew of that monk's
engagement with my field site in neighboring Burma, to add an ethnographic wrinkle to Tambiah's work. My attempts were soon discom-
fited, as each time I grew excited at what I could add, I looked deeper
into Tambiah's books and found that he had already reflected on this
or that aspect of social action and meaning, sometimes if only in a
protracted footnote.

I offer then, more in the spirit of amusing than enlightening our
Professor Tambiah, the following reflections on the legacy of Phra Phimolatham's efforts to revitalize Thai Buddhism by infusing new life
into meditative practice there, and of his efforts to propagate *vipassana*
(insight) meditation beyond Thai borders. Phra Phimolatham figures
prominently in both *World Conqueror and World Renouncer* (Tambiah
1976) and *The Buddhist Saints of the Forest and the Cult of Amulets* (Tambiah 1984). He was the abbot of Wat Mahathat (the principle monastery of the majority Mahanikai sect) and the ecclesiastical Minister of

the Interior who greatly advanced the propagation of lay meditation in Thailand.

My own perspective on this history is neither a "projection outward from the [Thai] village" nor "from a vantage point located high above the bustling metropolis of Bangkok." The view I offer is, if from anywhere, from Burma, where Phra Phimolatham traveled more than a dozen times in the attempt to import Burmese pedagogy for Abhidhamma study and the Mahasi method of vipassana meditation practice to Thailand.

The Abhidhamma is an abstract systematization and a philosophical theory offering a perspective on the nature of reality and an ethical program for liberation. In Burma, the Abhidhamma is accorded a great deal of attention. Vipassana meditation in its mass form developed following the influence of the renowned monk Mahasi Sayadaw (1904–1982). The briefest summary of Burma's lay meditation movement, which accelerated as a result of Mahasi's teachings and Prime Minister U Nu's support of them, can be stated as follows. Rather than allowing the extent of their practice of *sila* (virtue) to be limited to supporting the sangha through *dana* (donations) and attending to the layman's precepts, laity became intent on practicing *bhavanna* (meditation) in order to secure their path out of *samsara* (the cycle of rebirths) before the *Sasana* (Buddha's teachings) might disappear. The apostolic period of the Buddha was used as an implicit framework for validating laity's engagement in the highest soteriological goals. Mahasi's method introduced a systematic and methodical description of the stages of insight leading to the realization of *nibbana* (nirvana). Laity now perceived their engagement with the Sasana as one that not only distinguished categories of persons as renouncers and householders, but as enlightened (*ariya*) and unenlightened (*pothujjhana*).

A comparison of the development of the national Buddhisms of Burma and of Thailand reveals similar processes of religious reform and revival, as two incommensurate forms of power—one spiritual and the other worldly—were brought into closer alignment.

Burma's experience differed from the Thai experience due to its eighty-five-year history of colonialism. At the end of the nineteenth century and beginning of the twentieth century, several millenarian and revitalization efforts were already afoot in Burma, in reaction to the absence of a strong central authority that could purify and promote the sangha. The end of Burmese kingship and its supportive (and controlling) functions with respect to the sangha led to fractiousness within the sangha, whose efforts at self-purification promoted further sectarian divisions and rivalries. In response to these diversifying impulses, lay associations emerged. These attempted to fulfill the classical role and functions of kings, to maintain the sangha's adherence to the *vinaya* (monks' code of conduct) and to promote scholarship through lay sponsorship of scriptural exams and the conferral of titles. I have argued (Jordt 2007a) that a millenarian movement triggered by the loss of Buddhist kingship and the perception of the decline of society and the World Age gave rise to a lay meditation movement that sought to reinvigorate society and the religion in the face of British colonial policies that had separated church and state.

During the U Nu period (1948-1962), vipassana meditation was viewed as a revitalization of the Sasana following colonial rule. U Nu organized the sixth Buddhist synod, which signaled the efflorescence of meditation practice as tied to the project of revitalizing the texts. Thereby, a strong connection between *pariyatti* (text learning) and *patipatti* (meditation practice) was re-established. The texts would verify the experience of insight and vice-versa.

Phra Phimolatham's explicit goal was likewise to reconnect pariyatti and patipatti. This work became deeply entangled in Thai sectarian politics and rivalries, some in connection with royal reforms associated with the founding of the Thammayut sect under King Mongkut (r. 1851-1868). The following is Tambiah's description of the historical reforms instituted by Mongkut, especially as they implicated meditation:

> Mongkut's stated aim in founding the new sect was to improve upon the lax practices of the extant *sangha,* that is, the Mahanikai sect. . . . These ascetic practices of *arannavasi* tradition were not, however, combined by Mongkut with an emphasis on the practice of *samadhi* (concentration) and the cultivation of wisdom through insight meditation. Whereas Mongkut did stress that the exemplary Thammayut monks should combine scholarship with some proficiency in meditation, the latter pursuit did not become a central component in his conception of the monk's vocation. . . . It was because [Mongkut's] teachers could not provide the doctrinal and canonical explanations for the meditative practices that he became disenchanted with them and returned to Wat Mahathat to study canonical texts. (Tambiah 1984, 160)

This historical context is necessary to understand the nature of Phra Phimolatham's efforts at sasana revitalization and reform. It shows how the Thai efforts at integrating sasana practices relate to the centralizing efforts of the state. In as much as Phra Phimolatham drew inspiration from Burma it is worth reflecting upon how nationalist Buddhisms were being formed. I argue that national rivalries played a part in shaping the trajectories of Thai sectarian politics in which Phra Phimolatham took part. In his capacity as Sangha Minister of the Interior, Phimolatham had been promoting combining study (pariyatti) with meditation practice (patipatti). Meditation itself was a point of dispute in the sectarian struggles between the "reformist" Thammayut sect and the majority Mahanikai sect of which Phimolatham was aligned. From one perspective, the impulse for the revitalization reforms introduced by Phra Phimolatham came out of the perceived decline in the use of the pedagogic methods used to teach the texts in monasteries. Donald Swearer observes how "the government, through the Department of Religious Affairs of the Ministry of Education, has come to control religious knowledge, namely what is taught about Buddhism in both monastery and government schools" (1999, 216).

In 2007 I conducted interviews with a former monk ("Mr. C") who was a close supporter and trainee in Phra Phimolatham's revitalization program. According to Mr. C. the Dhamma learning situation in Thailand had become a shambles following the reforms instituted by the monk-prince Wajirayan. The reforms were seen as having simplified the Dhamma into "easy learning," thus eroding the original monastic learning style and watering it down. Phimolatham was interested in revitalizing meditation practice as well. Mr. C says that it was only after Phra Phimolatham could not find suitable Thai monks to teach meditation that he looked to Burma and the Mahasi method. We see that not only did there exist a vibrant criticism of the nineteenth-century reforms of Mongkut and of Wajirayan for pariyatti (scriptural) studies, there was also a perception that the patipatti (meditation practice) aspect of the teachings also required revitalization.

The sponsorship of meditation became a major source for sectarian rivalry between the Mahanikai sect and the Thammayut sect. Tambiah (1984) observes how Phra Phimolatham's "program of popularizing Vipassana meditation throughout the country" led to a counter-campaign by the Thammayut monks to popularize their provincial forest meditation teachers (155). He argues that support of the peripheral provinces' forest monks by the ecclesiastical and political center was part of the nationalizing and centralizing impulses of political authority. The contentiousness was crystallized in the personal enmity between Phra Phimolatham and Phra Mahawirawong, Supreme Patriarch (*Sangharaja*), who was instrumental in bringing charges against Phimolatham that led to his being forcibly disrobed and imprisoned.

I would like to draw attention to one section among the sixty-eight pages of charges against Phimolatham that illustrates also the relevance of geopolitical considerations at the time—particularly the fear of communist insurgency as well as a particular and deep-seated mistrust of the Burmese:

> The communists of Red China had been using members of The Sangha to spread their ideals and had set up an organization within The Sangha. Pra Pimon Tam [Phimolatham] was the head of this organization and its headquarters were in the Samnak Vipassana [meditation center] of Wat Maha Dhatu. The communists of Red China have also supplied the funds for the establishment of the Samnak Vipassana in Wat Maha Dhatu, as well as for sending bikkhus to Burma.
>
> The type of vipassana practiced in Burma is not really Buddhism, but a form of practice designed to trick the people into the ideals of the communist bikkhus. The method puts the mind of the meditator into a state where the teacher can pull the mind into believing the Buddhism of the communists. (Quoted in Apichat 1993)

Phimolatham's efforts to introduce Mahasi-style meditation represented a threat to the nation. Drawing on a widely perceived national rivalry between Burma and Thailand, this characterization of Burmese Buddhism illustrates the rhetoric used to evoke the sense in which a national Buddhism could be treated as a threat to Thailand's state.

Having laid the background to these politics of Sasana revitalization as a nation-state building endeavor, let me turn now to interviews I had with Phimolatham in 1988 (a year before his death). In these interviews we discussed his missions to Burma and his ideas about the state of Sasana in Burma and in Thailand.

> *Phimolathan* (paraphrased, through a translator): When it comes to education, the Thais learn rules, Vinaya, but the Burmese emphasize Abhidhamma. The Burmese learn profoundly whereas the

Thai learn generally and superficially. This is only my personal opinion. If I say that to another Thai monk they won't like to hear it.... When I sent Thai monks to Burma I had to answer diplomatically why they were going. I had to explain that they were going to learn some things they can't learn here. I had to be very diplomatic because there were many who didn't like it.

... Now Thai are studying Abhidhamma more analytically—less by rote. The Burmese learn the Pali grammar properly. They use the ancient method of learning. In olden days Thai used this learning method, but the king came and changed this style.... In Thailand there are two nikayas [sects] on account of political reasons.

If I gave you details and it were in ancient times, my head would be cut off, because I talked about the king. The king made the segregation. If you really analyze it, it is for political reasons. The fourth king, he was ordained here for many years at Wat Mahathat. He left the temple and after he left he had to be bigger and grander. That's why he established his own sect.

Jordt: Is it true that after King Mongkut, the fourth king, left Mahathat he found a Burmese Mon monk who taught him Dhamma? Why wasn't he satisfied with the Thai monks?

Phimolathan: I cannot say because it would be talking about the royal family.... Some truths can be known but cannot be spoken.

In considering the role of national sanghas and a universalizing revitalization effort, we can see in these excerpts a couple of noteworthy features. First is the idea that there is an authentic and original learning method that has been preserved by the Burmese. From Phimolatham's perspective, it is not therefore the "Burmese method" that is being adopted so much as the original "ancient method." King Mongkut's reforms are in this light a diversion from orthodox teachings for political purposes. (One need not delve deeply to find reference to sectarian rivalries here, and the place of the nineteenth-century reforms by Mongkut. There is also passing reference to rivalry with the Burmese sangha.) Phimolatham goes on to explain how these "ancient methods" allegedly preserved by the Burmese are misrecognized by the Thai sangha and laity for purely aesthetic reasons.

Phimolathan: Thai elderly monks, they don't like the Burmese monks because they are quite rough in their mannerisms, quite shabby robes. They like prim and proper styles. When they see Burmese monks like this they have a very bad impression. Thai are more delicate and refined and cultured in their mannerisms than

Burmese. The difference between the Thai and the Burmese monks can be seen in how they walk. The Thai monks, even if the planks are not nailed you will not hear them, but the Burmese monks even if the planks are nailed you can hear them.

In the Thai traditional way if elderly people are sitting there and a child will walk and they will hear the "tam, tam tam" they will use a stick and hit on the ankles. Thai custom, they train the children from when they are very young.

The Thais, when it comes to education, they learn rules, Vinaya, but the Burmese emphasize Abhidhamma. They observe the same two hundred twenty-seven rules. It's just cultural difference. The Thai monks say the Burmese monks' robes are too big, the measurements are a bit different.

In Thailand they all have one style in the temple—they wear the robes over one shoulder and when they go out over two shoulders. But in Burma they are confused which to choose and it depends on the conveniences and which nikaya they are in. There are so many nikaya in Burma. In Thailand you will never see the monks use their robes to cover their head. In Burma they do that. But it doesn't matter because it is a cultural thing, a national thing, it doesn't matter. Sometimes monks are short sighted, they don't have much wisdom and so they see all these things and then they criticize. Those who don't think that you can find the deeper meaning of the Dhamma in Burma, don't have *panna* [wisdom] to see. When I went to Burma, I didn't bother about all these rules, I wanted the gem [i.e., the Dhamma].

According to the Vinaya, monks ... are allowed to cover their collars, to make a collar with their robes. When it's hot they can make it into a coat. But in Thailand if you roll it up no one will give you food to eat. Thai people don't know the deeper Vinaya, so they criticize.

In both Thailand and Burma we can observe how the centralizing impulses of the state sought to tie the sangha to political authority. In Thailand, the collaboration of the Thammayut sect with political authorities had different nationalizing and centralizing objectives than those in the Burmese case. In Burma, U Nu aimed to transfer the centralizing authority and role of the king as chief supporter of the sasana to the populace, thereby aligning Buddhism and democratic governance in harmonizing institutional arrangements. This confluence of national political goals was compatible with classical sasana revitalization, with one innovative exception. It was the laity, in their invocation of the apostolic period of the Buddha as the metahistorical charter for organization and action, whose transformations through vipassana meditation practice would purify the monks and revitalize the state. This innovation was sparked by the abrupt removal of Buddhist kingship by the British colonialists and by the new overlords' refusal to undertake the classical functions of kingship through appointing a *thathanabaing*, or Chief Patriarch of the sangha.

Burma's sangha reverted to its monadic institutional form and a period of intense sectarian rivalry. Purification of the sangha, in the absence of a ruler's function to purify the sangha of heterodox elements, led eventually to the creation of lay associations and lay-owned centers in which laity could control monks within their institutional walls. Monks who did not maintain their code of conduct were asked to leave. Part of the laity's justification for undertaking this role (typically reserved for kings) was the fact of their having become vipassana practitioners, that is, individuals with direct and intuitive knowledge of the teachings. Patipatti meditation practice became institutionalized on a grand scale under U Nu and Mahasi, becoming simultaneously a verification of the texts, a revitalization of Buddhist society in the absence of a Buddhist king, and the conferral of political legitimacy on the populace through aligning an enlightened lay society with parliamentary democracy. Nation-state building and sasana revitalization found institutional and ideological compatibility.

Now I mentioned earlier the role that Mahasi Sayadaw of Burma had played in the systematization of vipassana practice. It is also the case that Mahasi, with the great support of Prime Minister U Nu, sought to propagate the meditation movement beyond national borders. There is no space here to describe Mahasi's missions abroad; however, it would have been clear to many at the time that Phimolatham's proselytizing efforts were in no small respect drawing upon Mahasi's own methods of propagation. For example, Phimolatham spread vipassana through the branch monasteries much the way Mahasi did, therein drawing monasteries in the Thai peripheries to the center of Bangkok and Wat Mahathat. And he was also involved in proselytizing abroad. Often these missionary efforts abroad resulted in his creating a Thai temple to which *Burmese* meditation teachers were invited to teach.

What is interesting about this gesturing beyond national borders is not only that it begins to help us outline one of the cultural models by which Buddhism travels in the region and beyond; it also leads us to speculate upon what possibilities existed for Phimolatham (and for us today) for a nonsectarian and indeed a nonnationalist Buddhism. In the case of Thailand and of Burma—and with regard to the rivalry between the two, which, if studied closely, might yet yield signs of what Marshall Sahlins (2004) calls, after Bateson, "complementary schismogenesis"—the monkly exchanges Phimolatham and Mahasi engaged in can, in a different language, be thought of as a form of Buddhist diplomacy.

To wit, in 1949 Phimolatham met the Burmese ambassador to Thailand, U Hla Maung. Phimolatham expressed an interest in studying Abhidhamma from learned *theras* in Burma. It was at Prime Minister U Nu's own invitation that Phimolatham would come to Burma and meet Mahasi Sayadaw, with whom he conversed in the shared sacred language of Pali. Phimolatham brought with him a Thai monk from the university who could speak English and interpret for him, for the benefit of U Nu.

Mr. C described to me the reception given to Phimolatham, as related by Phimolatham himself. (Mr. C was one of the few Abhidhamma scholars to complete training under the Burmese monks who were subsequently brought to Thailand at the behest of Phimolatham.) He told me (paraphrased, through a translator):

> Luang Phor [Phimolatham] was treated like a king when he arrived. Many women put their hair down for him to walk upon. A lot of these women were the daughters and wives of government officials. U Nu was great and intelligent. The Thai and Burmese had been enemies before, now they treated Luang Phor like a king. They wanted him to know that he was most welcome, that there was no more conflict and that they were no longer enemies.

The "conflict" Mr. C referred to was the sacking and destruction of Ayuttaya, the country's former capital, in 1767 by the Burmese. The enduring acrimony over this has often been reported to me. In the 1960s Prime Minister U Nu at one point even made a public speech while on a state visit to Thailand offering a public apology to the Thai people on behalf of the Burmese, wryly observing that the people of Burma living today were not responsible for the atrocities committed by the Burmese in the 1700s, since "we were not born then."

Whatever the source of the rivalry between the two national sanghas, as it were, Phimolatham's trip to Burma was apparently a source of irritation for some members of the Thai sangha. Mr. C explained to me (again, paraphrased through a translator):

> They said he was fawning. They asked, "Why are you going to see your enemies?" Phimolatham's monk friend and translator whom he brought with him on his first trip to Burma became jealous at the kingly welcome extended to Phimolatham and upon returning to Thailand he related to the Sangharaja [Supreme Patriarch] that Phimolatham had broken his precepts by walking on women's hair as well as explaining that the sasana was not good in Burma. He reported that he saw monks buying tickets to movies and that women sit together with monks and so on. The Sangharaja reportedly scolded Phimontham for having given him a positive report about Burma, to which Phimontham was said to have responded, "Bad things are everywhere, I only wanted to bring the good things back."

There may be different versions and interpretations of the local politics that caused Phimolatham to be forcibly disrobed and imprisoned (from 1960 to 1966) on trumped-up charges for being a communist and for having broken his sangha discipline. In a sense, inasmuch as he focused his attention upon Phimolatham, Tambiah employed him to gain an advantageous "outward from the center of power perspective" from which to disentangle the cosmological-political rivalries that crosscut sangha and state, and brought into view the cultural power principle that animated an entire system. What is also suggested from Phimolatham's actions and from the executive positions he assumed within the sangha was his wish to revitalize Sasana (religion) beyond national borders. He was Thailand's representative in the Moral Rearmament Association, an international religious movement begun by Frank N. D. Buchman in the 1930s that promoted seeking change in oneself in order to change the world. Phimolatham traveled abroad to establish learning and meditation centers in Laos, Cambodia, Vietnam, Malaysia, Indonesia, Sri Lanka, India, France, Netherlands, Germany, Switzerland, the United States, Canada, Japan, and in several South American countries. He met with the Pope and various dignitaries in an effort to promote Sasana understanding. These projects abroad, as was true also for similar projects of Mahasi Sayadaw of Burma and other famous monks more proximate to our times, had implications also for the nationalist Buddhist projects of their respective countries. These accounts might someday be folded into an analysis of historical-to-contemporary trajectories of regional power systems and the globalization of Buddhism itself.

In my own work, I have looked within the phenomenology of vipassana meditation for clues as to how practitioner individuals are linked into cosmological schema, and to explain the power principle (sometimes materialized in pilgrimages and amulets) that has appeared to operate on a moral wavelength among the unstable ternary order of sangha, state, and laity in Burma. (I have found this same principle to be useful *in extremis* in my initial attempts to comprehend the "antipolitical" rebuke of the military regime in the 2007 monks' revolt in Burma.) The transportability of vipassana meditation as technique has taken me yet further into cognitive territory and a fascination with the mechanisms by which communities of knowledge form and become nascent moral-political entities (Jordt 2007b). Each of these pursuits traces back in some overt or implicit way to the preoccupations of my teacher, Stanley Tambiah, over the course of his nearly five decades of scholarship, and one might aspire to no vainer ambition than to be regarded a worthy disciple. The reason for this might, on this occasion, be speculated upon plainly: that Tambiah's body of scholarship is reducible neither to a collection of free-standing theories that might be outstripped or made unfashionable (or yet fashionable) by fickle winds, nor even to a compilation of ethnography that serves humble purpose to historical narrative. Synthetic scholarship of this kind has the tendency to endure precisely because it is neither easy to emulate nor to supersede. Much will be gained by the effort to do both.

A Muslim King and His Buddhist Subjects: Religion, Power, and Identity at the Periphery of the Thai State

Irving Chan Johnson

In this paper, I explore how Thai villagers living in the Malaysian state of Kelantan creatively fashion cultural meanings for themselves by navigating through the conundrum of being the subject of two rulers—one Buddhist, but living in Thailand across the international border, the other Muslim, and part of the lived experiences of Kelantan's Thai residents. Seated on the throne in Bangkok is an idealized Buddhist monarch whose popular cult is based largely on media representations (pictures, books, news reports) and on an imagined sense of cultural citizenry rather than on historical associations.[1] Closer to home is the Muslim sultan who, despite being of a different ethnic and religious group, shares an intimate and historical bond with his Thai subjects through his symbolic patronage of the Kelantanese Buddhist establishment. Through an ethnographic discussion of the cult of royal power in a small Malaysian border village, I show how agency and history is produced and toyed with in the way men and women living along an international border reflect on issues of personhood and identity.

Located in the northeastern-most peninsular Malaysian state of Kelantan, Baan Phra Suung is a twenty-minute drive from the Thai border. The village of one hundred and twenty-five households is one of eighteen Thai Buddhist settlements in the predominantly Muslim Malay state. No one knows when Thais first settled in the area. "We have always been living here," was a refrain I heard time and again when I tried to enquire into the history of Thai settlement in the area. This was often followed by attempts to justify a historic Thai presence in the Muslim state—villagers spoke of ancient temple ruins no longer visible and of ancestral migrations from far-away places such as Sukhothai and Laos. Yet when these movements occurred no one knew, or even seemed to care. What was important was the present, and the fact that these Kelantan Thais live side-by-side with Malay Muslims in a contemporary Malaysia.

Despite being a demographic and cultural minority, Kelantan's nine thousand Thai Buddhists residents—accounting for no more than one percent of the state's total population—are very much a visible community. Many village temples have appeared in guide books and tourist brochures advertising Malaysia's northern frontier. Kelantan's ubiquitous Thai temples are home to massive statues. The longest Reclining Buddha in Southeast Asia and the thirty-meters-tall Sitting Buddha at Wat Klaang have placed Kelantan's Thai community in the public gaze. Along the pot-holed thoroughfares that slice through Thai villages travel boisterous Buddhist ordination parades as well as the plethora of pilgrims, tourists, kings, monks, smugglers, farmers, government officials, policemen, and others who navigate across older circuits of movement within the state, linking it with Thailand to the north and across the Malay Peninsula to the south.

Baan Phra Suung's residents are active participants in global flows of communication. Village houses, whether traditional constructions of wood with zinc roofs or modern mansions of concrete and marble, have one or more large televisions on which residents watch a continuous stream of Thai and Malaysian programs. These range from hugely popular Korean soaps and Thai romantic serials to news features and Hollywood blockbusters. Many households also own personal computers. The installation of telephone cabling in the village allows technologically savvy village youth to surf the Web, chat with friends in cyberspace, and check personal e-mail accounts. By 2012 many villagers possessed cellphones, and their community appears on Facebook pages. Temple ceremonies are filmed with smart phones, and their moving images have been uploaded onto a number of You-tube channels.

Between 2001 and 2002 I lived in Wat Nai, one of two Buddhist temples in the village. Not having a computer with me, I relied on the temple's computers to check my e-mail and do word processing. One day I noticed that one of the computer screens was wallpapered with tiled images of Thailand's Queen Sirikit, wife of King Bhumibol Aduyadej. The selection of tiled images first appeared on August 12, 2002—Queen Sirikit's birthday and Mother's Day in Thailand. The images remained on the computer screen through September. I asked my friend Khun[2] Dee why pictures of Thailand's royalty and not the state's Malay sultan had been chosen as the wallpaper.[3] This paradigm of political-versus-cultural identity perplexed me. Kelanta-nese Thais often told me how proud they were to be Kelantanese and Malaysian. They spoke of their community's long historical associa-tions with the sultan and how they felt the surge of patriotic fervor each time they heard Malaysia's national anthem play. In our conver-sations, they emphasized their difference from people in Thailand, often in language that painted Thailand in a negative light. Despite being a cultural bastion of Theravada Buddhism, Thailand was also associated with corruption, religious decay, and HIV. "So why the image of a Thai sovereign?" I asked, cheekily attempting to play the devil's advocate. Khun Dee was quick to respond. "The Thai king [and by extension, his consort] helps the people. He visits villages and even assists the farmers in planting rice. What has the Kelantanese sultan ever done for us? When he does visit our village he just zips by in his motorcade."

Khun Dee's response was nothing new. When I asked Kelantanese Thai villagers why they displayed pictures of the Thai royal family in their homes, I received answers of a similar type, revolving around the Thai king's good works. When King Bhumibol's sister passed away in January 2008, many Kelantanese Thais made the long trip to Bang-kok's Grand Palace to pay their respects. One Thai temple near Baan Phra Suung had taken this royal fervor a step further by organizing a special celebration each year on December 5, to mark the king's birthday. On this day monks chanted Pali scriptures to shower bless-ings on the king and his family. No such rituals were performed on the Kelantan sultan's birthday, which to many Thais was a non-event marked only by the flutter of colorful state flags and banners along state roads, proclaiming subjecthood. Kelantan's present sultan was criticized by many of my Thai friends for his seeming lack of interest in the affairs of his subjects, and in particular, in the affairs of the state's non-Muslim residents. The old personal relationship that once upon a time had structured systems of religious patronage between the Malay court and Kelantan's Buddhist monks had diminished as issues of radical Islamization and national policies of affirmative action had been brought to the fore. Nevertheless, framed photographs of the sultan and his queen continue to share wall space in many a temple and home with pictures of the Thai king and his family, sacred Buddha statues, and revered local monks.

In his book *World Conqueror and World Renouncer* (1976), Stanley Tambiah spells out the need to situate local communities within larger macrohistorical processes. For instance, he notes that to understand Buddhism in a contemporary Thai village, it is important to look at both the recurrences and structural transformations in royal and monastic power in the center of the polity from which the influence of that power radiates. This coupling of Buddhism and polity, Tambiah warns us, is subject to "dialectical tensions, paradoxes and ambiguities" (515) that result from diverse historical moments.

My work here moves Tambiah's analysis of "dialectical tensions" to the furthest peripheries of the state, where two pulsating polities collide and intersect. Rather than focusing on the centers of royal and religious power that were the concern of *World Conqueror and World Renouncer,* I look at how people living on the extremities of traditional states imagine kingship, and, with it, history in the present. It is within these interstitial spaces framed by national borders that the ambiguities and tensions inherent in the interaction of religion and polity are most clearly and ambiguously experienced. From this dialectic emerges the distinct sense of personhood that is celebrated by the Thai villagers of Kelantan. Yet as Tambiah has so rightly reminded us, present cultural forms can only be understood through a recourse to the past from which they receive much of their inspiration. How does this totalization of the Kelantanese state and its pulsating dynamics of power and religion affect the lives of the people who inhabit it? Through listening to the way Baan Phra Suung's residents speak of these entanglements with royal power, I discuss the means by which contemporary ethnocultural identities are conceptualized in a Muslim polity far from the centers of Buddhist hegemony in Thailand's Chao Phraya delta.

Tambiah points out that the traditional (pre-colonial) Southeast Asian state, which he calls the *galactic polity*, was constructed according to the principles of the Hindu-Buddhist *mandala*. The mandala comprised a powerful center around which orbited satellite political units drawn to the center's cosmological, ritual, and administrative magnetism. This system of smaller social and ritual planets held in place within a galaxy of more powerful centers was unstable. Tambiah writes that "the galactic polity was no effective cybernetic system; it lacked finely fashioned regulative and feedback mechanisms that produced homeostasis and balance" (1976, 122). Alliances between territories were often shifting and fleeting, usually tenuously held in place by systems of tribute-paying and recognitions of ritual superiority. But it was common for ambitious satellite rulers to contest overlordship by proving superior ritual and political status, and rebellions were frequent occurrences in the galaxy. Before the British took over the administration of Kelantan from its Siamese overlords in 1909, Kelantan was a Malay satellite of the Siamese court. Although theoretically pledging loyalty to the Buddhist ruler in Bangkok, the Muslim sultans of Kelantan were largely autonomous political leaders except during moments of administrative and civil upheaval, when the intervention of Siam was courted. This pattern of galactic control took on a new form with the ratification of the Malayan-Siamese border in 1910. The British were new players in the traditional game of shifting spheres of political influence. Working within European notions of the bordered polity, they enhanced the power of Kelantan's Malay Muslim sultan by removing Siamese political dominance. But this was a spatially defined power that was circumscribed to the boundaries of the state. As in British colonies elsewhere, the central players in the administrative game were the British governor and the civil service. The Kelantanese sultan shifted from being a satellite ruler of Siamese power with a great degree of political autonomy to being a cultural and Islamic figurehead. Even though it had conceded Kelantanese territory to the British, Siam—and since 1939, Thailand—continued to monitor developments in the state from afar, and in particular developments in all matters pertaining to Buddhism. The traditional galaxy continued to move, albeit in a new way.

For the Thais of Kelantan, this shift in political strategizing reinforced the power of the Muslim state while building up a system of Thai Buddhist cultural patronage emanating from the older mandala that was Bangkok. This was most evident in the organization of the Kelantanese Thai order of monks (*khana song mueng Kelantan*). By the late nineteenth century, the Thai monastic establishment had become increasingly bureaucratized as the incipient Siamese state attempted to control and standardize Buddhism as a tool of national consciousness throughout the polity (Tambiah 1976). Kelantan's Thai population was by the early twentieth century absorbed into the rigid religio-political maneuverings of a Siamese polity bent on reinforcing state power through religion. Kelantan's monastic establishment, in clear galactic fashion, mirrored that of Bangkok, yet remained subservient to it. The formal appointment of titled monks rested in the hands of the Thai king and his senior monastics, reflecting a traditional system in which the ruler was the chief patron of Buddhism in the polity, while at the same time it was from Buddhism that he received his mandate to govern.

This system of Buddhist rulership, based on ideals of political statecraft developed by Emperor Asoka in India, becomes confusing when one enters Theravadin communities in distant non-Buddhist areas. According to early Asokan models of the state and governance, the king was supposed to be the chief protector and patron of the Dhamma (Buddhist doctrine) and its monkly representatives. In Kelantan the situation was somewhat different. Here, a Muslim ruler took on the role of the Buddhist monarch. To this day, the ritual appointment of the chief monk of Kelantan (*jao khana rat*) needs to pass through the office of the Kelantanese sultan. It is only after the candidate's approval by the palace that the monk can receive his formal appointment from Bangkok, via the workings of the Royal Thai Consulate in the Kelantanese capital city of Kota Bharu.

On November 23, 1908, a Kelantanese monk by the name of Kiu received the monastic title *phra khru* from King Chulalongkorn in Bangkok. Villagers speak of Kiu fondly as the first monastic head of the state. Phra Khru Kiu maintained a personal association with the Malay sultan, of whom he was a personal friend. Than Iak, the present head monk of Kelantan, recalled hearing of how the old monk was a frequent visitor to the Kota Bharu palace and could walk into its vast compound without being stopped by the palace guards. This close relationship was cemented through the participation of senior Buddhist monks in the ritual and sometimes personal affairs of the Malay ruler. In 1918, Kiu participated in a Buddhist purification ceremony at the sultan's palace after a flag pole there had been struck by lightning. The subsequent chief monk of Kelantan, Than Jao Khun Khron,

was a renowned practitioner of magic, and stories of his intimate association with the Malay palace abound. One such story I heard was
of the monk healing the sultan's wife from a psychological disorder
just after the Second World War. The Thai monk was friends with the
Muslim ruler until his death in 1962, and his funeral pyre was lit by
the sultan himself.

Kelantanese Thais speak proudly of their senior monk's relations
with the Malay palace. Visits by palace officials to Thai temples are
greeted with pomp and pageantry, and stories of monk and ruler
friendship continue to be told. This system of traditional patron-
clientelism has been complicated by recent practices of nationalism
on both sides of the border. The celebration of Thai royalism by Sarit
Thanarat, Thailand's Prime Minister from 1959 to 1963, through the
culture of the visual image has impacted on Kelantanese Thai villages
in ways never before seen. Sarit's aggressive policies of cultural nationalism saw the establishment of a national cult of the kingly image throughout the Thai-speaking world, drawing non-Thai citizens
into the nation's folds through the dissemination of monk missionaries and teachers from Bangkok to the country's distant borders and
beyond. Sarit and subsequent heads of state have viewed Thailand's
borderlands as places of danger—rife with banditry, Islamic rebels,
and Communist insurgents. It was felt that the people who lived in
these feared zones were in need of a centralizing discourse which
would ensure that they remained patriotic to the Bangkok government. Kelantanese Thais were encouraged by the Sarit government
to take up land offers across the border, and the forested interiors of
Thailand's southern province of Narathiwat, which fronts Kelantan,
were cleared and developed. Roads, schools, homes, and television
stations were built, bringing Thailand a step closer to the realities of
Kelantanese Thai life. Each night Thai residents in Kelantan tune in
to televised news broadcast from Thailand. News reports carry constant images of the Thai king and his family, often in scenes of public
service. New circuits of travel and communication such as packaged
tours, internet websites, and so forth have meant that Kelantanese
Thais are now privy to experiences of Thailand previously unavail-
able in their small communities. These are coupled with a paucity
of public representations of the sultan. Photographs of the Muslim
monarch are restricted to newspaper reports and official portraits
available only from government departments. The sultan seldom
appears on television, and his representatives rarely visit Buddhist

temples and their religious elites. Hence, to many a Baan Phra Suung resident, the Thai king represents the idealized Dhamaraja ("king of the Dhamma"). They speak of him in a language of cultural nationalism that extends beyond the frontiers of the state. The present-day sultan, despite being widely seen as incompetent and lax by many of his Thai subjects, is still at the center of the classic galactic polity, a position he maintains with his formal approval of monastic headship. And it is to this satellite center that residents in the periphery pledge their political allegiance. Yet ritual and cultural allegiance gravitate towards the mandala's cosmic center in Thailand. It is in this interstitial cultural zone betwixt and between two historical galactic polities that Kelantanese Thais locate themselves.

The residents of Baan Phra Suung and their imaginings of past and present royal and monastic power add another facet to Tambiah's rich analysis of the relationship between politics and religion in Theravadin societies. Through looking at the cracks in the galactic polity—where one polity ends and another seemingly begins—and moving one's gaze back and forth between the past and the present, we get a better picture of the dynamic nature of personhood in contemporary states. Colonialism and the development of nation-states have not destroyed older systems of political association for people who inhabit the furthest reaches of the state. Concepts of kingship and ritual leadership and shifting ideological alliances continue to perpetuate themselves.

This short piece has shown how Tambiah's analysis of history, religion, and the ambiguous nature of political spaces in precolonial Southeast Asia continues to be relevant to the everyday lives of contemporary people. My ethnographic vignettes, taken from a small Thai village beyond the frontiers of the Thai state, expand Tambiah's original framework by showing how people make sense of the galaxies they inhabit. The pulsating nature of the galactic polity remains strong, albeit in a newly bordered world. Kelantanese Thais living on the frontier of two colonially imagined states continue to define themselves based on the way powerful centers of power impact on their lives. Today this impact is brought about in a variety of ways, ranging from the placement of a picture of royalty on temple computers to the hanging of photographs of kings and queens on the wooden walls of small coffeeshops. Muslim systems of statehood are reformulated according to classical Theravadin definitions of ideal rulership in Kelantan. Nonetheless, the power of boundaries established by

European treaties remains uncontested, and negotiations of power in both these instances occur within a new language of national sovereignty. The galactic polity therefore remains significant even if at the level of ideology. It does not fade away with the solidification of a border. Rather, it flows through that border, impacting on the lives of the people who live along it.

PART II

Cosmologies, Ideologies, and Localities

Economies of Ghosts, Gods, and Goods: The History and Anthropology of Chinese Temple Networks

Michael Puett

Stanley Tambiah's work in linking history and anthropology for the study of Thailand and Sri Lanka has been a constant inspiration for my own attempts to do something of the same for the study of China. In particular, I have been inspired by Tambiah's studies of the inter-relations of religious, political, and economic anthropology in ways that force us to rethink our old distinctions between tradition and modernity.

What I will be focusing on in this piece is the history and current workings of temple networks in China. These networks once spread throughout China and Southeast Asia, ran much of local society in China, and played a crucial role in the development of the huge maritime economy in Asia that developed over the several centuries before European colonization. And, right now, the networks are emerging again. The study of these networks opens up several issues in the history and anthropology of China.

To explain why this might be of interest, allow me to sketch a widely accepted narrative of recent history in China—a narrative with which I will take issue in this paper.

Traditions of Modernity

It is often—and I will argue mistakenly—asserted that the connections between early and contemporary China should be explored in terms of a basic distinction of tradition and modernity.

According to such a view, traditional China should be characterized as having maintained an assumption of harmonious monism—in other words, as having seen human beings as part of a cosmos in which everything was linked by chains of inherent correlation, and in which humans and the natural world were in harmony. Such a cosmological vision of harmonious monism was part and parcel, the story goes, of a traditional agricultural world based upon harmonizing with the shift of the seasons, themselves read as the natural movement of the larger cosmos. This traditional world was also a lineage-based system, in which the living were, as the saying goes, "under the ancestors' shadow."[1]

Modernity, under such a paradigm, would be defined as the breakdown of this assumption of a harmonious, correlative universe and the emergence—for better or for worse—of a humanistic ethos, a free-market economy, and an entrance into a global economy. Things as different as environmental degradation, capitalism, and individualism are often attributed to this shift to modernity. Such a modernity argument still underlies a surprisingly large body of social scientific theory.

I disagree strongly with this paradigm on several grounds, but let me begin with an empirical disagreement. As I have argued elsewhere (Puett 2001 and 2002), there was no assumption of a harmonious, correlative cosmos in pre-twentieth-century China. Such a claim arose during the past two centuries as a means of distinguishing China from either the "West," or "modernity," or both. There are certainly texts one could point to from pre-twentieth-century China that argue that the cosmos is harmonious, but these were always claims made against contrary positions, and were never assumptions.

In conceptualizing, therefore, the complex ways that past practices—be they ancestral rituals or temple networks—are currently re-emerging and being appropriated in contemporary China, we need to begin with a different vision of what these earlier practices were, and we need to have a better understanding of the historical appropriation and utilization of the practices throughout subsequent history.

Domesticating Ghosts, Creating Gods

To sketch an alternate view, let me begin with a seemingly odd place: ghosts. Ghosts (*gui*)—often, and equally accurately, translated as "demons"—are pervasive in China.[2] The landscape in China, from as far back as our written sources go, is a haunted one, a world filled with ghosts.

In fact, ghosts are the natural result of every death: when someone dies, their energies are released and form highly dangerous ghosts, often seething in resentment at those still alive. Their fury is often directed particularly at their close relatives, and to a somewhat lesser extent at others with whom they had associations—those they knew while alive, or those involved in professions similar to those the deceased enjoyed while alive.

Ancestral rituals are an attempt to control these ghosts. One set of souls, associated with the personality of the deceased, is placed in a tomb. The tomb is filled with the objects that the deceased enjoyed while alive, and exhortations are given for the souls to remain there and leave the living alone.

The spirit of the deceased, on the other hand, floats to the heavens. The goal of the rituals for the spirit is to make it into an ancestor, to give it an ancestral tablet, and to place it within a lineage based upon its descent rank. This ancestor is then offered ancestral sacrifices at the proper time, in ranked order with the lineage of other ancestors. With the sacrifices come exhortations to the ancestors to act as ancestors, to support the living as their descendants—in other words, to give the living benefits instead of haunting them and throwing disaster upon them.

Parts of these ritual exhortations involve claims that what the descendants are planning to do is but a continuation of things the ancestors initiated. Such ritual exhortations are undoubtedly the origin of the view that in premodern China the living worked under the ancestors' shadows and saw themselves as simply followers of what the ancestors wished. But this is to take a ritual exhortation as a belief. The reason one makes such exhortations is that one is trying to convince the ghosts to act as ancestors, to see the living as descendants, and to see what the descendants want as a continuation of what the deceased had already begun. One is *making* the ancestors and *creating* such claims, not stating a belief.

But if the goal is to transform ghosts of one's relatives into ancestors, those ghosts who are not domesticated in this way will continue to feed upon the living. Such ghosts are frequently the product of bad deaths, or of people who have died without a family. In these cases, the ghost will often attack those associated with the way the deceased died, or those who are involved in the profession the deceased maintained in life. Sacrifices offered to try to domesticate a ghost of this type would come not from members of the family of the deceased but rather from those associated with the deceased's way of life (or death). To give one of the most famous examples in the anthropological literature, Mazu was a girl who drowned in the tenth century, and who as a ghost would therefore drag living humans to their deaths in the sea as well. Accordingly, it was primarily fishermen—those who had to go on the sea and thus face Mazu's attacks—who initially began sacrificing to Mazu to pacify her (J. Watson 1985).

If the ghost in question responds to the sacrifices, it can often be domesticated to become supportive of the living. Except in this case, the ghost is not domesticated into an ancestor; it is domesticated into a god. Whereas the number of potential supporters of an ancestor-ghost is limited to those who are members of the lineage in question, the number of potential supporters of a god is limited only by the perceived efficacy of the god in question. The larger the number of offerings given, the more likely the ghost would be to continue functioning as a beneficent god or goddess, and the more that god or goddess would be empowered and thus willing, the supporters hope, to use that power on behalf of the living who are making the offerings.

And in this way began the formation of temple networks. As a god or goddess came to be seen as efficacious, more people would start making offerings to it. Moreover, since the god would be associated with particular activities, others dealing with such an activity would be inclined to join in the worship. Once the worship of a particular god or goddess became widespread enough, in fact, one would *have* to join in order to gain the support of others within that profession. Thus, entire crafts and practices would become associated with a particular god or goddess—fishermen with Mazu, health practitioners with Baosheng Dadi (the deity name of the doctor Wu Tao, who died in the ninth century), and so forth (Schipper 1990).

There was thus an inherent tendency toward expansion in the worship of a particular god, both because more practitioners meant more empowerment and domestication of the ghost, and because a deity with ever-growing power was a deity to whom more and more people would want to make offerings. Rituals thus developed to allow such expansion. Through a *fenxiang* (cutting of the incense) ritual, the ashes used to worship a deity in one temple would be taken to create an altar of worship in a new temple, and the temples would thus be linked in their common support of a particular deity (Schipper 1990). This could go on and on, with the creation of new temples endlessly. Indeed, the network of temples could become so powerful that the networks themselves would fund the creation of yet new temples in other areas.

As Kristofer Schipper has argued,

> [T]he great vital and creative forces of exceptional living creatures (animals, humans, or demons) once captured, recovered, and directed towards the good—that is, towards life—will continue to expand indefinitely. Worship—perfect ritual action constantly renewed—contributes to the spiritual power of the gods which in turn results in the spread of their glory and influence. In the beginning, the worship of these demon spirits is primarily propitiatory and purely local. But a minor demon can, through the liturgy of the people, become a great god, a patron saint, a protector of a region or of an entire nation, an archangel, an emperor of Heaven. (Schipper 1993, 42)

Over the past several centuries, the result of this process was the spreading of temple networks throughout China and much of Asia. In many areas, the networks became so powerful that they would run much of local society, including schools, the building of infrastructure, and so forth. In southeastern China, the networks emanating from Fujian ultimately spread throughout Southeast Asia and Indonesia and became the basis of enormous trade networks throughout the South China Sea.[3]

An Economy of Gods and Goods

A full recounting of the history of these lineages and of these temple networks in late imperial China is beyond the scope of this essay.[4] Suffice it to say, however, that, as such figures as Kristofer Schipper (1977, 1990), Hugh Clark (1991), and Yuan Bingling (2000) have brilliantly demonstrated, entire economies formed around these networks, and much of the huge Chinese diaspora was based in the temple networks as well (see, most recently, Kuhn 2008). The networks that spread throughout Southeast Asia were in many ways an equivalent to the Hadrami networks recently studied by Engseng Ho (2006) and the Manangi trade networks studied by Prista Ratanapruck (2008), and they formed a crucial part of the vast Eurasian trade network prior to the imperial expansion of the Western European states.Given their tremendous strength and economic force, it is not surprising that these networks always maintained a complex relationship with the state. In late imperial China, the state would constantly try to promote the gods into its own bureaucracy as a means of appropriating both the gods and their networks, an appropriation that was frequently resisted at the local level (J. Watson 1985; Duara 1988; Szonyi 1997).[5]

More recently, when European powers started moving into the region, the explicit goal was to control the economy of East and Southeast Asia through a colonial structure. The networks came under direct attack at this point. Then, in the twentieth century, successive attempts at dramatic state centralization in mainland China itself, under a call for "modernization," led to recurrent efforts to destroy the temple networks (Schipper 1990; Goossaert 2000).[6]

So how should we understand all of this? Before discussing the further implications of these temple networks, a theoretical interlude may be in order.

Domesticating the World

I began this discussion with ghosts, and it is to ghosts that I now return.

As we have seen, it is human rituals that transform ghosts into ancestors or gods. Such a statement might at first glance appear to be the product of an anthropological thinking based a bit too much on Durkheim and Girard, overly committed to the view that it is ritual that creates deities. In particular, it may appear to be an overly modernist reading, based upon unmasking the beliefs of traditional societies: in the case at hand, human action is posited as creating the gods who are then claimed to rule society. The problem with such a formulation, of course, is that it fails to take into account the indigenous belief system within which such rituals are understood.

But, in fact, the view laid out here is found explicitly in indigenous formulations, and in a form that is quite different from anything one would find in contemporary Western theory. Indeed, the primary ritual classic from China—the *Book of Rites*—argues precisely this position (Puett 2005 and 2008). The world in its natural state is fragmented and discontinuous, and dominated by highly dangerous ghosts. Humans thus created rituals to transform these ghosts into ancestors and gods. These ghosts and ancestors would in turn be used as mediators in a larger effort to domesticate the entire world: by taking pieces of what were deceased humans and transforming them into ancestors, families would be able to link themselves to these remains and create lineages, and by taking remains of other deceased humans and transforming them into gods, links could be made to other, unrelated groups. By creating these descent lineages into the past and these temple networks across spatial boundaries, humans would be able to form the groups necessary to domesticate the past and domesticate the natural world. What was once a fragmented world is thus transformed into a unified, harmonious system, in which gods and ancestors serve as the mediators linking humans to each other and to the rest of the natural world.[7] (The numerous statements in modernist writings that see a monistic, harmonious cosmos as having been an assumption in premodern China come from taking the desired results of such human action—namely, the creation of a full cosmos in which everything would be linked through the domesticating acts of humans—as a starting assumption.)

Far from living under the ancestors' shadow, the vision here is one in which the ancestors and gods are creations of the living, made in order to forge links to the constructed past and to forge vertical and horizontal links to the rest of the world in the present.[8]

Overcoming Discontinuity

But if these are the indigenous formulations, how can they be brought into a general anthropology?

Michael Scott (2007), building upon the work of Claude Lévi-Strauss (1966, 224–25) and Marshall Sahlins (1985), has made a distinction between ontologies based upon continuity and those based upon discontinuity.

For an ontology of continuity, the problem is seen to be one of asserting discontinuity. Many cosmologies are based upon such a claim of continuity, but I would here like to focus on the fact that much of contemporary theory is based upon continuity arguments of this kind. Indeed, all modernity arguments, which posit a traditional worldview of cosmic order and a traditional society of controlling lineage structures, from which a modern world with its celebrated assertions of individualism and free will is breaking, are based upon such a vision.

Ontologies of discontinuity, on the other hand, are those that see the fundamental problem as being one of creating links to connect what is perceived to be an overly fragmented, discontinuous world. As Scott correctly points out, such ontologies are under-explored and under-theorized in the anthropological literature.

The ontologies from China under consideration here are clearly based upon discontinuity: the world is fragmented and fractured, and filled with capricious ghosts. Within such a cosmology, the goal is to work endlessly to create continuity—to make connections, to form networks, and to domesticate the world such that these networks grow, flourish, and expand.

Stanley Tambiah has noted a comparable type of discontinuity vision in Trobriand thought:

> The structuralist view is that since the world out there is in flux and a continuous process, man in his cultural garb imposed on this flux a classificatory grid which introduces discontinuities; the intervals or spaces that divide the categories then become ambiguous, sacred, and tabooed. I wish to suggest a classificatory perspective that accords with Trobriand mental dispositions and proclivities; it gives the structuralist formulation a new twist. It is my sense that Trobriand thought actually operates on and manipulates the classificatory system in such a way that categories already separated are then collapsed or brought into conjunction so that these meeting points are viewed in themselves as, or as sites for, heightened manifestation, extraordinary events, and highly charged "excessive" acts. (1985c, 313–14)

As Tambiah correctly points out, much of structuralist thought has been based upon a continuity vision: the world is continuous, and humans impose discontinuity upon it. But, Tambiah argues, if we take Trobriand thought seriously, we see a vision in which the key is to take a discontinuous series and bring the phenomena that comprise it into conjunction.

In China, one finds entire social practices based upon a comparable cosmological vision, as well as an extraordinary body of ritual theory focused on the implications of such a cosmology. One of the reasons we have missed this is that by reading China according to a tradition/modernity paradigm, we have blinded ourselves to a fascinating body of thought.

Resurgence

But the problem is not simply that we have failed to deal with a body of indigenous theory that can help explain a fascinating side of earlier Chinese economic history. For recently there has been a tremendous resurgence of the temple networks in southeastern China. As Kenneth Dean has demonstrated beautifully in a number of groundbreaking works on Fujian (1995, 1998, 2003, 2006; see also Lagerwey 2001), the networks are once again beginning to take a leadership role in the running of local society and the development of local economies. Much of the funding for the restoration of the temples and the re-creation of temples' activities in the region came initially from the old *fenxiang* networks. Recently, for example, the Ciji Gong temple, a major node in the huge Baosheng Dadi network, has been rebuilt, with significant support from the *fenxiang* network outside of China. And this has long been the case in Taiwan, where the networks have been thriving for decades (see in particular Sangren 1984 and 1987, Weller 1987, and Chipman 2007).

The full implications of this resurgence will only become clear over the next few decades, but even a quick discussion of some of the possibilities will give hints of issues to consider. The growing significance of the networks for the running of local societies and economies in China has tremendous political implications for the future of entire regions of the People's Republic of China; the rebuilding of the network lines between the southeast coast and Taiwan has obvious and very significant implications for relations between China and Taiwan; the regrowth of the networks among the large diasporic populations in Southeast Asia and southeast China has potentially significant transnational implications; and the resurgence of the trade networks throughout Southeast Asia has tremendous economic implications for the entire region.

All of these developments, meanwhile, are occurring completely out of sight of virtually the entire spectrum of the social sciences apart from anthropology. When economists, for example, look at the economy of China, they do so almost entirely from a modernist paradigm of seeing a China breaking from its traditional, agrarian economy of the past and allowing rational individualism and free-market capitalism to emerge. They thus focus exclusively on things like the national GDP, the Shanghai stock market, the number of companies being privatized from the state, and so forth.

Such a paradigm not only misconstrues the economy and society of so-called premodern China, it also misses a very significant aspect of the resurgence of these older economic patterns. To account for what is developing, we will need very different economic models. And, in the case at hand, we actually have an extraordinarily rich indigenous body of theory from China that has barely been mined at all.

The Anthropology of History

In his articles "Cosmologies of Capitalism" (1988) and "The Sadness of Sweetness; or, The Native Anthropology of Western Cosmology" (1996), Marshall Sahlins has argued that capitalism is itself a cosmology, and that different cultures, with different cosmologies, have played a crucial role in the workings of the global system. Although Sahlins was focusing his discussion on the capitalist system as it emerged in the nineteenth century, his point can be enlarged to discuss both earlier and later periods as well.

Such arguments have not had much influence outside of anthropology, but I suspect that will change dramatically as non-Western economies once again become more and more dominant in the world. Much of contemporary theories of modernity will have to be rethought as these very different economies and cosmologies continue to emerge—many of which are based upon appropriations of very old economies and cosmologies that bear little resemblance to a so-called traditional order over which capitalism and individualism were supposedly triumphing. Suddenly, both the past and future will look very different.

An anthropology worthy of its name is one that will take non-Western theories of the self, ritual, statecraft, and economy seriously and allow them to help us question the Western narratives and frameworks that are still too often taken for granted.[9] Such an anthropology will also be fully historical, looking in detail at long-term patterns in history that force us rethink our modernity frameworks.

This is a vision of anthropology that has long been espoused by Stanley Tambiah. Let us hope that the rest of us will finally start catching up to the vision he began laying out decades ago.

Trade, Religion, and Civic Relations in the Manangi Long-Distance Trade Community

Prista Ratanapruck

It was the work of Stanley J. Tambiah that transformed me from a student of economics into a student of anthropology. At a time when I was feeling a growing dissatisfaction with the field of economics, I enrolled in a social studies seminar on the history of economic thought taught by Steve Marglin, an economist at Harvard. While discussing the topic of economic rationality, we read Tambiah's "Magic, Science, Religion, and the Scope of Rationality" (1987). I was fascinated by the author's comparative analysis, and set out to find out who Stanley Tambiah was. Learning that such comparative, historical, and philosophical work was also in the domain of anthropologists' pursuits, I followed the course catalogue to sit in on Tambiah's economic anthropology course. He introduced the course by saying, "This is a course in economic anthropology in which we will be reading a lot of obscure ethnographies. It is not an introduction to economic theories; Ec 10 is designed for that."[1] It was from this course that I learned how economic facts are social facts. I continued to be fascinated by Tambiah's analysis of ritual efficacy and the framework of "causality" and wanted to learn more, but enrollment in his "Magic, Science, and

Religion" seminar was limited to graduate students. This led me to apply for graduate study in anthropology.

An important part of Stanley Tambiah's work is devoted to critically examining how cosmologies are embodied in ritual actions. He describes rituals as "totalities constituted of both word and deed" (1985b, 1). In this paper, I attempt to show how his perspective led me to see an articulation between ritual and religious practices and trade practices in the Manangi long-distance trading community, as these practices share a certain "cosmology"—or a "cultural logic"— about how Manangis view the relationship between individuals and the collective.

During the last seven years, I have been following extensive trade and kinship networks of the Manangis, who are Nepalis of Tibetan ethnic origin. They are descendants of caravan traders who used to trade in salt and grains between Tibet and India.[2] Over the past century, their trade has shifted and expanded to northeast India, Burma, Thailand, Malaysia, Singapore, and Indonesia. Today, Manangis are skilled gem and handicraft traders; some are airline shareholders, and some are owners of hotels, factories, and real estate in Nepal and elsewhere in South and Southeast Asia.

In the established historiography of transregional trade and commerce in Asia, the role of Asian merchants was eclipsed by eighteenth-century Western colonial trade and expansion (Van Leur 1955, Steensgaard 1973). How have Manangis continued to thrive?[3] Unlike European company merchants, Manangis were endowed with relatively little economic and political capital. They did not have claims to sovereignty from their mother countries, backed up by guns and armies, to influence trade in foreign countries. They also had insufficient capital to accumulate large stocks of commodities to manipulate global market prices through monopoly. Endowed with relatively little economic and political capital, Manangi traders developed external social relations and kinship ties with local communities. Through local marriages, they gained special entry into local markets, including access to supplies of local resources, cheap labor, and knowledge about commodity production—access that would have been harder for larger company merchants to acquire. Yet, despite local marriages and successes in foreign lands, Manangi traders abroad did not naturalize into their adopted communities. They instead remained part of the Manangi community by maintaining cross-cultural kinship ties and a larger transnational community.

While turning external social relations into internal social ties within their expanding community, Manangis also seek to reinforce particular kinds of social relations within their community. Abroad, they establish communal rooming houses, share knowledge about their trade internally, and develop a system of mutual trust. At home in Kathmandu, they pool trade surpluses to organize elaborate religious and social gatherings, taking turns to sponsor the events through a system of rotation among households. These partnerships, which may be described, using a phrase from Aristotle, as *civic relations*, make up the cultural logic that governs the relationships between individuals and the collective, both in the domains of trade and beyond. It is this cultural logic that has enabled Manangi trade and social networks to sustain and expand, cutting across various forms of boundaries and connecting local and translocal societies, economies, and cultures.

I came to learn about this "cultural logic" purely by chance, but it was through eyes made perceptive by Tambiah and his work that I was able to see its significance. In the initial phase of my field research, I had ventured only into the domain of Manangi trade activities abroad. It was not until I spent time in their home community in Kathmandu that I realized that trade was only one side of their social life. When I visited the homes of Manangi traders, I was repeatedly told by their daughters that their fathers had gone to a *gompa*, a Tibetan Buddhist monastery; they had left at dawn and would return at dusk. Upon learning that such a routine was going to last almost three weeks, nearly the entire length of time leading up to their next trading trips, and that they would conduct such weeks-long ceremonies five times per year, I became curious about what they did there. If the activity at the gompa occupied so much of their time, what was its significance?

During the following years, I had opportunities to observe and participate in many of the Managis' community-wide social festivals and religious rituals, for which they have a very sophisticated system of organization and sponsorship. Some involve households signing up twelve years in advance to contribute labor and money for hosting the events. One of the most austere religious practices is the eighteen-day *Nyungne* fasting retreat, during which Manangis eat and drink only every other day and gather at a monastery to chant, prostrate themselves, and count prayer beads. The merit earned during this austere event is significant—a matter concerning life and rebirth. If one can, within

one's lifetime, let go of worldly attachments for the full period of eighteen days, one can, according to the Manangis, avoid being reborn as
a lower living being—as an insect, for example. Higher rebirth is important because humans, unlike lower beings, can accrue merit using their intelligence rather than their instincts to guide their actions.
The counting of prayer beads, as a form of meditative practice, also
helps create a consciousness that generates virtuous minds, speech,
and actions that eventually lead them out of the cycle of suffering.

Sponsoring and participating in religious events also allow Manangis to transform the material value of their wealth—their profits from
trade—into a more enduring and meaningful asset. Although money
has productive economic value in the Manangi community, as investment capital and as a means for material sustenance, its value is limited to its use within one's lifetime. After one's death, its value is static,
locked in material objects, and becomes useless. By converting wealth
into religious merit, which can accompany one in rebirth, one makes
the value of money available to oneself in another space and time. The
value of money becomes portable. Manangis often comment that one
should not hoard material wealth, but rather give it away in the form
of donations, pointing out that only religious merit can accompany
one into a future life. In this way, the religious merit accrued through
charitable giving, and the spiritual enlightenment gained from ritual
practices, is the most valuable asset of all.

Religious merit and spiritual enlightenment are assets that are
gained collectively as well as individually. Every evening at the fasting retreat, Manangis add up the number of beads that each person
has counted. At the end of the eighteen days they calculate the total
number of beads counted by all the participants. This number is then
announced by the head monk, who congratulates the community for
their collective achievement. The counting of prayer beads, therefore,
is not just an individual pursuit directed toward an individual's goal
of eventual higher birth. It is also a community effort to create religious merit, and the collective accomplishment belongs to everyone
equally, regardless of their unequal contributions, money, labor, and
abilities.

This framework, this cosmology of social relations embodied in ritual, is also visible in other domains of Manangi social life, including
their trade practices. What I witnessed at the fasting retreat reminded
me of the story that Chesang Ba, an eighty-four-year old former trader,
told me. Chesang Ba narrated how he and forty-eight other Manangis,

who had sought their fortune in gem mines in Burma, tried to smuggle their remaining gems out of the country after the Burmese military take-over in 1962. Before that time, many Manangis had shares in Burmese mining concessions. After the military took over, "no one could leave the country without being stripped naked." Chesang Ba, however, figured out a way to smuggle the gems out in a few double-layered baskets. First, he said, they had to soak the baskets in water to make the rattan soft so that they could hide the gems between the two layers. When the rattan dried, the woven strips became tighter and the gems became invisible. In these "rattan suitcases" Chesangba packed his own gems as well as those of the forty-eight other Manangis, along with gems worth 200,000 Indian rupees (200,000 INR) belonging to a Calcutta merchant, who promised to give Chesang Ba 40,000 INR if he could get the merchant's gems out of Burma.

From the gem-mining town Chesang Ba and the other Manangi walked to the Indian border. To cross into India they had to cross a river, but there was a guard near the bridge. They had to ford the river, but the fast-flowing water was neck deep. But with forty-eight heads, one of them figured out a way that they could cross without being washed away: by walking in a double line, with twenty-four people forming parallel lines and holding each others' hands. After they crossed the river into India, however, there were even tighter checkpoints along the way from Manipur to Nagaland. Chesang Ba and his friends learned of a Naga "smuggling" village, and Chesang Ba agreed to a plan proposed by three of the villagers. He and his friends would cross the border into Nagaland empty-handed, and for a payment of 1,500 INR the villagers would deliver their baskets to them later.

Four days later, Chesang Ba waited anxiously at the agreed-upon location, not knowing whether the Naga porters would show up, while his friends were relaxed. He was tense because he felt responsible not only for his gems, but also for those of his friends, who had trusted him to be in charge of the arrangements. At exactly 4:00 p.m., the Naga porters arrived. Chesang Ba was convinced that they did not know what they had been carrying. Again in possession of their "rattan suitcases" and their precious stones, Chesangba and his friends went on to Calcutta to sell their gems. Chesang Ba received the additional 40,000 INR from the Calcutta merchant, and distributed it all among his Manangi friends.

The smuggling of the gems and the organization of the fasting retreat have something in common. They share the same cultural logic about social relations and the same concept of partnerships. In the Manangi community, partnerships are formed so that the actions of individuals result in the common good. As a collective, Manangis were able to cross a deep river with rapid currents and smuggle gems across the border. Not everyone had the same ability to contribute to the collective effort, nor did everyone bear the same level of responsibility and anxiety. But the fruits of their effort were distributed equally. Likewise, at a fasting retreat, Manangis cooperate to host and to pursue religious practices on a scale much greater than what each one would be able to achieve individually. As a community, they have raised funds to build a stupa in Lumbini, a rest house in Bodgya, and many new monasteries in Nepal, which support almost a fifth of their population.

Partnerships in the Manangi community, however, are not merely instrumental for individuals' advantages. There is something more to the partnerships. They are motivated by concern for the good of the collective, and also for the good of other individuals in that collective—concern that is not only material, but also moral and spiritual. Such relationships, as reflected in the ways Manangis think about the merit accrued from collective religious projects, and in the ways Chesang Ba shared his windfall gains, may correspond to what Aristotle described in *The Politics* as relationships in a civic community. These are political relationships that bind individuals together as a society, as a state, making them different from partnerships in a joint-stock company.

John Cooper, elaborating on Aristotle's ideas of relationships in a civic community, describes how civic relationships—relationships among fellow citizens of a city-state, a polis—differ from relationships under an "oligarchic constitution," in which individuals come into association merely "for the sake of possession," for the purpose of "preserving, exchanging, and increasing possessions for their [own] economic value" (Cooper 2005, 51). In a joint-stock company, for example, individuals work for their common profit but aim for their own advantage by means of advancing the company. In such a commercial setup, the standard of political justice is based on the unequal contributions that participants bring to the common stock. In a civic community, by contrast, the standard of political justice is based on the common advantage, and there is equal access to the communal good if one has made a contribution toward that good according to one's ability.

In a city, a *polis*, according to Aristotle, individuals come into association with one another "for the sake of living well."[4] Even when they
do not need direct assistance from one another, it is also the common
advantage that brings them together, allowing them all to live well,
both as a collectivity and separately.[5] It is thus the mutual good will,
the mutual trust, and the shared respect for norms that make partnerships in a civic community different from partnerships in a commercial arrangement.

These salient characteristics of partnerships in the Manangi community may also be discerned in other social contexts outside of
trade and religious practices—in their community-wide ritualized
gambling activities, for example. Every year, the Manangi community
in Kathmandu organizes a two-week-long archery festival, which all
members of the community aged eighteen and above are required to
attend; failure to do so results in a fine. All are required to take part
in the archery contest and to place bets on the games. Again, they take
risks collectively and share the consequences of those risks equally,
even in the present of unequal contributions.

In an archery game, Manangis place bets collectively by forming
two competing teams, with participants on each team pooling their
money (with sums ranging from 500 to 1,000 Nepali rupees) to bet
against the other team. When a team wins, it gets to keep the money
from the losing team, an amount that will be distributed equally
within the winning team. Thus, within a team, everyone bears the consequences of winning and losing equally regardless of an individual's
skills. But despite the unequal contribution, the accomplishment of
the collective is shared equally, in the same way that the number of
prayer beads counted are added up and the religious merit is accrued
and shared equally at the Nyungne retreat.

In one exceptional case, however, a skillful player gets to keep more
prize money than others. This occurs when an individual player
shoots an arrow and lands it at the exact center of the target—an occurrence that makes his team win immediately and ends the game
without further shooting. In such a situation, the winner gets to keep
all of the prize money, without having to split it with other team members. Such a practice may seem at first to violate the main principal
underlying civic life in the Manangi community. But in fact it creates an opportunity for reinforcing even further the cultural logic of
common advantage. Upon shooting the winning arrow, the player is
invited to the center of the archery ground so that everyone can join

in congratulating him. His wife offers him a jug of beer, puts an auspicious *khaata* scarf around him, and showers him with white wheat flour, after which he is covered in white. To reciprocate, to thank her, he offers his wife the same—a jug of beer, a *khaata* scarf, and a shower of white wheat flour. During this exchange, the drum beats and both the winning and the losing team cheer.

At the archery contest, anyone who wins a bet is required to contribute 15 percent of the prize money to the community fund. But when an individual wins a large amount of prize money, after contributing 15 percent to the community fund he usually spends the rest of the money on everyone in the community, buying beer for men and juice for women and children. This is a token of sharing the wealth that the winner has just earned. If one sees bottles of beer and tetrapak juice floating around, one looks for the person covered in flour who has just landed an arrow at the center of the board and feasted the whole community. The ceremony thus makes public the wealth accrued from a windfall gain and demonstrates the generosity of successful individuals in the Manangi community.

The ways Manangis share their windfall gains from the archery contests mirror the ways Chesang Ba shared his earnings from the gem smuggling, as well as the ways Manangis share religious merit accrued at the Nyungne fasting retreat. Despite unequal contributions towards a collective pursuit, the fruit of that collective effort is shared equally, while the unequal contribution is acknowledged socially. Such social recognition of unequal contribution toward the collective good perhaps helps Manangis to sustain the ideal of common advantage in the presence of differing abilities among individuals to contribute to that collective.

In a city, a polis, unlike in a joint-stock company, fellow citizens are concerned for one another's well-being and personal good, including the moral good. And it is this individual good that constitutes the good of the collective, which is a part of everyone else's good. This makes partnerships in an ideal city-state, as Aristotle envisioned, not merely collaborations for meeting material benefits. They are partnerships for the sake of "good living," whereby individuals come to live together for the sake of wanting to live together and to share a civic life. In the Manangi community, such civic life is manifested in the ways individuals and households form partnerships to pursue their trade abroad, as well as to organize social and religious life to pursue their spiritual purposes at home in Nepal.

The Manangi community trade, ritual, and religious practices parallel one another not only because they share the same cultural logic, but also because they are connected to one another in a particular way. When pooling donations for religious projects and ceremonies, and when collecting money from gambling activities, Manangis raise funds that are first circulated as loans for investment in new trade ventures before these funds are expended on their intended social and religious purposes. The circulation of funds in the community through social and religious gatherings allows the redistribution of surplus and the expansion of trade, which generates further surplus. This in turn facilitates social and religious practices and hence the availability of more funds to fuel the expansion of the Manangi economy. The dialectical relationship between trade and religion facilitates the expansion of both. The flow of resources between the two domains invigorates the economy while allowing Manangis to fulfill other social and religious purposes. The creation of social values and cultural logics deemed positive in the community also creates the material conditions that enable the reproduction of that same set of social values. These are values that have been important for the viability of the Manangi community, both as a trading community and as a devoted Buddhist community. I have come to see the connections between these various domains of social life in the Manangi community because I have learned from Tambiah to look for the cosmologies—the cultural logics—that are embodied in both ritual and nonritual actions. These are the totalities that are constituted in words, thoughts, and actions, in the domain of religious life and beyond.

In the spirit of Tambiah's comparative analysis, I end this paper by drawing attention to the sharp contrast between the relationship of trade and religious expansion in the Manangi community, and the economic monopoly and military expansion of European empires—that is, state mercantilism. The cosmologies and the aspirations of the Manangis appear to be very different from those of the European empires. The pursuit of material wealth in these two societies is rooted in two very different nonmaterial ends. Unlike capital accumulated from trade by the Europeans, capital in the Manangi community always comes back to circulate through Manangi social and religious institutions before leaving those domains for circulation in long-distance trade. And when it circulates in long-distance commerce, through various territories, it does so without the support of an army.

In light of this comparison, I would like to propose rethinking two broad assumptions. First, must the pursuit of global commerce be coupled with armed states, raids, and wars? Is global free commerce a possibility or is monopoly, as described by Braudel (1979), unavoidable? After all, the Manangi diasporic community, dispersed across a large transregional space but conceivable as a society in its internal relationships among fellow citizens, has pursued its entrepreneurial and social endeavors despite the absence of its own sovereignty, army, and large capital stocks. Second, given what Manangis have achieved both in and beyond their material domains, fulfilling social purposes according to what they value, might their history complicate the unilinear Eurocentric economic history and the narrative of the rise of the West?

Cosmologies of Welfare:
Two Conceptions of Social Assistance in Contemporary South Africa

James Ferguson

Many anthropologists today seem unsure of what their discipline is about, or how it is to be distinguished from other forms of social and cultural analysis. I myself feel no such anxiety, since it seems obvious to me that anthropology's distinctiveness and value lie neither in a unique subject matter nor a trademark methodology, but rather in an intellectual tradition. I feel so confident about this, I think, because that tradition was conveyed to me in very convincing terms, and at a tender age, by an exceptional constellation of teachers. And of these teachers, none was more influential than Stanley Tambiah in showing me how to think about a problem anthropologically.

The question of what it means to approach a problem anthropologically is of some significance to my current research project, because it deals with a topic, social assistance, that has not historically been regarded as an anthropological one. Sociology seems to be where the topic is thought to belong, and sociologists have indeed written libraries' worth of books and articles about welfare, pensions, social grants, social work, the rise and fall of the Keynesian welfare state, and other related topics. That anthropology has produced no parallel

literature is worth pondering.[1] One might think that this is an arti-
fact of the conventional geographical division of labor between the
two fields (with sociology conventionally claiming the industrialized
First World, and anthropology the underdeveloped Third World). But
in fact anthropologists have from the beginning worked dispropor-
tionately with people who were directly engaged with systems of social assistance (Native Americans in the United States and aboriginals
in Australia come to mind, among many other examples). And many
of the modern Third World nation-states that have been the focus of
study and have produced the richest troves of anthropological work
have elaborate and well-established welfare regimes of long standing
that loom large in the lives of the poor and marginal peoples that anthropologists have so often studied. (One might think, for instance,
of South Africa, Brazil, and India.) An anthropology of welfare, then,
would appear to be overdue.

Yet how are we to approach this topic anthropologically? And
what might an anthropological approach be able to contribute to the
work already done by our colleagues in sociology and other fields?
I suggest that Tambiah (who himself made the journey from sociology to anthropology) can give us a clue. It is perhaps fortuitous that
I learned my economic anthropology from a scholar best known for
his studies of ritual and religion. For as Tambiah explained it, producing and exchanging, buying and selling, markets and prices—all
had to be situated within encompassing schemes of classification and
valuation that economistic perspectives inevitably left invisible and
unacknowledged.

Because anthropologists have historically taken seriously social
and conceptual systems that are very different from those of the
modern West, we tend to take far less for granted than do other social
scientists. The anthropological starting point is that different sociocultural worlds are in fact *different*. They are not simply different arrangements or valuations of the same basic set of familiar elements.
In fact they contain, and are made up of, altogether different *things*.
Analysis must in some sense *begin*, then, with the question of classification and cosmology, where the most basic question is: what are the
things in this world, and how are they related to one another? Michel
Foucault, of course, is one valuable source for thinking about such an
"order of things," and his work continues to guide my analytical approach to what he termed "the formation of objects." But the classical
traditions of anthropology in some ways converge on the same set

of issues and provide distinctive conceptual tools for their analysis—
tools to which I find myself increasingly returning as I work on my
new project.

As Tambiah put it in his introduction to *Culture, Thought, and Social
Action* (1985b), cosmologies "are frameworks of concepts and relations
which treat the universe or cosmos as an ordered system, describing it
in terms of space, time, matter, and motion, and peopling it with gods,
humans, animals, spirits, demons, and the like." Such frameworks, he
pointed out, "tend to be viewed as enduring arrangements of things
and persons," and members of a society ordinarily "accept them as
given in 'nature' and as the 'natural' way the world is ordered" (3–4).

This conceptual starting place helps me to think about some recent transformations in the domain of social assistance policy in contemporary South Africa. An older understanding of the world of the
social, which prevailed throughout most of the twentieth century, appears to be coming undone, and some familiar figures from that old
world appear to be losing their focus, changing form, or disappearing
altogether. At the same time, new ways of thinking are appearing that
evince not just new views about the familiar objects, but substantially
new kinds of things-in-the-world.

The older cosmological framework of welfare is one that we could
term *social democratic*. It was peopled not with gods, animals, spirits,
and demons, but with a rich set of equally obvious, taken-for-granted,
and socially constructed figures, ranging from entities (such as the
family, society, the employer, the worker), to relations (such as dependence and solidarity), to existential conditions (such as unemployment and disability). Most inhabitants of this world (as well as most
of the social scientists who have studied it) have taken for granted
this cosmological structure, and debate and discussion have centered
on how these obvious things in the world are, or ought to be, related,
reformed, or regulated.

Recent debates around the question of social assistance in South
Africa, however, reveal that this world of objects and relations has
changed. In an emerging cosmological frame that I term *neoliberal*,
some objects have appeared which simply did not exist before (such
as human capital). Other objects have familiar names, but their roles
have changed so much that they are hardly recognizable (such as enterprise, dependency, or the informal economy). At the same time,
some features of the older social-democratic cosmology appear to be
at risk, if not of disappearing altogether, then at least of being shunted

into a far less visible background (I am thinking of such things as society, the family, and—as I will show in a moment—unemployment).

I wish to emphasize that these changes are not (as is often supposed) simply a matter of anti-welfare neoliberals imposing their asocial and minimalist vision of government, while the defenders of the downtrodden struggle to defend a welfare state that cares about the poor. Rather, the contemporary cosmological shift is something that cuts across the political spectrum, and is visible in the modes of reasoning and styles of argumentation of both pro-welfare and anti-welfare actors. Perhaps the most vivid way of showing this is to point to the way that arguments in favor of one recent "pro-poor" policy proposal in South Africa (the campaign for a Basic Income Grant) rely upon, and make effective use of, the new cosmology of welfare. I will suggest that this demonstrates some of the political possibilities (as well as the more obvious dangers) of the new world that we now find ourselves in.

The idea of a Basic Income Grant (or BIG) has been advocated in recent years in South Africa by a broad coalition of church groups and labor unions.[2] While it has not, so far, been accepted by the government, it has achieved broad and significant support within progressive social movements and NGOs, and from some significant factions within the ruling African National Congress party (ANC). The proposal calls for a modest payment of about R100 (about $16) per person per month to be paid to all South Africans, irrespective of age or income. The argument is that such a universal system of direct payments is the most efficient way to directly assist all poor South Africans. Better-off South Africans would also receive the grant, but the funds they would receive (and then some) would be recuperated through the tax system.

The arguments in favor of the BIG do not dispense entirely with the social-democratic cosmological frame that I briefly outlined. But the familiar objects of welfare-state social policy lie side-by-side with other, much less familiar ones, which come from the brave new world of neoliberalism. In noting this, I do not mean to say that the BIG promoters have "sold out" to neoliberalism. Rather, I suggest that discursive and conceptual figures that appear at first blush to be part of a simply anti-welfare world view are in fact being creatively put to work in the service of pro-poor and pro-welfare political arguments.

Consider the following distinct arguments that are presented in pro-BIG discourse:

1. Perhaps unsurprisingly (in these times), the social-democratic theme of social obligation is largely replaced in BIG rhetoric by the theme of "investment in human capital." The poor individual is explicitly conceptualized as a micro-enterprise. The BIG would (as the BIG Coalition website claims) "enable working families to invest more of their incomes in nutrition, education and health care—with corresponding productivity gains" (Tilton 2005). So hungry people, for instance, might appear to need to eat, but really what they need is "to invest more of their incomes in nutrition" in order to build up their "human capital," with "corresponding productivity gains." Pro-BIG arguments are generously seeded with this sort of language, which recasts social spending as investing in a kind of capital.[3]

2. A second theme is a critique of dependency (one that neatly reverses the usual right-wing arguments against social payments). It is the *existing* "safety net," the BIG promoters argue, that breeds dependency. Today, any economically productive poor person is surrounded by dependents who must be supported. This dependency constitutes a "tax" on the productivity of the poor, which both creates a disincentive to work and degrades human capital. The "dependency" of absolute poverty is a drag on productivity, and it makes workers unable to be economically active, to search for better jobs, and so forth. What's more, insecurity breeds passivity, inhibiting entrepreneurship and "risk-taking behaviors." A poor South African thinking of starting a small business, for instance, under present circumstances must consider the terrible risk of falling into destitution and hunger in the event of failure. The same person with a monthly BIG payment would be empowered to be much bolder. Providing basic income security for all, it is claimed, will enable the poor to behave as proper neoliberal subjects (i.e., as entrepreneurs and risk-takers); the status quo promotes dependency and prevents that behavior.

As a key government report (the Taylor Committee Report) put it, "By providing . . . a minimum level of income support people will be empowered to take the risks needed to break out of the poverty cycle. Rather than serving as a disincentive to engage in higher return activities, such a minimum (and irrevocable) grant could encourage risk taking and self-reliance. Such an income grant could thus become a springboard for development" (Department of Social Development 2002, 61). In this way, the BIG would provide not a "safety net" (the old-style, circus-derived image of welfare as protection against hazard) but a "springboard"—a facilitator of risky (but presumably empowering) neoliberal flight.

3. BIG arguments also borrow from established neoliberal critiques of welfare paternalism (such as the old Thatcherite complaint about the "nanny state" that tries to run everybody's life in the name of the needs of "society"). The existing social-assistance system, BIG advocates point out, makes moralizing judgments about "the deserving poor" and requires surveillance, normalization, and so on, which is both objectionable in itself and expensive and inefficient. What's more, recipients are publicly labeled as such, and thus set apart from the general population; in this way, they may be subtly stigmatized. The Basic Income Grant, on the other hand, would be paid to everyone; citizens would access their funds (in the ideal scheme) by simply swiping their national identity cards in an ATM. They would use the funds (as good rational actors) in the way they saw best. There would be no policing of conduct, no stigmatizing labels, no social workers coming into homes—and no costly bureaucracy to sort out who does or does not qualify. Through the radical step of eliminating means testing (and, in some versions, replacing documents with biometric technology [Breckenridge 2005]), it is proposed that the "formalities" of social assistance might be streamlined in a way that might make social payments catalytic of, rather than contrary to, the vital economic logic of informality. The state is here imagined as both universally engaged (as a kind of direct provider for each and every citizen) and maximally disengaged (taking no real interest in shaping the conduct of those under its care, who are seen as knowing their own needs better than the state does).

4. Perhaps the most striking (and in some ways, disturbing) change from traditional social democracy is the explicit rejection of formal employment as the "normal" frame of reference for social policy (let alone as an entitlement to which all have rights). The Taylor Report notes, "High unemployment, including the massive net loss of formal sector jobs, and a growing shift towards so-called 'atypical' work, has reduced the incomes of the poor" (Department of Social Development 2002, 32). And it sees no prospect for an end to this shift away from formal employment. Indeed, the Report goes on:

> In developing countries, where stable full-time waged formal sector labour was never the norm, it is increasingly unlikely that it will become the norm. (ibid., 38)

The reality is that in the developing world formal sector employment may *never* become the norm that it is in Europe. (ibid., 154;
emphasis added).

The need for assistance, then, is not about being "between jobs"
or correcting for dips in the business cycle. Formal employment is
not (and never will be!) the normal state of affairs. Social assistance
is here radically decoupled from expectations of employment, and,
indeed, from "insurance" rationality altogether. Instead, the Taylor
Report re-understands the condition of unemployment not as a hazard, but as the normal condition (most people, most of the time, will,
for the foreseeable future, live that way), and seeks not to prevent that
condition, but to make it productive.

5. How can unemployment be productive? Here, the "informal sector" appears in a newly central role, appearing not as it did through
most of the twentieth century as a problem to be solved, but instead
as the solution itself. To be economically productive, BIG advocates
point out, does not require formal sector employment; social payments are most significant not as temporary substitutes for employment, but as a way of promoting greater productivity, enterprise, and
risk-taking in the "informal" domain within which more and more
South Africans are expected to earn their living. BIG payments, then,
are understood neither as temporary relief nor as charity, but as a
means of enhancing production by enabling both job seeking and,
crucially, entrepreneurial activity.

There is a history dating back to at least the late 1970s, of course,
of plans to "develop" what Keith Hart originally termed the *informal
sector,* based on the realization that "informal" economic activities
were both productive and capable of supporting large portions of
the population where formal employment was scarce (for a lucid review, see Van der Waal and Sharp 1988). But the vision in this older
literature was still broadly developmental. The informal was seen as
a point of entry into larger-scale enterprise, which would eventually
provide pathways into the formal sector; the informal sector was in
this way understood, as Van der Waal and Sharp have put it, "as the
formal sector in the making" (1988, 143). What is new in the more
recent representations of informality is the acceptance, even celebration, of informality itself. For in the scenario envisioned by at least
some of BIG's most effective champions, the informal economy is not
to be overcome or incorporated, but enhanced and expanded.

This is a striking vision of the future, where the informal economy is the new, exciting growth sector, and broad formal-sector employment a receding, twentieth-century relic. As two leading advocates of the BIG, Guy Standing and Michael Sampson, note, this neatly reverses the temporal vision of the great mid-twentieth-century development economist Arthur Lewis, who saw the heart of economic development as a transfer of surplus labor from "the traditional, informal sector" to the "modern, formal sector." Instead, in South Africa and elsewhere, Standing and Sampson argue, "economic informalization is growing" and "the proportion of people working in informal activities is rising." Under such circumstances, the very notion of an "unemployment rate" is archaic—"a mid-twentieth-century indicator that is inappropriate for a twenty-first-century economy and society" (Standing and Sampson 2003, 2).

It is easy to see the political dangers in the disconcerting shift that makes familiar twentieth-century social-democratic objects (like unemployment) simply disappear. What is harder—but, I have argued elsewhere (J. Ferguson 2010), essential—is to see that possibilities, and not only dangers, are opened up by the new objects and modes of reasoning that have taken their place. A host of new forms of anti-poverty politics, in Africa and elsewhere, are taking advantage of the new cosmological terrain that is opening up, and the news is not all bad. To understand these new politics, however, we have to be able to see that they involve schemes of classification as much as struggles over resources, and that such schemes are always, as Tambiah once put it, "thought as well as lived" (1985b, 4).

"A Recurrence of Structures" in Collapsing Nigeria

Victor Manfredi

From Tambiah to Nigeria

According to a leading school of anthropological thought, Lévi-Strauss (1945) deployed Jakobsonian structuralism to split the "atom of kinship"—an emic node of "arbitrary" mental representations organizing small human groups. Then Leach (1954) adapted this idea to analyze four centuries of "structural variability" among part-time kingdoms in Burma's Kachin Hills, and Tambiah (1976) further expanded the view, positing a Maussian "totalization" of "dialectical tensions" through two millennia, from Aśokan India to Southeast Asian Buddhist states. In shifting the visual metaphor from microscopy to astronomy, Tambiah also updated the implied linguistic analog of social relations, from a phonological feature grid to a syntax of recursive rules ("transformation yet felt continuity"; 1976, p. 527) generating infinite outputs ("the set or family of occurrences ... that particular Southeast Asian religio-political systems [as indeed individual actors] portray in varying mixes and strengths"; 1976, p. 516).[1] These innovations notwithstanding, Tambiah's treatment of politics remains Lévi-Straussian in other respects: diachrony is intrinsic to the model, and the proper object of analysis is internal to the mind ("La parenté ... n'existe que pour se perpétuer. ... [N]ous sommes en plein symbolisme"; Lévi-Strauss 1945, pp. 49, 53). There is also carry-over of ethnographic substance ("the production of wider systems of social solidarity and political integration" involves "[m]arriage or unions ... as has been demonstrated by Lévi-Strauss, Leach and Need-ham"; Tambiah 1976, p. 117 n. 13), and even an echo of the maestro's Olympian style ("[M]yth and reality are closer than we think"; Tam-biah 1977, p. 74).

Having already met these themes in Tambi's classroom thirty-something years ago, I should have immediately perceived the signifi-cance of a typewritten history of Ágbọ̀ ("Agbor" in colonial spelling) which was handed to me in September 1976 by the anthropologist M. A. Ọnwụejìọ̀gwụ̀ ("Onwuejeogwu") when he introduced me to the author, Chief A. E. Ìdúùwẹ. Ọnwụejìọ̀gwụ̀ had written a preface high-lighting Ágbọ̀'s multimodal politics and noting that the phenomenon is not rare. Nearby examples include the Ìgbo-speaking Óru ("allu-vial") mini-states (Ǹzímìro 1972); Okpẹ, the Ùrhobo ("Sobo")-speaking kingdom of which Otite drily says that its "political system cannot be regarded as being in equilibrium" (1971, p. 56); Isẹkiri ("Jekri"), the Yorùbá-related enclave which went from having "[i]n 1800 ... a highly centralized government" (Lloyd 1963, p. 207) through an 88-year in-terregnum before the crown was revived in 1936 in the multi-ethnic crossroads of "Warri" (Ikimẹ 1969, pp. 253–70; cf. Moore 1936, 1970; Edevbie 2004, p. 265f.; Imobighe et al. 2002; Eke[h] 2007); and Ẹ̀dó (known to Europeans as *Benin* and to Ìgbos as *Ìdúù*), the antique and pluridynastic imperial capital that the British pillaged in 1897 before restoring its monarchy in 1963 (Bradbury 1967, 1968).

This cluster of political ambivalence in the Atlantic trade zone of southern Nigeria, cutting across linguistic and ecological lines, attests to the overlap of two larger subregional patterns: i) crowned priests of tutelary divinities in Ẹ̀dó- and Yorùbá-speaking walled market towns (Fádìpẹ̀ 1940, 1970), and ii) gerontocratic lineages in Ìgbo-speaking and Cross River horticultural villages practicing the "occasional state"—a temporary union of autonomous communities facing ex-ternal threat (Áfììgbo 2006, p. 40). The empirical blurring of these di-vergent types was noted by the government folklorist N. W. Thomas (1910, and later amplified in Bradbury 1969), although Thomas was sacked when his grassroots research threatened to undermine the conceptual footings of Indirect Rule (Lackner 1971). Saving the dichotomy of "centralized authority" versus "stateless societies" (Fortes and Evans-Pritchard 1940, p. 5; cf. Meek 1937, pp. 3, 185) needed studies like Forde and Jones 1950—a classic of the trend to lump protostates together with "tribal" organization (Fried 1957; Sahlins 1961). Thanks to official groupthink, Lugard's 1914 contraption called Nigeria stayed stuck in an orientalist "kingdom- and empire-oriented . . . straitjacket" (Áfììgbo 1996, p. 3f.), and, eventually rebranded as a sovereign state, it failed to attain the "amalgamation in . . . culture . . . and even cosmology" (Áfììgbo 2003, p. 46) wished for by nationalists and modernization theorists alike. Instead it spawned a distinctively crumbling civic ethos and a new sociological term of art: "the chaotic complex" (Láwúyì 2002; cf. Áfììgbo 1972, 2005b; Qláníyàn and Àlàó 2003; Eke[h] 2007).

Successor regimes became successively more top-heavy (Fáwọlé 2003) and more adept at gerrymandering the federating units (Ẹ̀lá[h] 1983), yielding to date 37 insolvent states and more than 740 unaccountable local jurisdictions. Proliferation of vacuous administrative domains may be ethnographically insincere, but it obeys an unassailable double logic: to defuse game-theoretic power blocs at the center (Dudley 1973) and to instrumentalize public goods at the periphery. The money interest is hard to exaggerate. In 2007, for example, one local chairman in Ẹ̀dó State disposed of an unaudited annual "security vote" equal to US$100,000 (roughly the same as his official salary) plus had a free hand to distribute cars and other valuables irregularly sourced by the state house from ruling party godfathers.[2] Commodification of customary politics is even more blatant in the Efik-led trade kingdom known to Europeans for 400 years as "Calabar":

> [T]here was a Palace Crisis in 2004 over the matter of fake clans and villages. A number of *Etuboms* [kingmakers] maintain long lists of villages that do not exist, on account of which they themselves are considered Clan Heads. . . . One of the *Etuboms* owns 22 fake villages and is personally paid for 18! . . . All the *Etuboms* who were either not part of this scam or were suspected of harbouring sympathies for those who wanted to stop the malpractice have since been shut out of the Palace. . . . The total effect of this exclusion is that seven out of the 12 Efik Principalities are not represented at all. (Edem and Ekeng 2008, p. 7f.)

In sum: for at least a century, historic palaces in Nigeria's Atlantic fringe—sometimes called the "South-South"—have been continually reshaped by the respective occupying power; but why?[3] What "deep structure" regenerates this flickering phenomenon through time and space? Before turning to particular cases, here's a general guess.

In the 17th and 18th centuries, under the financial stimulus of slave exports and the civil pressure of raids (Rodney 1969), the ancient gift economy gorged itself on inflated rents and marriage fees (Fálọ́lá and Adébáyọ̀ 2000, p. 100f., citing Fádìpẹ̀ 1940) and entrenched "the necessarily political character of middlemen" (Manfredi 1993, p. 4). As chiefly *pourcentage* became the format of retail politics in Atlantic Africa, a distinctive jargon evolved for trade-inducing bribes: first as *comey* (from Portuguese *comer*, "to eat"), then as *custom* and *dash* (Geary 1927, p. 82; Jones 1958, p. 52), and now more gerundively as *seeing* and *settling*. Graft by whatever name was hardwired into the Royal Niger Company's 19th century gunboat concessions and grandfathered into the post-1914 chieftaincy "warrants" which the occupier doled out along with the right to siphon export rents on vegetable fats (cocoa and palm oil), precursors of today's smuggled hydrocarbons. Periodically, systemic gravitation aligns these mediating networks into galaxies, big and small.

That a politics sustained in this way tends to fluctuate, follows by analogy with the Asian cases cited above. Small scale structural "oscillation" of the Kachin conical clan (Leach) can be explained as neomarxist "evolution/devolution" in a context in which social reproduction is not locally assured (Friedman 1975). And in Buddhist capitals, "outcomes of a pulsating kind" expressed in a "cosmological idiom together with its grandeur and imagery ... [are] a realistic reflection of the political pulls and pushes of these center-oriented but centrifugally fragmenting polities" (Tambiah 1977, p. 74). So too in Ágbọ̀, Ìdúùwẹ the titled organic intellectual willingly donned the mantle of a *"gumlao* revolutionary leader" (Leach 1954, p. 263) as a partisan of "voluntaristic action" conscious of "many pasts and ... an open-ended future" (Tambiah 1992, p. 170).

This paper retells the story of Ágbọ̀ (§3) in between briefer comments on better-known Ogoni (§2) and Biafra (§4). An appendix (§5) provides excerpts from Ìdúùwẹ's remarkable manuscript.

Vultural Ecology

In the current league table of "blood for oil," Nigeria can't compete with occupied Iraq, but the rankings may change if Africa's western equatorial coast becomes "the next Gulf" (Rowell et al. 2005; cf. Ghaz-vinian 2007). Anticipating such a development, U.S. planners recently predicted Nigeria's "outright collapse" (National Intelligence Council 2005, p. 16), but their presentism is misplaced: a "tendency towards disintegration" (Rodney 1969, 24) has marked the West African sub-region since the 16th–19th centuries, when tributary lineage systems met the nascent capitalist world-economy, and the same anomic quality persisted throughout a long 20th century of fruitless nation-building. In recognition of this, a more reasonable question is not when "outright collapse" will arrive, but why it hasn't yet.

No answer can ignore chiefly corruption (Ǹzímìro 1984). This is-sue was at the root of the "judicial murder" of nine Ogoni citizens, including the world-class writer Kenule Saro-Wiwa, in Port Harcourt on 10 November 1995 with the apparent complicity of top manage-ment of Anglo-Dutch Shell (Ámadí 1996, p. 161; cf. Ghazi 1995; Lean 1995; Wiwa 1996; Rowell 2009). General Abacha's "Special Tribunal" held Saro personally responsible for the lynching on 21 May 1994 of four Ogoni chiefs who "were on a list of 10 'vultures' that Mr. Saro-Wiwa had made public the previous October because of what he said was their opposition to his aggressive campaigning for Ogoni rights against Shell" (Lewis 1996; cf. Òkóntà and Douglas 2001, Òkóntà 2007b, p. 226).[4] The marsupial court invoked an Orwellian doctrine of guilt-by-presumed-conspiracy (Ámadí 1996), and then Saro's ex-ecutioner prolonged Ken's hanging with repeated flubs (Ọlọ́rúnyọ̀mi 1996, p. 24). Nor did Nigeria's collective torture mercifully end when Abacha himself dropped dead of unknown causes on 8 June 1998. During the next eight years of "President" Ọbásanjọ́—the khaki-clad boss of 1976–1979 dredged up from retirement in 1998 and draped in proverbial *agbádá iná* and *ẹ̀wù ẹ̀jẹ̀* (Délánọ̀ 1966, p. 11) by the anti-democratic and unpopular People's Democratic Party (PDP)—"more than 10,000 Nigerians ... died in violent clashes along intercommu-nal lines" (Human Rights Watch 2007) and "more than three million Nigerians were internally displaced" (Reuters 2006). Some of these killings were at state hands (Fálána 2002, Ìgè 2008) but most of the mayhem was dished out by auxiliaries, in tune with global trends (Smith 2001; cf. Ágbụ 2004, Pratten 2006; Òkóntà 2007a).[5]

Saro-Wiwa's incandescent tragedy illuminates Nigeria's political landscape. He began his literary career in 1962 as a scholar at Univer-sity College Ìbàdàn. Classed as an ethnic "minority," he spurned the Ìgbo-led National Council of Nigeria and the Camebecause (NCNC) of his "own" Eastern Region (see §3) to join the relatively exotic Northern People's Congress (NPN) representing the Sókótó Caliphate (Ọmọruyì 2008). Escaping doomed Biafra in 1969, he signed on as a civil commissioner in army-run Rivers State, but became disenchanted by federal reassertion of "the Crown's rights over minerals and land" in 1973 as had been first claimed by the "Obnoxious Ordinances" of 1945-1947 (Coleman 1958, p. 282; Saro-Wiwa 1989, pp. 217, 387). Saro's public disaffection from the extractive state may explain why he was "cheated of the opportunity" to participate in 1977 constitutional talks, after which he "avoided all political parties" (Saro-Wiwa 1996, p. 73). The 2nd Republic unraveled at the end of 1983, and General Babangida seized power in 1985 and coopted Saro in 1987 to run an ill-defined parastatal of "mass mobilization" with the bulky acronym of MAMSER. Saro resigned from MAMSER in 1988 and in 1990 launched the nonviolent Movement for the Survival of the Ogoni People (with an oddly similar acronym, MOSOP) in five out of the six Ogoni districts—also called "kingdoms" or "clans" (Saro-Wiwa 1995, p. 66; Òbí 2001; Òkóntà 2007b, pp. 179, 209). MOSOP launched anticorporate campaigns, joined the Unrepresented Nations and Peoples Organization, and boycotted Babangida's military-to-civilian "transition without end" (Diamond et al.1997). The grinning general's *chakkavatti*-like conceit was to draw in effect a "cosmological topography" (Tambiah 1976, p. 102) of dual parties, center-left and center-right, planted like ornamental shrubs in symmetrical cement bunkers in more than 700 local government headquarters across Nigeria. Presidental nominations were repeatedly aborted by micromanagement, but in June 1993 the procrastinations ran out, Chief Moshood Abíọlá swept the vote, and the army pulled the plug (Ọmọruyì 1999). After a few months, General Abacha emerged from behind the curtain (but never from behind his aviator shades) and Saro soon met his martyrdom in the glow of "sHellish" flares.[6] Babangida, after recycling Ọbásanjọ́ in 1999, withdrew to his home town of Minna and into a German-built custom labyrinth.

These events were dramatic but not new. Southern Nigerian peasants had deposed their chiefs in 1904, 1929-1930, and 1968-1969 (Gailey 1970, Áfììgbo 1972, T. Adéníran 1974, Beer 1976, Ọhadíké 1991, Pratten 2007) and more generally "the presence of classes within the lineage mode of production" (Terray 1975, p. 96) is documented in a literature extending from Crowder and Ikime (1970) to Vaughan (2000) and Watson (2003), supporting the thesis that "kinship assumed the role of state surrogate during the centuries of the slave trade" (Eke[h] 1990, p. 661; cf. Meillassoux 1986). External entanglement caused medieval West Africa to miss out on any counterpart of the "feudal revolution"—the internal process by which medieval Western Europe passed from rogue knighthood to fiefdoms with financial accountability (i.e., from personal to territorial-bureaucratic authority) (Duby 1962, p. 68f.; Bisson 1994, p. 39). That transition was forestalled by a system whose "terrible logic . . . caused the African chiefs to cling to the Atlantic slave trade as their staple economic activity, even after it had become an anachronism . . ." (Rodney 1970, p. 118). Thus Joseph (1987) could find "prebendal politics . . . in the Second Republic" of Nigeria and Saro (if not misquoted) could spot human "vultures" scavenging the delta's political terrain. In wider perspective, West Africa's "patrimonialism" (Reyna 2007) resembles South Asia's "fetishized" political Buddhism (Tambiah 1992, p. 59) as the vehicle of waxing and waning power.

Ágbò in Its Firmament

Ágbò Kingdom covers Ìká North and South Local Government Areas in the present Delta State (Ònyéchè 2002). Its capital, Íme-Óbi, "the king's precinct" (< íme "inside," ò-bí "dwell-er"), perches at the delta's northwest edge on a sandy plateau where the east-west road crosses Òrogodó stream. Next door is the sprawling market whose official name, Bójìbọjì, commemorates a waterside bivouac of colonial expeditionary troops (< Yorùbá bọ̀jú-bọ̀jú "face-washer"). In 1901 the British camped in front of Ágbò palace, but the post retreated to Bójìbọjì in 1906 after an angry crowd killed District Commissioner Crewe-Reade (alias "Rédì") in revenge for beating a old man to death while press-ganging Ágbò youths as load carriers. Ìdúùwẹ writes that Rédì's violent end gave Ágbò an "official reputation for truculence."

Ìká North East and South together have just 5% of the population of the whole delta region—today's Delta, Bayelsa, and Rivers States—but Ágbò Kingdom is not culturally atypical of its neighborhood. Ìgbo-style ọ̀fọ́ (patrilineage symbols of indigenous bamboo ringed in iron bands; Figure 1) coexist with Ẹ̀dó-style coral and brass regalia (referencing royal monopolies on salt-water wealth and the death penalty; Figure 2).

The dualism extends even to dance steps: aerobic Ìgbo acrobatics (Beier 1957) coexist with the lead-foot Ẹ̀dó choreography performed by

Figure 8.1. Ọ̀gwá ndi ichèn, Ògbe Ńmụ̀ Déin, Ágbọ̀, 1982. (Photo by V. Manfredi.) In the ọ̀gwá ndị ichèn (elders' parliament), the oldest lineage male sits before the ọ̀fọ̀ sticks offering food, chalk, and money to the collective ancestors, ńdị nmọ̀ (cf. Ọ̀nwụejìọ́ gwụ̀ 1981, p. 39). In the royal lineage Ńmụ̀ Déin (Déin's descendants), the oldest male is called Íregwàị—a name that might be glossed as "the tongue that informs us." Here, Ìdúùwẹ is two seats from the Íregwàị Ébọnmà, but he eventually attained Íregwàị status before himself becoming an ancestor.

dancers wearing cowrie-laden ùbulúku smocks depicting the dry-land locomotion of Óloòkún, the fish-tailed ocean god (Galembo 1993).

As Ìdúùwẹ's manuscript makes clear, Ágbọ̀ was the transmission gate between Ẹ̀dó and Ìgbo. Although this intermediation is largely overlooked today (Nzímìro 1972, Èjiọfọ́[r] 1982, Ọhadíké 1994, Okpehwo 1998), the fractal pattern of dispersion is proved by abundant evidence and is well suited to a Tambian metaphor comparing Ágbọ̀'s position between its Ìgbo-speaking satellites and the wider orbit of Ẹ̀dó to a small solar system in a bigger galaxy.

For example, the big trading town of Ọ̀nịcha ("Onitsha") now calls itself "Àdó City" (see for example http://ikmartins.5u.com/) because it claims to have been founded by "Ézè Chíìma" from Ẹ̀dó (automatically pronounced "Àdó" in the Ọ̀nịcha dialect of Ìgbo; cf. Éménanjọ 1971). But this attribution is imprecise. Ẹ̀dó has no name resembling Chíìma, but Ágbọ̀ still recalls the eastward escape of "Prince Kímẹ́" circa 1700 during a succession dispute (Ìdúùwẹ ms.; cf. Meek 1937, p. 11 fn. 1; Ọ̀nwụejìọ̀gwù 1972; Oguagha 1992, p. 363; Manfredi 1991, p. 278f.). By

Figure 8.2. Íkenchúku's father Òbíkà in festival regalia outside the Ágbọ̀ palace. (Photo reprinted from Beier 1963, p. 190f.; courtesy of the Ulli and Georgina Beier Center for Black Culture and International Understanding, Òṣogbo, Òṣun State, Nigeria.)

regular phonetic shifts, the closest match in Ọnịcha for [kímẹ́] is precisely [chíìma]. Three other separate details confirm that Ágbọ̀, and not Ẹ̀dó, was the direct model for the Ìgbo-speaking "Ézè Chíìma" states. First, Àbọ́ claims that its founder and Ọnịcha's were brothers who "left [Ẹ̀dó] together, separating at Ágbọ̀" (Nzímìro 1972, p. 7). Second is the presence in one of the "Ézè Chíìma" towns of a ward called "Ọ̀gwá Chìmè" ("Chímè's assembly," Èjìọfọ́ 1982, p. 345), with the final [e] making a telltale match to the Ágbọ̀ form of the proper name. Third, Ágbọ̀'s royal lineage is called Ńmụ̀ Déin ("Déin's children") after the founder of the current dynasty, and Ụ̀mụ̀ Déin—the Ìgbo translation of this phrase—is also the name of a royal line in Àbọ́, Ọnịcha, and Úgwutà towns (Nzímìro 1972, pp. 29, 196, 217), whereas no name like Déi(n) can be found in Ẹ̀dó.[7]

Ẹ̀dó influence in Ágbọ̀ is extravagantly dramatized in the Ágbọ̀ festival called Ọ̀sị́ Ézi ("A friend from outside."[8]) (See Ìdúùwẹ ms.; Figure 2; Beier 1963; Ị̀máhị̀agbe 1981). Less obviously, however, the "centralized" polity of Ẹ̀dó shares some basic structures with the "stateless" east. At Ẹ̀dó's ritual apex sits Ọ̀mọn N'Ọ̀ba ("Ọba's legitimate child"), the culture-heroic king, but there are three more chiefly sets to reckon with (Bradbury 1956, 1967, 1968). The *kingmakers* are autochthonous and hereditary; the *town chiefs* are "big-man" commoners who exchange wealth for lifetime knighthoods (cf. Sahlins 1963); the *palace chiefs* are royal dependents, hereditary or appointed, with the formal status of house servants but from a household that covers half of the old imperial capital (Bradbury 1969). Two of these Ẹ̀dó grades—kingmakers and town chiefs—have counterparts throughout the "stateless" Ìgbo-speaking east.

Predictably, Ẹ̀dó's political authority was most fluid in 1897 after the British toppled Ọ̀ba Òvọ́nrànmwẹn and sacked the palace of its brass and ivory treasures. To quell civil resistance, the occupiers had to ally themselves with town chiefs and condone de facto "joint rule" between their client Ọ̀ba Ẹ̀wẹ́ka II (whose father Òvọ́nrànmwẹn died in exile) and the Ìyàsẹ́ (the Yorùbá-style town leader). But abuses by the town chiefs disadvantaged their party, the Action Group (AG, led by Yorùbá Chief Ọbáfẹ́mi Awólọ́wọ̀, alias "Awo") in the 1951 Western Regional elections, which were won instead by the National Council of Nigeria and the Camerouns (NCNC, led by the Ìgbo Chief Ǹnàḿdị̀ Àzíkàíwe, alias "Zik"). During the 1951 campaign, Òwegbe, the palace's masonic auxiliary, "unleashed a wave of violence throughout Benin Division" (Bradbury 1968, p. 247) against the AG's elite cadre, the Reformed Ògbóni Fraternity (a Christianized form of Yorùbá freemasonry). In 1963, Ẹ̀wẹ́ka's son Ọ̀ba Ákẹnzùa II endorsed the NCNC's plebiscite to remove the Midwest from the Western Region (Vickers 2000), which had the effect of substantially restoring Ẹ̀dó monarchy after 66 years. The Midwest secession also deemphasised the monarchy's mythical link to Ifẹ̀ (called "Úhẹ̀" in Ẹ̀dó) and this remains a sore point, earning the current Ọ̀ba a public smackdown from the Yorùbá establishment (Àjàyí 2004; cf. Ẹ̀rédiaùwá 2004, Àlùkò 2004, Èghárevba 1934, Ryder 1965, Horton 1979, Adédìran 1991, Ọbáyẹmí 1991).[9]

That such kingdoms fluctuate between "a *weaker* form, which was perhaps the more usual state, and a *stronger* form, which was perhaps achieved during exceptional periods" (Tambiah 1977, p. 82) is borne out by yet another example, which I observed at first hand. On 8 September 1976, my mentor M. A. Ọnwụejìọgwù presented me to A. Ẹ. Ìdúùwẹ (Figure 1; Figure 3), an accomplished elder of Ágbọ's royal lineage.

Ìdúùwẹ had by then already been an activist for half a century, since helping to found Ágbọ Patriotic Union, a club of migrant literates in Lagos. In 1939, he wrote to the British in his capacity as APU secretary, that "…apart from language, Ágbọ people have everything in common with the Yorùbá and the Benin [= Ẹdó]. And we pray you do not listen to irresponsible grumblers and newspaper men."[10] These disparaging epithets transparently refer to Zik, who founded the *West African Pilot* in 1937 and who in 1949 told the Ì[g]bo State Union that "the God of Africa has specially created the Ì[g]bo nation to lead the children of Africa from the bondage of the Ages" (Coleman 1958, p. 347). In 1948 the colonizers disregarded Ìdúùwẹ's advice and reclassified Ágbọ Kingdom as an Ìgbo-style cluster of ten "Ịká clans," ensuring that "clan heads rotated the post of presidency in the district council" (Ìdúùwẹ ms.; cf. Coleman 1958, p. 314).[11] But in 1960, Ìdúùwẹ's pro-Yorùbá sentiments were rewarded by the Ágbọ monarch Òbíkà (1916–1967; Figure 4), an AG minister at the time, who conferred on him the title Òdíì, glossed as "leader of [the king's] legion and deliverer of the royal gifts."[12] Around the same time, Ìdúùwẹ wrote "History of Greater Ágbọ," whose title diplomatically conveys the pre-1948 centripetal idea of Ágbọ Kingdom without technically contradicting the decentralized constitutional position of the day.

After the 1963 plebiscite, Òbíkà switched parties to become a Minister in the NCNC's Midwest administration.[13] This was inevitable: "Just as the British colonial government expected kings and chiefs or native authorities to ensure its success among their people, so did the Midwestern State government expect the same type of rulers to promote its interests" (Otite 1975, p. 78).[14] But two army coups ended civil rule in 1966, and when the Ìgbos finally lost the Biafran War in 1970, Òbíkà's son Íkenchúku felt autonomous enough to sell a large tract of lineage land to Chief Vincent West Ẹgbárin, a multi-industrialist with the portentous alias Ọrịkaézè ("He [who] resembles a king"). In October 1976, Íkenchúku celebrated the Ọsịézi festival in high style on national TV, and the lineage assembly (Figure 1) sent Ìdúùwẹ to contest the land sale in court as a violation of collective usufruct (cf. Úchèndù 1977, 1995).[15]

On the morning of 9 September 1976, as state radio announced the death of Mao Ze Dong, Chief Ìdúùwẹ invited me to see "where my

Figure 8.3. Chief Augustin Ẹ̀gwabọ́ Ìdúùwẹ in front of his house in Ògbe Ńmù̀ Déin, Ágbọ̀, 1982. (Photo by V. Manfredi.)

father is buried." We crossed the old highway, a war-torn moonscape where ducks bathed in puddles between paved spots, and entered a sandy path, when two motorcycles zoomed up. The riders, scrawny *ìchásùn* (palace lackeys), accosted my elderly host and knocked him to the ground. As I helped him to his feet they called me a spy and grabbed the portfolio containing my passport. That evening, Chief and I discussed the assault with Ọnwụejìọ́gwụ̀, and the next day I walked alone to the palace, primed with a repertoire of antiquarian blandishments for the king:

Dóo Dein, ágwọ ekèlíkà, ẹ́ka oghei, ògí-ázụ gbome Òhimi, nwá tùtú!

[Hail dynastic founder, multicolored snake, unchecked hand, whose domain extends up to the Niger, demonic child!]

My performance amused the *ịchásùn*, but Íkenchúku returned my passport only on condition that I conduct my studies in a distant village under loyal supervision.

By my next visit in 1980, much had changed. In 1979, General Ọbásanjọ́ rigged Awo's party (then called UPN) out of the presidency and handed Lugard's baton back to the Caliphate's NPN—resuming the script of 1960 that had been interrupted by coups and war. Also in 1979, Chief Ọ̀rịkaézè dropped dead in an NPN meeting and Íkenchúku was mysteriously shot at night somewhere outside of Ágbọ̀. Following an autopsy in the University of Benin Teaching Hospital (O. Ẹ̀bọhọ́n, p.c.), Íkenchúku's corpse was refused legitimate burial by Ògbe Ńmù̀ Déin (Ìdúùwẹ manuscript, excerpted below), complicating the succession of his infant son (Figure 3). Ìdúùwẹ's lawsuit was granted by default, following the respondents' deaths.[16]

After these decisive events, Ìdúùwẹ finished rewriting his "History of Greater Ágbọ̀," but he still had to collate the different drafts prepared during the kingdom's successive phases. While we fiddled with scissors and paste, another editorial problem arose. Ìdúùwẹ still used a colonial-era spelling, which had been overtaken in the 1960s and '70s by the official orthography with subdots (Èkére 1961, Ọ́gbàlụ́ 1975, Elugbe 1984, Williamson 1985), but this well-argued policy was scarcely known, far less applied, in a small speech community like Ágbọ̀. The job was over my head and beyond my means, but Ìdúùwẹ was patient and in January 1982 presented me to his ọ̀gwá in ebullient mood.[17] The NPN was overthrown by populist soldiers at the end of 1983; then in August 1985 General Babangida turned the wheel of *dhamma* once again, spinning Nigeria further down the drain. Meanwhile both Ìdúùwẹ and Ọnwụejìọ́gwụ̀ have joined their ancestors, and Íkenchúku's son has assumed the Ágbọ̀ throne. Ìdúùwẹ's book remains unpublished, to my great regret.

Figure 8.4. The infant Kíagbòekúzi three years after his father Íkenchúku's reign. (Photo culled from a local almanac.)

"The Ìgbo Have No Kings"

When General Abacha's dead hand slid off the lever of power one June night in 1998, a tangential consequence was to reprieve the annual Ìgbo studies conference which had been banned by an eccentric satrap in Ímò State, the very pentacostal Colonel Zubairu (Ílozùé 1999). The next meeting in November 2000 was thrown in turmoil, however, as Ìgbo's twinkling political constellations morphed into a neo-Biafran Rorschach test. The thesis of the 16th Àhịajíọkụ́ Lecture, delivered by a professor of physics, is adequately represented by the following excerpt:

> The precolonial traditional government of the Ìgbo without kings imbued in them the characteristic traits that prompt the saying that "*Ìgbo énwé ezè.*" ... Most Ìgbo governed themselves without giving power to chiefs or kings. ... Nobody had any special privilege because of ancestry. ... Perhaps we should say more about self-reliance, which is strongly influenced by the legacies of *Ìgbo énwé ezè.* ... The Biafran war tested the self-reliance of Eastern Nigerians, especially the Ìgbo, to its limit. ... Then Biafran scientists and engineers began to fabricate grenades, mines, bombs, mortars, rockets, pontoons, plated vehicles etc. ... We find some parallels between scientific culture and the legacies of *Ìgbo énwé ezè.* Scientific culture recognizes no kings and chiefs with divine knowledge ... Our conclusion is that the implications of *Ìgbo énwé ezè* are democratic, self-reliant, scientific, modern and in tune with the best traditions of humankind. (Ọnwụmèchili 2000)

Prof. Áfiìgbo, then the dean of Ìgbo historians and co-organizer of the event, reports that this hackneyed panegyric was rewarded with a "vile attack" (2002, 2005a, 478) from Prof. Ọnwụejìógwù̀ (2001) in the form of a reply entitled "*Ìgbo nwe ézè,* Ìgbo Have Kings: The Evolutionary Development of Complexities in the Ìgbo Political System." Áfiìgbo himself replied with a more social-science inflected restatement of Ọnwụmèchili, resting on two remarkably traditional planks.

Áfiìgbo's Plank One is the diffusionist idea that "advanced social technology (more centralized political systems)" was not indigenous to Ìgbo-speakers but the result of external "conquest" by a "second wave of migrants ... who came in from the middle belt savanna" (Áfiìgbo 2002, 2005a, 483). The sole evidence cited for this story is an imaginative equation of the ethnic term *Ìgbo* LL with "the phoneme [sic] *gbó* ... found among the Yorùbá to be indicative of bush" (p. 482). To be taken seriously, the etymology would have to explain the opposite tone of the two roots, *L* versus *H*—but Áfiìgbo doesn't mark tones—and would also need to justify the reconstruction of a word spanning the unrelated meanings of *farmland* and *forest/bush* (p. 482)—but no such word exists in any Nigerian language known to me.[18] Linguistic howlers aside, Áfiìgbo's story is a neat ideological match for Ọ̀nwụmèchili's premise, that any example of Ìgbo-speaking kingship is an "exception" (2000), echoing civil war propaganda that "Biafran society is traditionally egalitarian" (Òjúkwu 1969) and re-hashing Meek's Hamitic theory that "[k]ingship is not and never was a feature of the Ìgbo constitution. Where it occurs it is clearly of exotic origin" (Meek 1937, p. 185). Once upon a time, Áfiìgbo had called Meek's idea "prejudiced" and "based on rather very slender evidence" (Áfiìgbo 1981; cf. Zachernuk 1994), but by 2002 he had decided that it provided "some of the key to our problems" (Áfiìgbo 2002, 2005a, p. 482). What had changed meanwhile?

Áfiìgbo's Plank Two is equally familiar from 19th century and colonial literature. He puts it as follows:

> Ìgbo political theory, by which we mean the theory which underpins and supports the Ìgbo polis, is ... basically organic and natural being based on blood descent. ... With such a political theory it is not surprising that in an Ìgbo polity, the *number one* political authority is that which derives from correct standing in or descent from the blood line. (2002, 2005a, p, 484, emphasis original)

A few pages later, Áfiìgbo repeats the idea that "traditional rulership in Ìgboland" is based on principles related "to hereditary rights, to ascription, to the blood line" as distinct from "charisma and achievement" (p. 488). One hundred forty years before, a counsel to the British Rāj in India wrote: "The history of political ideas begins, in fact, with the assumption that kinship in blood is the sole possible ground of community in political functions" (Maine 1861, p.129).

Áfiìgbo's 2002 thesis has one great difficulty, apart from its disfigurement with childish taunts.[19] Any attempt to marginalize Ìgbo examples of "centralized kingship" at the same time that one asserts the ubiquity of Ìgbo "traditional rulership" based on a pre-contract, tribal organization based on "blood" is an incorrigibly static position that must attribute all change to the *deus ex machina* of immigration. Áfiìgbo may have missed the words *evolutionary development* in the title of Ọ̀nwụejìọ́gwụ̀'s 2001 pamphlet, and he probably also overlooked the main point of Ọ̀nwụejìọ́gwụ̀'s 1981 book which contextualizes Ǹri within the wider Ìgbo-speaking area by showing that its centralized political structure was not an isolated "exception" (Ọ̀nwụmèchili's term) to the stateless tribal stereotype. Building on Ǹzímìro (1972), Ọ̀nwụejìọ́gwụ̀ disproved the colonial theory that Ìgbo politics can be reduced to "mutually balancing segments" (Fortes and Evans-

Pritchard 1940, p.16) and showed on the contrary that "where wealth differentiation and associational groupings are marked,...segmentary opposition becomes a minor feature of the political process" (1981, p. 134). This is not a matter of Nri alone: differentiation and association of this kind runs right across the Ìgbo-speaking area, and not just in the big trading entrepôts. Áfììgbo's quaint appeal to "organic and nat-ural...blood descent" also ignores an elementary ethnographic point unknown to Sir Henry Maine, that all kinship terms are in principle *classificatory* and not limited to literal, "organic," or *biological* refer-ence (cf. Ọ̀nwụejìọ́gwụ̀ 1981, p.135 fn. 15). By insisting, on the contrary, that kinship is objectively separate from politics, Áfììgbo can blame the hubristic and authoritarian Lord Lugard for the "careerism and impudence" of Ìgbo "warrant chiefs" in 1912-1929, characterizing that era as "the time when the principles upholding the Ézè-ship in-stitution in precolonial Ìgboland were violently breached (Áfììgbo 2002, 2005a, pp. 487, 491). But to be consistent, Áfììgbo should also blame the hubristic and authoritarian Lord Ọbásanjọ́ for the "career-ism and impudence" of today's Ìgbo-speaking "political godfathers" of the PDP, such as the Anambara State brothers Chris and Nnàm̀dì "Andy" Ụ̀bá[h] (Ńnàńnà 2004, Ayọ̀adé 2006). Áfììgbo never considers the possibility that these monstrous "big men" are not aberrations, but predictable expressions of long-standing Ìgbo political order.

Intellectual vacuity is plain whenever a historian resorts to *post hoc propter hoc*. Offering the excuse that "since 1896 much water has run under the bridge," Áfììgbo pardons the failure of the committee by "the military administration of the defunct East Central State ap-pointed in 1975" with himself as "Chairman ... to restore to the in-stitution [of traditional rulers] in Ìgbo land its 'tradition[a]lness' by laying emphasis on the correct genealogical position of an occupant of the stool" (2002, 2005a, p. 490). Continuing the self-pity, he laments that "[f]or some time we have been sliding back into the warrant chief era" (p. 490)—as if the verification of genealogy is a job for the army. The worst thing that Áfììgbo manages to say about Ọ̀nwụejìọ́gwụ̀'s cul-turally and historically grounded 1981 study of Ìgbo kingship is that "only the first chapter does not address a political question," and that it is "*by and large political anthropology more or less along the lines of* high-noon colonial anthropology" (1996, 12, emphasis added). Maybe high noon is when the national clock stopped.

Appendix

Excerpts from Ìdúùwẹ's "History of Greater Ágbọ̀"

Page 43

In the late forties political parties sprang up. [Òbíkà] remained neutral for sometime, while his subjects supported the two parties NCNC and AG. The majority became NCNC partisans. They wanted their natural rulers to support them but this honourable ruler hesitated to support any political party, as he is the father of all. They then victimised him with the false slogan that he caused the Western Nigerian government whose party was AG to increase taxation. They marched to his palace, caused damages to his car and property and attacked some of his chiefs—Akpara, Oguden and others—and drove them into the woods. The leaders of the party were arrested and jailed in 1954.

Òbíkà's character was undaunted despite all his worries, and he was obliged to become an AG partisan. In the election of 1959 he showed himself as an able leader and won for the AG 5 seats out of the 14 seats in his clan, and the majority in the Ika Local Council of 42 seats in which the AG won 22 against NCNC's 20. The Òbí was therefore congratulated and the Western Region Government made him a Minister of State without portfolio and Edward Anuku a junior Minister in the Ministry of Economic Development and Planning. But because of the crisis of 1962 in which the Government of Western Nigeria was seriously involved, the Òbí crossed the carpet to NCNC during the campaign for the creation of Mid West, and the Òbí won for his new party great support for the Midwest Region. The Government of the new Region made him to continue as Minister of State.

Page 45

The installation and coronation of Íkenchúku was marked with the greatest enthusiasm ever witnessed in Ágbọ̀, despite the cloud of the civil war which had begun in 1966. . . . He proved himself a patriot during repressive incidents in the civil war. Íkenchúku could be called a saviour of his people and of the strangers within his gate. . . .

At last after the third year he became despotic and oppressive and there was unrest in the kingdom. He died on 29th April 1979 survived by 4 daughters and two sons of 2 and 1 year old. He was not given the usual burial ceremony but his son was untimely crowned privately by the palace chiefs without the knowledge of his royal family Ògbe Ńmụ̀ Déin people and [kingmakers] Àlị Íjèmisí.

People and Ideas Travel Together: Tambiah's Approach to Ritual and Cosmology in Brazil

Mariza Peirano

Chances and Odds

The first time I read Tambiah's work was in 1973, in a masters seminar on symbolism held by Peter Silverwood-Cope at the Universidade de Brasília. At that time, Tambiah's article "The Magical Power of Words" (1968b) had recently been published in the journal *Man*, and "Form and Meaning of Magical Acts" (1973), still in manuscript form while the seminar met, would be available in print later that year. When the fieldwork of Edmund Leach's students in the Vaupés region of Colombia came to an end, Christine and Steve Hugh-Jones headed back to England, but Peter Silverwood-Cope decided to move to Brazil. As an enthusiastic admirer of Tambiah, both as a scholar and on a personal level, he introduced his students at the Universidade de Brasília to Tambiah's ideas.

The purpose of this personal introduction is to set the record straight regarding how Tambiah's work landed in Brazil more than three decades ago: it occurred by means of the mere casual fact that Leach had a keen student teaching in Brasília (of all places in Brazil). By another coincidence, some years later, in 1976, as a second-year graduate student at Harvard, I was thrilled to come across Tambi (as his students and friends called him), who had recently transferred from the University of Chicago to teach there. In fact, in those days of slow communication, I had believed him to be far away, in England.

Of course, Tambiah's strong influence in Brazil nowadays does not result only from chance involving former students, though this is indeed a significant part of it. After all, people and ideas travel together. But a more sociological explanation is also in order. The question becomes this: how is it that, despite Tambiah's main ethnographic interest being located geographically, culturally, and ideologically very distant from Brazil, his work has been so significant for many anthropologists in Brazil? I offer here some short answers.

Anthropology in Brazil

A powerful feature of the practice and teaching of anthropology in Brazil lies in the fact that we tend not to separate ethnography from theory. In general, this means that a monograph is read for its ethnographic evidence and for its theoretical framework, both dimensions fused together. Of course, this is how classical monographs are (or were) also read in the United States, and perhaps elsewhere, in graduate seminars usually titled "History and Theory" or the like. But in Brazil this practice is generally extended to contemporary monographs—that is, present-day ethnographies are read and evaluated as possible new *Argonauts of the Western Pacific*, not because of a particular interest in Melanesia, but rather for the theoretical claims made by Malinowski by way of the Trobrianders. Thus, in the same vein, Tambiah's *Leveling Crowds: Ethnonationist Conflict and Collective Violence in South Asia* (1996a) is read not for a special interest in South Asia, nor for an exclusive concern with collective violence. It is read for its innovative approach to riots as rituals and the cosmological implications of that approach; for the new analytical tools Tambiah provides; and also, because nation-building is a continuous concern in Brazil, for its powerful portrayal of the (difficult) experience of the nation-state project outside Europe. In this perspective, we may say that although theory and ethnography tend to be inseparable in Brazil, the first encompasses the second.

A question then immediately surfaces: why this theoretical eagerness? Not unlike in other places, the modernization project of the 1930s in Brazil included the institutionalization of the social sciences for at least a twofold purpose: to prepare new political leaders to govern the country on a solid democratic basis, and to attain levels of scholarly excellence so as to allow communication with the world academic centers on an equal basis. Theory thus became a (noble) path to many ends: a modern political elite needed fine analysis to unveil what was supposed to be "Brazilian social reality," and, in due course, to transform it, which would be achieved by way of good analytical tools that would instigate sound theory, in turn making Brazilian social scientists conversable with the world.

Waves of Marxism, structuralism, poststructuralism, postmodernism, and so on came into vogue during this time. But, of course, obsession with theory has its down side: when ideas are adopted just for their fashionable appeal, the result is often a loss of analytical power. Lévi-Strauss once remarked that his experience in Brazil as a teacher in the 1930s showed him that students could be so much ahead of their professors in terms of the latest theoretical turn that only the most recently proposed approach seemed interesting to them.

To this day, one striking feature of anthropology in Brazil has been its disinterest in exoticism, though a fascination with "difference" has remained fundamental to the research agenda. A concern with indigenous peoples and their contact with regional populations first defined the field, and this trend dominated the scene until the 1960s; in the following decades, the inclusion of the peasantry was immediately followed by the addition of larger urban contexts; in the 1980s, social scientists' intellectual production itself became an anthropological subject; and, in the 1990s, with globalization came ethnographic interest in the experiences of Brazilians living in other parts of the world, and increased interest in conducting research abroad. The result has been a steady incorporation of new topics and an enlargement of the discipline's research universe. Today, all these modes of conceiving otherness coexist in an attempt to develop an anthropology "made in Brazil."

This relative freedom may be explained by various factors. First, Brazil has never experienced historical resentment for having been the object of anthropological curiosity for the metropolitan centers. Second, a concern with the notion of "Brazilianess" has always been present, from the traditional interest in indigenous peoples within the national territory to the new concern with Brazilians abroad, and, even more recently, an engagement with the populations of other former Portuguese colonies. And third, the Portuguese language has produced a relatively isolated community of social scientists—including sociologists, anthropologists, political scientists, and historians—who are close interlocutors, peers, and mutual critics. Thus, as in many contexts in which anthropology developed as a field of knowledge during the twentieth century, a large variety of intellectual influences were brought to bear on topics of particular local concern, and striving for theoretically significant contributions became the path toward a much-desired, though frequently frustrated, international dialogue.[1]

Tambiah in Brazil

It is within this scenario that Tambiah's approach has become an important inspiration for many anthropologists in Brazil. Though well known, his work is not faddish or trendy—or, at least, it has not yet become the focus of a fad or trend. Instead, Tambiah's approach is seen as providing a solid foundation for those who are determined not only to combine ethnography and theory, but also to ground continuous theoretical advances in solid ethnographic scholarship. His work has thus provided a firm counterbalance to the dominant emphasis on theory alone.

We have benefited immensely from Tambiah's constant reminders that the intellectual dichotomies that thrive in academic circles may be reconciled and combined for the sake of sound interpretation: that, for instance, structural analysis and cultural accounts are not conflicting analytical frameworks; that the union of form and content is part of cosmology and essential to the performative character of ritual; that social action and thought are not contradictory but inevitably complementary domains; that both semantic and pragmatic meanings are implicated in transference; that microevents may clarify macrohistories, and vice versa.

Furthermore, Tambiah has elucidated two complementary orientations. First is the idea that anthropology is a collective project, permanently revived, renovated, and expanded. We can see this conception at work in his brilliant re-analysis of classical monographs and in his ongoing conversations with interlocutors past and present (and here I include his splendid Leach biography).[2] Second is his interdisciplinary approach, as demonstrated in his habitual crossing of boundaries to adapt, recreate, and include (albeit not without a twist) achievements from other disciplines, such as linguistics and philosophy, in order to energize anthropology's own understanding. His broad vision is nowhere more evident than in his influential work on ritual and its relation to cosmology—in which ritual serves as a means of analyzing social events in the broadest sense, thereby enlarging the focus of a phenomenon so familiar to anthropologists.

A brief survey of monographs, articles, books, theses, and dissertations reveals the extent to which Tambiah's approach has inspired a great variety of ethnographic themes, all of them sharing the idea that rituals do not conform to a particular anthropological definition. Instead, the perceptive researcher recognizes as rituals the special events that enlarge, focus, highlight, and justify what is ordinary in a given society. In this way, ritual becomes an analytical tool that allows us to detect cosmologies in ordinary events. Following this approach, new ethnographic data not only "surprise" us anthropologists, but, by allowing us to enter into dialogue with and expand upon previous assumptions, they constitute a sound pathway to theoretical refinement.

Examples of what Tambiah has inspired can be found in many studies related to politics as a whole. One such case is an analysis of the two-month-long "National March of the Landless Peasants" (in which three columns of demonstrators covered more than 1,000 kilometers of highway to establish and traverse a moral as well as a physical path) by Christine Chaves (2000). There are also studies of religious-cum-political phenomena, such as short marches to Brasília, Brazil's capital (Steil 1996 and 2001) and of the relationship between political rituals and local festivities (K. Silva 2003, Chaves 2003). Carla Teixeira has investigated processes by which congressmen lose office due to a lack of decorum (1998), later coupling this work with a focus on boasting (*bravata*) as a ritual genre of politics (Teixeira 2001). Studies of the struggle for land on the outskirts of cities and the significant event venues in these contexts have also been inspired by Tambiah (e.g., Borges 2004), as has the examination of the ways in which peasant meetings reveal the link between social morphology and the power of leadership (Comerford 1996 and 1999). Comerford soon expanded his 1999 investigation to become an ethnographic examination of the relationship between kinship, locality, and moral reputation as the foundations for institutional structures of the state and the church (Comerford 2003).[3]

At least three studies based more on the traditional definition of ritual but emphasizing its performative aspects are indebted to Tambiah. One deals with the relationship between regional and national festivities, where the fascination with exoticism (which is the basis of international tourism) is contrasted with anthropology's own past inclinations (J. Silva 2007). A second looks at the elections of the General Assembly of the United Nations as a paradoxical event in which the values of equality and symmetry can be attained only in the context of a firm heirarchy and behind closed doors (Góes Filho 2001 and 2003). A third looks at the Rio Earth Summit from the perspective of an observer who is both a journalist and an ethnographer (Little 1995).

Tambiah's insights into the ways in which small events can indicate the presence of the state in daily life have led to studies such as those that look at legal IDs as modern amulets (Peirano 2006, 2009, and 2011). An inspired analysis of the ritual aspects of the many rehearsals that lead to a symphonic orchestra recital also follows Tambiah's approach (Trajano Filho 1984), as does an analysis of a theater piece by Nelson Rodrigues (Moreira Santos 2001) that is well known in Brazil. An important study of the ritual genre of telling stories to make political statements was carried out among the Tapuio Indians of the state of Goiás (C. Silva 2002).

Western cosmologies *per se* have been the subject of at least two studies, one of them an examination of messages carried by the Voyager spaceship in the hope of finding extraterrestrial life (Aranha Filho 2001), and the other focused on the conjunction of science and religion in the search for UFOs (Ferreira Neto 1984).

Crossing Brazilian territorial borders over the last two decades, anthropologists have produced research on rumors as a narrative genre for nation-building projects in Guinea-Bissau (Trajano Filho 1993, 1998, and 2004); a study of public administration state-formation rituals in East Timor in relation to the larger scenario of international cooperation (K. Silva 2004); work on the presence of the dead in state affairs in South Africa, as documented at burial sites and the public policy of land restitution (Borges 2007a and 2007b); and research on the foundation of cities in Argentina as analyzed from sixteenth-century sources (Boixadós 1994). Tambiah's interest in Thailand was ethnographically re-situated to Brazil in a study carried out at the Thai Embassy in Brasília, focusing on the relationship between religion and politics in the diplomatic dealings with local authorities (Taminato 2007).[4] Finally, a three-day seminar that was a tribute to Tambiah was held in 2000 and resulted in a collection of essays by anthropologists who had been inspired by his approach to ritual (Peirano 2002).

Ritual as an Analytical Strategy and Ethnographic Approach

All the studies mentioned above derive from Tambiah's transformation of ritual from a classical empirical subject into an analytical tool. Based on the idea that ritual does not have an absolute definition, that it is for "the natives" (be they politicians, common citizens, or even social scientists) to point out what is a "special event," Tambiah's original proposal about the performative force of ritual not only helped solve the old puzzle about the efficacy of social acts, but also opened up the possibility of gaining insight into actual ethnographic theories (such as a "South Asian theory of democracy" or a "Thai theory of the state"). When rituals are conceived not as events that are qualitatively different from everyday occurrences, but rather as more formalized, more stereotyped, and more structured versions of them, then all of these events become equally revealing of public cosmologies.[5] This heightened aspect of ritual was of major interest in the studies developed in Brazil, making ethnographic theories parallel to cosmologies.

Furthermore, focusing on rituals puts us into the realm of social action. In the context of shared world views, communication between individuals reveals implicit classifications among human beings and between human beings and nature, human beings and objects, and human beings and gods (or demons, or constitutions), for example. Communication may be carried out by means of words or acts; these differences in media do not minimize either the action's purpose or its efficacy, given that the use of language is also a social act. Tambiah thus helps us reach a fundamental conclusion: anthropology always incorporates, implicitly or explicitly, a theory of language. Charles Sanders Peirce, Roman Jakobson, and J. L. Austin are invited to join us in the effort to interpret speech (as a communicative event) in the context of cosmology, and to include both with ethnography.

Tambiah's *Leveling Crowds* (1996a) is the great example of such breadth.[6] By looking at riots as rituals, Tambiah shows us their patterns in terms of the triggering events, sequences, participants, places of incidence, organized and anticipated features, recurrent phases, and the elements selected from routine forms of sociality. His work leads us, first, to the recognition that the cultural repertoire of South Asia does not offer a foundation for the Western European model of the nation-state, and second, to the conclusion that electoral politics and collective violence may be integral components of democracy at work.

The book's combination of theory and ethnographic material has been of great interest. Although the first part of the book is officially dedicated to cases of violence in different places and times in South Asia, and the second to a dialogue with Gustave Le Bon, Emile Durkheim, E. P. Thompson, and subaltern studies, this division is blurred when, for example, a consideration of microevents in the first part leads to concepts of much larger dimension, or the theoretical discussion of the second part demands mention of newly discovered data about specific events. This is a grand picture of what anthropological analysis is capable of when microethnography and macrosociology are combined. Investigating collective violence by means of ritual analysis, Tambiah indicates how old theories may serve new purposes when the empirical object is properly delineated in the tense confrontation between native ideals and values, on the one hand, and anthropological comparison on the other.

In university libraries, *Leveling Crowds* finds its place in the sections devoted to political science, anthropology, religion, violence, and South Asia. Transported to the graduate classroom, the book has become one of the modern classics of social science theory.

A Debt to Tambiah

I conclude by looking ahead. Despite all the recognition Tambiah has received for his work, our indebtedness to him has not yet been expressed fully. Nor have his contributions been fully explored. For instance, the notions he presented in *Leveling Crowds* about the dynamic transformation of microevents into major issues, and vice versa, release us from the commonsense grid of what is conceived as local, national, and global. The concepts that he calls *focalization* and *transvaluation* refer to the processes by which a series of local, small-scale conflicts, involving people in direct contact with one another, build up into ever-larger clashes.[7] The first process strips local incidents and disputes of their contexts; the second distorts, abstracts, and aggregates the incidents into larger collective issues (Tambiah 1996, 81). In addition, he presents us with the concepts of *nationalization* and *parochialization*, the first referring to the radiating out of a local cause or event to become a condensed symbol, the second referring to a process in which a national issue is reproduced in diverse local places, "exploding like a cluster bomb in multiple context-bound ways" (Tambiah 1996, 257). In a world where distortion is often the basis for incidents and clashes that are later combined into larger collective issues, and in which larger issues reproduce themselves in multiple places, Tambiah has given us analytical tools for the present and for the future. Though not anticipated, these four kinds of actions are not randomly or arbitrarily situated, as one would tend to imagine at first. Instead, Tambiah has shown us their structural movements and their possible developments in terms of the path that leads from the micro to the macro level, and vice versa. Indeed, he has given us a blueprint for the challenge that the perlocutionary effects have always represented for the anthropologist and the sociologist when thinking about social action. It is for us to carry on the investigations he has inspired.

Paradoxes of Order in Thai Community Politics

Michael Herzfeld

Oscillation between hierarchical and egalitarian models is a feature of the political life of the Shan of Burma, as Edmund Leach (1954) famously argued. But it is also of more general significance; indeed, it characterizes the uncertainty of anthropologists themselves as they try to put Southeast Asian societies into one or the other box. In the Thai context, older anthropological notions of "loose structure" (see Embree 1950 and cf. J. M. Potter 1976; but see also Textor 1977) seem to be incorporated in a certain studied informality in some interactions, but these performances vie with a heavy emphasis on models of hierarchy that draw heavily, if not always directly, on royal symbolism. Yet even that seeming contradiction may be more the result of the way in which Thailand has become a Western-style state, governed—and analyzed—according to a positivistic understanding of the meaning of data and order and yoked to a Western-derived progressivist model of the past: the "pulsing galactic polity" that Stanley Tambiah offered as the mandala-based dynamic of the early Siamese state (see *World Conqueror and World Renouncer,* 1976) has been displaced to an idealized past. Today, the earlier polity is treated with a nostalgic condescension worthy of the Eurocentrism that the modern Thai state has so assiduously sought both to cultivate and to deny, a feat it has achieved by reifying the idea of a unified Thai tradition in a manner strongly reminiscent of many European nationalisms over the past two centuries.

I make these remarks, then, in the context of a conviction that arguments about "where modern Thai culture came from" are bedeviled by simplistic etiologies of origin: the either-or formulations of "the West versus China" are no more satisfactory than the simplistic insistence that everything about modern Thailand, including the seemingly obsessive positivism of much of its political elite, can be traced to Buddhist models. To say that there is much in Thai political and cultural life that is obviously of Western inspiration means neither that it is a straightforward imitation—indeed, it rarely is that—nor that Thais are unaware of the geopolitical conditions that have seemed to necessitate a creative use of Western prototypes. Indeed, I would argue that the country's "crypto-colonial" condition (Herzfeld 2002) and the concomitant insistence that Thailand must achieve a certain degree of "being civilized," *khwaamsiwilai* (Thongchai 2000), are precisely what have made the apparently uncritical adoption of a positivistic model of society and culture all but inevitable. That does not mean, however, that Thais are fooled by the claims of positivistic discourse, only that they have learned to use it well and in a distinctively local way; ironically, they may sometimes be far more aware of its contingent character than were its Western originators. The representation of the West and Asia as mutually opposed is as unproductive as the binarism of loose structure and hierarchy, and is indeed often read into the East/West stereotype as a dictatorship/democracy dualism that is equally unhelpful in disentangling the complex realities of modern Thai politics.

It would also be unrealistic to insist on such "pure" explanations and neatly Cartesian dualisms in the context of a rapidly globalizing and increasingly complex world economy. In my own fieldwork in Rattanakosin Island, Bangkok, earlier in this decade, I found that middle-class populations (such as those of the Phraeng Phuthawn, Wat Sakaet/Phukao Thong, and Tha Phrachan locations) were far less interested in pursuing community identity as a strategic goal than were those groups—notably the Pom Mahakan community, of which much more in a moment—whose desperate economic plight and fear of eviction made concerted action a more attractive alternative. Local observers often commented that they found much more of a sense of community in these poorer communities (and again, Pom Mahakan seemed to be the most striking example, although Tha Wang was certainly another) than in the middle-class enclaves, in sharp contrast to official insistence that squatter populations, as the poorer groups were considered, could not be considered true communities at all. Thus, even the dynamics of self-definition were clearly constrained by economic factors.

While I am no economic determinist, and nor, certainly, is Tambiah (see especially Tambiah 1990), we cannot ignore the material conditions that favor one or another perspective, that favor a particular invocation and conception of "Thainess," or that encourage or undermine collective action. While such considerations are certainly tempered by cultural specificities, they also serve to direct such specificities within a larger context of globalized values—what I have elsewhere dubbed the "global hierarchy of value" (Herzfeld 2004). As a result, amid all the protestations of Thai-Buddhist values, the language of protest is often English even for those who do not speak it; in Pom Mahakan, the first major preferred slogan was "STOP THE WAR—STOP THE EVICTION." The use of English was simply a practical recognition that this is the way to get attention, as protesters in China (to cite the famous example of Tiananmen Square) discovered very early on.

What has persisted into the present, in an intriguing symbiosis with the Westernizing and positivistic rhetoric of both the state and the NGOs (it is striking how quickly "NGO-ese" gets adopted by the community residents, reinforcing the impression of their competence[1]), is a distinctive pattern of "high-wire" (Paine 1989) tension between extremes of egalitarianism and authority. Models abound: the self-presentation style of two recent governors of Bangkok, Samak Sundaravej (later briefly prime minister) and Apirak Kosayothin, embodied the contrasted ideals of the Thai *phuu nam* (leader); Samak appeared as an authoritarian father-figure whose apparent lack of good manners became a particular problem when he became prime minister of the entire nation, while Apirak portrayed the restrained and thoughtful listener. Within the Pom Mahakan community, too, the collective leadership that the community evolved to avoid raising unnecessary conflict provided a flexible means for meeting a huge variety of different situations, since the relationship of the community with the municipal authorities seemed at times to vary almost from hour to hour.

It might seem strange, in the context of a society ostensibly as concerned with calm compromise as Thailand, to invoke the agonistic models that Robert Paine derived principally from a Mediterranean, Christian, and European prototype (see Campbell 1964). But appearances are deceptive. Paine showed that the "high-wire" image could be used to explain sexual comportment in an overtly Muslim society whose values appeared to conflict with the very possibilities that the ethnographer had observed. In this way, ethnographic observation opens up some of the intimate spaces of social life that official ideology deliberately occludes. In much the same way, a comparison of Thai community politics with those of more openly aggressive societies shows that politeness does not necessarily mean an absence of proactive, strategic, and even aggressive modalities of social interaction. On the contrary, politeness itself, with its intimations of hierarchy, can provide a subtle weapon in the play of power, one that allows social actors to use selective speech acts in order to lay claim to positions of authority. This is, broadly speaking, what is meant by the English expression "taking the moral high ground": adopting a pose of lofty detachment or smiling conciliation can be a very aggressive play for recognition in a society that values such things.

It was the very ambiguity of models of social hierarchy that sustained the galactic polity, but that also led to its periodic "pulsing" (an oscillation that reflected repeated expansions and contractions of power, not unlike the oscillation between the *gumsa* and *gumlao* models observed by Leach). In the same way, the apparent stability of community life in the face of adversity conceals a considerable amount of anger, debate, and dissension, the management of which is handled by assigning specific roles and moments to leaders of particular character. It is this alternation and persistent ambiguity, not the positivistic rhetoric of Thainess and democracy, that represents a more identifiably indigenous strain in the political thought of the residents and their leaders. Whether it should be attributed to "Buddhism" or instead to a hypothetical substrate of Thai culture is perhaps more a matter of terminology than of factual precision. What is clear, in any case, is that we should avoid essentializing origins and identities to the point where they overcome analysis.

The most obvious expression of the tension between hierarchy and egalitarianism appears in the political uses of the expression *phii-nawng*, a compound of "older siblings" and "younger siblings." In the most inclusive political context, this has apparently become the preferred idiom for expressing the hierarchical relationship between Thailand and Laos. But there is something paradoxical even in this self-evidently hierarchical formula. Inasmuch as Thais regard Laos as representing the older, uncontaminated form of their own culture, with all the disadvantages that attributions of tradition can bring to any entity struggling to establish its own lien on modernity, we can only explain the idea that Thailand is the "older sibling" as an expression of this modernist ideology: tradition does not mean maturity in the global hierarchy of value.

When the expression is used in the context of community politics, the ambiguities intensify. NGO activists have especially cultivated this usage as *ostensibly* egalitarian, yet it is clear that their own skills place them in a *phii* (older sibling) position in relation to the relatively dependent *chaobaan* (residents). When they as well as community leaders use the expression to address the community as a whole—at one point the Pom Mahakan residents were meeting collectively two or three times a week—they appear to be invoking a more generalized principle of parity. When Governor Apirak came to visit the community and addressed the residents with this term, it would normally have seemed simply a repetition of common political rhetoric, had it not been for his very humble mien and his refusal to use a microphone, address the residents *de haut en bas,* or more generally to employ gestures and language that would belittle the residents; instead, he chose to sit on a low stool before the seated elderly members of the community, inviting them to express their concerns rather than lecturing them as others had done. Yet even here it is clear that, politically at least, the governor was seizing the moral high ground in a way that increased his moral authority and deepened the residents' respect for him. Later events confirmed his willingness to take them seriously and gained him a strong following in the community.

That such encounters are rife with theatricality is a commonplace of anthropological observations of politics in Southeast Asia (see, e.g., Geertz 1980). In this case, there was a literal rehearsal, as the community leaders hastily coached the children in a collective *wai* (formal greeting with the palms pressed together) of homage when they learned that the governor was, unexpectedly, about to arrive with his entourage. By consigning this role to the children, the leaders certainly meant no disrespect, and in fact went out of their way to be extremely polite in their conversations with the governor, who reciprocated their courtesy. But children, as the youngest group, could *wai* without fear of incongruity; older people do not *wai* their juniors except under conditions of strong hierarchical difference, in part because to do so would imply that the younger person should die first.[2] The children's act of homage also showed the visiting delegation the psychological and social good health of the community—an especially important move, inasmuch as the previous municipal administration had accused the community of being riddled with drugs and violence. The clean, well-dressed, and respectful children, playing openly in the paths and squares of the community's space, were the best evidence that such a reputation was underserved and unjust. That the *wai* is usually performed first by younger people to their elders did not in fact preclude the use of the *wai* as a sign of respect for the governor by any of the residents, but the children's performance dramatically emphasized the normative character of both the residents' collective comportment and the community's respect for the governor's high office.

The oscillation of authority and egalitarianism that I observed in the many community meetings I attended was a more complex matter. Much always depended on how threatened the community felt at the time. This again recalls Tambiah's description of the galactic polity (1976, 115): the effective condition of rule was a marriage between the ruler and a commoner. This is the same logic whereby protesters in Thailand until recently almost never split into party-political factions with distinctive flags or other symbols, but instead demonstrated under the aegis of the royal portraits and the national flag—a feature that was very prominent at Pom Mahakan.

Within the community, however, the "pulsing" is perhaps more palpable than the encapsulation. It is illustrated by an oscillation in the operation of the community's collective leadership, which encapsulates possibilities for authoritarian control and relaxed folksiness alike; as Tambiah presciently remarks (1976, 103), anticipating what was soon to appear as the most distinctive aspect of practice theory (see, e.g., Karp 1986), these conceptual structures are constantly "emergent" in the actual social performance of perceived structures. And here *performance* is indeed the operative term; we are speaking of some very self-conscious role-playing, through which the play of authoritarianism and egalitarianism defines the acceptable limits beyond which the local polity cannot "pulse" without risking collapse

from within or destruction from without. The performances themselves are reminders of these dangers and of an almost stereotypical
pattern of confronting the dangers with displays of adaptability.

Thus, when a few residents challenged the otherwise generally
agreed-upon plans for confronting the authorities, a leader with a gift
for humorous chatter would be trotted out first. When important decisions had to be made, it was often the most openly aggressive and
intransigent of the leaders who would take the helm. At one meeting,
at which the community was called upon to decide whether to ask the
United Nations Commission on Cultural, Economic, and Social Rights
for a letter of support to be sent to the national government, and that
I was videotaping so that the community would have evidence that
they had followed democratic procedure, this man harangued the assembled residents for quite a few minutes about the importance of
speaking out if they disagreed with the idea—an idea that he himself
quite evidently supported.

Now it is clear that his actions on that occasion were also motivated by a desire to provide the necessary evidence that no one was
intimidated from opposing the plan. In fact, of course, his rough
manner and hectoring speech were interpreted by some, on this and
other occasions, as precisely the opposite—as an intimidating use of
authority. This was not the "ritual" sense of a meeting that Hinton
(1992) insists is typical of such situations, but it certainly could not
be read in a completely literal fashion either. Rather, it was indeed
a performance—and as such it was material, or "performative," in
the sense that it produced results. (I return below to the sense of the
word *ritual*, which for Hinton is clearly an obsession with empty form
and political occlusion, whereas for Tambiah it raises important and,
in my view, much more useful questions of efficacy; the question is
about *what* it produces rather than about *whether* it is productive.)

Tambiah offers an original insight into the coexistence of hierarchy
and mutuality in Thai lay society, placing it in its complex historical
context (especially in the context of the transformation of the "pulsing galactic polity" into a territorial and bureaucratic nation-state).
The multiple leadership styles that we see in Pom Mahakan illustrate
both the pulsation and the recognition that each *moeang*—each unit
at each level of the segmentary system of nested political entities—
stands, in practice, in a metonymic relation with all others.[3]

This was well understood by the community leaders in another
important respect: the treatment and representation of the age and

significance of the several spirit shrines that dotted the community's living space. There was a big shrine next to the main entrance; when the front area was taken over by the Bangkok Metropolitan Administration (BMA), this shrine was moved to a safer, interior space—the residents had no illusions that the authorities would respect the sacredness of such objects if they had already shown themselves to be prepared to destroy *bodi* trees, which are regarded as descended from the original tree under which Lord Buddha had achieved enlightenment. This large shrine was considered to belong to the entire community; others were dedicated to particular family ancestors, some with characteristics that betrayed a foreign, usually Chinese, element. But when the threat of eviction became acute, all the shrines were suddenly recast as shrines to the ancestors of "the Thai people." The destruction of the shrines became, in this representation, an act of sacrilege directed against the nation.

Here we see the segmentary logic of which Tambiah saw traces in the early Siamese and related polities, operating at the conceptual level of the relationship between a community and its encompassing nation. Just as the royal portraits and the national flag allowed the residents to represent their cause as a specifically Thai cause, buttressed by an elaborate series of invocations of *khwaampenthai* ("Thainess") and assertions that "we are Thai people" (and therefore have a right to live on this land, which by extension became conceptually a miniature Thailand in its own right), the shrines served as a condensing device through which the residents of Pom Mahakan could represent their cause as a national one.

The same flexibility appeared in the community's post-tsunami self-representation. Despite their desperate poverty, residents responded to the call for aid much as did other, wealthier Thais, with greater concern for the collective good than for their own individual welfare. Indeed, the rhetoric in Pom Mahakan was very much along the lines of arguing that it was precisely the suffering they had endured in their long struggle against eviction that gave the residents their understanding for, and empathy with, those whose lives were materially disrupted or destroyed by the disaster. One of the leaders made a powerful speech arguing that, as true Thais, they should display the Buddhist virtue of loving kindness (*maetha*), a virtue they had previously accused the municipal authorities of lacking in confronting the Pom Mahakan residents themselves. Significantly, too, this leader yoked the image of compassion to a call for comprehensive aid that would not be selectively given to Buddhists or to Thai nationals alone; at a moment of true crisis, it was, he suggested, a sign of Thainess that the residents should avoid discriminations of that sort and assert their moral superiority—their high ground—by an act of inclusiveness. Here again we get a fleeting glimpse of a "pulsing" view of the world—a view that swells to enclose, but can also shrink to resist and repulse.

I do not want to argue that the flexible politics that have allowed the residents to resist eviction for two decades, and that have been explained away through the invocation of an ideal of Thai willingness to compromise, can be traced back to a mandala model of the kind described by Tambiah. In an earlier era of anthropological thought, such an analysis might have carried conviction, but there is no evidence of such explicit configuration of the community in terms of the mandala's sacred geometry. Indeed, I think it is very important to resist the reductionist temptation to "explain" every aspect of modern Thai life in terms of a specifically Buddhist, Thai, or any other kind of delimited past; to do so is to accept an official ideology that simplifies the experienced realities of these urban dwellers to singular origins, and that endorses—indeed, co-opts—their devout desire to view every aspect of their lives through the prism of their religious system.

Rather, I suggest that we begin from Tambiah's recognition that the mandala model favored a segmentary view of political life even in the absence of the agnatic kinship that was usually seen as a precondition for segmentation (see Fortes and Evans-Pritchard 1940). Segmentation does not, logically speaking, require any specific kind of kinship at all (Karp and Maynard 1983; see also Herzfeld 2005, 112). But it does require a model that will not collapse between generations and eras. Had segmentation been totally dependent on unilineal kinship, too great an emphasis on the "cross-cutting ties" of uterine kinship and of affinal connections would render it irrelevant and unmanageable in a society, such as most Thai communities, where agnatic ideology is relatively weak (see, e.g., S. Potter 1977). (Ironically, it may be that the increased importance of agnation in such matters as royal succession is itself the result of an externally derived—and perhaps imposed—model of European origin [see Loos 2006].) The mandala model is one such option, and it may have paved the way for a persistent political relativism amid the present-day demand for clarity that is the hallmark of the modern, positivistic, data-focused state. So it is segmentation, rather than the more specific mandala model, that partially explains the political adaptability of small Thai communities.

And segmentation can take dramatic forms, in which the key paradox of loyalty to multiple levels of identity emerges in performance. To many foreigners, the spectacle of Thai community protest under the aegis of royal portraiture and national symbols is puzzling; they tend to think that protest means attacking authority in general—*any* kind of authority. In the dominant mode of political protest in most of Europe, for example, factionalism is immediately infused with party-political identities, and the flags one sees are mostly party flags, not national ones. Nowhere is this demonstrated more dramatically than in Italy, where loyalty to the nation-state is at best a problematic notion, albeit one with persistent bourgeois underpinnings and enjoying new leftist forms of endorsement as a means of fighting a political right wing too closely tied to anti-immigrant calls for separatism in the more prosperous parts of the country. One rarely sees national flags at Italian protests of any kind, still less portraits of the national president or prime minister.

In Thailand, however, no sense of inconsistency arises from such demonstrations of national loyalty on the part of those who sometimes quite raucously protest against authority. On the contrary, it is arguably the only strategy available to them. For to refuse it would be a dangerous act of disloyalty—especially given the severity of the *lèse-majesté* laws still in force and often invoked for political advantage—that could easily be used to undercut any claims the community might have to legitimacy in the eyes of the encompassing nation. Embracing this symbolism—and, more generally, the "three pillars" of monarchy, people, and religion—infuses the microcosm of the local community with the presumed "energy" (*palang*) of the virtuous ruler, and allows its leaders to articulate their opposition to authority within a larger and more coherent moral universe.

The use of flags and royal portraits is, be it said, a Western invention, and forms part of the ritualistic display that Thailand adopted as part of its crypto-colonial inheritance. Even the colors of the national flag recall those of Britain, France, Russia, and the United States. But note that the portraits are associated with religious reverence. Such partial reworkings of familiar Western models are diagnostic of the intimate spaces within the crypto-colonial model, whereby a people constrained to accept an externally defined model of their own dependence effectively recast that model and its associated symbols in

terms that are not immediately legible—to use James Scott's (1998)
helpful metaphor of high-modernist governance—to the foreign patrons. Inasmuch as "transparency" can paradoxically serve as a mask
(R. Morris 2004), unity within a segmentary system that looks to overseas patrons can also disguise a high degree of internal fragmentation. This has become especially clear from the numerous recent calls
for national unity. These calls reveal, to borrow a phrase from Michael
Taussig (1992), the "nervous systems" of easily alienated modernities
that claim to be derived from the supposedly stable traditional orders
of the past.

Within that framework, we can reinterpret the ritualistic character
of both protest and formal meetings. Unlike Peter Hinton, who (as I
have remarked) saw meetings as simply an exercise in political performance, and in a manner that comes much closer to Tambiah's interest in performativity (see especially Tambiah [1979] 1981), I regard
these symbolic displays as ways of reorganizing what might seem to
an outsider to be transparent forms of loyalty and protest as a means
of deploying the former in defense of the latter. In this pragmatic
logic, a consistent performance of loyalty (compare the British "loyal
opposition") becomes the enabling condition of protest.

Especially since the rise of the Assembly of the Poor (Missingham
2003), political protest in Thailand has boasted a highly recognizable
format, with discourse and symbolism that have ramified throughout
the polity and that certainly have produced recognizable echoes in
Pom Mahakan. The stylized "conversation" between an NGO activist and a community leader that dominated my first experience of a
Pom Mahakan protest in 2003, for example, reiterated the Thainess
of community life; the importance to national history of the older
buildings in the space occupied by the community; and even the legitimacy conferred by the visit of a foreign scholar—myself—the extent of whose involvement was as yet unknown but whose presence
was presented as a recognition of the community's contribution to
national pride.

That this was indeed a highly ritualistic performance did not in the
least undermine its performative force. On the contrary, as I personally felt the drama of the moment pulling me inward, I experienced
a sense of solidarity within a larger framework, a feature that this
framework shares with the mandala model. When local bureaucrats
attacked the residents' claim to community status on the grounds of
the heterogeneity of their origins and I responded by emphasizing

their cultural diversity (*khwaamlakhlaai thang watthanatham*), the residents picked up the term within a day; they were, once again, discovering a model and a terminology that allowed them the formality of collective representations as an instrument of internal differentiation.

I am not sure how useful it would be to characterize this oscillation between encompassing and differentiating stances within a common, consistent model as "typically Thai." It seems to me that, following Tambiah's lead (1989a, 1992, 1996b), we ought to resist such facile essentialisms, especially as they are often the core of unpleasant forms of exclusive localism—something, incidentally, that the Pom Mahakan leadership recognizes as a real and present danger, one that conflicts with their insistence on the value of a compassion that transcends all forms of ethnic and religious discrimination. But it would not be fanciful, I suggest, to argue that this kind of oscillation is, at the very least, compatible with the general principles of the pulsing galactic polity, overlaid as they are by a Western-derived idiom of legalistic rigidity and a positivistic understanding of the nature of knowledge. To elucidate what "is" Western and what "is" Thai in these matters (see, e.g., Thirayuth 2003) is perhaps less interesting than the perception that Westernness and Thainess themselves have become instruments of political negotiation in a complex field in which the wielding of agency may express subjection to a crypto-colonial reality as much as it expresses the temporary authority of local elites. That field is now globalized to the point where talk of origins, important though these are in Thailand (see, e.g., R. Morris 2000), must itself be an integral part of that political instrumentality rather than a literal excursion into a literalistic history of which the actual traces are now surely, and conveniently, lost amid the shadowy ghosts of the ancestors as they fade into an endless dusk increasingly deepened by the neon lights of modernity.

PART III

Violence, Political Conflict, and Humanitarian Intervention

Structural Work:
How Microhistories Become
Macrohistories and Vice Versa

Marshall Sahlins

The most wonderful things are brought about in many instances
by means the most absurd and ridiculous; in the most ridiculous
modes; and apparently by the most contemptible implements.

—EDMUND BURKE, *Reflections on the Revolution in France*

The Politicians have long observed that the greatest
Events may often be traced to the most trivial Causes,
and that a petty Competition or casual Friendship, the
Prudence of a Slave, or the Garrulity of a Woman[!!] have
hindered or promoted the most important Schemes,
and hastened or retarded the Revolutions of Empire.

—SAMUEL JOHNSON, *The Rambler*

Early in 1841, the irascible British Consul in Honolulu, Richard Charlton, fired off one of his habitual letters of complaint to the Governor
of O'ahu. "Sir," he wrote, "I have the honor to inform you that some
person or persons are building a wall near the end of the bowling alley belonging to Mrs. Mary Dowsett, thereby injuring her property
and violating the treaty between Great Britain and the Sandwich
Islands" (BCP, 8 February 1841). Most absurd and ridiculous, as Edmund Burke might have judged, Mr. Charlton's letter is thereby all the
more suggestive of the general theme of this article: how small issues
are turned into Big Events; or in somewhat more technical lingo, the
structural-cum-symbolic amplification of minor differences. The focus is on the historical dynamics by which relatively trivial disputes
over local matters (such as the trespass complaint of Mr. Charlton)
get articulated with greater political and ideological differences (as
between Britain and the Sandwich Islands), and are thus promoted
into conflicts of world-historical significance. Critically in play are

the structural relays between lower and higher levels of sociocultural order, as in the Honolulu case between the relationships of neighbors and the relationships of states. Higher-level oppositions are interpolated in lower-level conflicts, and vice versa, in this way compounding the animosities of each by the differences of the other. By nationalizing the personal relations in the case of Mrs. Dowsett's bowling alley, and thereby personalizing the national relations, the British consul hoped to create an international showdown—or at least dissuade some guy from building a wall.

These structural relays indeed work both ways, dialogically synthesizing microhistories with macrohistories, whence their power of amplifying lesser into greater conflicts. For in giving collective identities to local relationships, and local identities to collective relationships, they also give to each the interests and sentiments of the other. Collective subjects such as nations, "imagined" as they may be, take on the flesh-and-blood qualities of real-life subjects—injured Britannia will be played by Mrs. Mary Dowsett—and are accordingly acted out in interpersonal dramas, with all their attendant feelings and emotions. Yet if abstract collective entities are thus substantialized in acting persons, the concerns of these persons become correspondingly abstract. Endowed with collective identities, the real-life subjects thereby put at issue the larger political and ideological differences they are authorized to represent. That wall encroaching on Mrs. Dowsett's bowling alley is now imposing on the sovereignty and good will of the British Empire. Note that the abstraction does not dissolve the original contention but on the contrary makes it all the more intractable. Thus overheated and overdetermined by greater causes, parochial discords may escalate into fateful events.

But nothing of the sort happened in the case of Mrs. Dowsett, for several reasons. One was the historical infelicity of the property dispute. The injury done to the Haole lady could not upset either the foreign or the local people of Honolulu. Whether as interpersonal melodrama or the evocation of national grievances of longer memory, it was not a good metaphor. Besides, the greater forces whose intervention was being evoked, Great Britain and the Sandwich Islands, were not themselves in a state of contention. Fifteen years earlier Mr. Charlton's complaint would have been somewhat less absurd. As an Englishman and a merchant, he was then aligned with the Hawaiian king in a struggle against a set of usurping pious chiefs, who for their part had made the American missionaries the priests of their own pretensions to rule. Moreover, this conjuncture did have considerable historical resonance. The link between Britain and the Hawaiian kingship goes back to the advent of Captain Cook, whose (purported) remains continued to ritually sanctify the rule of the famous Kamehameha, father of the king in Mr. Charlton's time—even as the governor to whom Mr. Charlton addressed his letter was a member of the same anti-royal faction that succeeded in stripping Kamehameha's heirs of their sovereign authority. Imposing the oppositions of England versus America and merchants versus missionaries on the conflict between the Hawaiian king and his ambitious chiefs, this dust-up of the 1820s in the Sandwich Islands could serve as a good illustration of the dynamics of structural amplification. But like Mr. Charlton's complaint, this is an old story and already well told two or three times (Kirch and M. Sahlins 1992; Mykkänen 2003).[1] Here I offer instead a few equally revelatory incidents.

They are, in order: the recent affair of the Cuban refugee child Elián Gonzalez in the United States, the agrarian disputes of Catalan peasants in the Cerdanya in the seventeenth through the nineteenth centuries, and the civil strife in Greek city-states during the Peloponnesian War. The last discussion will be the longest, as I take the opportunity to address some high-flying issues raised in Thucydides' analysis of factional conflict. Indeed all of the cases, although they may not be familiar ethnographically, will bring to anthropological mind certain structural dynamics that have had a considerable theoretical run in the discipline: notably, the *segmentary relativity* famously described by Evans-Pritchard (1940, 135f.), the *complementary schismogenesis* of Gregory Bateson (1935 and 1958, 175f. and 265f.), and the processes Stanley Tambiah (1996a, 192–93, 257–58) has more recently identified as *transvaluation* and *parochialization*.

The Iconization of Elián

> One of the most interesting things about the Elián case to me was how it changed from a very small issue into a wide community-based problem. Initially, it was really older Cuban-American exiles that were fighting this war. Eventually, it was younger Cuban-Americans from all social classes.... This started really as another "bosarito," another young rafter.

> And it ended being an epic of the community and the nation
> at large. The dynamics of that process are fascinating.
>
> PBS *Frontline* 2001, Damian Fernandez

There was nothing at all ridiculous about the way the Cuban community of Miami made the shipwrecked Elián Gonzalez quite literally a poster child, turning the family conflict over custody of the child into an international incident involving American and Cuban officials at the highest level of government. As you will recall, five-year-old Elián was the survivor of an ill-fated attempt of a small party of Cubans to cross the Florida Straits in November 1999. The sinking of their unseaworthy vessel cost the life of Elián's mother—who had been estranged from his father, still in Cuba. But it would take seven months of legal wrangling, public debate, mass demonstrations, and ultimately the armed intervention of U.S. federal agents, to return Elián to Cuba and his father—over the strenuous objections of his relatives in Miami, the great majority of Cuban-Americans, and a certain segment of the U.S. public and Congress that thought an individual's "right to freedom" more compelling than "family values" any time. Since I have recently discussed this story in print (although in a somewhat different context), I mention here only a few dimensions most relevant to the way millions of Cuban and American citizens and their respective governments got involved in the child-custody dispute of an obscure and not altogether reputable family (M. Sahlins 2004).[2]

Hurricane Elián confirms the point made in connection with Mrs. Dowsett's bowling alley: that not just any old story will do to whip up a collective hullabaloo. As in the popular Latin American *telenovelas* that likewise fold national issues into family melodramas, there needs to be a good old story, one with sufficient structural and historical iconicity to evoke a widespread political response. Many a commentator in the U.S. media remarked that if it had been Elián's father who died and his mother who remained in Cuba, he would have been repatriated immediately and without notice, as anything else would have been a blow against motherhood—proverbially one of the two greatest American values, along with apple pie. But the pathos of a mother's death and the ensuing drama of love and spite among close kinsmen made Elián's plight a ready common ground of widespread empathy and sympathy—especially among Cubans, who were all too familiar with narratives of extended families torn apart by immigration. The Gonzalez family could share this poignant history even with

Fidel Castro, who once won a similar battle for the custody of his own son, and whose own nephew, U.S. Representative Lincoln Diaz-Balart (R-Fla.), figured prominently in the attempt to prevent Elián from rejoining his father. Congressman Diaz-Balart gave Elián a Labrador puppy, among the other strenuous arguments he made to show that the boy would be happier in America. Also well remembered was the notorious Operation Pedro Pan of 1960–1962, when over 14,000 Cuban children between the ages of 6 and 16 were separated from their parents and shipped to foster homes in the United States. Organized by the Catholic Church in America, working in secret agreement with the U.S. government, the operation was given impetus in Cuba by the circulation of rumors that Castro was going to take the children from their parents for political indoctrination. According to Gabriel García Márquez (2000), among the "even crueler lies" being broadcast about Cuba, apparently by the CIA, was that "the most appetizing children would be sent to Siberian slaughter houses to be returned as canned meat"—a cannibal refrain that was revived in Miami about Elián; indeed the U.S. Congress heard sworn testimony from a Cuban American that Castro would eat Elián were he to be repatriated (*Newsweek* 2000). That many of the Pedro Pan children—currently in their 40s and 50s, some never reunited with their parents—supported the cause of keeping Elián in America suggests that they could indeed be taken from their homes for political indoctrination.

Elián's youth was another felicitous aspect of the affair, given the aging political causes of the Cubans on the island and in America, now more than four decades removed from their original fervor. Both the tired revolution in Cuba and the waning counter-revolution in Florida saw in Elián the opportunity to recuperate their increasingly uninterested young people. Both sides made Elián the focus of a politics of youth. All across Cuba, schoolchildren were turned out for mass demonstrations demanding the return of the "boy hero." While Elián was in Miami, his empty school desk in Cuba was publicized as a symbol of perfidious capitalism; when he returned to Cuba, his empty school desk in Miami was publicized as a symbol of perfidious communism. As a prominent Havana newspaper put it, Elián "had been converted forever into a symbol of the crimes and injustices that imperialism is capable of committing against an innocent" (*Miami Herald* 2000a). The Cuban media in Miami put out endless variations on the refrain that returning the boy to his father would only subject him to communist brutality—or as one of his Miami relatives observed after that happened: "They're teaching him to be like Che [Guevara], an assassin and an asthmatic" (*Miami Herald* 2000b).

Represented in such terms as *freedom, communism, democracy*, and *imperialism*, the conflict over the custody of Elián was thus amplified to the point of irreconcilability. Moreover, these transfers between the political macrohistory and the familial microhistory were right on top, apparent enough, for example, to be articulated by a popular Miami priest: "I am absolutely certain that communism began in Cuba by dividing the family," he said, "and communism is going to end in Cuba when this family is reunited" (*Washington Post* 2000c). A corollary regarding the iconicity of Elián was well put by the afore-quoted Damian Fernandez, professor of international relations at Florida International University: "Elián represents a nation—the young nation, the nation that will be. And both sides wanted to guide the future of that nation" (*PBS Frontline* 2001).

Aside from the aspects of a classic schismogenesis, the magnification of a domestic dispute to a showdown between communism and capitalism resembles the process of transvaluation described by Tambiah in connection with the development of ethnonationalist riots in South Asia. Transvaluation likewise involves the assimilation of the particulars of local disputes "to a larger, collective, more enduring and therefore less context-bound cause or interest" (Tambiah 1996, 192). The original petty discords are absorbed in burning issues of race, religion, or ethnicity, which attract all the more hostility in the measure that they are abstract and unconditional. Tambiah also speaks of a corollary process of *focalization* in which disputes are cumulatively aggregated into large clashes involving antagonists only indirectly connected to the original incidents, the particular context and character of which get lost in the expansion. However, what is different about the Elián case, as well as some others considered here, is the retention and integration of the original incident in the larger cause, so that precisely communist morality and capitalist freedom can take on the ethical and emotional charge of kinship relations—a father bereft, a mother who sacrificed her own life for her child's freedom. The universal causes are allegorically identified with these particularistic relations, giving transcendent consequences to the way the family melodrama is played out.

In this connection, one might take note of the mediocrity of the persons upon whom history had thus devolved. Among the main characters in Elián's Miami kindred were his great uncle Lazaro Gon-

zalez, an unemployed auto mechanic, and Lazaro's brother Delphin—
the two of whom, it has to be admitted, on a combined score of DUI
(driving under the influence) charges had almost as many qualifica-
tions for leadership as George W. Bush and Richard "Dick" Cheney.
Others close to Elián included Lazaro's daughter Marysleysis, whose
"anxiety attacks" put her in the hospital six or eight times during
Elián's stay. Taken as a sign of her spirituality and suffering, Marysleysis' faintings made her all the more beloved in the Little Havana community, although to WASP-dominated America at large, she came off
as unpleasantly hysterical. Then there were the two cousins who often
came to play with Elián, both felons with long rap sheets. In sum, the
people who thus had greatness thrust upon them would not seem to
be sterling examples of Hegel's "cunning of reason." Their characters
are more reminiscent of Marx's remark about Louis Napoleon: that
the class struggle in France had "created circumstances and relations
which allowed gross mediocrity to strut about in a hero's garb."

Meanwhile, on the larger American scene, Elián was also being used
as an epitomizing argument by a variety of political interest groups
aligned in complex relations of opposition in principle and alliance
of convenience. For example: the endorsement given by Senator Joe
Lieberman, soon to be the Democratic vice-presidential candidate, to
the bill introduced in Congress by conservative Republicans to make
Elián an honorary U.S. citizen (and thus circumvent the immigration
laws). This was a very rare sort of legislation, heretofore reserved for
the likes of Mother Theresa and Winston Churchill. "I don't think it's
in [Elián's] best interest to send him to a place where the government
can tell him what he thinks and what he'll become," said the Republican sponsor of the bill that would authorize the U.S. government to
decide Elián's best interest and what he would become (*Washington
Post*, 2000a). Many liberal Democrats, on the other hand, were opposing measures such as the Elián citizenship bill—on conservative Republican principles. The way that Maxine Waters, African-American
Congresswoman from California, argued on national television for
returning Elián to his father on the grounds of "family values" and
"natural rights" (*CNN Crossfire* 2000).

Long a Republican sacred cow, the issue of "family values" effectively split and seriously weakened the American political Right.
For when a number of its spokespersons came out for repatriating
Elián on grounds of family values, the remaining libertarians were
pushed to the shrill extreme of attempting to trump family values by

the higher rights of possessive individualism. "A father's right can never supersede those of a child," said a prominent academic disciple of Ayn Rand, and in any case, if the father is a committed Communist, "that disqualifies him from being a parent" (*Capitalism Magazine* 2000). This sage professor of Ayn Rand doctrines put Elián's own right to freedom on a par with the other such divine rights the U.S. Attorney General was attempting to abrogate at the time, namely the free trade of Microsoft and cigarette manufacturers. "Whether the issue involves a whole industry, a single company or a single individual," he said, "the fundamental principles are the same. Either people possess the right to their own life, which includes the right to trade freely with other men, or they do not" (*Capitalism Magazine* 2000).

But opinion polls were showing that Americans in general were decidedly in favor of sending Elián home. Even beyond the question of fathers' rights, there was abroad an uncomfortable doubt that Elián's future as an American kid would be as beneficial as the champions of his "right to freedom" were claiming. Nor were the many published images of Elián being overindulged with toys and other goodies—including the toy guns he liked to shoot off—reassuring to a lot of Americans coping with problems of teenage violence and drug abuse. Elián's story broke the same year as the massacre at Columbine High School in Colorado. Expressing a sentiment that had many parallels in the media, a rather conservative columnist wrote: "Under the cloak of freedom we have lavished Elián with toys, made him a celebrity, handed him a puppy, taken his picture, raised his hands in a victory sign, and then asked him if he wants to go back to icky old Cuba." Imagine a foreign country refusing to repatriate your child "because our society is permeated with drugs, sex and violence" (*Chicago Tribune* 2000b).

Back in Miami, however, the Cuban community was developing irrefutable cosmological reasons for keeping him. Elián had become a religious icon. Part Jesus, part Moses, and part *Orisha*, he was a manifestation of divine salvation, destined to restore the exiled Cubans to their homeland. Talk about raising the symbolic stakes of a family argument! Hailing Elián as "the child king" and "the miracle child," representing him as crucified by the Clinton administration, the Miami Cubans also added a lot of Marian symbolism to this Christological topos—natural enough, given the fate of Elián's mother. The Virgin Mary appeared twice: once inside the Gonzalez house and once on the window of a bank some blocks away. This Virgin of Totalbank,

468 NW 27th Avenue, was unmistakable according to one of the tellers, even though "you could not see the body or the face" (*Washington Post*, 2000b). Mothers brought their babies to press against the windowpane. One skeptic, however, was heard to opine that the so-called Virgin was a residue of Windex. As for Moses, his mother too had set him adrift in hopes of sparing his life, as a deft Cuban American exegete observed. Then, he continued, "The daughter of the pharaoh took in Moses and changed the history of the Hebrews. . . . Moses lived to lead his people out of Egypt to the promised land of Israel after a captivity of 40 years—about the same as our exile from Cuba" (*Chicago Tribune* 2000a). An eclectic folk mural, often paraded in the crowd that gathered daily at the Gonzalez house, shows Elián on the sea in an inner tube together with the patron saint of Cuba and two Santería deities, while dolphins circle and protect him; overhead the hand of God holds a small virgin and child; a large scale of justice frames the scene with the head of Pope John Paul II on one side and President Clinton on the other; in the background are two shadowy images of Fidel, a frowning Statue of Liberty, an archangel holding another scale, and Jesus himself.

That Elián was saved by dolphins who surrounded his inner tube raft was the standard opinion of the Cuban exile community. A common theme on local talk radio, the buzz in Cuban coffee shops, the story was confirmed by the official Elián website. On this, gringo opinion was overwhelmingly skeptical. A cartoon in the *Miami Herald* depicted the dolphins that surrounded Elián's raft as hulking men garbed as fully helmeted and padded football players—the Miami Dolphins (the city's professional team). But there were some believers on the American Right. Peggy Noonan, former speechwriter for President George the First and sometime downchannel talking-head supporter of George the Second, filled a column in the *Wall Street Journal* with banal pieties about the Elián "miracle." "Too bad Mr Reagan was not still president," she said. "Mr Reagan would not have dismissed the story of dolphins as Christian kitsch, but seen it as the best possible evidence of the reasonable assumption that God's creatures had been commanded to protect one of God's children" (10 April 2000). There you have it. Miracle! Miracle! Read all about it in the *Wall Street Journal*—a tract that in any case has always believed in the Invisible Hand.

But now for something completely different in cultural content, if similar in structural dynamics.

French and Spanish Nationalism in the Catalan Cerdanya

That cantankerous British Consul in Honolulu, Richard Charlton, would have envied the success of Catalan peasants of the Cerdan valley in making international issues out of petty trespassing. In his influential work *Boundaries*, Peter Sahlins (1989) tells how Catalan peasant communities on either side of the border between France and Spain that was uncertainly established in the seventeenth century, how these peasants over the next two hundred years brought these nations into their parochial quarrels over pasturage, water rights, and the like. In the process, moreover, they respectively gave themselves the identities and virtues of Frenchmen and Spaniards, while attributing the complementary derogatory aspects of the opposed nationality to their peasant adversaries—with whom, nevertheless, they continued to share the same Catalan ethnicity. Here again the relay between the totality and the locality worked in both directions: "a nationalizing of the local and a localizing of the national," as Peter Sahlins puts it (1989, 165). Indeed it was the Catalan peasants of the valley, by their agrarian disputes, who were finally able to fix the national boundary that Madrid and Paris failed to explicitly determine in the 1659 Treaty of the Pyrenees, obsessed as they were with the geopolitical ideology that since ancient times the Pyrenees Mountains formed the natural frontier between the Spaniards and the Gauls. It took some time and effort for the central governments to understand that they had rather vaguely drawn the boundary right through the plain of the Cerdan Valley.

But even as the French and Spanish authorities were nostalgically longing for the protective enclosure of their kingdoms within natural mountain frontiers, the Catalan communities of the Cerdanya were manifesting a degree of parochialism reminiscent of a classic peasant *esprit de clocher*. Their patriotism did not generally run beyond the boundaries of the village—which, however, they were often prepared to extend at the expense of neighboring villages. The Cerdanya had known some district and valley-wide organization in the past, although not so politically institutionalized as in other Pyrenean valleys. In any case, the division introduced by the 1659 Treaty left each of the 80 or so villages rather in the condition of a *pays* unto itself (cf. Soulet 1974, 37f.; Weber 1976, 45). Peter Sahlins speaks of "closed corporate peasant communities" on the model of those described for Latin America and elsewhere by Eric Wolf (1957). Highly endogamous, differentiating their co-resident "neighbors" from "foreigner" others, holding common rights in pastures, forests, and other resources, maintaining their own moral and political regimes—as defended ritually or violently by their young men—these villages manifested a concern for their own identity and sovereignty that was the antithesis of national belonging. Referring to analogous village dispositions in the nearby Rousillon (in the period 1780–1820), Michel Brunet invokes Pierre Clastres' celebrated formula of "Society against the State" (Brunet 1986). But then, the Catalans of the Cerdanya had their own homebred enmities. The intervillage affrontments that were so fateful after the Treaty of the Pyrenees were already endemic before it: disputes over land, water, pasturage, pilgrimage sites, firewood, and the other local interests that made up what Marx and Engels called "the idiocy of rural life."

All the same, the Catalan villages of the Cerdanya were not so narrow-minded as to ignore the advantages of nationalizing their local causes, once the interest of France and Spain in the international boundary afforded the opportunity. Again I make remark here of a certain structure of alliance and hostility, of a kind one generally finds in such symbolic amplification: the criss-crossing or chiastic system of oppositions in which differences between higher-order collectives, in this case France and Spain, are laid onto lower-order discords, thus adding the force and meaning of the greater antipathy to ongoing local differences. Just so in the Cerdanya, as each contending Catalan village invoked its superposed national identity, the antagonisms of countries were added to the arguments between communities, in this way inflating the peasant disputes all out of proportion to their original reasons. The effect was dependent on the familiar structural dynamic of segmentary relativity, as Peter Sahlins points out: the tactic of maximizing the social distance between contending villages by their assumption of maximally contrasting group identities. Ignoring their Catalan commonalities, the villages displaced their contention to the more inclusive and opposed categories of France and Spain. By thus marking the greatest possible difference between them, they would mobilize the greatest possible support to their respective causes.

Something has to be said, then, for the higher-level conjuncture, the state of affairs between the adjacent nations. The disputes between Catalan communities along the borderland would have come to nothing were it not for the problematic relations at certain periods between France and Spain. In much of the eighteenth and nineteenth centuries those relations encouraged the generalization of peasant conflicts to the level of the state, indeed gave the local conflicts ever more fateful stakes. Until 1722, the almost incessant incursions of French and Spanish armies into the Cerdanya generally ignored the international boundary stipulated by the Treaty of the Pyrenees in favor of a military frontier that would include the whole valley. At this time the Catalan peasants were more united in their opposition to the occupying powers than they were divided among themselves, and they largely prosecuted and settled their intervillage conflicts without outside help. Over the course of the eighteenth and nineteenth centuries, however, France and Spain progressively—if also fitfully, and unevenly—consolidated their national territories, indeed defined their sovereignties as national and territorial, thus giving increasingly consequential values to the definition and defense of their borders in the name of "the integrity of the nation." This complex process of nationalization entailed aligning juridical, ecclesiastical, and fiscal jurisdictions that had corresponded neither with one another nor with the boundary of 1659. It entailed also a shift from the Old Regime form of royal sovereignty over subjects to the state administration of territories. Of course, the French Revolution was a decisive factor in these respects. Moreover, in politicizing, secularizing, and territorializing the *patrie*, the Revolution made a moral boundary of the French frontier—notably with Catholic Spain. Spain could now add its revulsion for an apostate nation to its old fears of heresies, from the Cathars to the Huguenots, emanating from the north. Finally the Revolution, the Empire, and the Restoration set the stage for the recurrent internal conflicts of the nineteenth century, in Spain and France both, between liberal and royalist or ultra factions—which gave whatever party was in power in one country, liberal or royalist, reason to fear the success of the counterposed party in the other country. In 1821, the French set up a *cordon sanitaire* on the border, as much against political ills as against the cholera in Barcelona, and French troops remained in the Cerdanya for a considerable part of the nineteenth century. All this did not prevent intercourse between Catalans of the two sides of the valley. On the contrary, relationships across the international frontier actually intensified in the nineteenth century—including the communal conflicts of border villages. The conflicts became still worse from 1853, when France and Spain began proceedings to definitively delimit the border. The fifteen years it took to come to a conclusive treaty gave the villagers their last good chance to make national hay out of claims to their neighbors' stubble.

But already from 1722 the developing interest of France and Spain in consolidating their jurisdictional limits encouraged the Catalans of the Cerdanya to claim that, in prosecuting their own trespass cases, they were upholding the rights of their respective monarchs. They began to appeal to their national authorities to get the offensive "foreigners" (their Catalan neighbors) off their land. At first they only spoke of themselves as "subjects" of their respective kings, but they did not hesitate to identify their peasant enemies as "Spaniards" or "Frenchmen," with all the opprobrium that implied. As in the petition of 1740 from the syndics of La Tor de Carol to the French authorities complaining of the "Spaniards" of the neighboring village of Guils:

> It would be sad if the inhabitants of La Tor de Carol had to resort to armed force over a measly pasturage, yet this is precisely what there is to fear. For the inhabitants of La Tor de Carol are sensitive to the insults of the Spaniards which they have long experienced, and one day they could lose their patience. They do not fear their foreign neighbors, and the injustice inflicted upon them will one day force them to chase the Spaniards from the land. Despite the haughty and insulting manners of the Spaniards, the inhabitants [of La Tor de Carol] have refrained from retaliating, if only because of the profound respect they have for His Majesty. But the inhabitants of La Tor de Carol, seeing themselves pushed to the limit, could easily retaliate. They hope that His Majesty will have the good will to have the boundaries of this valley established clearly. (quoted in P. Sahlins 1989, 162–63)

Notice that the Catalan adversaries of La Tor de Carol in the community of Guils are being attributed the ideological defects of "haughty Spaniards," in this way adding insults of national character to the injuries of a "measly" pasturage dispute. In later years, the events of the French Revolution, the resistance to a French occupation of the Cerdanya in 1793–1795 and to Napoleon's occupation of Spain combined to up the ideological ante involved in chasing foreign cows off one's land. No longer reticent about identifying themselves as Spanish, for example, the peasants on that side of the border were defending their agrarian interests in the righteous guise of pious and glorious Spanish warriors in battle with ungodly and domineering Frenchmen. In July of 1825, at the important Feast of the Rosary celebrated in the principal Spanish town of Puigcerdá, hundreds of people turned upon and stoned the attending musicians and villagers from the French Cerdagna. "Kill the *gavatxos* ['dirty Frenchmen']," they screamed, "they have ruled Spain far too long" (P. Sahlins 1989, 235).

The "massacre" at Puigcerdá, as the French mayor of La Tor de Carol would call it, is a good example of the explosive conjunction of higher- and lower-level oppositions. "The nationalism displayed at this Feast of the Rosary arose from the intersection of a local dispute over a canal and the international political crisis of the early 1820s which brought national struggles and party politics into the French-Spanish borderland" (P. Sahlins 1988, 249). The local dispute was already several centuries old, though it had intensified during the French Revolution. The canal, Puigcerdá's only water source, originated on the French side, where it ran through the village territories of La Tor de Carol and Enveig. Puigcerdá had often complained that these communities habitually diverted the water to their own fields and meadows: a "usurpation" all the more serious in the hot summer of 1825, because spring storms had clogged the canal with debris and water was scarce. Recent political events, moreover, added conflicts of greater portent to the problems of Puigcerdá's water supply, notably including the struggle between constitutional liberalism and absolute monarchy in Spain that in 1821 brought the troops of a now-reactionary French regime to the border. The Spanish liberals had gotten the upper hand until an important French army, 100,000 faithful "Sons of St Louis," invaded Spain in 1823 and restored the powers of King Ferdinand VII. Considering also the expulsion of Napoleon's army from Spain not long before, one can understand how Puigcerdá's water crisis signified that the *gavatxos* had "ruled Spain for too long."[3]

"Narcissism in respect of minor differences," as Peter Sahlins calls it, is a phrase that could evoke Bateson as well as Freud in theorizing the escalation of complementary differences among feuding peoples. The schismogenesis achieved a cultural climax in 1867, when the mayor of French-Catalan La Tor de Carol, referring to relations with Spanish-Catalan Guils, implored the French authorities to establish "a dividing line to separate from now to eternity two villages of foreign nations and of different mores" (P. Sahlins 1988, 258). But by then, the Spanish and French governments, while likewise interested in a definitive boundary, were concerned to make it peaceful, and they could no longer be roused to dispatch their customs officials, constabularies, or soldiers in defense of some village's grazing rights. Treaties of 1866 and 1868 finally established the international boundary, and remaining local claims were adjudicated by an International Commission set up in 1875. Without the concourse of the larger national totalities, the intervillage conflicts across the border were reduced to their original rustic proportions. In the twentieth century, given the different courses of development on the French and Spanish sides, and the differential cultural integration of French Catalans in the nation, that once-arbitrary and long-contested line running through the Cerdan valley now marked a "dead" frontier.

Stasis *at Corcyra*

The civil strife (*stasis*) of 427 B.C. at Corcyra (modern Corfu), an ally of Athens, was unprecedented in severity; although according to Thucydides, it was the prototype of similar struggles in many other Greek cities that likewise became battlegrounds of the larger issues of the Peloponnesian War.[4] An uprising of the so-called few against the rule of the many, the privileged citizens against the democratic regime of the people, the *stasis* at Corcyra degenerated into a frenzy of destruction that included the main institutions of civil order among its victims. Sacred values of kinship, justice, and religion were drenched in blood and set to naught. In Thucydides' view, often repeated these days, such are the consequences when a brutal human nature is unleashed against an always-flimsy conventional culture. Otherwise perceived, however, the violence could well be a case of too much culture rather than too much nature: that is, a structural compounding of local politics by the sentiments and forces of pan-Hellenic war—including causes to die for, such as "equality" and "freedom," that were never known to humanity in the state of nature. (But then, neither was the state of nature.)

Just as local disputes were endemic in the Cerdanya before those in certain locations were internationalized, so civil strife was common in the Greek city-states before and apart from those that got mixed up in the great showdown between Sparta and Athens. *Stasis* was "a continuous, serious and ultimately unresolved problem in the polis world" (Manicas 1982, 680).[5] Aristotle devoted an entire book of the *Politics* to these "revolutions." And if one may be allowed to speak of an Aristotelian form in the many particular examples he adduced, it would be the recurrent factional opposition between a minority party of the rich—plutocrats who could also be landed aristocrats—and the popular party of the people, who were generally poor. Given the property basis of political privilege, classicists reasonably talk of "class warfare," although the main issue was the distribution of power in the state rather than control of the means of production (let alone a revolution in the mode thereof). In the context of the Peloponnesian War, these struggles came to be essentialized as "oligarchy" (supported by the Spartans) versus "democracy" (supported by the Athenians). Their beginnings, however, were not so momentous.

On the contrary, in regard to a certain set of cases, Aristotle explicitly recognized the process of structural-cum-symbolic amplification, particularly in the dimension of transvaluation (à la Tambiah). These uprisings were singled out for the apparent anomaly that their precipitating causes were relatively trivial private matters, even though their ultimate consequences involved changes in the constitution of the state. Or, as Aristotle actually put it, "factions arise not about but out of small matters, but they are carried on about great matters" (*Politics* 5.1303b).

This finality of factional strife was brought about by the relay of the conflict from the private to the public sphere, as conditioned by the standing of the parties to the private dispute in the city at large. The "small matters" from which *staseis* grew were the likes of quarrels over boy lovers and marriageable heiresses, contested inheritance claims and aborted marital agreements. As they concerned notables of the city, however, such personal issues were joined and prosecuted by opposed classes of citizens, so that in the occurrence they had politically fateful outcomes. Obviously, it was not the lovers' quarrel or the breach of promise that made the incident seditious, but the fact that it involved people who were in a position to enlist others in their interests. To cite what amounts to an ideal-typical example from Aristotle:

> in general the faction quarrels of notables involve the whole state in the consequences, as happened in Hestiaea [in Euboea] after the Persian wars, when two brothers quarreled about the division of their patrimony; for the poorer of the two, on the ground that the other would not make a return [i.e., a disclosure] of the estate and of the treasure their father had found, got the common people on his side; and the other, possessing much property, was supported by the rich. (*Politics* 5.1303b)[6]

Aristotle does not offer further details about how the factions were mobilized, although it is obvious from this and other examples that the transvaluation of the initial interpersonal conflict to class interests entailed a motivated ideological inflation: namely, poor brother is to rich brother as the common people are to the plutocrats. "Obvious," and obviously too simple. To take a comparative viewpoint for a moment, these Greek leaders were not like the Germans as described by Tacitus or the Fijians by Hocart, whose ruling chiefs hierarchically encompassed the whole society, such that their bodies personal were identified with the body politic, and what they suffered was necessarily suffered by their people collectively (cf. M. Sahlins 1985, ch. 2). Or consider even Edmund Burke's apologetics for the English monarchy, including the argument that the inheritance of the crown, as opposed to an elective kingship, similarly united the people with the person of the king by tying their fate to a royal family: an assimilation of kinship with kingship that metaphorically endows the powers of the king with the sentiments of the kin. By inherited succession, Burke claimed,

> we have given to our frame of polity the image of a relation in blood; binding up the constitution of our country with our dearest domestic ties; adopting our fundamental laws into the bosom of our family affections; keeping inseparable, and cherishing with the warmth of all their combined and mutually related charities, our state, our hearth, our sepulchres and our altars. (2001, 185)

By contrast to such systemic relays between the domestic microcosm and the political macrocosm, in the classical Greek polis the leading men would have to work at organizing their people. They had to fashion their followings pragmatically, as by galvanizing their extensive networks of friends and kinsmen or acting the demagogue— literally the "leader of the people"—in the assembly of the city. This dependence of politics on achievement, as opposed to the authority vested in lineage, was actually a developing historical trend in fifth-century Greece—which also helps account for the kind of volatility and strife that Thucydides found in Corcyra and elsewhere.

Following Thucydides, Aristotle took note (*Politics* 4.1296a) that during the Peloponnesian War the engagement of the Spartans and the Athenians, on the side of the rich and of the people respectively, exacerbated the usual class conflicts of the polis.[7] A higher structural level was added to the endemic oppositions of the city. Even apart from the direct intervention of outside forces and high-stakes ideologies, the war could act at a distance on local power struggles by encouraging now one faction now another to take action, depending on changing fortunes of Sparta and Athens in their greater battle for pan-Hellenic hegemony. Relevant in this connection is the number of revolts from Athens recorded by Thucydides after the Athenians' catastrophic defeat at Sicily. Some of these uprisings were aided by Spartan triremes, even as some were influenced by the renegade Alcibiades, yet the seriousness of the civil strife was not all due to the outside-in and top-down impetus. Account has to be taken also of the reciprocal possibilities of action-from-below opened by these outside powers: how their intrusion, or potential intrusion, afforded the opportunity for enlisting them in all sorts of parochial animosities. Any polis is many poleis, observed Plato (*Republic* 4.423), for in the first place it is divided into a polis of the rich and a polis of the poor, which are at war with one another, and each of these is divided into many smaller groups. Articulating factional differences among these groups to high-flying external causes could thus make matters all the more acrimonious. The Peloponnesian War could be inserted into almost any and every fissure in the city's social structure—which is apparently what happened at Corcyra (Thucydides, 3.70–3.85; cf. Conner 1984, 98f.; Orwin 1988).

By Thucydides' account, the troubles at Corcyra began with the return of certain ransomed citizens—evidently of the higher classes—who had been held by the Corinthian allies of the Spartans, and had conspired with their captors to overthrow the democratic regime of the city and sever its alliance with Athens. Or more pertinently, the "enslavement" of Corcyra to Athens, which was the ideologically amplified charge brought by the conspirators against a prominent leader of the people. When that suit failed, the would-be rebels found themselves victimized by a counter-suit that violated the norms of religion and law both, to which they in turn responded by staging a bloody coup d'état. Now in control, the "oligarchs" (as Thucydides identifies them) or "revolutionaries" (as the Athenians would dub them) declared Corcyra neutral, assuring the citizens that their action "would save them from being enslaved by Athens." However, when a Corinthian ship came in bearing Spartan envoys, the rebels were emboldened to again attack and defeat the natural allies of the Athenians, the *demos* (the people). The oligarchs now summoned mercenary support from the Peloponnesian mainland—a provenance that implies connections with Sparta. But the people, by promising the slaves of the city their freedom—note the magnification of the stakes—got the better part of them on their side; and with the aid of women hurling tiles from the houses, the popular forces put the oligarchs to rout. Combining revenge with ideological amplification in each counter-attack, these reversals of fortune were in themselves conditions of increasing violence.

After the failed attempt of an Athenian general to effect a settlement, successive interventions by Spartan and Athenian navies made things even worse. To abbreviate a complex story, the Spartan fleet, having achieved a certain victory at the expense of some poorly commanded Corcyrean triremes, stole away on receiving news of the approach of a large contingent of sixty Athenian ships. The Athenian commander Eurymedon, finding himself in complete control, now cordoned off the city and delivered the oligarchic faction to a bloody massacre by an out-of-control democratic mob:

> During the seven days that Eurymedon stayed with his sixty ships, the Corcyreans were engaged in butchering those of their fellow-citizens whom they regarded as their enemies, and although the crime imputed was that of attempting to put down the democracy, some were slain also for private hatred, others by their debtors because of the moneys owed to them. Death thus raged in every shape; and, as usually happens at such times, there was no length to which violence did not go; sons were killed by their fathers, and suppliants dragged from the altar or slain upon it; while some were even walled up in the temple of Dionysus, and died there. (Thucydides, 3.81.4-5)

The reign of terror at Corcyra, while apparently more violent than any previous *stasis*, was only the first of its draconian kind, according to Thucydides: "struggles being made everywhere by the popular leaders to bring in the Athenians, and by the oligarchs to introduce the Spartans" (3.82.1). Like his earlier account of the plague at Athens, Thucydides conveys the sense of an epidemic diffusion of these political "convulsions," becoming ever more malignant as they spread from city to city. For Thucydides, however, this was not a matter of compounded symbolic escalation but something of the opposite: the disintegration of cultural order by the eruption of human nature. What the atrocities expressed was a universal underlying human acquisitiveness, "always rebelling against the law and now its master," as it was unchained in one city after another by the stress of war. "The cause of all these evils was the lust for power arising from greed and ambition, and from these passions proceeded the violence of the parties engaged in contention" (3.82.8). True that the explicit justifications were higher-minded: "the cry of political equality for The People," on one side; and that of "a moderate aristocracy" on the other. But as Thucydides also famously observed, in these maelstroms of moral inequity and self-interested hypocrisy, "words had to change their ordinary meaning and to take that which was now given to them" (3.82.4). Cautious plotting became "self-defense"; moderation, "unmanliness"; prudence, "cowardice." No oath was proof against the advantages of breaking it, even as such treachery was taken as the sign of a superior intelligence. The only principle left, as W. Robert Connor observes (1984, 99), was "the calculation of self-interest." And the effect was total anarchy: "Now all the conventions of Greek life—promises, oaths, supplications, obligations to kin and benefactors and even the ultimate convention, language itself—give way. It is Hobbes's *bellum omnium contra omnes*."

For all the suppositions in antiquity that man was naturally social (Aristotle) or in origin blessed (Hesiod), it could also be supposed that in the course of time an equally fundamental baseness of human character would give rise to continuous strife and misery. For Aristotle, human appetites were by nature unlimited, especially the appetite for gain, and this was a major source of the corruption of any and all forms of political regime (Aristotle, *Politics* 2.1267a–b, 2.1271a, 3.1286b). As for Hesiod, his description of the human fate in this age of iron reads like Thucydides on *stasis* in Corcyra:

> Father will have no common bond with son,
> Neither will guest with host, nor friend with friend;
> The brother-love of past days will be gone.
> Men will dishonor parents....
> Men will destroy the towns of other men.
> The just, the good, the man who keeps his word
> Will be despised, but men will praise the bad
> And insolent. Might will be Right, and shame
> Will cease to be. Men will do injury
> To better men by speaking crooked words

And adding lying oaths; and everywhere
Harsh-voiced and sullen-faced and loving harm,
Envy will walk along with wretched men.

(*WORKS AND DAYS*, LL. 180-94)

But then, Thucydides also had the dubious benefit of a sense of *nomos*, or "convention," which by the end of the fifth century, in comparison with *physis* or what was "natural" to humankind, was only local, changeable, and prejudicial: "It was, obviously, an ethically significant phenomenon in linguistic history when the expression [*nomos*] which usually meant either 'by law' or 'in accordance with accepted *mores*' also took on the sense, not only of 'subjectively,' but of the latter adverb with an unfavorable connotation, i.e., erroneously" (Lovejoy and Boas 1935, 106). One basic human nature, many superficial cultures—the second as no match for the first—this idea is still too much with us, as Bruno Latour (2002) has recently argued.

There is good reason to argue that Thucydides' conception of the natural human condition is also still with us: in the form, as Connor suggested, of Hobbes's *bellum omnium contra omnes*. In the Hobbesian state of nature, each man's singular pursuit of his own good demanded an equally relentless and destructive pursuit of power, both to secure his own well-being and to harness the powers of others to that end. "So in the first place, I put for a general inclination of all mankind, a perpetual and restless desire of power after power, that ceaseth only in death" (Hobbes, *Leviathan*, ch. 13). In the *Leviathan* as in Thucydides' *History*, all sorts of actions and words with other apparent meanings could be resolved to their self-serving power-effects (Hobbes, *Leviathan*, ch. 10 et passim). Liberality is power because "it procureth friends and servants"; good reputation is power "because it draweth with it the adherence of those that need protection"; indeed, "what quality soever maketh a man beloved, or feared of many; or the reputation of such quality, is power, because it is a means to have the assistance, and service of many." (One is reminded of the current obsession with "power" among anthropologists and cult-studs, involving the similar reduction of the most diverse *nomoi* of peoples all around the world to the one and the same function of power-effects.) The good reason for pairing Thucydides with Hobbes, however, goes beyond these analogies of intellectual terrorism. It is because Thomas Hobbes was the first translator of Thucydides directly into English. Hence a number of classical scholars have seen in Thucydides' description of the *stasis* at Corcyra and the plague of Athens the prototype of Hobbes's war of each against all (cf. Brown 1987; de Ste Croix 1972, 26-8; Orwin 1988, among others). Which does indeed bring us up to date, insofar as Hobbes's state of nature was destined for its own brilliant career as a charter myth of bourgeois-capitalist subjectivity.

Nevertheless, as Rousseau said of philosophers who have felt the need to return to the state of nature, none of them ever got there. Nor would anthropology or archaeology confirm that anything like a *bellum omnium contra omnes* was the origin of the human career. What they do show is that whatever our natural drives and dispositions may be—whether egoistical or sociable, sexual or nutritional—they have come under conceptual definition and control: that is, as regards their objects, occasions, practices, social relations, and morality. Encompassed in diverse symbolic worlds, the natural proclivities are then diversely sublimated and expressed—or repressed. Indeed, if Hobbes is making sense in asserting that affability, liberality, belovedness, friendship, hospitality, and battle are so many forms of the natural lust for power, then clearly the natural lust for power has no particular cultural necessity.

In this connection, it is difficult to credit Thucydides' contention that words lost their meanings at Corcyra, so much as the hypocritical use of them made people all the angrier at the evident deceit, and thus added large doses of moral outrage to differences of party interest. (Living as Americans have under a regime that in the oxymoronic name of *compassionate conservatism* enriched the superwealthy at the expense of the society, one is entitled to doubt that such cynicism changes the meaning of *compassion* so much as exposes the deceit of those who abuse the word. It's not for nothing that Bush was the most hated president since—well, since Clinton.) But to reduce the hostility discharged by moral contradiction to the expression of natural frenzy is to practice the same kind of verbal deception one is purporting to unmask. More generally, it verges on absurdity to attribute the violence occasioned by the use and abuse of words, thus symbolically incited and constituted, to a preverbal human disposition. Better the take of the classicist Marc Cogan (1981, 62-64) on the *stasis* at Corcyra: that the intervention of the Peloponnesian War gave new and unconditional values to the internal rivalries of the cities—rendering them, one might say, as irreconcilable as they were ideological. Values like "freedom" and "slavery," "equality" and "subjection."

"Athens and Sparta," says Victor Davis Hanson, "are states in a real war, but they are also metaphysical expressions of opposite ways of looking at the universe" (1996, xi). Competing with each other as the leading cities of Greece since the late sixth century, in an exemplary process of complementary schismogenesis, they became cultural antitypes. Athens was to Sparta as a sea power to a land power, as cosmopolitan to xenophobic, commercial to autarchic, luxurious to frugal, autochthonous to immigrant, logomanic to laconic—"one cannot finish enumerating the dichotomies" (Aron 1961, 108). Special weight attaches to the dichotomy between democracy and oligarchy, as respectively championed by the Athenians and the Spartans. First attested as distinctive forms by Herodotus in the mid-fifth century, "democracy" and "oligarchy," as Martin Ostwald (2000, 21f.) points out, take on the sense of political-ideological antitheses for the first time precisely in Thucydides' description of the civil war at Corcyra.

Yet everything suggests that a more general opposition between equality and hierarchy was centuries old before it was thus politicized by Athens and Sparta. Ian Morris (2000) makes a sustained argument from textual and archaeological materials that this recurrent contest of political forms began in the eighth century (B.C.), with the birth of the *polis* and the idea of the state as a community of "middling citizens." The idea, however, would have to do battle with an older aristocratic tradition of a heroic, interpolis elite, linked by pedigree to the gods above and adorned with the intimations of divinity they acquired in the form of luxury goods imported from the Orient. Morris charts the diverse outcomes of this cultural clash at different times and places, culminating in the victory of the middling stratum at the end of the sixth century and the institution of democracy as such (particularly at Athens). Here, clearly, is another take on the great transformation in cosmology and polity analyzed by Jean-Pierre Vernant in well-known works (1982, 1983). The turn was from a hierarchical system under the sovereignty of god or king, Zeus or *basileus*, who by divine might subdues all rebellious elements and creates a stable order of distributed statuses and privileges—Hesiod's *Theogony* provides the mythical model—from this hierarchical system to a cosmic as well as human constitution in which power is diffused equally through the totality, among elements whose reciprocal interaction at the center generates a stable, balanced, and just regime—Anaximander's cosmology is the model. Vernant explains the contrast introduced by the *polis*:

We see here the birth of a society in which the rapport of one man to another is conceived as a relation of identity, of symmetry and of reversibility. Rather than forming, as in mythical space, a world of levels with the king at the summit and below him an entire hierarchy of social statuses defined in terms of domination and submission, the universe of the city presents a constitution of egalitarian and reversible relations, where all the citizens are defined in relation to one another as equals on the political plane. One can say that in having access to the circular and central space of the agora, the citizens enter into the framework of a political system ruled by equilibrium, symmetry and reciprocity. (Vernant 1983, 211; cf. Détienne and Vernant 1974, ch. 3)

So analogously, the cosmological scheme developed by Anaximander in the mid-sixth century dispensed with the divinely imposed, hierarchical order of earlier myth for a self-equilibrating universe, established through the reciprocal interaction of its opposed elements (Fairbanks 2001; Hahn 2001; Kahn 1960; Kirk et al. 1983, ch. 3; Vernant 1983; G. Vlastos 1953). Accordingly, modern scholars generally celebrate Anaximander's cosmology as a revolutionary breakthrough of secular and rational thought (Couprie et al. 2003). Like the *polis* of equal powers centrally met in the *agora*, in Anaximander's system the earth is fixed at the center of the universe by its equidistance from other bodies of the celestial sphere. And in the same way as the constituent elements of which these bodies were composed, their conflictual opposition as equal forces ensures that no one among them will dominate the others. As Vernant put it (1983, 33): "The elements are in effect defined by their reciprocal opposition, as forces in conflict. It is necessary, then, that they always stand to one another in a relation of equality—equality of power." Moreover, as it is in the macrocosm, so in the microcosm; the health and well-being of the human body is a function of the balance of corporeal qualities or powers:

Alcmaeon maintains that the bond of health is the "equal rights" of the powers, moist and dry, cold and hot, bitter and sweet, and the rest, while the "monarchy" of one of them is the cause of disease.... Health on the other hand is the proportionate admixture of the qualities. (Kirk et al. 1983, 260)

This doxographic notice of a late sixth-century treatise by the physician Alcmaeon contains in essence the notion of a "cosmos of health" that would continue to flourish in the writings of the Hippocratic doctors (Kahn 1960, 132-33, 159-60). Here, then, was a challenge to hierarchy that ran from cosmology to biology, by way of society.

Given these parallels of the polis system in the conceptions of the universe and the body, one is tempted to follow the lead of many classical scholars in understanding the cosmological and biological constructs as reflexes of the political realities: something along the lines of the good Marxian tradition of ideological superstructures in relation to more pragmatic infrastructures. Alternatively, the analogies could mean that these several conceptual domains were not so differentiated in ancient cultural practice as they are in modern theory— that they were perhaps more of the character of homologies than analogies. Most noteworthy in the present context is Plato's repeated conflation of the body politic and the body natural in *The Republic*, the one described in the terms of the constitution of the other, including a discussion of the factional warfare between oligarchic and democratic parties in the soul as well as the city that is only a thinly disguised version of Thucydides' account of the *stasis* at Corcyra (*Republic* 8:555-61). (Plato also forestalls Aristotle in remarking that the circumstance setting off party warfare "may be very slight," thus recognizing the phenomenon of structural amplification; as for Thucydides, the parallels in Plato include the exacerbation of internal warfare by external accomplices and the perverse distortions of language by partisan interests.) And where political principles were hardly to be distinguished from the biological or the cosmological, would they be any less "ideological"?[8] We are told that *isonomia*, "equality," if it was the organizing principle of the Athenian democracy, was by the same token "a slogan"; then again, it was "an idea, indeed a whole set of ideas, by which the partisans of democracy justified the rule of the people" (Vlastos 1953, 362, 347). By the fifth century, in any case, *isonomia* was not only in the superstructures: it was in all the structures. One might thus say it was in the cultural basis. *Isonomia* in cosmology, polity, and physiology—Athens was on the good side of ontology.

Just so, as the call to arms of the democratic many against the privileged few, *isonomia* was Athens' trump card in the battle with Sparta for the allegiance of the cities. "The fairest of all names," as Herodotus (*Histories* 3.80) called it, *isonomia* offered the just alternative to an oligarchic regime in which the many had to share the dangers to the polis while the few took the profits (Thucydides, 6.39.2). At issue was something more than "equality before the law [for male citizens]" as we would understand it, though this is the usual translation of *isonomia*. In a direct democracy, *isonomia* had a more inclusive political value, involving also equal participation in the making of law and state policy and the happy condition wherein "all share alike in ruling and being ruled in turn" (Aristotle, *Politics* 7.1332b). Hence Athens' appeal, especially to the *demos* of the cities in the final phases of a long, long struggle against hierarchy:

> the Athenian order seemed to be able to inspire a deeply felt positive affection. Its most notable achievement responsible for evoking such sentiments was the establishment of an admirable degree of justice for all its citizens through legal equality (*isonomia*) at a time when the old aristocratic orders (*eunomiai*) were deteriorating everywhere. (Fleiss 1966, 132)

But this was only one aspect of a complex ideological chiasmus. If, on the one hand, Athens was on the good side of the opposition between hierarchy and equality, on the other hand, Athens was more and more through the fifth century the detested "tyrant city"—since, as an imperial power, she was on the bad side of an equally profound opposition between the cherished independence of the classical polis and its humiliating submission to another. Athens' ideological position was ambiguous to the point of being contradictory, as was Sparta's in a symmetrically opposed way. Interfering abroad, Athens could advocate equality of the citizens, but at the cost of the freedom of the city; which gave Sparta the opportunity to act as liberator of the city, if at the cost of the equality of the citizens. The allegiance of *poleis* such as Corcyra to Athens in the fifth century entailed inclusion in her empire and submission to her increasingly exploitative and repressive domination. By the time of the Peloponnesian War (431 B.C.), the erstwhile allies who had willingly accepted Athens' leadership of the Delian League (in 477 B.C.) had explicitly become her tributary subjects. Aside from annual tributes to Athens, they had to suffer the presence of posted Athenian officials; sometimes also Athenian garrisons and the expropriation of lands for Athenian settlers; the transfer of judicial control to Athens in the case of certain serious crimes; and, not least, obeisance to Athens' city god by participation in the spectacular processions of the Grand Panathenaia, bearing vestments and sacrifices to Athena. Yet if Athenian hegemony was widely considered a tyranny, as even Pericles admitted (Thucydides, 2.63.3), it was not only because of the burden of these impositions, but because they violated the famously cherished values of the freedom of the city. Given the values of freedom, autonomy, autarky, and their corollaries, the resentments provoked by Athenian domination could well be out of proportion to its impositions. A measure of this disparity is the success the Spartans had in conflating Atticism, the submission of other cities to Athens, with "slavery," as we have seen in the *stasis* at Corcyra. Just as much as the antithesis between democracy and oligarchy, that between slavery and freedom became a general issue of the Peloponnesian War. Indeed the Corinthians had urged this war on the Spartans to "win future security for ourselves and freedom for the Hellenes who are now enslaved" (Thucydides, 1.124.3). Despite the attractiveness of Athenian democracy, then, when the Peloponnesian War broke out, sentiment in Greece was running in favor of the Spartans:

> Men's feelings inclined much more to the Spartans, especially as they proclaimed themselves the liberators of Hellas. No private or public effort that could help them in speech or action was omitted.... So general was the indignation felt against Athens, whether by those who wished to escape the empire [or those who] were apprehensive of being absorbed by it.... (Thucydides, 2.8.4–5)

The high value the ancient Greeks put on the independence and self-sufficiency of the *polis* was a kind of sub-Olympian version of the autonomy and completeness of their gods. (In this respect, Aristophanes' depiction of the Athenians as birds, interposed between heaven and earth where they can intercept the sacrifices destined for the immortals, was not altogether Cloudcookooland.) In its own aspirations of autonomy and permanence, as well as its power over its inhabitants, the *polis* was the human institution most like the god—a "mortal god" (to adapt another Hobbesism). A state was only a state, as Aristotle put it, if it had the finality of a complete and independent life (*Politics* 3.1280b). The alternative was indeed slavery: "for surely it is quite out of the question that it should be possible to give the name of state to a community which is by nature a slave, for a state is self-sufficient, but that which is a slave is not self-sufficient" (*Politics* 4.1291a; cf. 7.1326a–b). So far as this value of independence was cosmological, the Spartans would be in the best position to purvey it. The "moderate oligarchy" they supported in the cities could recall an aristocracy of heroic origins, even as their own kings and Lycurgus

himself descended from Heracles. In any case, they did actively inter-
vene in Corcyra and elsewhere in the cause of restoring the forfeited
independence of the cities. Better a free city under a moderate oligarchy than equal participation in a state of subjugation.

Hence when Athens and Sparta got involved in the endemic factional strife of the cities between the plutocrats and the people, they
added a criss-crossing system of fateful causes to the chiasmus of contending forces. To reiterate: the equality of the citizens promoted by
the Athenians would cost the freedom of the city; while the freedom
of the city promoted by the Spartans would cost the citizens their
equality. Where liberty thus contradicts equality, the victim will be
fraternity. Engaging in complex ways the strength of extramural powers and the compulsions of transcendental values, internal discord
spins out of control. Whether the greater forces and causes mobilize
the people in the interest of pan-Hellenic war or the people mobilize
the larger forces and causes in the interest of their own "small matters," the oppositional field offers the opportunity of numerous maneuvers from one factional pole to another—without ostensible loss
of virtue. It takes a lot of culture to make a state of nature.

Summary: Structural Dynamics

From civil war in the Greek *polis* to the fracas over Elián Gonzalez,
passing by way of dust-ups in Catalonia and the Sandwich Islands,
these conflicts knew a common basic dynamic of escalation. All
shared a certain *elementary form of structural amplification* (as I am too
pretentiously calling it): some more than twice over, by recursively
adding greater oppositions to lesser ones (Figure 11.1). By inclusion
or segmentary relativity, feuding local groups assume the identities of
larger collectivities—the way Catalan villagers, for example, became
Frenchmen and Spaniards—and thereby engage these collectivities
in their own petty issues. The structural effect is a chiastic pattern
of affinities and enmities, as the greater entities also enter the lists
against the lesser factions of the other side. In the upshot, the local
causes are prosecuted as larger oppositions, and the larger oppositions as local causes. More complex struggles, for example the *stasis*
at Corcyra and the Elián affair, are constituted by superimposing or
redoubling the same elementary form at higher levels of order—the
way the oppositions of the Peloponnesian War were added to, and exacerbated, internal strife in the cities; or how the bitter antagonism

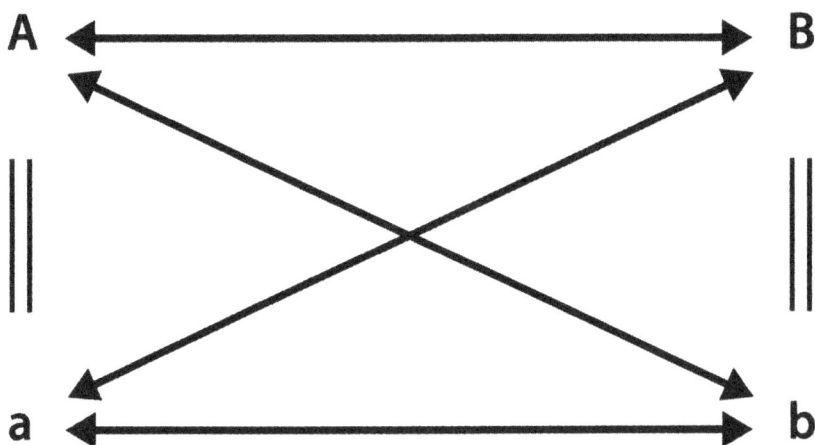

Figure 11.1. The elementary form of structural amplification. The local dispute between (a) and (b) engages the larger opposition (⟷) between (A) and (B), through the identities (a) = (A), (b) = (B). In the occurrence, (B) is engaged against (a) and (A) against (b). The original dispute between (a) and (b) is thus amplified by the larger forces, causes, and differences involved in the opposition of (A) and (B). The dynamics of amplification include well-known processes of segmentary relativity (Evans-Pritchard), schismogenesis (Bateson), and transvaluation (Tambiah).

between Cubans in Miami and on the Island was reverberated by correlated divisions in the American public and the lingering differences of the Cold War.

In two related respects, which I have been calling *structural* and *symbolic* (though without further explanation), this elementary form has intrinsic properties of escalation. In principle—this is the structural dynamic—the intensification of any one opposition is likely to engage and aggravate all the other antagonisms in the chiastic set. The principle is the familiar one of "the friend of my enemy is my enemy," "the enemy of my enemy is my friend," and the other three-place permutations of the binary pair, friend/enemy. At the same time, any such structural magnification of differences is likely to be a symbolic one, since the integration of higher with lower levels of order also entails the combination of universalistic ideals with particularistic interests. This because the higher structural levels or wider communities engaged in the fray—the classes, ethnicities, races, nations—are for their part imagined in terms of abstract and discriminatory ideals. Hence upping the structural ante intensifies the battle, insofar as it now joins unconditional antipathies of morality and political ideology, not to say cosmology, to petty disputes that otherwise would be negotiable. The bigger the fight, the better the reasons for it.

From this it follows logically—as has already been suggested empirically—that the amplification of lesser disputes depends on the state of the relations between the larger collectivities to which they are articulated. In the elementary form diagrammed here, the escalation of the differences between (a) and (b) depends on the relations prevailing between (A) and (B). This we saw in the Cerdanya, in the way the amplification of peasant disputes among the Catalans responded to varying relations between France and Spain.[9] The Elián affair indicated that something also has to be said for the symbolic felicity of the case, something about the meaningful and conjunctural conditions that make a cause *célèbre*. But beyond that, we have to look to the larger correlation of forces. The lingering antipathies of the Cold War notwithstanding, the American and Cuban governments had mutual interests in controlling emigration to the United States and loosening the American embargo on trade. The greater structure of the conjuncture dampened the lesser oppositions in play. By contrast, the rebellions in Corcyra and other cities were, so far as Sparta and Athens were concerned, so many tactical conditions of the war between them: terrains to be defended or seized—which of course made the civic strife so much the worse. One is reminded of Thucydides' famous observation on the "truest cause" of the Peloponnesian War, as opposed to the local incidents that set it off: the dispute of the Corinthians and Corcyreans in 433 B.C. and the Potidaea affair of 432 B.C. These incidents may have precipitated the Peloponnesian War, but its "truest cause," said Thucydides, was "the growing power of the Athenians and the fear this inspired in the Spartans"—the larger correlation of forces.

Perspectives on the Politics of Peace in Aceh, Indonesia

Mary-Jo DelVecchio Good and Byron J. Good

Stanley Tambiah laments in *Leveling Crowds: Ethnonationalist Conflicts and Collective Violence in Southeast Asia* (1996), "something has gone awry in center-periphery relations throughout the world." Identifying widespread ethnic conflicts as characteristically "amongst enemies intimately known," noting "the internationalization of the technology of destruction" and "ethnonationalism," Tambiah evokes an overwhelming "disillusionment of our epoch," of "our contemporary world suffused by violence" (1996a, 3-11). His impassioned 1986 monograph on Sri Lanka and ethnic fratricide between dominant Sinhalese and minority Tamils details the escalating "dismantling of democracy" in postcolonial Sri Lanka and the ill-fated demise of the British colonial legacy of governmental institutions and ideologies of tolerance (*Sri Lanka: Ethnic Fratricide and the Dismantling of Democracy*, 1986). At the time of writing this essay, armed conflicts between the Sri Lankan government and the rebel Tamil Tigers continued, and civilian casualties and insecurities of daily life were all too common (Sengupta 2008a and 2008b; Associated Press 2008). The nation's bellicose military and political leaders ("two brothers") were "aggressively [seeking] to end the quarter-century-long ethnic conflict by crushing the Tamil Tigers militarily" (Sengupta 2008a). In 2009, the Tamil Tigers conceded defeat and the civil war was declared to be over.

Tambiah's studies of the painful national crisis afflicting contemporary Sri Lanka and ethnonationalist conflicts around the world resonate with our own efforts to understand and respond to the "remainders of violence" associated with the generational conflict in the province of Aceh, Indonesia, a region long "suffused with violence" in which center-periphery relations have "gone awry." Anthony Reid, a noted historian of Indonesia, titled his 2006 edited collection on Aceh *Verandah of Violence*, a word play on Aceh's historical role over centuries as the veranda of the journey to Mecca for Muslim Hajj pilgrims from Southeast Asia and China, and on the worldwide reputation of the Acehnese for fierceness and military prowess (Reid 1995). A province of over 4 million people at the northern tip of Sumatra, part of a nation whose population of 245 million makes it the world's fourth most populous, Aceh holds symbolic potency in the Indonesian nationalist imagination as the first province to declare independence in 1945. Aceh's separatist impulses, referenced below, are anathema to Indonesia's national political leadership.

But Aceh is also a reminder that sites of conflict may, at some moment in history, also become laboratories for reworking center-periphery relations in society. On December 26, 2004, the Indian Ocean tsunami wrought devastation in both Sri Lanka and Aceh. In Sri Lanka, 36,000 persons were killed and an estimated 1 million people displaced along the island's coast, with Tamil regions hit hardest and Sinhalese communities widely affected (Jayasinghe 2006). In Aceh, an estimated 130,000 to 168,000 people were killed, with over 400,000 persons displaced (Borrero et al. 2006). However, while the tsunami and humanitarian interventions seem to have exacerbated the conflict in Sri Lanka, in Aceh they pushed forward a peace process, already underway but with a far from certain outcome, to a final agreement between the Government of Indonesia and the Gerakan Aceh Merdeka (Free Aceh Movement), or GAM, signed in Helsinki on August 15, 2005, just over seven months after the tsunami. More than that, they launched a peace process which has become an important site for exploring new forms of center-periphery relations in Indonesia.

How then do crises, such as natural disasters or conflicts, and a society's accommodation to humanitarian responses, reveal larger social and political forces usually hidden from view? (See Fassin and Vasquez 2005 on the 1999 Venezuelan disaster.) In the Indonesian case, what do the responses to the tsunami by the central government and provincial authorities and the evolution of the peace process in Aceh, both of which developed in interaction with the global humanitarian "apparatus," tell us about the reshaping of relations between Indonesia's political center and its peripheries? In our conversations with Stanley Tambiah—our dear friend Tambi—these questions always took on a comparative cast. Why, we often discussed, did the local and national leaders of Indonesia and Sri Lanka respond so differently to the tsunami? Why did the tsunami and the humanitarian intervention lead to increased violence in Sri Lanka and to a quite remarkable peace process in Aceh? And what is the future of the peace process in both places?

Although this topic is too large to explore fully in this brief essay, here we address several dimensions of center-periphery relations between the nation-state of Indonesia and the Acehnese, drawing from our personal and ethnographic observations while serving as scientific consultants for the International Organization for Migration's mental health projects in high-conflict-affected regions since June 2005; from conversations held during an October 2007 conference that we convened (The Peace Process in Aceh: Remainders of Violence and the Future of Nanggroe Aceh Darussalam), bringing together leading Acehnese and Indonesian government peace negotiators at Harvard's Asia Center; and from recently published academic, intergovernmental organization, and media publications and unpublished reports, including two astonishing documentary films on the Aceh conflict.[1] We then return, in our concluding comments, to preliminary thoughts about the Indonesia–Sri Lanka comparison.

Aceh's Colonial and Postcolonial Struggles

Aceh's reputation as a fiercely independent "nation" is historically rich, remarked upon by many travelers across the centuries—from Marco Polo to Raffles and other Europeans (see Reid 1995). Valorized for long resisting Dutch colonial rule, for being the first province to declare its independence in the Indonesian nationalist struggle, successfully forcing out the Dutch, British, and Japanese occupying forces at the end of World War II, the Acehnese have also gained renown among other Indonesians as challenging and difficult compatriots.

When promises of provincial autonomy, pledged during the nationalist struggle, were abrogated by Indonesia's first president, Sukarno,
during the early independence period, Acehenese resisted forcefully;
Batak troops from North Sumatra were sent to the province to curb
threats of separatism, but in the end Sukarno was forced to grant the
Acehnese provincial status and special consideration. Seeds of struggle with "Jakarta" (the capital) and the national government, closely
associated with Java and the Javanese, were sown. Discovery of vast
reserves of natural gas off the coast of Aceh, exploited by the central
government with little return to local communities or economic development, rekindled the Acehnese sense of betrayal. A popularly
supported Free Aceh Movement, known as GAM, was launched in
1976, and grew by the late 1980s into the most powerful political force
in Aceh. By 1989, the Indonesian military—largely special forces of
the army—were engaged in open military conflict with GAM and
more generally with those communities known to be "bases" of GAM.
Zones of insecurity began spreading throughout rural Aceh, as villages became GAM villages or contested villages, and the conflict intensified. Although colored by ethnic contests that had historically
grown up between Javanese and Acehnese, the Free Aceh Movement
was a provincial movement. Conflict with the national military and
police forces occurred exclusively on Acehnese soil, in contrast to the
Tamil-Sinhalese conflict in Sri Lanka, where Tamil fighters carried the
conflict to Sinhalese towns and cities. Particular village communities
with ties to GAM became "hot spots" (Jesse Grayman's term) in the
conflict, with many Acehnese feeling squeezed between the national
military and GAM (Good et al. 2006, 2007). As the conflict between
the Acehnese and the TNI (the Indonesian national military) spread,
urban, rural, coastal, inland, and highland communities experienced
insecurity, violence, torture, and chronic trauma, weakening the political and social ties to the central national government and for some,
even to the nation of Indonesia.[2]

The Tsunami of December 26, 2004

The province of Aceh came into global popular awareness on December 26, 2004, when the Indian Ocean earthquake (9.2 on the Rich-
ter scale) triggered a massive tsunami, killing between 130,000 and
168,000 persons in Aceh alone, and approximately 230,000 people in
the eleven countries affected (Borrero et al. 2006). In Aceh, nearly a

half million people were displaced, their houses, animals, and lands destroyed, many swallowed by the sea. Indonesia's Metro TV featured round-the-clock coverage of an endless loop of video taken by a wedding videographer as he struggled to escape the rising water twisting houses, vehicles, and people into its blackness; videos and photos sent by private citizens and string reporters conveyed early forays into this devastated land, while a newly composed song, "Indonesia Menangis"—"Indonesia cries" (or grieves)—became the disaster's broadcast theme.

The Indonesian government, overwhelmed by the loss of local communications and effective government, reluctantly granted permission to foreign military and humanitarian workers to step ashore, risking international witnessing of consequences of decades of deadly conflict. Into this state of astonishing natural disaster poured thousands of emergency responders from a documented 132 international and local humanitarian organizations. When the tsunami struck, the International Organization of Migration (IOM), an intergovernmental organization with over 120 member and 19 observer states, was among the few international humanitarian organizations already based in Aceh. Under contract to the Indonesian Ministry of Law and Human Rights, IOM had been charged with resettling communities displaced by the conflict between GAM and the national military and police. Post-tsunami, IOM rapidly mustered a highly visible and largely successful emergency disaster response, providing emergency shelter and relief and contracting to build homes in the demolished areas. Its outreach teams, vehicles with blue and white IOM logos, and refugee services were soon easily recognized and widely appreciated by victims throughout the tsunami-affected areas.

IOM (pronounced in Indonesian with a lilt, as "*eeyom*") quickly added temporary health clinics and maternal health outreach programs to shelter projects, and IOM's health officer sought international donor funding to develop new initiatives in "psycho-social and mental health." As part of her effort to expand IOM's portfolio, she recruited an Acehnese psychiatrist from the medical faculty at Syiah Kuala University to lead these initiatives; we joined him as IOM consultants. The popular understanding of trauma as a response to natural disaster legitimized for donors and humanitarian organizations the need for mental health responses; it also opened the way for recognition of trauma to enter post-conflict humanitarian interventions.

Brokering the Peace and the MOU

Many Acehnese speak about the tsunami as sent "by God" to end the long conflict between GAM and the Government of Indonesia. Indeed, the Memorandum of Understanding (MOU) signed in Helsinki on August 15, 2005, by representatives of GAM and the Government of Indonesia unleashed a project with near-revolutionary consequences for the province of Aceh, its people, and its local political world. Under Suharto's New Order regime (1966-1998), the Acehnese struggle to control local politics and natural resources, particularly a vast natural gas reserve off the coast, became the focus of GAM resistance. In 1976, GAM called for greater autonomy; by the turn of the millennium, GAM was calling for independence from the Indonesian state. Many of its leaders, studying and working in Europe, the United States, and Malaysia, engaged in a concerted effort to internationalize the GAM cause and to appeal their case to international human rights organizations and leadership. During the 1990s the armed conflict between GAM and the Indonesian national military and police forces (TNI and BRIMOB) intensified, as local resistance and popular anger spread in reaction to "the militarization of predatory economics" (Kingsley and McCulloch 2006) and the stripping of Aceh's oil and gas wealth, its forests and plantations, even its fish and coffee. Local villagers, loggers, farmers, fishermen, merchants, businessmen, and traders were extorted and terrorized. Zones of military operation (*daerah operasi militer*, or DOM) were zones of heightened insecurity for ordinary citizens (Drexler 2008). The violence was particularly intense in Aceh's northeastern districts from 1989 to 1998, and again in 2003-2004; before the tsunami, it had been interrupted by two short and unsuccessful cease-fires under the post-Suharto presidencies. The loss of East Timor increased the nationalist military's resolve, and the odds of noncombatants suffering relentless chronic conflict and aggression increased throughout Aceh after 2001.

The Acehnese have a saying, "The mountain goat eats the corn, the village goat takes the beating." It was the source of Aryo Danusiri's title for his prizewinning 1999 film *The Village Goat Takes the Beating*, in which villagers recount the humiliation, torture, and violence they experienced at the hands of the national military. Through decades of conflict, while GAM guerilla forces (the mountain goats) waged their battles against the TNI from remote bases in the hills and forests, many civilian Acehnese (the village goats) were beaten and tortured in their own communities by forces intent on destroying GAM "at its roots"—at the household, kinship, community, and economic levels.[3]

A Scene from the Field Survey

In February 2006, IOM undertook a psychosocial needs assessment in 30 villages in three districts known to have suffered particularly high levels of conflict and violence during the two previous decades of armed conflict between the forces of the Government of Indonesia and the Free Aceh Movement (GAM). Villagers described sustained violence by Indonesian Special Forces against their communities, with houses and schools razed or burned, and villagers beaten, tortured, or killed—often in retaliation for attacks by GAM on the Indonesian military. Men and women told us of being forced to watch spouses killed and sons taken to the forest to be executed, and of their own beatings and humiliation. They complained of waking up with vivid images of what happened and being unable to return to sleep (Grayman, Good, and Good 2009), the constant fear and sadness that made daily activities difficult, and their anger and inability to forget inflicted traumas.

By mid-March, we began our statistical analyses of traumatic events and psychological symptom levels, to produce the IOM psychosocial needs assessment (PNA). Of the 596 randomly selected adult villagers, 78 percent had experienced combat and firefights; 38 percent had fled burning buildings; 39 percent reported being beaten; 25 percent of the men and 11 percent of the women reported being tortured; 41 percent had had family members or friends killed; 8 percent of women had had husbands killed; and 5 percent of all adults reported children killed in the conflict. We had not known if the stories we heard during our February field trip represented particularly egregious events suffered by a limited number of individuals in the most severely affected villages, or if they were more representative. As we scanned the data, we were stunned at how widespread acts of violence against civilian communities had been. Within this population, 65 percent scored symptomatic for depression and 34 percent scored symptomatic for Post Traumatic Stress Disorder (PTSD), with no significant difference between men and women; 69 percent scored symptomatic for anxiety, with women scoring significantly higher than men, 75 percent vs. 64 percent (Good, Good, Grayman, and Lakoma 2006).

A Village "Trauma Clinic"

Interviewers had alerted the IOM outreach medical team of a village population that had suffered *particularly* severe torture, interrogation, house burnings, and destruction of property.[4] The community asked the medical team to make a visit. It was rainy season, and the dirt road to the village was deeply rutted and slick; the IOM vehicles, all with four-wheel drive, slithered clumsily up the hill. People passed on motorcycles and on foot. Villagers had been notified of our arrival earlier by cell phone. We were received not with solemn greetings but with amusement, playfulness, and coffee in the market place. The market street was covered with trash, flies, and garbage. Shop shelves were mostly bare. Citrus and snake fruit brought from town, along with cigarettes and coffee, were for sale. TVs flickered in the backs of shops. Cloudy skies cast a dank grayness. We drank sweetened coffee sitting with village men as they spoke of soccer and *rantau*—trips in their youth, seeking fortunes, adventure, even wives—to Jakarta and elsewhere throughout the archipelago. Slowly yet spontaneously they began to talk of the violence suffered by the community before the peace agreement, the MOU. A man told of his brother who witnessed his two sons shot by the military; "he is depressed," he said. He then told his own story: "they" were going to shoot him, but his Javanese wife stood in front of him, arms wide apart, and shouted at the Javanese troops: "I am Javanese, shoot me, not him!" We heard this story a number of times that afternoon, along with many others.

Soon women of all ages, most dressed in new brightly colored and pressed sarongs and head scarves, emerged from the back of market stalls and village houses, along with their children and the village men; with our psychiatrist colleague and the IOM medical team, we merged into a village procession to the *meunasah*, a community center typical in Acehnese villages. The IOM vehicles followed us closely—lurking security. In front of the meunasah, a tall thin man awaited the medical team, choking, sobbing, embraced by village men. The psychiatrist raised his eyebrows, asking what had happened. "He was accused of telling GAM to run." "They [the military] took him in the night, in the very early morning, they hung him with a plastic bag over his face, strangled him." "They hung him like a goat, they beat him in the head, beat him senseless." "He has depression and trauma." "He can't breathe, he can't work," his men friends lamented. "He was tortured." The women whispered to me, Mary-Jo, "He cries because he

can't work and he can't earn money for his family. He can't be a man."
All present looked upon the man with compassion and concern. He
had been sobbing uncontrollably for months, his friends said, since
before the tsunami, when the villagers had been sent away from their
homes "for security reasons," only to return to find their houses shot
up, their belongings gone, with "not one plate left!"

The group climbed to the second floor of the community house;
a succession of men, women, and children dressed in their best continued to arrive throughout the afternoon. The psychiatrist settled on
a straw mat and leaned against a wall; the young female doctors and
male nurses set up medication and examination stations along another wall. I sat, with my friends from the university, with the women
and children. The psychiatrist examined the inconsolable man, spoke
briefly to calm him, held his hand, laid him gently on a straw mat, and
injected him with a sedative. The suffering man soon fell into a deep
sleep. "Trauma clinic" had begun.

Five hours later, the psychiatrist drew clinic to a close. He was rewarded with a traditional body massage by a professional soccer player
in the village, who had talked with us at the coffee house upon our arrival. The village men looked on appreciatively, expressing sympathy
for hard work done graciously and well, and satisfaction that one of
their own could offer a gift of caring and healing in exchange. As we
left the meunasah, people asked us into their homes, urged more coffee, wished us safe journey. "Trauma stories," "trauma healing," and
"witnessing" took on special meaning that day, as the villagers told
their stories to the IOM medical team, the local university research-
ers, the American anthropologists, and to each other.

This visit led to the conceptualization of a mental health outreach
program staffed with Acehnese general practitioner physicians and
nurses trained in mental health and trauma treatment services and
psychiatric medications, with support of the district health services.

Post-Tsunami/Post-Conflict Aceh

The tsunami profoundly changed the dynamics of efforts to broker
a peace agreement between GAM and the Government of Indonesia.
All post-Suharto presidents of Indonesia—B. J. Habibie, Abdurrahman Wahid, and Megawati Soekarnoputri—had vowed to stop the
bloodshed in Aceh, but negotiations had failed, ceasefires had fallen
apart, and both President Wahid and President Megawati had insti-

tuted martial law, unleashing new violence. President Susilo Bambang Yudhoyono, who in 2004 had become the first president directly
elected, and many of his supporters, particularly Vice President Yusuf
Kalla, were deeply invested in brokering peace with GAM, but they
too had been unsuccessful prior to the tsunami (Aspinall 2005). The
tsunami had brought widespread international attention to Aceh,
and the massive humanitarian response made continued violence
by the military against the people of Aceh politically and morally
unsupportable.

The August 15, 2005, peace agreement signed in Helsinki was far
more wide-ranging than the previous cease-fires, initiating a serious
peace process under the watchful eye of a multinational Aceh Moni-
toring Mission staffed by European Union and regional observers. The
Helsinki Memorandum of Understanding led to a cessation of combat
and a near total end to incidents of violence, the immediate release of
Acehnese political prisoners, the demobilization of the GAM forces,
and the gradual withdrawal of non-Acehnese national military forces
from the province. Politically, the government of Indonesia granted
increased provincial autonomy to Aceh; in exchange, GAM leadership renounced claims to independence and were granted increased
control of Aceh's natural resources,[5] special political autonomy, including the right to hold direct elections for provincial governor and
district heads, and the right of Acehnese, including GAM members,
to form local political parties and run for office without membership
in a national party (Aspinall 2005).[6] GAM and other Acehnese comment positively on the peace accord, often wryly asking, "Why did
God send the tsunami? To punish us for our sins of evil living [a negative comment about the Shari'a and its supporters], or to bring about
an end to the conflict, human rights, and peace?" (MDG field notes,
February 2006).

Having developed a working relationship with members of President Susilo's government during early phases of the peace process,
IOM continued to be responsible for implementing "DDR" (Demobilization, Demilitarization, and Reintegration) activities specified in
the MOU agreement. Given the political success of the first and second psychosocial assessments, the World Bank and donor countries
supported IOM's development of a pilot mental health intervention
for high-conflict-affected villages. By January 2007 IOM launched
mobile mental health teams to work in collaboration with the district health offices. The teams of young Acehnese clinicians served

25 villages; by June of 2007 they had screened 15,000 villagers and placed 700 people under their care, 70 percent of whom were receiving medications for trauma, depression, or anxiety; a few were receiving psychopharmacological treatment for severe disorders such as schizophrenia or bipolar disorder. The decentralization of care from the national Ministry of Health to the District Health offices and to IOM was one way the government of Indonesia sought to address remainders of past violence.

The peace process itself was of course the greatest public mental health intervention in Aceh. Although villagers continued to exclaim, "Saya masih trauma!" ("I still have trauma!"), many clearly improved as the occupying "inorganic" military forces withdrew and peace and security appeared to be more the norm, reducing the symptoms of a "nervous state" and society (after E. James 2008, Taussig 1992). Nonetheless, psychological remainders of violence continued to affect many. After IOM published a second psychosocial needs assessment covering 14 districts in Aceh, the World Bank encouraged IOM to expand their mental health outreach to an additional 50 high-conflict-affected villages and to extend care to an additional 1200 people (Good, Good, and Grayman 2010).

On the Road with a Mobile Mental Health Team

In 2007, we joined one of the IOM outreach teams on a lengthy trip deep into the district countryside. The area seemed remote, though homes were strung for electricity and TV satellite dishes perched on roofs. There was no market center; the team's general medical clinic was held in the village meunasah, a large, simple unpainted wooden structure set in an open field. For almost four months, the team had been screening villagers and offering basic mental health care to those deemed in need, under the supervision of IOM's Acehnese psychiatrist. This village was among those chosen from conflict-affected villages. Medical visits bring out crowds. On the day of our visit, men, mostly older, and women and children of all ages arrived as soon as the medical team settled. Approximately a hundred persons filled the open-sided community center. The senior IOM psychiatrist spoke to community members as he observed the team physicians and nurses carrying out their examinations. We anthropologists were joined by a psychiatrist from Harvard who had tutored the team in psychiatric diagnosis and counseling on an earlier visit.

Toward the end of the treatment session, we spoke with some of the many women waiting to be treated. "Women here seem strong—who owns the houses?" There was much laughter; in chorus the women responded loudly, "Women do." An obviously silly question, lady! (Mary-Jo was checking out James Siegel's [2000] interpretations about female triviality and ownership.) Women then told how they responded to aggression from armed forces who swept into their villages. "We defended our land." Said one, "If I am to die, I will die bravely [*berani*]." Another, "I will die with my children, and I will die defending them and defending my land." Daughters, they said, were sent to town or other safe places during periods of conflict; sons accompanied their fathers into the forest. The women stayed behind in the houses they owned, with their small children, to guard their land and offspring. They described how soldiers "pulled my hair" or "crushed my toes with their boots." Their comments rolled forth. Told with fierce toughness, these brief stories seemed to be less victim talk and more solidarity talk—"these things happened to us and we resisted and persisted"—reflecting a community of defiance.

Many of the older men at clinic, thus the less well, were quiet, appearing sad. After this visit, when we had spent clinic time also playing with and taking digital pictures of small children, adolescent girls, and their mothers, we wondered, looking into their faces, what were the consequences of years of chronic conflict and family separation for community and families? What does the future hold for these children of Aceh who grew up in zones of insecurity and military conflict? What was the subjective reality of these parents, these children, of the youth soon to become adults? What were these villagers' imaginings about the future, and what does the current situation portend for their children? We wondered how they really felt about the peace process (they exclaim their approval), and what being an Acehnese and an Indonesian means in this post-MOU era.

A Post-Election Field Visit

We joined a medical/mental health outreach team almost a year after the visit noted above and after many district and gubernatorial elections had been held. Former GAM members were elected to almost all public offices. Those once imprisoned included the governor of the province, Irwandi, a University of Oregon–educated veterinarian (DVM) who had been swept out of prison by the tsunami, which had killed many of the inmates. Nurdin Abdurrahman—a teacher who had spent twelve years beginning in the 1970s in and out of jail and had suffered terrible torture, who had then established a foundation to treat trauma inflicted on political prisoners with EMDR (Eye Movement Desensitization and Reprocessing), and who had fled to Australia to pursue a master's degree and a new life—was elected *bupati*, or district head, in the district where IOM carried out its work. GAM insisted he return after the MOU and run for office in this most politically difficult and conflict-affected area. New leaders from the internet and cell phone, G3-savvy crowd of young highly educated Acehnese are also the face of the new politics in Aceh.

The "Peace Pill" and the Politics of Treatment

Following these many successful elections, and just prior to additional provincial assembly elections, we returned to Aceh. We accompanied the IOM medical mental health outreach team. Praise for the clinicians and stories of appreciation seemed truly genuine, especially given that Acehnese tend to be straightforward and not shy if they regard a service as less than acceptable. However, even if biased the response and stories of therapeutic benefit were impressive. An elderly village woman who described herself as an activist explained how after two months of treatment for depression and PTSD—due to conflict-related chronic trauma and anxiety—she awoke one day suddenly able to see in a new way. For years, she said, everything had seemed to be behind a scrim (a darkish screen), nothing was bright, everything was fuzzy and dark (she was not wearing glasses). One recent day, she awoke, and colors were bright, she could see people clearly, the brightness of the sky, the green leaves of the plants. She laughed as she described the change, delightful and vivid. She described her life before the MOU and the new politics—always tense, always worried about the soldiers searching for her sons, having to buffer her sons from the military. Her husband was much older than she and "did not leave the house much." Her son was shot on his motorcycle while trying to escape soldiers harassing young men in the village. He died later from his wounds. She told how she and others were exhausted by buffering the men. The women had to teach their young grandchildren—all the villages' young children—from the time they were toddlers to protect the men, their fathers and grandfathers and uncles. We taught them, she said, "*When you see the si'pai run, hide . . .*

if they ask you a question, say nothing . . . if they show you a gun and ask if your daddy has one of these, say no, if there is a gun in the house, say no . . . run, hide, do not speak to them." The term *si'pai*, as in other settings including Java and Basque country in Spain (see Good forthcoming, Aretxaga 2008), has a long lineage. It was a title for Ottoman landed warriors defending the empire's borderlands; a reference to the Indian soldiers of the British colonial army who fought in World War II and before; in Java, for a local soldier in the Dutch colonial army, seen as a Javanese betrayal of other the Javanese. In the pre-MOU era, were these "si'pai" betrayers of their own compatriots, enemies intimately known and feared—Indonesians, who should have been compatriots but were now part of the postcolonial forces?[7]

A woman in her forties from the same area was also suffering from a long depression in response to losing her sons, who fled to the city away from the conflict. One had been injured in a traffic accident, and had been near death before recovering. During our visit, the woman told us that after being treated for two months, she felt her normal self, could cook and farm; her husband confirmed that she had been deeply depressed and was now herself again (also a change occurring very recently, as she, like the woman above, had been treated for only three months). Her husband was excited and voluble, wanting to talk about more than just depression and recovery. He laughed as a small group of men and women gathered round, talking about how excited they were that they could directly vote for their own choices. He gave me a paper flag of the Partai Aceh, the newly formed political party formally representing much of the old GAM structure, and asked Mary-Jo what she thought it meant. She laughed—"You tell me." Euphorically he responded, "In the past you could be killed for having this flag on your wall. Now, now, we can celebrate it!" The once-depressed wife smiled gently as her husband expressed with laughter how he felt "inside" about being able to vote for his party, for his people—that he could be psychologically free to support those he trusted.

The provincial assembly election was to be held in a few weeks. Party flags were flying everywhere in villages, on highways, in towns, on private as well as public spaces, in party buildings painted red if they belonged to the Partai Aceh party, or blue if they belonged to one of the others. As we drove back the five hours to Banda Aceh, it seemed that not all politics lead to trauma, and that in Aceh we were witnessing some Acehnese citizens experiencing a certain kind of politics as having a healing effect. Certainly the politics of peace appears to provide some balm to those who have suffered trauma from years of conflict.

Is Aceh a Laboratory for New Modes of Governance?

The successful negotiation of the Memorandum of Understanding between the Government of Indonesia and the Free Aceh Movement, signed in Helsinki August 15, 2005, represented more than an agreement to end fighting between the two parties. It represented a commitment to profound changes in the relations between Indonesia's central government and one of its most contentious provincial "peripheries." The agreement that Aceh should be allowed to form local political parties, rather than field candidates exclusively through existing national parties, as required for other provinces, was one of the most intensely contested elements in the negotiations—and later in the parliament's ratification of the MOU—but it was the crucial gain for GAM, who gave up all claims to independence in the final signed agreement. The election of former GAM leader Irwandi Yusuf as Governor of Nanggroe Aceh Darrusalam, the "nation" of Aceh, in December 2006 marked a critical step forward in the transformation of relations. He, like other GAM leaders in subsequent district elections, ran as an "independent" candidate rather than under a party banner, another innovation in governance allowing for GAM to be transformed from a resistance movement into a local, perhaps somewhat "ethnonational" political movement within the context of the unitary state of Indonesia. The formal registration of Partai Aceh in July 2008, which brought together a significant portion of the diverse GAM leadership under a single party banner, as well as the registration of several other local parties, each representing different elements in the nationalist struggle, moved this transformative process dramatically forward.

The massive response to the tsunami and the emergence of a complex peace process have generated numerous new institutions linking the central government to the province of Aceh in quite new ways. The Aceh-Nias Rehabilitation and Reconstruction Agency (BRR), which managed international and national funds for post-tsunami reconstruction; the Aceh Reintegration Agency (BRA), charged with a significant role in re-integrating former combatants into civil society; the Forum for Communications and Coordination (FKK), which provided a formal central government and military representation in the peace negotiations; along with many other formal institutions and a burgeoning group of civil society organizations, all provided new structures for reconstituting relations between Aceh and Jakarta.

It was, however, the ruling by the Supreme Court of Indonesia that local elections throughout the country could field independent candidates in local and provincial elections, citing the precedent of Aceh, that makes clear that what is happening in Aceh has the potential to provide new models for center-periphery governance throughout Indonesia. Similarly, and of longer standing, the central government support for the institution of Shari'a law in Aceh—undertaken for complex political reasons in the midst of the conflict, against the wishes of many, perhaps a majority of Acehnese—has also provided a model closely watched by other provinces and districts, highly contested throughout the country. What these and many other innovations in the relations between Aceh and Jakarta suggest is that Aceh has emerged as a kind of laboratory for new forms of governance, undertaken in the context of a broader process of decentralization launched during the presidency of B. J. Habibie.

Although the peace process has continued without any major incidents for more than three years at the time of the writing of this paper, the outcome remains very much in question. Threats by some national political party leaders to divide Aceh into three provinces, supposedly to accede to the desires for ethnic minority Gayo people and others in Aceh's central highlands, and rumors that the military is quietly rebuilding village posts throughout the province are reminders that many in the central government have not fully accepted the new forms of sovereignty in Aceh. And many Acehnese who have watched cycles of peace and conflict throughout their lifetime remain skeptical. From an optimistic view, many Acehnese, young and old, are participating in a precarious but exciting experiment as they redefine their political subjectivity, from having been activists, combatants, or exiles during the conflict to becoming active participants in new forms of governing Aceh. For nearly all persons in the villages in which we work, the desire for peace is paramount, as is the excitement of rebuilding Aceh under the banner of Acehnese local parties and emerging forms of autonomy. We remain guardedly optimistic that all sides recognize how much there would be to lose should the conflict begin again, and that the peace process has a genuine opportunity to develop new forms of governance in Indonesia.

Epilogue: Reflections on Aceh and Sri Lanka

Aceh and Sri Lanka both represent postcolonial conflicts (Good et al. 2008). For Aceh, the narrative of the Acehnese struggle for independence against the Dutch, linked to a remembered history of an Acehnese nation or sultanate, vies with the national narrative of a joined struggle by persons from around the enormously complex archipelago against colonial powers as part of the making of the Indonesian nation, a narrative in which Aceh plays a significant role. Memories of betrayals by "Jakarta"—first by President Sukarno, then by his daughter President Megawati—are told by villagers with a deep historical consciousness, and are linked to the history of colonial si'pai and betrayals. We have suggested that the steps taken by President Susilo Bambang Yudhoyono and Vice President Yusuf Kalla, newly and directly elected, reflecting their commitment to resolving the Aceh conflict even before the tsunami and supported strongly after the signing of the MOU, has made possible the reconstituting of relations between Aceh and the central government. Taken in the context of the sprawling island nation, of which Aceh is a tiny part, the conflict never engulfed the whole of Indonesia, as in Sri Lanka, and the massive international influx and outpouring of Indonesian sentiments following the tsunami allowed for a significant change in center-periphery relations.

It is not our place to suggest exactly why similar processes did not follow the tsunami in Sri Lanka. Namalie Jayasinghe, in her Master of Science thesis for the London School of Economics, "Post-Tsunami Sri Lanka and Ethnic Conflict" (2006), identifies many failures of the Sri Lankan government to provide an equitable use of international tsunami funds for the afflicted Tamil and Sinhalese populations. Of particular relevance is her argument that in contrast to GAM, which had human rights international status as a separatist group, the Tamil Tigers were categorized as terrorists, and were therefore unable to receive international funds or provide local relief to regions where the government was unwelcome. This difference in legal status meant that the localization of recovery was blocked; postdisaster power was not shared and therefore negotiations were less likely to grow out of the disaster. Jayasinghe lays greatest blame on the Sri Lankan political leadership for its lack of just distribution of relief and its fueling of ferocious ethnic hostilities in Sri Lanka through the aggressive use of military force and its ideology of ethnonationalism.

What we want to suggest, simply, is that sustained comparative examination of ethnonational conflicts as advocated by Stanley Tambiah has great potential for enhancing our understanding of emerging forms of governance in postcolonial societies. Such understanding is urgent, given the terrible spread of violence in what were once described as "traditional" societies. Tambi's work provides a model of scholarship and passion that need to be brought to such work and to the role of anthropologists working in such complex settings if we are to contribute to processes of human rights and peace building.

A Tale of Two Affects:
Humanitarianism and Professionalism
in Red Cross Aid Work

Liisa Malkki

This brief essay represents a fragment of a research project on the ethics and politics of humanitarian practices in the International Committee of the Red Cross (ICRC) and a related national-level organization, the Finnish Red Cross (FRC). I have worked mostly with Finnish medical professionals—nurses and doctors—who have gone on international ICRC and FRC missions, and, to a lesser extent, with Red Cross professionals who work domestically in Finland. I have also interviewed FRC staff in logistics, finance, administration, transportation, and other areas. In an effort to understand the forms and uses of affect among these aid workers, and in the institution they serve, I have in addition interviewed Red Cross therapists who offer counseling to the workers.

Here, I will try to give an account of two of the key affective regimes or sensibilities that are both present in Red Cross work and yet appear to be incommensurable. (This is not to say, of course, that there are not other kinds of emotions also at play.) The first of the two is a "humanitarian sensibility" that hails a generalized suffering humanity, or, in another well-known formulation, the "suffering stranger";

the other is an unsentimental, consummate professionalism. I will end by suggesting that these two very different, sometimes opposed affective sensibilities are nonetheless "recursively and dialectically related" (Tambiah 1985b, 13), often for good reasons

The opposition between the sentimental and the professional parallels another. On the one hand, there is the humanitarian sensibility that expects to encounter need and suffering on a cosmological, universal scale (generalized human suffering) and attributes mythico-historical significance—extraordinariness—to it. Figures that enable the visualization of this human suffering include the famished young child and chaotic masses of refugees. On the other hand, there are forms of need and suffering that are encountered as mundane and ordinary—that is, not *necessarily* especially meaningful in a moral, cosmological sense. One representative figure here might be a grown man panhandling. He might provoke discomfiting guilt about "our society" and its inequalities, but not automatic discussions about bare human suffering (Arendt 1979, Agamben 1998).

I begin with an anecdote to draw the difference more sharply. On a summer evening in Montreal, my family and I attended the engagement party of a young Hutu couple from Burundi. They had both been granted asylum in Canada after fleeing genocidal violence and were beginning life in the "New World." I stood outside a community hall, one in a large crowd of people milling about. Suddenly a very young girl ran up to me. She looked like a little wedding cake in her extravagance of white lace. She tugged at my dress urgently: "Je dois faire caca!!" Hesitant to take her to the bathroom, I asked, "Where is your mother?" She snapped: "Ma mere est morte!" And then, with impatient emphasis, she repeated in English: "My mother is dead!" I automatically assumed that her mother had died in one or another episode of genocidal violence in Central Africa. It turned out that she had, in fact, died recently of cancer in Canada. I had assumed, in other words, an extraordinary and yet generic death that somehow stood, metonymically, for "human suffering" in Africa. What had actually happened was quite particular and cruelly ordinary. This abrupt shift in my thinking from the general to the particular revealed a humanitarian sensibility in my own habits of thought and feeling—or, perhaps better, a kind of habituated, affective humanitarianism.

Clearly, humanitarianism is not only a matter of institutions and international law, mandates and interventions; it is also a mobile "affective state" with significant effects (Stoler 2004). Sometimes—in the form of a widely shared sensibility—it takes on the structural heft of an ideological apparatus in an Althusserian sense. At other times, it appears in the form of something more contingent and individual—perhaps as a private rush of emotion.

In his essay "Capitalism and the Origins of the Humanitarian Sensibility" (1998), Thomas Haskell traces the historical interrelationships among capitalism, the abolition of slavery, and key perceptual shifts in "conventions of moral responsibility" (238) between 1750 and 1850. He points out that while emotion has "the power to influence perception," perception can also shape emotion, and both are affected by (historical and cultural) convention (239). It is convention (not self-deception or "false consciousness"), he writes, that delineates perceptions of moral responsibility (249). "These conventions allow us to confine our humane acts to a fraction of suffering humanity without feeling that we have thereby *intended,* in any way, or *caused,* in any morally significant way, the evils that we do not relieve" (249; emphases in the original). I would suggest that at issue is not only the reckoning of causality and the calibrating of responsibility, but also the social imagination and affective visualization of suffering in itself, sometimes regardless of how relationality is experienced. Some kinds of suffering assault contemporary emotions and sensibilities (especially in the wealthy North) much more sharply than do others. The suffering of children and animals (especially baby animals) is often experienced as a categorical abomination an order of magnitude greater than that of, say, again, grown men. It gets "under one's skin." This sort of sensibility is easy to condescend to in the name of "real politics" and "real aid." Yet, it is far from trivial as a sociopolitical phenomenon and as an aspect of humanitarian practice.

The humanitarian sensibility that I have so briefly sketched here is (like internationalism) peculiarly robust in the Nordic countries. It is cultivated through innumerable gentle pedagogies, among them calls for citizens to make hand-knitted socks and sweaters, blankets and toys, for people in need. The annual Hunger Day (Nalkapaiva) has been a nationwide Red Cross event with distinct ritual qualities since 1981, and its blood drives are also a familiar post-Second World War practice (Hytonen 2002). Humanitarian organizations like the Red Cross have long exercised such pedagogies of power, and have in this sense been a part of the sentimental education for citizenship.

The Finnish Red Cross operations budget comes from three principal sources: individual donations, the Finnish Foreign Ministry, and the European Union. It is the private donations that are the primary connecting point between the humanitarian sensibility and the other affective configuration that I will trace here. The Finnish Red Cross, like other national Red Cross and Red Crescent societies, and indeed like the ICRC, depends financially upon the public's humanitarian sensibility. The Red Cross—like so many other organizations—is keenly aware of the importance of appearing and acting as a humanitarian organization. Many of the citizens who make donations and pay their annual membership dues are motivated and moved by a humanitarian sensibility of the kind described by Haskell.

In the autumn of 2006, the Finnish Red Cross sent out a call to its entire membership, drawing special attention to the predicament of children in political conflicts and natural disasters around the world. The call was also published in a 2006 knitting book by Anu Harkki, whose brainchild the campaign was; it was also featured in several magazines and circulated on the web. The public in Finland were invited to knit so-called aid bunnies (*apupupu*, singular) to comfort these children in their hospital beds, in camps, or in other frightening contexts. The aid bunnies are a version of the older "Trauma Teddy" long used by the British and Australian Red Crosses. They belong to a class of objects often referred to as "therapy toys." In the Finnish campaign, then, precise instructions were given as to the materials to be used, the size and shape of the bunnies, the details of their faces, and so forth. An impressive 11,000 aid bunnies had arrived at the central Red Cross logistics center of Kalkku in the city of Tampere by the time of my visit there in the summer of 2007, and by the end of the campaign at Christmas of that year, more than 25,000 had been donated. Many knitters expressed disappointment and frustration (online and in conversation) that no more bunnies were accepted after that. The campaign that followed—"Pipoapua Pohjolasta!"—called for warm woolen caps and mittens. It did not capture the public's imagination to the degree that the aid bunnies had done.

A Red Cross program officer commented on the aid bunny campaign: "People here [in Finland] get very excited about [this way of helping].... [O]ne elderly lady brought in 130 bunnies when the Red Cross celebrated its anniversary." She had knitted all of them. In conversations with Red Cross staff, the aid bunnies sparked quite a bit of good-humored joking. But the staff also seemed to be respectful and even moved by the woman's gesture.

In a group discussion with Red Cross staff, one man said: "Since it's a lot of work [to make these bunnies, the donors] want to know, 'So, where's this one going?'" Another added that it is understandable to feel that way, "since the bunnies are made by hand all by oneself; it's a very personal way of participating." A young woman explained, "We always tell them that we can't individualize [*yksiloida*] anybody. We can't determine whether it will go to a certain country or a certain group. How they get distributed depends on the need there [abroad]." The bunny is felt to be a part of its maker; like an *aide-memoire,* it is an *aide-imagination* enabling its maker to imagine a world to which s/he is connected.[1]

One young man explained earnestly: "[T]his is a really good model because it's a concrete way of doing something, and since it is targeted at kids on top of that, it appeals even more.... It's great that the schools are [involved] in [these craft projects], too.... The Red Cross becomes better known and more generally attitudes [may change for the better] and then, later, your purse strings will open more easily if you know more and can *imagine* [where the aid goes]." Then one intensely quiet man spoke up: "We've got 11,000 aid bunnies here; we're *drowning* in them.... The countries that request aid from us, well, they're not familiar with aid bunnies! They don't *request* bunnies!" The group of us dissolved in laughter. Then the conversation continued:

> *Kaija* (a logistics expert): You know, the bunnies also involve marketing issues.... It feels silly to market aid bunnies...
>
> *Matti* (grinning): [Yeah, There you are, saying,] "And we even have these bunnies for you!"
>
> *Ilona:* Offhand one could suppose that parents would think that their child needs proper shoes—so, umm, at that point that aid bunny could even be irritating somehow.
>
> *Mikko:* The bunny or the shoes...
>
> *Kaija:* After the Bam earthquake, [so many people] donated balls and everything...and how much time it took to sort out these [toys] when we were really busy with real things and essential supplies!! Balls and bunnies must come after these.

At least some shipments of aid bunnies have been held up or never delivered. This was the case with a shipment to Lebanon. As of this writing, the bunnies are still on standby in Jordan and, as one person quipped, "Maybe they'll get through somehow—maybe as stow-aways." The bunnies had been turned away at the border because they had failed to conform to international toy safety standards; they were handmade and the knitting wool lacked fire retardant. (Ironically, pure lambswool is naturally quite nonflammable, and synthetic fire retardants have been shown to be carcinogenic.) Many bunnies have gotten through, however. Shipments have gone with the Red Cross aid deliveries to Nepal, Mongolia, China, Palestine, Morocco, Tunisia, Ukraine, White Russia, and Tadjikistan.

So, what about the aid bunnies as an object of critical analysis? First, they help to demonstrate how a domestically cultivated humanitarian sensibility enables a widely shared, universalizing social imagination of human need and suffering "out in the world" (*maailmalla*). Soft and colorful, the aid bunnies are a concrete, home-made bridge for the humanitarian imagination to travel. Second, they suggest that children as sufferers, as symbols of a suffering humanity, are good to think (Tambiah 1985b). Perhaps they are also *good to feel*.

But here is the interesting thing: the humanitarian sensibility historically so strongly cultivated by the Red Cross and other like organizations is *at odds* with the *professional* dispositions of actual Red Cross aid workers today. These workers' de facto *ideal* is that of the consummate professional. They are highly trained and specialized. These people conform at best uneasily to the mass-mediated figure of the (stereotypically Western, and Northern) humanitarian as Good Samaritan (Waters 2001) slogging away in faraway crisis zones on behalf of a suffering world.

Professional practices never quite fit the institutional mandates or affective structures that produce them.[2] They are negotiated in real time, often in the chaotic and hard-to-decipher realities of specific circumstances. Maybe these professional practices are always, simultaneously, more and less than the lofty codifications of mandates and the social imagination of human suffering in the abstract. In trying to think about the internationalist professionalism that came through so clearly in the Red Cross interviews, I went to Emile Durkheim. Writing about how diverse and even incompatible professional ethics can be (and *should* be), Durkheim observed:

> As professors, we have duties which are not those of merchants. Those of the industrialist are quite different from those of the soldier, those of the soldier different from those of the priest, and

so on .... We might say in this connection that there as many
forms of morals as there are different callings, and since, in theory,
each individual carries on only one calling, the result is that these
different forms of morals apply to entirely different groups of
individuals. These differences may even go so far as to present a
clear contrast. Of these morals, not only is one kind distinct from
the other, but between some kinds there is real opposition. The scientist has the duty of developing his critical sense, of submitting
his judgment to no authority other than reason; he must school
himself to have an open mind. The priest or the soldier, in some
respects, have a wholly different duty. Passive obedience, within
prescribed limits, may for them be obligatory. *It is the doctor's duty
on occasion to lie, or not to tell the truth he knows.* A man of the other
professions has a contrary duty. Here, then, we find within every
society a plurality of morals that operate on parallel lines....
*This moral particularism—if we may call it so—which has no place in
individual morals ... goes on to reach its climax in professional ethics,
to decline with civic morals and to pass away once more with the morals
that govern relations among men as human beings.* (Durkheim 1957, 5;
emphases added)

In the passage above, Durkheim speaks of each of the different professional occupations—soldier, priest, merchant, scientist, doctor—as
a *calling*. There is much of that in contemporary humanitarian practices, as in our own scholarly practices. I assumed that this was what I
would find among the Finnish medical professionals.

One of my early approaches to the question of humanitarianism
as "service to humanity" was to ask the Red Cross nurses and doctors
in Helsinki what ideals or professional role models they might have. I
offered as possible models famous, idealized medical humanitarians
such as Nurse Nightingale, the classic Lady with the Lamp; Mother
Teresa; Albert Schweitzer; and even the late Princess Diana. Later, I
proffered the United Nations soldier or peace-keeper. In retrospect,
I realize that these models were not just ideal-typical models for me;
they were also caricatures. I had assumed, ungenerously, that I would
hear a great deal about the importance of earnest international service and "doing good" on behalf of an always distant suffering humanity. My respondents usually raised an eyebrow at this. They answered thoughtfully, but critically, with a refusal. A former director of
the international section of the Finnish Red Cross told me early on
that the very term *humanitarianism* was a troubled one. I should have

paid more attention to her passing comment. Instead, I persisted in looking for evidence of a calling in service to humanity.

I asked a nurse who was a veteran of many ICRC missions: "Does anyone expect a Nurse Nightingale or Princess Diana figure of you? How do you react?" Amused and slightly impatient, she answered:

> I don't believe anyone expects that sort of Mother Teresa of me. In my opinion those are not values—for me personally. I don't aspire to anything like that. For me, it's important how I do my work, and how I get a contact to those people I'm helping. I don't see myself as a person who'd like to become the flagship of some system or organization. Of course, if one must, if the importance of the issue demands it, perhaps then.... [But no], I don't think anyone expects [a Mother Teresa] of me, and least of all do I expect it of myself. Because, personally, I don't see it as important—to be some extremely "important" person. It's the work, what I do; that's what's most important to me—that the community can grow and that those being helped can come to foreground more than me.

I asked a doctor this time: "Is your work a calling or a job or ...?" She replied with a mischievous smile:

> Well, the Red Cross pays good salaries. So that already drops you from the pinnacles of self-sacrifice. Those [interested in self-sacrifice], they go to the MSF [Médecins sans Frontiéres, Doctors Without Borders] where they pay minimum wages—people who have that kind of concern uppermost.... [T]hose who have only the most cursory understanding of this [work], they say, "Oh, I admire you so much for going there to do something good.... I remember when we were on a [ten-week] training course in Copenhagen; there was a girl there who had come ... We were all doctors. ... She had these sorts of ideas that she was going "to do good in India"—but she fell back to earth pretty quickly. She quit the course after two weeks. At the Red Cross course, there was no one who was so exaggeratedly that way [bent on self-sacrifice]. There [abroad], in practice, I haven't seen any sort of Nurse Nightingale thing among the nurses or doctors. But perhaps those people more often go [on international missions] through religious organizations? In my opinion, you don't need those sorts of people there. I think it should be people with a pretty solid grip [*jämäkkä ote*] who get sent there.... Of course, the two [models, of the calling and the solid professionalism] don't necessarily exclude each other.

In short, the FRC people were not stereotypical humanitarians with a calling to help humanity, let alone to sacrifice themselves for its sake. They were not soldiers, either—and certainly not missionaries. They were internationalist professionals both in practice and in occupational disposition.

Yet these generally unsentimental professionals were also entangled with (and sometimes relied on) humanitarian affect. In the most obvious sense, they knew perfectly well that their aid work depended to a significant degree on fund-raising that could mobilize humanitarian affective states. But further, most of the people I worked with recognized that their professional and ethical motivations for this work and their emotional reactions to it were always in some measure shaped by and articulated in relation to the humanitarian sensibility (even if this was often a relation of opposition). Many sought to put a critical distance between themselves and that sensibility, but at the same time recognized the perennial possibility of their own emotional vulnerability.

What's more, the "performative efficacy" (Tambiah 1985b) and the *reception* of the Red Cross as a neutral, impartial, and *specifically humanitarian* organization protect the aid workers in significant political, diplomatic, and physical ways. So, curiously, the medical and other aid work accomplished by highly professionalized teams around the world can be said to take place under the enchanted blanket of the more sentimental humanitarian ideal.[3]

There was an additional protection afforded by cool-headed, unsentimental professionalism: that professionalism could act as a strong and necessary psychic shield for aid workers. One therapist explained that in crises like the Rwanda genocide, the surgeon just "operates and operates and operates" without having to think about the individuality or particular personhood of the body under the sheet. Thus, professionalism shelters people from different forms of excess: weepy sentimentalism, compassion fatigue, and emotional breakdowns.[4]

The contemporary humanitarian social imagination can visualize great horror in zones of crisis and emergency—in states of exception, as some would argue. Agamben and others have written about states of exception as sites where law and normality are suspended. Concentration and refugee camps have often been characterized as exceptional in this sense. If we think, for example, of refugees as "bare humanity" trapped in these zones, it is possible to see states of exception, at least from afar. But if we shift the lens to *occupational categories* in the camps—the doctors and nurses, transport and logistics officers—then we do not see bare humanity; we see aid workers for whom the camp is by no means a state of exception. It is a site for the implementation of mundane, standard procedures and coordinated teamwork. At this level, it is ordinary. This is not to say that the aid workers I interviewed never felt shock. Each of them had memories of moments or relationships that made a crack in their psychically sheltering professionalism, and each had had experiences that were in fact singular and *extraordinary*. (This is the subject of another paper in which I discuss emotions that are neither professional nor humanitarian.)

So, delicate balancing acts may be necessary for aid work to proceed. The pendulum can swing too far—from an excess of emotion to its chilling absence. There was the case, for instance, of the surgeon who went on an international Red Cross mission solely to get an intensive stretch of war surgery under his belt, as this would help him to do his work better in his highly specialized medical job in Finland. The therapist who mentioned this case clearly considered it an instance of troubling coldness.

Referring to a particular natural disaster, the therapist described how doctors, mostly men, but some women too, began to behave under stress: "There was competition as to who could stay awake the longest. . . . That was totally idiotic [and irresponsible]! . . . The doctors would be in a real *hurmiotila* [a trance or a state of ecstasy] in very intensive work situations. [One can] develop a *himo* [a lust, a craving] for these extreme conditions." In *Regarding the Pain of Others* (2003), Susan Sontag discusses "the perennial seductiveness of war" (122). Clearly, practices like medical aid or peace-keeping can have a similar pull. Trance states and cravings are not exactly devoid of affect, of course, but they do tend to trouble the humanitarian sensibility as well as the expectation of professionalism.

The hoary old opposition between reason and emotion is not what is at issue here. It is not the case that Red Cross professionalism is interchangeable with rationality while the humanitarian sensibility is synonymous with emotion. Otherwise put, it is not the case that professionalism is a form of practical reason and humanitarianism a kind of emoting or magical thinking alone. A therapist I spoke with dismissed the opposition quite neatly: "If a person is totally without feelings, she may not be able to recognize dangers [early enough] nor to evaluate situations [astutely]. . . . This is some kind of urban legend or illusion—that the so-called 'sensible people' [*jarkevat ihmiset*] don't emote [*tunteilla*] and *that* is why they are sensible."

I have tried here to describe the contrast between the humanitarian sensibility, on the one hand, and the professional sensibility, on the other, as two mobile affective states. I also want to suggest that while these two sensibilities are incommensurable in important ways, they are dialectically related and interdependent. Thus, professionalism is not a lack of affect. Rather, it is itself a kind of affect. Both affective configurations facilitate the work that needs doing. The humanitarian sensibility is not therefore irrelevant to the professionals' work. This is not a matter of which affect or sensibility is genuine; both are affects-for-use—they are *good to feel*—and both may be necessary to the job at hand.

At the Base of Local
and Transnational Conflicts:
The Political Uses of Inferiorization

Emiko Ohnuki-Tierney

Magisterial theoretical contributions, always based on solid and ex-
haustive historical and ethnographic data, are what first come to
our mind when we think of Stanley Jeyaraja Tambiah. But I am now
keenly aware that his work, as most evident in his *Leveling Crowds*
(1996), has also been rooted in his passionate concern with injustice and inequality in the realpolitik of the past and present, when
the forces of Western imperialism have not abated after decolonization but increased in ferocity as the United States has become a new
center of imperial domination. Tambiah sees a close connection between political, economic, and cultural inequality in geopolitics and
violence at the local level. His effort to analyze the factors that cause
violence has been driven by his commitment to domestic and international peace. His goal has been to seek "plausible and coherent answers" to the question of why ethnicity and ethnonationalism have
been "potent bases for collective mobilization and are powerfully at
work in many modern contexts at a time when global processes of
modernization and homogenization are alleged to be dominant cur-

rents" (Tambiah 1996a, 138). He identifies the root cause as imperialism, which prompts ethnonational resistance to it:

> The liberal democracy at home in Western Europe and the United States could assume the fierce shape of authoritarian rule abroad, the exploitation of native labor and resources, and the inferiorization, if not erosion, of the cultures of the colonized. This inferiorization and threat of cultural extinction in large part lies behind the rise of Islamic fundamentalism, Buddhist "nationalism," Hindu nationalism, and other such reactions, and their retaliatory attitude to Western economic affluence and domination, political supremacy, alleged consumerist values, celebration of sexual eroticism, erosion of family durability, alleged "privatization" of religion and separation of religion from affairs of state, and so on. (Tambiah 1996b, 14)

In Tambiah's analysis, geopolitical inequalities sow the seeds of local violence. Virulent forces of various "nationalisms" have risen as a result of the authoritarian rule executed by nations that espouse liberal democracy for their own citizens.

Let me first emphasize that Tambiah's theoretical formulation is deeply contextualized in a given sociopolitical local context, which is in turn embedded in geopolitics. Therefore it is basically different from the "Othering," Orientalism, and other related concepts in cultural studies and in some quarters in anthropology that are not situated in sociopolitical contexts. Thus, in 1996, Tambiah offered a brilliant blueprint predicting the mess that the United States currently faces: authoritarian rule abroad, the exploitation of natural, human, and economic resources, and the inferiorization of subject peoples. As the years pass and a more sober understanding of the Middle East is emerging, we understand that the galvanizing point for Osama bin Laden and other "militant" leaders has been the humiliation and suffering of Muslims imposed by non-Muslims (Bin Laden 2005), a dynamic that cannot be reduced to the theological arguments of Islamic fundamentalists that some Americans have identified as the cause of terrorist attacks, thereby assuming the cause to be located only within.

In this essay, I extend Tambiah's insights into transnational conflicts—the processes through which "enemies" of empire are inferiorized—by examining popular and academic explanations of those

who destroyed the World Trade Center, which has become the
Ur-model for multifarious instances of contemporary terrorism.
This example involves the construction of the "brown menace" at
the time of the September 11 event, for which the "yellow menace"
was summoned as a precedent. This article is neither on the current
"terrorist attacks," nor about the Middle East. Nor is its purpose to
whitewash the Japanese aggressions and their consequences. The
example is used to illuminate a broader issue that Tambiah has
raised—the construction of the Other for political purposes by powerful nations.

The Master Narrative for the September 11 Event

Many historical facts are placed in the dustbin of history, to use Walter
Benjamin's well-known expression. But rarely do we see a caricature
repeatedly replacing historical information, as happened in the case
of the *tokkōtai*, known outside of Japan as *kamikaze*, which became
synonymous with reckless, inscrutable, fanatic chauvinists.

Using this image and the fear that it arouses in the popular imagination, the American government and mass media framed 9/11 with
the master trope of Pearl Harbor: the attack on the Twin Towers in
New York and the Pentagon was the "homeland attack," analogous to
the attack on Pearl Harbor by "kamikaze" pilots that initiated the Pacific Front of World War II. The attack was framed as war when it was
not, enabling the scenario to end with the symbolic recapture of the
homeland by the raising of the American flag at ground zero in New
York, just as the Marines did on Iwo Jima. The kamikaze became the
model for interpreting suicide bombers in the Middle East and elsewhere. Let me first show how the master narrative was presented and
how I interpret it.

The major frame used exclusively by the government and predom-
inant in the mass media, as in the double-column article in the *New
York Times* of December 2, 2001, may be schematized as in Table 14-1.

The World Trade Center attack was as visually spectacular as it was
historically significant. The perpetrators on 9/11 were a brown menace to the American homeland, and their racialization was reinforced
by another racial metaphor, the Yellow Peril that attacked Pearl Harbor. The United States declared a divine right to impose "democracy"
on its inferiors even when the entire population might be killed off,

Table 14-1. The Narrative Frame

The Day of Infamy:	12/7, 1941	9/11, 2001
The Homeland Attack:	Pearl Harbor	The Twin Towers and the Pentagon
The Evil:	Yellow Peril	Menacing brown "Arabs"
The Leaders:	Tōjō/Emperor Shōwa	Osama bin Laden and Saddam Hussein
The Ideology:	Shintoism	Islamic fundamentalism
Homeland Recapture:	Iwo Jima flag hoisting	NYC flag raising
Shock and Awe:	Atomic bombs	Massive military attack on and occupation of Iraq
After the Victory:	Successful democratization	"Reconstruction" and "democratization" of Iraq

as long as their oil fields were left intact. Since the Japanese had been "tamed" by the successful introduction of democracy in Japan, the U.S. government tried to convince the American people that the Iraqis too would be pacified and embrace democracy, the gift of the United States to the world.

The constructed analogy between the two events made it possible for the government to construe 9/11 as the homeland attack; "*devoir de mémoire*" (Todorov 2000) was to be engraved in the minds of citizens. The overall effect of this master trope may be similar to what Michael Silverstein, using Vygotzkian complex thinking, shows so effectively, with devastating humor, about George W. Bush's speech:

> Such thought-about but unfocused narrative relations, if seized upon by a pregnant captioning label of image, suddenly make the whole analogical series take on a definitive identity—in fact retrospectively a *necessary* identity that we now recognize as so many examples of one underlying principle, conceptually implicit, even immanent. "So *that's* what it is!" (Silverstein 2003, 23)

This master narrative succeeded in becoming the dominant interpretive frame even after its key elements began to fall apart, with the identity of the evil enemy leader shifting from Osama bin Laden to Saddam Hussein as the two were said to be connected, even though no weapons of mass destruction were found in Iraq.

As the Middle East crisis intensified, the mass media daily reported deadly attacks by suicide bombers not only in Iraq and Afghanistan but in the Israel/Palestine conflict zone and beyond, in Chechnya, in Indonesia, and in the Philippines. For all those who "kill themselves in order to kill the enemy," the Japanese kamikaze became the model of the inscrutable Other. On the need for a historical precedent for an understanding of a current phenomenon, Niall Ferguson, a prominent British historian at Harvard, explains: "As for the tactic of flying planes directly at populous targets, what else were the 3,913 Japanese pilots doing who killed themselves and many more American servicemen flying kamikaze missions in 1944 and 1945?" (Ferguson 2001, 77–78). The "kamikaze" pilots at Pearl Harbor were different from those at the end of the war to whom Ferguson refers. The planes for the Pearl Harbor attack were equipped for the pilots to return to the aircraft carrier waiting off Oahu, whereas those at the end of the war were sent on missions meant to be one way. At any rate, as the days and weeks went by, the use of the "kamikaze" as the model for Middle Eastern terrorism intensified and remained in the forefront of major newspapers.

History as Ideology; or, Metaphors We Are Deceived By

Let us now examine the 9/11 narrative against historical facts. It has become clear that U.S. intelligence agencies failed to detect the 9/11 plan in advance, though they had been aware that Al Qaeda posed a danger. The attack on Pearl Harbor was not as unexpected and unprovoked. Japan's plan for aggression had been known for quite a while, and even the site for the attack was made known in advance to U.S. leaders (Persico 2004; Vlastos 2001). The Pearl Harbor attack was carried out by military order by uniformed armed forces of a nation-state at war. In contrast, the 9/11 attack was carried out by a small number of individuals who did not act as members of a nation-state at war. They were said to be motivated by Islamic fundamentalism. The attacks on the World Trade Center and the Pentagon were directed at the economic and symbolic center and the military center of the American empire. During World War II Hawaii was not the American "homeland"; it was a colonial possession, annexed and made a territory by the United States in 1898. Hawaii became the fiftieth state only in 1959, close to twenty years after the attack on Pearl Harbor.

Its largely nonwhite population made it a marginal place, and it had a great deal of difficulty being admitted to statehood. Moreover, Pearl Harbor was a major U.S. military base, the headquarters of the entire Pacific Fleet. The Japanese attack on the base intentionally avoided civilian casualties. The attack on the Twin Towers was aimed exclusively at civilians, though the Pentagon was certainly a military target. The dramatic finale for 9/11 was the raising of the American flag by New York City firefighters, which was seen as analogous to the hoisting of "Old Glory" on Iwo Jima. But the two are quite different: six Marines hoisted the flag on Iwo Jima during (not after) a fierce battle (Bradley 2000), but Iwo Jima was not a part of either the Japanese or the American homeland.

U.S. military leaders considered that only the catastrophic results of the atomic bomb would end the war, since the Japanese, who would kill themselves as kamikaze pilots in 1944 and 1945, were the utterly inscrutable Other. Despite the effort by George Taylor, the British historian of China, to "convince the U.S. military that they did not have to engage in acts of genocidal annihilation to end the war," presidents Roosevelt and Truman, their advisers, and military leaders "were convinced that the Japanese were 'culturally incapable of surrender' and that they would have to fight to the very last Japanese citizen" (Price 2002, 18).

Iraqis too were portrayed as utterly Other in the U.S. media. It was alleged that like the Japanese, the Iraqis—or at least the "Saddam loyalists"—would not surrender until their country had been destroyed, justifying the invasion of Iraq by the massive military forces of the "coalition of the willing," primarily American and British, in order to crush any possible opposition. The aftermath, too, was imagined as a process of democratization, as had been carried out in Japan.

Despite rising criticisms of the invasion and occupation of Iraq, through the "dangerous use of historical analogy" (Vlastos 2001) or the use of a "flawed and disturbing analogy" (Cummings 2001) the construction became historical fact. Newspapers and broadcast media featured the juxtaposition of Pearl Harbor with the fiery collapse of the World Trade Center.[1] On December 2, 2001, the *New York Times* published an article by Greg Ryan with a double column for "The Day of Infamy." The column included the two flag-hoisting scenes, on Iwo Jima in 1945 and at ground zero in New York in 2001, together with a caricature of the Japanese, with a Tōjō, with round glasses, buck teeth, and hands with animal claws on one side, and Osama Bin Laden as Satan on the other. The caption for the Tōjō caricature reads:

> Magazine covers, comic books, posters, and political cartoons regularly portrayed the enemy—especially the Japanese—as brutish animals. Although clearly racist, the images were effective in whipping up and sustaining war morale.

The Japanese had done the same, depicting the Americans and the English as pigs and other animals. Demonization and dehumanization were the tactics by which the enemy was made into the utmost Other, not only inferior but nonhuman, deserving of annihilation.

Just Who Were the Kamikaze Pilots?

> To be honest, I cannot say that the wish to die for the emperor is genuine, coming from my heart. However, it is decided for me that I die for the emperor . . .

These words from Hayashi Ichizō, a graduate of the Imperial University of Kyoto who died on April 12, 1945, succinctly portray the death imposed on the young men who died as kamikaze pilots. They did not commit suicide, and no Japanese ever thought they did.

Towards the end of World War II, when an American invasion of the Japanese homeland seemed imminent, Ōnishi Takijirō, a navy vice-admiral, invented the *tokkōtai* ("special attack force") operation, which included airplanes, gliders, and submarine torpedoes, none of which was equipped with any means of returning to base. Ōnishi and those closest to him thought that the *Japanese soul,* which was believed to possess a unique strength to face death without hesitation, was the only means available for the Japanese to save their homeland, which was surrounded by American aircraft carriers whose sophisticated radar systems protected them from being destroyed by any other means. Of the approximately 4,000 tokkōtai pilots, about 3,000 were so-called teenage pilots, who were drawn from newly conscripted and enlisted soldiers and enrolled in a special pilot training program. Close to 1,000 were "student soldiers," university students whom the government graduated early in order to draft. Unfortunately, the teenage pilots left almost no written record, but the writings left behind by the student soldiers offer invaluable testimony to these young men's struggle to sustain their connections to the rest of humanity amid the wrenching conditions of war and to make meaning of a death they felt was decreed for them. These extraordinarily well-educated youth were reflective and cosmopolitan, able to read the classics as well as philosophies and literature from Germany, France, Russia, and elsewhere, sometimes in the original language. They drew on their knowledge of philosophy and world history to try to understand the situation in which they inadvertently, but inescapably, were placed. Many of the student soldiers were political liberals, or even Marxists or other "radicals" (Ohnuki-Tierney 2002, 2006).

Since the end of the nineteenth century, as Japan began to modernize, the Japanese government had faced the fact that Western colonialism was encroaching into the Far East; Japan was the only Far Eastern nation that was not colonized. The first task for the Meiji Government (1868-1912) was to build a strong military, for which they adopted the motto, "Thou shall fall like beautiful cherry blossoms after a short life." This motto was relentlessly disseminated through textbooks, school and popular songs, films, theatrical performances, and other media, in addition to being formalyl preached to soldiers on the base. This was the darkest period in Japanese history for young men. From elementary school onwards, they were told that their lives should be sacrificed for Japan-cum-emperor. The Tōjō Cabinet (1941-44) twice shortened the duration of university studies, and all "graduates," other than those in education and the sciences, were drafted.

Those who "chose the fate," as Bourdieu put it (personal communication), to be kamikaze pilots repeatedly said they feared the fear of death, and many said that they would rather die soon than wait for death. They did not commit suicide. Some stated that the government was murdering them. They were similar to those soldiers from any nation or society who were drafted and sent to battlefields where death was guaranteed.

These young pilots read thousands of books, trying to find meaning and to rationalize their deaths at such an early age. Most of them were not married, and while some had experienced only platonic love, others were intensely in love with women they had to leave behind. As their death approached, they wrote more and more poems, crying out for their mothers and lovers. Hayashi Tadao, another graduate of the Imperial University of Kyoto, wrote the following poem the night before his death on July 27, 1945—that is, the day *after* the Potsdam Declaration:

Dusk, that most beautiful moment . . .
With no pattern
Appear and disappear
Millions of images
Beloved people.
How unbearable to die in the sky.

(quoted in Ohnuki-Tierney 2006, 96)

Kasuga Takeo, who looked after the daily routines of the student soldiers at the Tsuchiura Navy Airbase, describes how the night before
their final flight would turn into mayhem. They drank cold sake. Some
broke hanging light bulbs with their swords, others threw their chairs
through the windows, while others tore white tablecloths. While some
shouted in rage, others wept aloud. They thought of their parents and
lovers. Although they were supposedly ready to sacrifice their precious young lives the next morning for Imperial Japan and for the
emperor, they were torn beyond what words could express. Some put
their heads on the table, some wrote their wills, and others danced
in a frenzy manner while breaking flower vases. The next morning,
they all took off wearing the Rising Sun headband. Kasuga wrote that
this scene of utter desperation, which he saw with his own eyes, had
hardly been reported. He added that they had gone through strenuous training, coupled with cruel and torturous corporal punishment
as a daily routine, only to be sent off to their deaths (Ohnuki-Tierney
2006, 9–10).

In sum, none of the Japanese pilots volunteered, committed suicide, or died for the emperor; many were highly educated; and their
targets were military, not civilians.

Suicide Bombers/Terrorists in Western Portrayal

Although contemporary suicide bombers/terrorists are not the focus
of this essay, a brief discussion is presented here to drive home Tambiah's insights on the inferiorization of the Other.

After 9/11, many rushed to offer explanations for the suicide bombers. They were *terrorists*, a term first used by the British government to
label the IRA and INLA (Sluka 2002). Michael Walzer defines terrorism as "the deliberate killing of innocent people at random, in order
to spread fear through a whole population and force the hand of its
political leaders" (Walzer 2002, 1; see also Walzer 2006, 201–02). Some

assumed that there was a straight line from the Quran to the minds of the suicide bombers/terrorists, imagining one unitary tradition of Islam locked in a time capsule. However, we learned that despite significant differences between the Sunni and Shia traditions, Islam places a strict ban on suicide, and that the motivations of the suicide bombers are often secular in nature (see Caryl 2005 for a review of key books on suicide bombers). Many are highly educated, intelligent individuals, like the Japanese tokkōtai pilots. If most of those pilots did not die for the emperor, neither do most suicide bombers die for Allah.

The label *terrorism* itself is telling. As early as 1977, Edmund Leach pointed out in his Munro Lecture that the term *terrorism* is used only for *them*, just as he most famously stated that *their* religion is called *magic*, but *our* magic is called *religion* (Leach 1966b). In light of 9/11, what Leach said about the still-unsolved "Christmas bombing," the event in which a powerful bomb was placed in a coin-operated locker at La Guardia on December 29, 1975, remains astonishingly relevant:

> The La Guardia Airport bomb of 1975 is the same kind of outrage against commonly accepted morality as the dropping of the atom bomb on Hiroshima in 1945. Both these examples of wholly indiscriminate terrorist killing required that the bombers, an unknown criminal in one case and the President of the United States in the other, should think of the potential victims of the bomb as "people quite unlike us," sub-human others. . . .
>
> However incomprehensible the acts of the terrorists may seem to be, our judges, our policemen, and our politicians must never be allowed to forget that terrorism is an activity of fellow human beings and not of dog-headed cannibals [as Pope Gregory IX depicted the Mongol princes]. (Leach 1977, 30, 34–36)

What Leach and Tambiah told us long ago is not to label "their" acts as *terrorism* but not our acts, such as the invasion of Iraq; and not to justify *our* terrorism in killing their soldiers and civilians by characterizing them as the Other—inscrutable, inferior, nonhuman, or even "evil."

Since the initial reaction to 9/11, many have rushed to offer explanations for the events. Although there are many (see, e.g., Lifton 1999), major lines of explanation include the "disenchantment of the world" precipitated by industrialization as the major target of militant Islamic fundamentalists. Islamic fundamentalism's attack on capitalism and capitalism's impact on people who have become egocentric "economic man" in a ceaseless quest for material accumulation is seen as a result of Western/American imperialism. A more recent line of explanation posits the Counter-Enlightenment as the universal seed for non-Western revolutionaries. John Gray (2003) sees the "intellectual roots of radical Islam . . . in the European Counter-Enlightenment" (25), while Ian Buruma and Avishai Margalit (2004) consider Marxism and German Romanticism to have provided the intellectual inspiration for many non-Western political leaders of twentieth-century atrocities, such as Pol Pot. In these discussions, Nietzsche's nihilism looms large, as it did in the explanation of the Nazi mentality (Golomb and Wistrich 2002). According to Kermani (2002), it is *not* the Quran, but Nietzsche's nihilism—that is, the "will to nothingness"—that is the spiritual source for some of the suicide bombers. Kermani sees the 9/11 attacks as an extreme expression of modernism. In a similar vein, Khosrokhavar (2001) points to Heidegger, mediated by Henri Corbin, who also had a crucial influence on the neo-conservative Iranian intellectuals.

Identifying Western Counter-Enlightenment philosophy as the inspiration of modern revolutionaries and others who have taken to violence is the opposite of identifying the "terrorists" as "them." It is also the necessary corrective to the image, emerging right after 9/11, that "they" are simple, uneducated, chauvinistic zealots. It is an effort toward recognizing "them" as another face of "us."

This identification highlights the cosmopolitan nature of intellectuals the world over, including some of the Japanese political leaders, such as the wartime Prime Minister, Konoe Fumimaro, who was a devotee of Oscar Wilde during his university days, as well as tokkōtai pilots, to whom Romanticism, historical determinism, and the aesthetics of nihilism gave comfort when they were desperately trying to rationalize the death that was decreed for them (Ohnuki-Tierney 2006).

We have a distinguished tradition of scholarly work on "fire in the minds of men," as Billington (1999) has aptly called it. Billington examines the thought of nineteenth-century revolutionaries primarily in Europe, such as those who frequented the cafés of the Palais-Royal, or Filippo Giuseppe Maria Lodorico Buonarroti of Italy, but also elsewhere. Lilla (2001) probes the "reckless" minds of Martin Heidegger, Carl Schmitt, Walter Benjamin, Alexandre Kojève, Michel Foucault, and Jacques Derrida—intellectuals who became involved in politics, often without realizing the consequences of their activities and how they might be utilized by the regimes under which they were working. Milosz's *The Captive Mind* (1953), Aron's *The Opium of the Intellectuals* (1957), and Sartre's *Plaidoyer pour les intellectuels* (1972) also fall into this line. In his biography of Andrei Sakharov, Lourie (2002) describes the "hypnotic" power of mass ideology (139) and how Sakharov closed his eyes for a long time with a belief that "the elementary catastrophe that both poets and revolutionaries assumed would cleanse the world was not long in coming" (12).

If Rousseau cannot be declared to have planted the seed for Robespierre, or, for that matter, Nietzsche for the Nazis, even though these regimes used these philosophies to their advantage, we cannot draw a straight arrow of causation from the Counter-Enlightenment to the thoughts of non-Western revolutionary leaders. Nonetheless, it is quite important to be reminded that intellectual currents have crossed political borders in the past and continue to do so at present, with peoples in various societies passionately involved in Western intellectual and artistic developments and, to a much lesser degree, vice versa. Most importantly, young people in all sorts of societies have hitched their idealism onto these intellectual currents, misrecognizing the state's misuse of the aesthetic of nature and other symbols, as with the case of the brutal manipulation of the beauty of cherry blossoms by the Japanese military state (Ohnuki-Tierney 2002).

While Tambiah (1996a) has critically examined various influences of Western philosophies, especially that of Johann Gottfried Herder, on the nation-state in crisis, as an outstanding anthropologist he does not stop with a study of leaders, but is committed to an understanding of the way a large number of people are mobilized in the name of nationalism and ethnonationalism—the phenomenon Tambiah has called "leveling crowds" (1996b). Such crowds are often galvanized by the inferiorization of the people in the context of political, economic, and/or cultural imperialism (on cultural imperialism, see Ohnuki-Tierney 1999, 265–66).

Elsewhere, using the Japanese historical experience, I have emphasized that the birthplace of nationalism and patriotism is at the interface of the transnational and the local (Ohnuki-Tierney 2002, 249–51). Indeed, the postcolonial period world over is replete with what Berlin (1992), using Schiller's expression, labeled the "bent-twig" reaction, as felt collective inferiority gives rise to virulent nationalisms. As John Kelly (1998 and 2003) repeatedly reminds us, the watershed of the shift from European to American imperialism came after the end of

World War II; as Benedict predicted at the end of the war, the power of the United States in the postwar decolonization process cannot be exaggerated (Kelly and Kaplan 2001, 15-17). Nowhere is this more strikingly evident than in the words of Bin Laden himself, who repeatedly points out the arrogance of the United States and how its government has imbued its media with terror in order to show its superpower status (Bin Laden 2005, 48).

If this article may seem to point a finger at the U.S. government and the American mass media, let me emphasize here that the wartime Japanese state was just as guilty in many ways. The Japanese had engaged in the inferiorization of other Asians since the end of the nineteenth century, generating a rationale for the Nanjing massacre and other atrocities for those Japanese soldiers who engaged in these heinous acts. The Japanese state and media engaged in intensive demonization of the Americans and English, depicting them as animals. The Japanese government and its people continue to be haunted by their wartime behaviors after more than sixty years.

This article is intended to point to the deeply felt, but never personalized, side of Tambiah's life work. It is his moral commitment to humanity, seeking theoretical understanding of human lives on the ground and how they are affected by injustice and inequality, both within their own society and without. He has not shied away from exposing the role carried out by some Buddhist leaders in the Tamil/Sinhalese conflicts in his own country (Tambiah 1992). This was an enormously courageous undertaking. His massive work on the leveling crowds seeks to examine the people engulfed in the violent conflicts whose causes lie at the intersection of the local and transnational, with the former involving the long historical process of inferiorization they have been subjected to and that persists even today. His theoretical pursuits always rise out of detailed analysis of the ethnographic and historical contexts.

Afterword. Galactic Polities, Radical Egalitarianism, and the Practice of Anthropology: Tambiah on Logical Paradoxes, Social Contradictions, and Cultural Oscillations

Michael M. J. Fischer

For Tambi

... the richness of the forms of life of other societies, knowledge of which will deepen and illuminate our own lives and societies. This is the reason and justification for the practice of anthropology.

—S. J. TAMBIAH

A Time, a World, a Voice, and an Anthropological Calling

From the teardrop-shaped island, there once came a group of extraordinarily talented social anthropologists; they brought with them perspectives, questions, and empirical fieldwork that helped reshape the discipline, its calling, and its composition.[1] They traversed the temporal and social seas from Ceylon/Sri Lanka's position as the educated jewel and model democratic state of the British Commonwealth (where they were raised and educated) to its subsequent descent into a form of postcolonial violence.[2] How could they not, then, also traverse the seas from the classical social anthropology in which they trained (in England and America), becoming some of its finest practitioners, to the battered landscapes of the late twentieth century, about which they also wrote with insight and passion?[3] They attended to geographies, polities, and cultural formations well beyond that of their homeland. They attended to the larger South Asian and Southeast Asian scene, pre- and postcolonial relations, and to the work of theory in the inclusive, comparative, and transnational field science called anthropology.

In the case of Stanley Jeyaraja Tambiah (or "Tambi," as he is known to his friends and students—literally "younger brother," meaning affectionate uncle, mother's younger brother[4])—the brother and nephew of Justices of Sri Lanka's Supreme Court who were trained in the transnational Anglo-colonial judiciary that sometimes rotated judges interchangeably from Asia to Africa, slowly building up a procedural system of adjudication between local conditions, traditional customary law, and codified statutes[5]—one cannot help but read an enriching projection of concern about his homeland in his work on Buddhism in Thailand, on sources of charisma and legitimation, on ritual and cosmological action, and on ethnic violence across South Asia.[6]

Tambiah's insistence that one should begin with a firm grasp of political economy and with local ethnographic grounding, rather than with cosmology and ritual, is rooted in his career trajectory. Trained originally as a sociologist at the University of Ceylon and at Cornell, Tambiah's first efforts were quantitative surveys (*The Disintegrating Village: Report of a Socio-Economic Survey*, 1957), village studies of kinship, land tenure, and polyandry ("The Structure of Kinship and Its Relationship to Land Possession and Residence in Pata Dumbara, Central Ceylon," 1958; "Polyandry in Ceylon," 1966), and rural community development for a UNESCO-Thai technical assistance project in northeastern Thailand. His trajectory was redirected by engagements with the English social anthropologist Edmund R. Leach, who had originally been trained in engineering, and whom Tambiah first met in 1956 at the former University of Ceylon, renamed the University of Peradeniya. Tambiah had returned there to teach and Leach was making a second visit to Pul Eliya, a village in central Ceylon built around an irrigation tank, where Leach had done fieldwork in 1954.[7] Leach was supportive and engaging but devastating about the quantitative survey approach, and he brought Tambiah to Cambridge for two years (1962–1964).[8] There Tambiah transformed himself into a social anthropologist, later editing with Jack Goody a classic volume in kinship studies (*Bridewealth and Dowry*, 1973), and absorbing as well Leach's incorporation of some of the then-new and intellectually challenging structuralist insights of Claude Levi-Strauss. Tambiah abandoned none of his earlier commitments; in his 1985 collection of essays (*Culture, Thought, and Social Action*) he continued to refer to himself as a development anthropologist and to invoke Sir E. B. Tylor's creed that anthropology is a reformer's science.

Much of Tambiah's stress on oscillating and pulsating models of politics and on dialectical dynamics parallels that of Leach, as evident in the latter's provocative work among the Kachin, *Political Systems of Highland Burma* (1954).[9] Tambiah remained a close friend and eventually became Leach's biographer (*Edmund Leach: An Anthropological Life*, 2002). Another of Leach's students, Nur Yalman (and Yalman's student Dennis McGillivray), would take up structuralist analyses in Ceylon in a more strictly Levi-Straussian fashion, but many of Tambiah's striking analyses deploy structuralist insights, particularly his brilliant handling of the cosmological and mythic reworkings of the histories of Ceylon/Sri Lanka, as well as, of course, his signature analysis of the world conqueror/world renouncer dualism in South and Southeast Asian "galactic polities." The effort to demonstrate how to integrate structuralist and historical analyses was also taken up by Marshall Sahlins in his work on Hawaii, Fuji, and classical Greece; and Tambiah's accounts should be read alongside those of Sahlins, since many of the same themes reappear, albeit handled methodologically differently. Sahlins's essay in this volume quietly acknowledges and illustrates this point, turning to the mythic dimensions of contemporary and historical ethnic violence.

I begin with the editors' provocative title for this volume, as a way of staging themes in Tambiah's work, and then move on to his analysis of galactic polities, charismatic circuits, collective violence, and ritual. Along the way I deal with the contributions this volume makes to these topics.

Radical Egalitarianism

Because of the crossings of generational time and situational space mentioned above, Tambiah's cosmopolitical analytic language is always carefully indexed to its sociopolitical origins and implications. Take the phrase devised by the editors for this volume's title: *radical egalitarianism*.[10] It captures aspects of Tambiah's moral commitments to the ordinary people of a society as opposed to development economists, modernization political scientists, and comprador local elites of the transnational political economy, as beautifully expressed in his "Anthropologist's Creed" (1985a). The phrase also captures (as perhaps the editors had in mind) Tambiah's invocation of Leach's quip that he is a radical at home in his own society but not in other societies

(cited in Tambiah 2002, 261),[11] and the closely associated rationale
for anthropology's repatriating comparativist creed of studying the
"richness of the forms of life of other societies, knowledge of which
will deepen and illuminate our own lives and societies" as "the reason and justification for the practice of anthropology" (1996a, 33).[12]
And yet *radical egalitarianism* is also a paradoxical and loaded phrase,
often quite negative, in the six primary usages that suffuse Tambiah's
writings on, and this volume's responses to, the troubled postcolonial
politics of South and Southeast Asia.

First there is the radical egalitarianism of the world-renouncer of
Buddhist-Hindu cosmology, represented in the role of monks, who,
Tambiah points out, are not apolitical (as they have been portrayed
in some idealist interpretations of the Hindu renouncer).[13] Buddhist
monks detach themselves from worldly ties in emulation of the Buddha, attempting to rise above ephemeral concerns, in order both to
pursue enlightenment and to guide the polity. In the context of South
and Southeast Asian polities, the *sangha* (corporate body of monks)
is supposed to function as a ritual and moral balance to legitimate
and guide power and kingship. As we have vividly seen in the modern
politics of Sri Lanka, Burma, and Thailand, this can turn totalitarian
as easily as democratic. The articulation of a revivalist Buddhism in
the postcolonial politics of Sri Lanka has been a powerful contributor
to the ethnic violence that has torn that country apart.

One of Tambiah's most important contributions, carefully deploying historiographic, literary-genre, mythic-structural, as well as ethnographic methods, is to deconstruct this chauvinist ideology and
show the countervailing alternative histories that have been erased by
chauvinism. There is, he asserts, "no reason to foreclose on this possibility [that the framework of current Buddhist nationalism can in the
future stretch and incorporate a greater amount of pluralist tolerance
in the name of a Buddhist conception of righteous rule], for there
are precedents that can be positively employed" (1992, 125). But, he
continues, forcefully putting forth an anthropological institutional
perspective against simple idealistic possibilism or wishful thinking,
"new perspectives can be forged only under social and political conditions which are themselves not frozen or restrictive" (ibid.). Much
of his brilliant analysis in *Buddhism Betrayed? Religion, Politics, and Violence in Sri Lanka* is dedicated to charting the freezing and restrictive
traps into which Sri Lankan politics has devolved since the 1940s, in
what he argues has been a dramatic transformation from Buddhist-

Hindu galactic polities to the cosmologies of unitary nation-states. The sin, of course, lies not only with Buddhist ideology or ritualized cosmology, but also with the British colonial rule against which the religious revivalism arose; and in a larger sense, the sin lies with the transformations induced by nation-state identity politics, and thus with what Tambiah calls (using a transformed Indian term) the *"juggernaut* of mass participatory politics" (1992, 172).[14]

Tambiah's title *Buddhism Betrayed?* is an explicit reference to *The Betrayal of Buddhism* (with no question mark), the explosive report issued in 1956 by a Commission of Inquiry of the All Ceylon Buddhist Congress, just before the fateful 1956 elections, a "singular climactic moment" in twentieth-century politics, "when a significant number of monks temporarily organized to win an election" (Tambiah 1992, ch. 7). The report was staged not only on the eve of the election but to mark cosmologically 2,500 years since the death of the Buddha and the coming to Sri Lanka of Vijaya, coded as the first Sinhalese and a prototypical mythic hero who comes from the periphery to violently conquer and establish a new center of righteous rule. The report is one of three texts that Tambiah analyzes from the 1940s and 1950s defending the role of monks as political actors, indicting British colonialism for using Christian missionizing to weaken Buddhism, and asserting a remedy program to establish Buddhism as the dominant religion and Sinhala as the only state language.

This is not merely old politics. In 2006, on the report's fiftieth anniversary and "the 2,550's anniversary of the Buddha's death," it was reissued as a warning reminder to the United National Party government of its defeat in 1956; and Buddhist organizations once again urged the government "to implement five proposals to arrest the decline of Buddhist values and culture in Sri Lanka. The Venerable Medagama Dhammananda of the Asgiriya Chapter, Kandy, read out these proposals at a meeting held at Ananda College, Colombo on October 3" (Perera 2006).[15]

The second radical egalitarianism, one that plays into the revivalist ideology of Sri Lankan Buddhist nationalism, is the "nostalgic fiction of a simple, homogeneous, egalitarian pre-colonial Sinhala Buddhist peasant society" (Tambiah 1992, 96). It feeds into a dangerous political economy of development ideology when used as the mythic charter for the multipurpose colonization schemes to resettle peasants from overcrowded areas onto new lands: the Gal Oya Multipurpose Scheme of the 1950s (one of a number of such post–World War II Tennessee Valley Authority-styled projects, and the one where the first postindependence riots occurred, with Tambiah as a witness and reporter[16]), and the $1.5 billion Mahavali Project of the 1980s, which was to provide irrigation to 37,000 hectares of already cultivated land plus 130,000 hectares of new land and double the hydroelectric power capacity of the country. Eighteen thousand families, mostly Sinhalese, had already been resettled on these lands by the mid-1980s. Tamils saw these projects, placed in what Tambiah calls the "shatter zone" between the Tamil north and east and the Sinhalese south, as Sinhalese land grabs. When the massive riots of May 1958 broke out, it was footloose wage-laborers living in labor camps, organized into a strike force by politicians to whom they were beholden, and urban thug *agents-provocateurs* disguised in monks' robes with shaved heads, rather than better-off landed peasants who rampaged to purify the land of Tamils, leading to Tamil "counterclaims of 'homelands' and Sinhalese majoritarian discrimination in settlement policy" (1992, 127). As Tambiah comments, "The elite bureaucrats of the island, the technically sophisticated economists, engineers, and architects, in collaboration with foreign experts and much foreign funding, plan highly 'industrialized' blueprints and use heavy technology for building the irrigation dams, the roads, communication facilities, and the like. But this same cosmopolitan elite, together with the leading politicians, then yokes this heavily capitalized infrastructure to a peasant form of cultivation. . . . The elite, living a different style of life and reproducing a different pattern of privileged domination in their role as planners and rulers, wish upon the vast mass of the people an indefinitely expanding network of peasant villages" (ibid., 127–28).

And, he continues, "the ideologues of the society, the activist scholar-monks, the populist literary circles, the vote-seeking politicians, and the creators of rituals of national development and television dramas unite to propagate this vision of a (utopian) past that could be a prospective (utopian) future"—a vision that "hinder[s] the envisioning of a more realistic and workable regime . . . that can accommodate minorities" (Tambiah 1992, 128). Under such circumstances the provision of free education in local languages had the effect of creating vast pools of angry, unemployed literate and semi-literate youth, who had invested hope in education, but in a society without the jobs to fulfill their ambitions.

The ideology of the egalitarian, self-sufficient village, a mini-kingdom built around, as populist novelist Martin Wickramasinghe put it, *vava* (irrigation tank), *dagaba* (temple), and *yaya* (paddy field), was explicitly invoked by the politicians as they opened and dedicated the new project lands. The egalitarian nostalgia is a fascinating reworking of the hierarchies of village life. The fantasy is one in which money is rarely used, the produce of the land is divided equally between the cultivator and the treasury, there is equality of income, and poverty is nonexistent. In India, this sort of division of labor is called *jajmani* and is accounted as a division of labor among castes in an organic whole. The hierarchy is explicit in the caste system, and Buddhist ideology differentiates itself from Hinduism even in the cognate term for the moral order: Sanskrit (Hindu) *dharma*, Pali (Buddhist) *dhama*. Buddhist *dhama* is paired with equity (*sama*), in dialectical opposition to Hindu *dharma*, always signifying inequality and hierarchy (ibid, 108). But, of course, the land in the Buddhist polities of Sri Lanka belongs to the king, and is allocated, along with its manpower, with finely graded castes and tenurial rights into monastic (*viharagam*) and temple (*devalagam*) endowments, noble estates, (*nindagam*) and royal estates (*gabadagam*), with specification of duties and work owed the king.

This is an explicit caste system, and it is more like a feudal structure, or as Tambiah acknowledges, a patrimonial structure as described by Weber, than it is an ideal egalitarian community. Indeed as Weber describes, the ministerial form of government is divided into royal household duties (with the highest offices being dualistically structured—Office of the Royal Bath, Office of the Royal Wardrobe), and the whole is legitimated, as Weber argues for ancient agrarian empires, with elaborate cosmological rituals. We shall return to the cosmology and ritual below, which as Tambiah is at pains to argue (in his critique of Geertz) is performative and constitutive, not merely reflective, mystifying, or theatrical. Tambiah argues for an understanding of this pre-nation-state patrimonial structure as flexible and inclusionary, allowing redundant and involuted bureaucracies to incorporate and assign roles to growing numbers of people, and similarly providing increasing occupational niches for immigrant groups of different origins and religious traditions and practices, which is quite different from the drive for unity and identity of the modern nation-state.

The third radical egalitarianism, of course, is the socialist one that projects backward into utopian history and forward into the utopian future the idea of an egalitarian community. Tambiah cites Henpitagedera Gnanasiha Thera, one of the more radical Buddhist monk-scholars, as thinking of Russian socialism as being based on principles similar to those of this Buddhist conception (1992, 108). And indeed such a conception is present in much vulgar Marxist and socialist thought, and is a key component of a turn to totalitarianism in both left and right traditions.[17] Parallel to today's Muslim fundamentalists, who argue that once a unitary Islamic society has been forcibly established, democracy, equality, and social justice will reign, so too argue Buddhist revivalists. Gnanasiha condemns divisive parliamentary politics for preventing the reaching of any national consensus. By contrast, he argues, Buddhist "democracy" requires only one party so that discussion can be carried on until there is consensus (ibid., 115). Further, much as under a Ministry of Islamic Guidance and Culture in Iran, "in a Buddhist-administered society, the action of man is directed to a good path not only by advice, but by closing the avenues that lead to wrong actions" (ibid., 119). Pannasiha, another monk-scholar, says of the issue of minorities, that to protect the hegemony of the endangered Sinhaha Buddhism, "when 74% of the population is united, what can the other 26% do?" (ibid., 124). He is complaining about the alleged favoring of Tamils in the civil service,[18] and arguing against enfranchising Tamil tea estate laborers, lest it change the electoral arithmetic.

The sangha itself, the Buddhist body of monks, is idealized as an egalitarian structure. According to the charter myth, the Buddha tells Ananada that after his death there should be no successor: only the *dhama* (doctrine) should bind the *bhikhus* (monks). The elders among the monks deserve respect, but can only teach and advise, not legislate or compel. The transactions of the sangha should be held in frequent assemblies (with procedural rules) where all are equal and decisions are consensual. All offerings to the sangha are to be shared equally and all increase should go into a common fund (1992, 114). But again, as Tambiah will outline in great detail for Thailand, reforms of the sangha are also state centralizing mechanisms and fraught with hierarchical maneuverings.

Three more egalitarianisms appear in these pages, two with strong ritual-performative characteristics and two with cosmological components: pooling-redistribution (see discussion of Ratanapruck below), social democratic welfare-politics transformed into neoliberal microeconomic discipline (Ferguson, this volume), and the juggernaut of mass participatory politics. This juggernaut of mass partici-

patory politics is the most significant and will be dealt with below as
a separate section parallel to the other key themes of galactic polities,
charismatic circuits, and ritual action.

Galactic Polities, Revitalizing Reforms, and Theater States

Rereading Tambiah's pair of books on Sri Lanka in the context of his
trilogy of better-known books on Thailand—*Buddhism and the Spirit
Cults in North-east Thailand* (1970), his master work *World Conqueror
and World Renouncer: A Study of Buddhism and Polity in Thailand against
a Historical Background* (1976), and *Buddhist Saints of the Forest and the
Cult of Amulets: A study of Charisma, Hagiography, Sectarianism and Millennial Buddhism* (1984)—and his essays on ritual performative action
(1985b, 1990), one recognizes the same key terms throughout, as well
as three overlapping dialectics and oscillations:[19] 1) between centralizing nation-states and previous fractionating *mandala* or "galactic"
polities; 2) between actual history and charismatic ritual action that
mobilizes mythic and cosmological charters; and 3) between the this-
worldly royal politics of the *chakravarti* (world conquerors, universal emperors; Pali *cakkavatti*, "through whom the wheels of dharma
turn") and the *dharmaraja* (righteous king) who purifies the sangha
in return for the sangha's legitimating of the royal rule, becoming
the "guides of the king's conscience and mentors of the people" (Wi-
jayawardena 1956, 513, cited in Tambiah 1992, 39).

Call these three fields of oscillation or dialectic *histories, myths,* and
cross-cultural structures. Histories have to do with kinship, marriage alliances, factions, migrations, occupational niches, conversions, wars
of conquest, and the political economies of patronage, trade, production, tax and revenue generation and redistribution. Histories of the
sangha have to do also with lineages of mentorship and ordination,
missions to recover or propagate meditation or textual traditions, and
establishment of educational systems aligned with or dissonant to polities and states. *Myths* have to do with double narratives of heroes who
from the periphery violently conquer and reaggregate a fragmenting
and demonic chaotic kingdom, and are themselves transformed into
benign, righteous, and virtuous rulers once they have reached and re-
constituted the center. *Cross-cultural structures* have to do both with
the mutual dependence of religious and political legitimacy (sangha
and king), a basic Indo-European topos, with merchants and farm-

ers as a third wheel, and with the structural binary of autochthonous versus immigrant founders ("natives of the soil" versus "sea-crossing elites") found from Fiji to Greece.[20]

The Buddha and Asoka (the third-century B.C.E. Mauryan chakra-vartin, who ruled over most of the Indian subcontinent) are the two prototypes of the world renouncer and world conqueror. The former is a prince who, witnessing human suffering, abandoned his royal function and founded the sangha; he himself is said to have claimed that he had many times previously been born a chakravartin. The latter becomes a convert to Buddhism after witnessing the carnage created by his successful war of conquest over the Kalinga kingdom. Vijaya, the "first Sinhalese," is the Sri Lankan prototype immigrant chakravartin: the immigrant debased prince crossing the sea from India to establish a righteous Buddhist kingdom on the island of Lanka/Ceylon.

The Thai sangha lineages about which Tambiah writes are linked by missions from India to Sri Lanka and thence to Thailand. Buddhism radiated as well to Indonesia, Burma, China, and Japan and as far west (we often forget) as the Mediterranean. The monastic meditative traditions and ordination lineages of Sri Lanka were renewed in the eighteenth century under the "foreign" matrilineal Nayyakar kingships of Kandy, which sent missions to Siam, returning to establish the Siyam Nikaya and to renew or build new *viharas* (temples) across the Kandyan kingdom. It was at this time that the Buddha's tooth relic was elevated to a central role in the annual *perahera* (ritual procession) in Kandy that previously had paraded only the four guardian deities of the realm. In parallel, but different, fashion, the reforms of the nineteenth-century Thai monk who succeeded to the royal throne, Mongkut, not only renewed the sangha but deployed it as a centralizing educational institution for an incipient modernizing nation-state.

As James Taylor and Ingrid Jordt elaborate in this volume, the reformist movements in Thailand, Sri Lanka, and Burma drew upon one another's maintenance of the old Pali texts and meditation traditions, but the reform movements in each setting developed dialectically different generative strategies. Mongkut sent two missions to Sri Lanka in the 1840s as had his grandfather, Rama I, in the late eighteenth century, in part as legitimating dharmaraja actions. Both Mongkut and the Sri Lankan forest monk Pannananda (in the early nineteenth century) also went to Burma for training in the Mon reform tradition (dating back to a fifteenth-century sangha reform under a Mon dharmaraja). But while Mongkut would build a close-knit cadre of disciples to propagate his Thammayut sect, and would use the printing press and a simplified Ariyaka ("purity") writing system (a Romanized transcription of Pali phonetics) to propagate his version of the Buddhist doctrine domestically and to surrounding nations, in Burma a mass meditation form was propagated among the laity by the monk Mahasi Sayadaw with the support of Prime Minister U Nu (1948–1962) as a means of revitalization after colonial rule. Mahasi Sayadaw's Vipassana (insight) meditation and Abhidhamma philosophical formulations stressed that the laity should not just give donations to the monks but should themselves meditate. Vipassana or insight meditation centers were established across Burma, Sri Lanka, Indonesia, and in the United States. Vipassana meditation was taken up in Thailand as well by the Mahanikai sect under the great abbot monk Phra Phimolathma. But with the rise of Mongkut's Thammayut sect as a centralizing and nationalizing instrument, Phra Phimolathma was forcibly disrobed and imprisoned. The Thammayut monks, Jordt says, also dialectically countered the meditation emphasis of the Mahanikai sect by stressing the importance of the Thammayut forest monk meditation teachers. A charismatic dialectic ensues of devotees seeking out meditating forest monks who retreat further away from the centers of population to pursue their detachment from the world, and thereby intensify their charisma, which in turn attracts devotees further into the peripheries, thereby acting as a kind of frontier expansion and marking of the state.

The sangha-royal dialectic creates polities that are theatrical and ritually charismatic, absorbing power into their centers and weakening on their peripheries in pulsating, changing dynamics that Tambiah memorably calls the *galactic polity*, evoking both the stars (transcendence) and this-worldly leverage. It is a form that Clifford Geertz called *negara*, using the Balinese term, but that Tambiah more deeply roots in the great but snow-flaky empires of the chakravarti such as Asoka, rulers of the worlds of South and Southeast Asia. ("Snow flaky" in the sense of being geometrically fractal and replicative or mandala like, and in the sense of being ephemeral, loose, disappearing, with new ones constantly forming. Tambiah says he intends *galactic* as a translation of the term *mandala*.) Tambiah's account of Thailand focuses on the nineteenth-century reforms of King Mongut that centralized and reformed the sangha as an educational pillar of a modernizing state.

Tambiah's argument with Geertz is instructive. Geertz famously describes the symbolic politics of the Balinese *negara* polity, comparing it, in the margins of his text, to the symbolic and spectacle politics of Washington, D.C. (Geertz 1977, 1980). Geertz thereby disrupts any contrastive idea that American politics is rational and instrumental, while those of other kinds of polities are cosmological and mystified. But his account of the nineteenth-century Balinese polities is, Tambiah says, "decidedly nonannalistic," too easily splitting off a still center of expressive action at the top from instrumental action at the base and periphery. While one could do a more generous reading of Geertz's account in the context of his notion of "cultural involution" under Dutch colonial rule, the support of ever-more-refined court rituals at the expense of a politics that could disrupt the Dutch control and extraction of revenue, nonetheless Tambiah rightly insists on looking to the precolonial "periodic campaigns and changing zones of control [having] to do with the capture of booty and manpower to resettle as 'slaves' or 'serfs' near one's centers of control," which is the general pattern of Southeast Asian polities, and which can be tracked also in the chronicles and oral histories of Bali. (Tambiah uses Hildred and Clifford Geertz's own oral history work [1975] to demonstrate this.[21]) Perennial rebellions and succession disputes, exacerbated by multiple ranked marriages and concubinages, ensure that there are few long-lived dynasties, and the cosmological state has to be continually re-imaged and reincarnated. The claim to be a chakravartin is a personal achievement that cannot be inherited, although once a ruler has achieved that status he can claim to be an incarnation or avatar of archetypal heroes. Kings make multiple marriage and concubinage alliances as means of binding lesser royal families to the center, and of asserting the patrimonial role of husband to the realm, but this then complicates succession maneuvers and fights.

Sri Lanka provides Tambiah with rich materials to demonstrate not only how a decidedly annalist reading can unpack the workings of mythic structures and cosmologically interpreted social action. More crucially, Sri Lanka enables him to show how one can find alternative histories critical to a political understanding of "how and why … incorporation and assimilation, or containment and insulation, or rejection and expulsion take[s] place with regard to outside Indian peoples and their practices, and how in due course … a narrative of composite yet distinctive Sinhala identity [can] be evolved" (1992, 150). This is the mythohistorical and practical work over the centuries that needs to be remembered as accommodating pluralism rather than erasing it. Invoking Levi-Strauss, Tambiah says "myths have their variants, . . . one should expect a corpus of related myths, especially if they are focused on themes existentially important to the cultures and societies where they circulate. . . . [S]uch are the paradoxes and puzzles . . . that one would expect the exploration of a number of solutions [to them]" (ibid., 149).

Take, for example, the eighteenth-century kingdom of Kandy where the royal line passed from patrilineal Sinhala to matrilineal Nayyakars, originally from Madurai in south India (Tamils). Tambiah gives us both the marriage alliances that began in the seventeenth century and two myths of the period that comment upon the incorporative mechanisms. The marriage alliances provide the way the succession passed after the death of Narendrasinghe in 1739 to a brother of a Nayyakar queen (wife of Narendrasinghe) presumably because she and her brother were of *ksatriya* status, whereas Narendrasinghe's only son by a Sinhala concubine was not of sufficient caste rank. That Nayyakar king, Sri Vijaya ("victory"), himself took a Nayyakar queen, and his heir in turn was his sister's son. To make the succession of Vijaya work, Narendrasinghe had him educated in Sinhalese laws and customs, and both Vijaya Rajasinghe (1739-1747) and his successor Kirti Sri Rajasinghe sponsored missions to Siam, the latter returning in 1753 to establish two important viharas of the Siyam Nikaya, elevate the role of the Buddha Tooth Relic in the annual perahera ritual, and refurbish and build new viharas across the kingdom, thus enacting their position as dharmarajas. These Tamil-origin south Indians still had some personal (Hindu) Saivite practices, and two prominent (Buddhist) monks were implicated in an assassination plot amid complaints about having a heretic, evil Tamil as king. The dharmaraja survived and managed what probably was an expression of the chronic factionalism at court.

Tambiah reads two foundation myths as commentaries on this pattern of incorporation of Tamils into Sinhala identity. The first, recounted in the chronicles at the time of the transition from the Sinhalese king Narendrasinghe to the Nayyakar (Tamil) king Vijaya, is the defeat of Natha, one of the four guardian deities of Kandy, by Pitiye, a Chola prince disgraced because he had killed a calf and the cow had complained to the king by ringing her bell. Pitiye invades Ceylon, proceeding from the east coast towards Kandy, along the way clearing land, creating rice paddies, initiating irrigation. Natha, losing the war of violence but winning a quest for salvation, is elevated to *bodhisattva*, while Pitiye is domesticated and becomes one of twelve regional deities, guardian deities of the *bandara* class. *Bandara* in turn seems to be from *pantarm*, non-Brahmin priests of the Vellala caste who came in the thirteenth century from various parts of south India with attendants, craftsmen, and mendicants of their Siva temples, and were given *radala* and *mudali* titles (the highest status rank in the Goyigama Sihanala caste of cultivators). The myth of the original Sinhala founding hero, Vijaya, is parallel: a disgraced prince, he enters the island, violently displacing the savage *yakkhas*, and with a *yakkhini* has children who are sent to settle the periphery.

These, as Tambiah points out, are widespread (cross-cultural, structural) myths of the origin of power and its creative transformation, proceeding from abroad and the periphery in acts of barbarism and violence, then domesticated and reconstituting legitimate order. They are as well more local charter myths of the domestication of the jungle for rice cultivation, often with imported Tamil labor. On an even grander cosmological register, the Buddhist genesis myth is also about the "creation of world as devolutionary differentiation," with disorder increasing through the workings of human desire, until a new order is re-established (not unlike the differentiation of Genesis and the story of the Garden of Eden).

Tambiah works through other examples of historical incorporation and exchange, including the Chola occupation of the island in the tenth and eleventh centuries and the return raid by King Bajabahu into Chola territory, recovering 12,000 Sinhala captives and bringing of 12,000 Chola captives back to settle and work the land in Sri Lanka; the fifteenth-century waves of Karava immigrants from south India incorporated into the lower subcastes of the Goyigama; the two rival Buddhist trading families from Kerala who controlled the coasts, and the probable arrival at that time of the cult of the goddess Pattini, originally a Buddhist and Jain deity (Obeysekere 1984). Similar caste incorporations occurred in the Hindu and Muslim-remaining Tamil-speaking north (the Jaffna Peninsula).

The point here is that there is a rich tapestry of incorporation, exchange, and reworking of traditions that often gets lost in mythic charters intended to advance particular interests at particular moments of competition, and that it is the anthropologists' calling to not allow such erasures to pass unremarked. Irving Chan Johnson (this volume) supplies another such example on the Malaysian-Thai border, where Buddhist communities under a Muslim sultan pursue their boisterous ordination parades, care for massive statues, and host pilgrims, monks, traders, smugglers, and tourists. For the past century the ritual appointment of the chief monk of the Malaysian state of Kelantan has passed through the office of the Muslim sultan, while the Buddhist king of Thailand is viewed through the television, photographs, and posters.

Indeed, *chakravartin*, Tambiah notes, might be best translated as "king of kings," in acknowledgement of the existence of lesser kings and the *mandala* structure of galactic polities. "King of Kings," *Shahanshah*, is the title of Persian rulers, divine insofar as just kings are endowed with the *farrohar*, the divine light, symbolized as well in the sacred sphere by the highest level of sacred fire composed of purified levels of many fires from the varied occupations of men, hearth fires collected into community-level ones, as well as natural fires such as lightning (Fischer 1973). Unjust kings lose their farrohar—one of the great themes of the Persian national epic, the *Shahnameh* ("Book of Kings"; Fischer 2004).

Tambiah describes the cosmic rituals of galactic polities as rites of dispersion and rites of aggregation. The former include agricultural cycle rites that begin in the royal palace, then proceed to provincial courts, and "ripple" down to the rice fields of villagers. The latter include annual Oaths of Allegiance as well as the royal multiple marriage arrangements, and the sequestering at court of members of lower allied royal or provincial families to ensure their loyalty. One is tempted to rethink the structure of early Islamic polities in these terms, with Muhammad's multiple marriage alliances made explicitly for precisely these political purposes, the sequestering of members of rival clans at court, and the *bayt* (oath of alliegance).

In one of the most fascinating of the chapters in this volume, Victor Manfredi rereads, assembles, and collates the fractious history of Nigeria as pulsating sets of galactic polities both at the national level ("adept at gerrymandering the federating units into now 37 insolvent states and over 740 unaccountable local jurisdictions," "defusing game-theoretic power blocs at the center") and at the level of the oscillations of political form in southeastern Nigeria between, on the one hand, Edo crowned priests of tutelary divinities centered in walled market towns, and on the other hand, Igbo gerontocratic lineages of horticultural villages practicing the "occasional state" formation when under external threat. *Gumsa/gumlao*, in Leach's Burmese categories.[22] (Hertzfeld, this volume, suggests a similar oscillation between two styles of leadership in Bangkok politics.) The dualistic oscillation includes patrilineal symbols (Igbo *ofo* of agricultural bamboo ringed in iron bands versus Edo coral and brass regalia, representing royal monopolies of salt water wealth and sovereign authority to impose death penalties) as well as dance steps (aerobic Igbo acrobatics versus "lead-footed Edo choreography under cowrie-laden *ubuluku* smocks depicting the dry-land locomotion of Olookun, the fish-tailed ocean god"). Manfredi, like Tambiah, looks first to the political economy: the slave trade exports, raids, and middlemen in the seventeenth and eighteenth centuries, and the "vultural ecology" of today's Shell Oil economy.

Charismatic Circuits

Tambiah's essay "The Charisma of Saints and the Cult of Relics, Amulets, and Tomb Shrines," which opens the present volume, is today perhaps best read back to front, for its parallel account of the enchantments of the Christian and Buddhist cults of saints and relics. Christian monks boasting of their ritual kidnappings of sacred relics—in the dark of night breaking into saints' tombs and Roman catacombs to steal bone and ash, nails, wood, and linen, with which to consecrate churches in new territories—seems more exotic than Buddhist circulation of relics in today's world of cosmopolitan tasters of many religions. We tend to forget that the Second Council of Nicaea in 787 C.E. decreed that no church was to be consecrated without relics; that a decade and a half later two more Councils would demand any altar without relics to be destroyed; that the technical definition of an *altar* in Roman Catholic canon law is a tomb containing relics of saints; or that the Vatican continues to maintain a supply room chock full of ash and bone and other relics to be used for consecrating new churches. For those tourists who have been to Malacca in Malaysia or Goa in India, the story of St. Francis Xavier, the Jesuit missionary who died on Shangchuan Island off the south China coast in December 1552, and helped found a long-lasting Christian presence in Nagasaki and southern Japan, will be a vivid reminder of this circulation of relics. In February 1553, his "incorrupt body" was taken to St. Paul's Church in Malacca and in December was shipped to Goa, where the body is entombed in the Basilica Bomb Jesus. His right forearm was ordered removed in 1614 by the fifth Superior General of the Society of Jesus,

Claudio Acquaviva, and was shipped to Rome to be used in the canonization of the saint (when miraculously, it is said, blood dripped from the wound) and then was put on display in a silver case in the Society's church. Another arm bone was sent to Macau, intended for Japan. In front of the ruins of Malacca's St. Paul's Church today stands a 1952 statue of St. Xavier, dedicated to mark the four hundredth anniversary of his missionary work in Melacca (1545-1552). On the day of its consecration, a casuarina tree fell and broke off the right forearm, the one that is in Rome and that he used to bless his converts. And so it remains.

Tambiah notes that, as in Buddhism, the Church changed its doctrines about the relics, originally treating remains as inviolable, but then instituting the partibility, distribution, and redistribution of relics. Helen, the mother of Emperor Constantine, famously brought back pieces of the cross to be distributed by Constantine across Europe as a form of legitimating patronage for his Christianizing realm. After the tenth century, the cult of the saints was universalized through deemphasizing local saints and focusing on relics of the Virgin, St. Peter, and the relics of Jesus such as his cross, crown of thorns, or shroud. More recently, late-twentieth-century Pope John Paul II began a drive to canonize more saints as a way to revive the Church through the cult of saints.

Structurally, the modalities of the saint and relic cults of Buddhism and Catholicism, Tambiah argues, are very much the same. While in the opening of the essay attention is given to the way in which relics and amulets partake in the formation of communities and are a way of circulating grace (Christianity) and merit (Buddhism), and a theological gloss is provided ("the personal, interiorized, mystical illumination of the saints is seen in these religious traditions as flooding the vast spaces of the world with their cosmic love"), in fact the thrust of the essay, as in much of Tambiah's work, gradually shifts to the political legitimation that religious charisma provides. The relics function as the palladia aspect of what Max Weber called the ritual legitimation techniques of the ancient empires. Patronage and exchange are the microcapillaries of this mode of legitimation; the complementary ritual functions of king and priest are the macrocirculation channels of legitimacy.

In the local traditions of northeastern Thailand, amulets are made with the image of the patron (royalty, generals, bankers) on one side and the image of the saint on the other: the Indo-European king-priest/monk and Buddhist sangha/dharmaraja complementarity. As these amulets circulate, are stolen and faked, they become saleable, stimulating further production and faking. Like the ashes and bone fragments in stupas that mark the Buddhist landscape, they are tokens for ordinary men to see and handle, yet belonging "not to this transitory world but to eternity."

Michael Puett (this volume) opens the door to an analogous Chinese world of religious charisma through temple networks and spirit-possession associations that have formed the backbone of maritime Southeast Asia and coastal China. This is a world that is stirring once again and taking on renewed importance, but as Puett says, largely "out of sight of virtually the entire social sciences apart from anthropology." Both colonial governments in Southeast Asia and the communist government in China have tried to suppress these networks, because and although, as he also says, in many areas these networks have run much of local society, including schools and infrastructure. Puett guides us through the haunted landscape of demonic ghosts produced by every death. One tries to control them with ancestral rites, fulfill unfinished business in their names, and domesticate them into gods with sacrifices. As gods (often associated with the occupation of the deceased) they may attract more people, and temple networks propagate and become points of attachment for new migrants. Like the Hadrami networks from the other direction, these Chinese networks extend across Indonesia and Southeast Asia and feed back again today to China. A new practice of women becoming spirit mediums in Southeast Asia is being imported to China, particularly in the coastal Putian (Fujian) areas from which many of these networks once originated.[23] Again there is a sea-land dialectic: coastal boat people and fishermen, as the silt filled in creating new land, established themselves on the land and claimed to have always been Chinese. In turn, then, the state attempted to incorporate or control them—in late imperial China, Puettt says, by promoting the gods into its own bureaucracy, against local resistance. The entire Southeast Asian maritime world is filled with networks of sea peoples whose histories are only slowly being recovered from their invisibility to terrestrially oriented historians. The lineage system is a more flexible organizational form than anthropologists once thought, allowing people to buy in or be recruited, adopt a common name, set up a clan house, and thereby claim to be of a common lineage. In modern Singapore, many temples are small shrines in high-rise housing developments, where on two days a week a medium may operate from, say, 6:00 to 8:00 in the evening. Like a nervous system with neurons and synapses, the channels of charismatic ritual and mythic structuring run everywhere.

Prista Ratanapruck takes us into yet another trading network that also uses pooling-redistributive mechanisms, both of the temple (or here, Tibetan monastery) form (as with the Chinese temple networks) and of the *cargo* (Sp. "burden") fiesta forms of agrarian Mesoamerica and the Andes highlands, the *kheirat* pooling systems of Iran (Fischer 1990c), or the Big Man redistribution systems in the Pacific, albeit with a Tibetan Buddhist inflection. The Manangis (Nepalis of Tibetan ethnic origin) were once salt and grain caravaneers between Tibet and India. In recent times, based in Katmandu, their networks extend from India across Southeast Asia, as they trade in gems, handicrafts, and other things. As in other trading networks, individual traders use local marriages to gain access to new areas. But for others, Ratanpruck describes a life on the road of communal rooming houses, sharing of knowledge, and mutual aid; and at home in Katmandu of pooling trade surpluses to put on elaborate rituals, including a two-week-long archery festival in which all men must bet and compete, with winnings distributed equally among the winning team; and if an exact bull's-eye is scored, the individual who wins must patronize the community at large. Money, the Manangis say, is of value only during one's lifetime and so it is best to convert into religious merit, including communal sharing and eighteen-day fasting retreats to count prayer beads for the accumulated merit of all.

Ratanapruck acknowledges the extractive mechanisms of pooling. She is primarily interested in the network expansion that pooling allows. But she also notes that many Manangis are monks (some nuns), and these require support from productive members of the family. In many traditions where religious values remain strong, surpluses are often put into support of religious institutions. In the case of Jains, a wealthier merchant community than the Manangi peddlers, surpluses often go into upgrading temples and community philanthropic organizations, as well as conspicuous ritual processions as a sign of both piety, merit making, and the power of the discipline and community. In the past Manangis paid Tibetan monasteries that provided loans for trade. In the present Ratanapruck describes various forms of protection money that have to be paid, as many Manangis still move around under the bureaucratic radar in an informal if ordered economy. Redistributive rituals in many traditions can serve as partial safety nets, without the legitimizing moral justifications of sharing and egalitarianism erasing of income disparities that exist among the Manangis, as elsewhere. (Ratanapruck tells, for instance, of three traders who once spread their hawkers' cloths next to one another on Bangkok sidewalks, one now owning a small hotel in his home village, the other two owning three-star hotels in Katmandu, and yet another Thailand-based trader having become a millionaire; and inversely monks, who are forced to leave the monastery because parents have died and they need to support siblings.)

Donations to community rituals are public; peer pressure and status competition are explicit coercive modes. Ratanapruck likens these carefully recorded and announced monetary contributions to a potlatch (2008, 209). This is not to say that the various rituals engaged in, chanting and counting of prayer beads included, cannot concentrate the mind and build social solidarity, or that pooling does not allow the community to produce collective goods such as roads, refurbished stupas, and support for monasteries. The *meetha* (village-wide archery festival), *nandi* mechanisms of joint hosting of festivals, and the new urban Kathmandu meetha including card games, board games, and lotteries are fund-raisers, solidarity builders, and merit-making. Gambling is said to instill a discipline of indifference to money loss, a separation from desire, the bolstering of a "big heart," and a turning outward toward the community.

Collective Violence and Humanitarian Intervention

The way in which democracy came suddenly to masses of people in South Asia is a type case of what Emile Durkheim, in a different context, called the sociological monstrosity of the destruction of mediating institutions between the national government and the citizen. Durkheim, contemplating the oscillating swings of popular opinion in plebiscitary or referendum politics after the French Revolution destroyed parish mechanisms of intermediate levels of governance, worried that stable government policies would be hard to achieve. For Tambiah, contemplating the arrival of mass democracy after colonial rule, it was the effort to transfer constitutional power to dominant groups and the sudden production of volatile vote banks that has similarly impeded judicious governance. He turns to Durkheim particularly for his account of affect-charged crowd "effervescence," that labile surplus of affective energy that can suddenly flip from pack attack to panic flight and vice-versa, and that is composed, in the case of modern ethnonationalist collective violence, of both anger and fear. In *Leveling Crowds: Ethnonationalist Conflict and Collective Violence in South Asia* (1996), Tambiah looks first to the ritualized riots of pre-modern moral economies described by E. P. Thompson, Natalie Davis, and others—my own account of riots against religious minorities in nineteenth- and early-twentieth-century Iran provides another starkly defined public processional and ritual form performed before state and religious authorities inscribing public truth upon the body, analogous to Foucault's description of punishment in the opening of *Discipline and Punish* (1977; *Surveiller et punir*, 1975), and repeated in executions of Baha'is in the early days of the Islamic Revolution of 1979 (Fischer 1973, 1990b).

But with others, Tambiah perceives a radical difference in modern mass violence, and he draws upon both the literature of modern crowd psychology (Gustave Le Bon, Georges Rude, Sigmund Freud, Elias Canetti) and Durkheim. Although Tambiah suggests that most of the South Asian ethnonationalist riots are short-lived, that the heightened affect and suspension of individual reason wanes as quickly as it arises, his own account of the traps in which mass "democratic politics and ethnonationalist politics are related in South Asia" and in which "violence as mode of conducting politics has become established and institutionalized" is considerably darker. "Industrial employment, professional skills and the practice of Western medicine" have become "recategorized as entitlements and sumptuary privileges indexed as quotas assignable to preexisting ethnic or racial or indigenous groupings" (1996, 342). Collective violence orchestrated to defend or contest these entitlements creates a massive internal contradiction. "Systematically organized ethnic riots by politicians, parties, and police" destroy and then, on the other hand, require repair by agencies of the same governance structures, particularly the health care system, hospitals, welfare agencies, refugee camps, and relief administration (ibid., 330). The language of the United Nations conventions of the International Law of Human Rights—the Declaration of 1948 and its two main Covenants of 1966 on civil and political rights, and on economic, social, and cultural rights; along with its eight further covenants on genocide (1948), refugees (1951, 1966), racial discrimination (1965), women (1979), religion (1981), children (1989), and indigenous peoples (draft 1993)—remain important hortatory ideals, but are contested and unenforceable even in signatory countries.

Time has moved on since 1996, and the debate about human rights versus humanitarian rights has intensified (Fassin and Pandolfi 2010). Mary Jo DelVecchio Good and Byron Good's contribution in this volume provides an important ethnographic case that extends both Tambiah's discussion and his more optimistic hopes. The struggle of Aceh separatists against the Indonesian central state was locked in a brutal civil war for twenty-eight years, or longer if one counts its roots in earlier broken promises. Aceh had played an important role in the struggle for Indonesian independence against the Dutch. Promises made then for provincial autonomy were broken by President Suharto, who sent Batak troops to put down resistance. Discovery of natural gas off Aceh was exploited by Indonesia with little return to the local communities, and this exacerbated Aceh's sense of betrayal. In 2004 a tsunami devastated the province's north and west coasts, and also brought the civil war to a halt. Almost miraculously, the Acenese independence movement and the Indonesian state were able to leverage the disaster into a peace accord and a new center-periphery set of relations—*almost* miraculously, because it took concerted effort on both sides, but nonetheless *miraculously* (with the help of an act of God or nature) because the tsunami also hit Sri Lanka, with no similar effect in bringing peace (which only came six years later in the form of a bloody crushing of the Tamil Tigers in May 2009). Mary Jo and Byron Good report on an extraordinary conference they convened at Harvard in 2007, bringing together leaders from all sides of the Aceh conflict, who in neutral territory could both talk and re-enact some of the emotional explosiveness.

More comprehensively, the Goods report on two mental health needs-assessment surveys they conducted in the interior villages where the struggle had been fiercest, and their subsequent effort to help build both mobile clinics and integrate them in a public health care system. Their work with the international NGO International Organization for Migration (IOM) and with local psychiatrists and health care workers goes to the heart of debates about the value of talk therapy and psychopharmacology, about donor metrics and timetables, about repair of torn social fabrics, and about renegotiation of center-periphery relations. The rewards of watching people return from extreme dysfunction and inability to work to social life belie extreme skeptics of medical intervention. Supporting local self-government slowly being rebuilt is equally fraught and rewarding. The "poisonous knowledge" of things done in the past, in other conflict areas of

Indonesia (for example, the still-traumatic aftermath of the 1965 anti-communist massacres) as well as elsewhere in the world, has become part of everyday reality. As a Balinese anthropologist observes about his society, you have to carry on everyday life with people who killed your family. This condition of knowledge is a widespread one, from Europe in the aftermath of the Second World War to the brutalities of the Second World War in Southeast Asia, from civil war in Beirut to postcolonial and post-Soviet ethnonationalist conflicts around the world. Difficult as these situations are, life does come back, and narratives that are alternatives to those that mobilized and locked people into mutually assured destruction can and do emerge—a hope that Tambiah repeatedly expresses for South Asia.

Liisa Malkki, Marshall Sahlins, and Emiko Ohnuki-Tierney each reflect on a different facet of these issues. Malkki reflects on the double binds between humanitarianism and professionalism in the world of dealing with refugees, and for NGOs such as the Red Cross. As work by Fassin and Pandolfi (2010) and others has pointed out, navigating between neutrality in the name of humanitarian emergency relief and de facto complicity sides to a conflict is easier to accomplish verbally than in reality, as the splits between the Red Cross, Doctors without Borders, and Doctors of the World have demonstrated.

Marshall Sahlins, citing his son, Peter Sahlins, picks up the theme of the amplification of minor differences through relays up and down the transformative scale of structural conflicts. Arjun Appadurai takes from Freud the phrase "narcissism of small numbers" for the title of his meditation *Fear of Small Numbers: An Essay on the Geography of Anger* (2006). Taking cues from Georg Simmel, Tambiah says, on the same theme, *"the greater the blurrings of and ambiguities between the socially constructed categories of difference, the greater the venom of the imposed boundaries, when conflict erupts, between the self and the other, 'us' and 'them'"* (Tambiah 1996, 276; emphasis in the original). As Sahlins pithily remarks, apropos the all-too-frequent glib references to Benedict Anderson's *Imagined Communities*, "collective subjects such as nations, 'imagined' as they may be, take on the flesh-and-blood qualities of real life subjects" under conditions of segmentary opposition, schizmogenesis, or what Tambiah calls *transvaluation-focalization* and *nationalization-parochialization*. Anderson in *Imagined Communities* (1991; 1983) and in a different way, Gellner in *Nations and Nationalism* (1983) focus attention on the materiality of print literacy in the production of nationalism. Tambiah (1976) and Taylor (in this volume) also pay attention to the materiality of print and orthographic technologies, as Rosalind Morris (2000) does to the more recent mediations of photography and video in the transfer of spirit mediumship and political violence in Thailand.

Two things are important here: the synaptic transfer across national boundaries sparking quite different social arenas of conflict using the same symbolic resources (e.g., the transduction of the Salman Rushdie affair or the Muhammad cartoon affair [Fischer 1990b, 2009]);[24] and the vertical transductions between local and national levels of antagonisms and conflicts.

Emiko Ohnuki-Tierney turns to a current example of cross-temporal analogizing that has deformed American foreign policy: the quick assimilation of the attack on New York's World Trade Center to the attack on Pearl Harbor and (much later) kamikaze attacks during World War II (see also John Dower 2010). What makes Ohnuki-Tierney's participation in this discussion so powerful and compelling is not the reference to "inferiorization" or the way in which "liberal democracy at home in Western Europe and the United States assumes the fierce shape of authoritarian rule abroad," however true those are, but rather her own remarkable work (2002, 2006) on the roughly four thousand teenage *tokkōtai* (kamikaze) pilots drawn from a thousand university students and some two thousand other teens, newly enlisted or conscripted toward the war's end, and their desperate attempts to find meaning and rationalize the deaths to which they were being sent. As with Tambiah, Ohnuki-Tierney exemplifies an anthropologist's calling to recover the humanity of people sacrificed to the juggernauts of mass politics, and to recognize their alternative ideals, motives, and possibilities.

Flying Canoes, by way of Conclusion

Along the trajectory of Tambiah's career he has written a series of experimental essays in the methodologies for analyzing ritual action, cosmologies, and classifications. Many of these emerge from an important, if now decaying, tradition of anthropological pedagogy: the reanalysis of ethnographies with new theories and analytical perspective, particularly of Malinowksi's of the Trobriand Islands and Evans-Pritchard's of the Nuer and Azande. Often this was done in term-length seminars devoted to one society to allow close readings and in-depth rethinking. Tambiah's essays also take place in that liminal space-time in which British social anthropology struggled to come to terms with Levi-Strauss's structuralism as well as to incorporate structural linguistics (particularly Roman Jakobson, but also J. R. Firth, C. K. Ogden, and I. A. Richards), symbolic and phenomenological analyses (Ernst Cassirer, Suzanne Langer, Peter Berger and Thomas Luckman, Erving Goffman, and Clifford Geertz), speech act theory (J. L. Austin), and ritual dramaturgy and performative rhetoric (Kenneth Burke, Victor Turner, Richard Schechner). Tambiah follows the lead of his mentor Edmund Leach and of Mary Douglas more than Levi-Strauss, but the latter is a constant presence to react against and metabolize, as is that other student of Marcel Mauss, Georges Dumezil, whose analyses of the tripartite structures of Indo-European myth lie only slightly below the surface of Tambiah's sangha-dhramaraja explorations.

It is the Brazilian anthropologist Mariza Peirano, another former student of Tambiah's, who in the present volume draws attention to this corpus of Tambiah's work, at the same time drawing attention to yet another national tradition of anthropology that Tambiah has influenced. Even the listing of Brazilian topics for which Tambiah's work has been used, and the research agenda convened around Tambiah's work, is remarkable.

There are many golden nuggets in Tambiah's experiments with logical and formal relations that myths and rituals perform, embody, and constitute. Among my favorites are analyses of Trobriand seafaring magic to speed *kula* deep-sea canoes (flying canoes) that serve as charter myths for male-female complementary powers and name the paths of *kula* trade routes; Thai animal classifications that puzzle through the analytic methods for explicating classification and ritual proposed by Levi-Strauss, Leach, and Mary Douglas; Sri Lankan exorcism rites that (like Levi-Strauss's analysis of Cuna exorcisms for the pains of blocked childbirth) act through a kind of abreaction, and utilize "maximal sensory intensity" to embody the demonic "indulgence of gross desires" that invade and are made to retreat taking the evil with them; and the Thai royal tonsure ritual that enacts the transformation from galactic polity to nation-state through the innovations of Mongkut's reign.

King Mongkut takes the public role of the god Shiva in the tonsure rite for his designated crown prince (an innovation in the previously "notoriously ambiguous and unstable Siamese kingdom with its frequent rebellions and usurpations"). Previously a king remained secluded while his representative Brahmin priest performed the public rite. Mongkut's "innovative step (which he repeated in other cosmic rites)," Tambiah observes, had three implications: a "modernizing motive to impress the foreigners" by allowing the king to be seen in public without their having to cast their eyes down on bended knee; "the political statement" of the king's increased power and sense of security ("a king confined to his palace relies on the dubious eyes and ears of his favorites"[25]); and "a ritual motive" that heightened the efficacy of the rite. Mongkut's move consolidates, as Tambiah puts it, an "emergent meaning" that enlarges the institution of kingship (Tambiah 1985b, 160-61).

But it is the analysis of Trobriand flying witches and flying canoes that remains my favorite. The magic used by their male makers to endow the female deep-sea canoes with their flying speed is gained by younger brothers from older brothers and fathers or from mother's brothers with a *pokala* payment. The form of this magic that today men retain is but an incomplete version of the original magic that made canoes fly. So too I hope my token *pokala* to my older "[mother's] younger brother," Tambi, will speed the anthropological canoes of our calling.

God speed, Tambi.

Felicity Aulino and Miriam Goheen

1. This collection is in large part the result of two events held in honor of Professor Stanley J. Tambiah: first, a double panel session at the annual meeting of the American Anthropological Association, November 2007, Washington, D.C.; and second, a double panel session at the International Thai Studies Conference, January 2008, Bangkok.

2. This is especially evidenced in *The Buddhist Saints of the Forest and the Cult of Amulets* (1984), as James Taylor shows in the second article in this volume.

3. Social totality here should remind us of Mauss's "total social phenomenon," the "collective mentality" of the Annales School, and "social formations" in structural-Marxist thought.

4. *World Conqueror and World Renouncer* (1976) is again an outstanding example of such work.

5. Tambiah once admonished a student who tried to disguise his use of Marxist theory in a class on peasant societies. It being the Cold War era, Marxist theory was laden with negative connotations for many Americans. Tambiah simply looked at him and said, "You use what works! Just explain the data, and don't read meanings into what are merely heuristic models to further understanding."

THE CHARISMA OF SAINTS AND THE CULT
OF RELICS, AMULETS, AND TOMB SHRINES
Stanley Jeyaraja Tambiah

1. Sox cites Peter Nichols as making this statement in *The Pope's Divisions* (Nichols 1981).

2. In November 1974, the Pope, then Cardinal of Cracow, venerated the Lanciano relics; in October the executors of the will of the last king of Italy, Umberto II, met John Paul II and handed over the title to the Shroud of Turin to the Holy See. John Paul made a pilgrimage to the

grotto of Lourdes in August 1983, and may have been the first Pope to have done so.

3. For example, a whole array of persons have been recognized as saints in Christianity—early Christian martyrs, ascetic saints of the desert or of Mount Athos, patriarchs of the Eastern Church, bishops of the Western Church, and so on. I maintain, however, that this spectrum coheres around a central dominant focus that emphasizes asceticism, contemplative life, austere personal life, charity, and compassion toward fellow beings.

4. From a general comparative point of view, it is important to recognize that in some religious traditions sainthood may have no place, or only a marginal place. In Judaism, sainthood is relevant only to Hasidism and therefore has only a minor place in the totality. We see the reverse situation in Islam, in which just one among many branches, the Wahabi movement, is inhospitable to the conception. I have yet to inquire to what extent sainthood has a place in Confucian religion.

5. The comparative project in the study of religion has been recently tackled by an array of scholars in the edited collection *A Magic Still Dwells* (Patton and Ray 2000). In the volume, issues posed by comparative study are variously probed in a positive critical spirit, and its possibility and value is largely affirmed. I have myself dealt (elsewhere at some length) with comparative issues relating to translation of cultures and their commensurability; the proposition that meaningful comparison between two (or more) phenomena is not possible without first establishing a "base of agreement" between them, from which meaningful similarities and differences can be projected; and the point at which we may have to conclude that the phenomena in question are incommensurable. See my *Magic, Science, Religion and the Scope of Rationality* (Tambiah 1990), ch. 6.

6. James also remarked that asceticism may be carried too far; moreover, pessimistic feelings about the self may motivate mortifications and torments, which may signify an irrational or obsessional phase among psychopathic persons.

7. Although certain kinds of Islamic saints, like the Sufi *wali* in Egypt or the *marabout* in Morocco, are not celibate, and although saintly charisma in these traditions is physically transmitted through descent and inheritance, the highest forms of sainthood in them are "achieved." I shall deal with some Islamic cases later. Karl Potter, in *Presuppositions of India's Philosophy* (1963), distinguishes two ways of attaining mystical freedom portrayed in Indian speculative philosophy. One is the *jativada* approach of gradual progress toward the goal through discipline, action,

and ritual (progress philosophy): these are necessary and sufficient conditions of observance and effort that "causally" lead to the liberation. In Hinduism, this approach is best exemplified by *yoga siddha*, and it well characterizes the quest of the Buddhist adept. The other is the *ajativada* approach of a "leap" attained by sudden knowledge or intuitive dawning (leap philosophy), which in Potter's description is "acausal." Practice and disciplined pursuit may be preparatory but cannot coerce the achievement of attainment. This approach is exemplified by *bhakti siddha*, the devotional saint. It seems that most hagiographies of devotional saints suddenly touched by the divine actually also stress their dedication to ascetic discipline and religious practice.

8. Trimingham traces the development of the orders through three stages, but admits, thereby softening his arguable evolutionary perspective, that "this is no more than a generalization of trends, and that in the final stage the three continued to exist contemporaneously" (1971, 102). "The stages (as affecting the individual) are 'surrender to God' (*khanqah* stage), 'surrender to rule' (*tariqa*), and 'surrender to a person' (*ta'ifa* stage)" (ibid.). The first Trimingham regards as "the golden age of mysticism," intellectually and emotionally an aristocratic movement, with a "master and his circle of pupils, frequently itinerant, having minimum regulations for living a common life, leading in the tenth century to the formation of unspecialized lodges and convents." The second stage, the Seljug period in the thirteenth century, he calls a "bourgeois movement" in which there is a "transmission of a doctrine, a rule and method," and there is "development of new types of collectivistic methods for inducing ecstasy." The third stage, the time of the founding of the Ottomon Empire from the fifteenth century onwards, is when Sufism becomes "a popular movement," characterized by "the transmission of an allegiance alongside the doctrine and rule" and the founding of numerous *tariqa* lines and orders fully incorporated with the saint cult (ibid., 103).

9. Also see Gilsenan's *Recognizing Islam: Religion and Society in the Modern Arab World* (1982).

10. I formulated similar ideas about the Buddhist saint in *The Buddhist Saints of the Forest and the Cult of Amulets* (Tambiah 1984).

11. It is personally gratifying that another anthropologist (trained in Australia and not associated with me) confirms in most respects all I reported and interpreted in the 1960s and 1970s concerning the cult of amulets in Thailand that centered on certain forest saints.

12. The coming together of the Buddha's dispersed relics and ashes and the reconstitution and resurrection of the body at the end of the Buddhist era is also a theme in Buddhism, albeit it is not as critical a doctrine as is its parallel in Christianity.

13. Ambrose had already previously received gifts of relics from Constantinople for his Basilica of the Holy Apostles.

14. I would add to this discussion some submissions in Georgia Frank's *The Memory of the Eyes: Pilgrims to Living Saints in Christian Late Antiquity* (2000). In her exposition of a "theology of vision" she says that the human eye was conceived as being able to see beyond physical appearances to gain a more complete understanding of biblical events. Pilgrims experienced this theology of vision when they traveled to see the Egyptian desert ascetics who were likened to Christ and his disciples. Of particular relevance to my essay is Frank's statement that visual piety, as reflected in relic veneration, enabled a pilgrim's eyes to project a deeply meaningful wholeness onto the fragment of a relic. (In later times the theology of vision found its most complete expression in the cult of icons.)

15. For example, a writer on the medieval Christian cult of the saints as practiced in Western Europe has this to say: "The bodies of the martyrs, unlike those of heroes, would not remain dead forever. Early Christians took literally Christ's promise of the resurrection and thus expected that on the last day the martyrs' physical bodies would be taken up again by their owners.... Christians believed that physical proximity to these bodies was beneficial, and that those buried near a saint's tomb would be raised up with the saint on the day of judgment" (Geary 1991, 33–34). As remarked earlier, these ideas of future reaggregation of relics and the resurrection of the Buddha and saints are not unfamiliar to Buddhist traditions as well.

16. On Moroccan saint shrines, I have found interesting information in the following sources: Edward Westermarck, *The Moorish Conception of Holiness* (1916); Clifford Geertz, *Islam Observed* (1968); Ernest Gellner, *Saints of the Atlas* (1969); Vincent Crapanzano, *The Hamadsha: A Study in Moroccan Ethnopsychiatry* (1973) and *Tuhami: Portrait of a Moroccan* (1980); and Dale F. Eickelman, *Moroccan Islam* (1976). Also see, for a different example, Emmanuel Marx, "Communal and Individual Pilgrimage: The Region of Saints' Tombs in South Sinai" (1977, 29–51).

17. Similarly, Crapanzano (1980) reports that "Moroccans speak of visiting a saint's sanctuary as 'visiting the saint.' ... Some Moroccans ... claim that saints are alive in their tombs" (16–17).

18. For this discussion of Christian relics I am indebted to Elizabeth Benard, "The Living Among the Dead: A Comparison of Buddhist and Christian Relics" (1988).

19. Thus St. Thomas Aquinas, in the course of discussing the crucifixion of Jesus, cites Gregory of Nyssa as observing that "the form of the

cross, radiating out from the centre in four different directions, denotes
the universal diffusion of the power and providence of him who hung
upon it." See Aquinas, *Summa Theologiae*, vol. 54, *The Passion of Christ*
(1965), 3a. 46, 4 (p. 17).

20. As John McCulloh puts it in "The Cult of Relics in the Letters and
Dialogues of Pope Gregory the Great" (1976), "It was particularly appropriate that martyrs, who had given their lives for the faith, should rest
beneath the altar on which lay the body of Christ, who had given His life
for men. The physical evidence of the martyrs' passions was a constant
reminder of the passion *par excellence*" (179).

21. *Dhatu* in Buddhist cosmology also refers to each of the realms of
desire (*kama*), form (*rupa*), and no form (*arupa*).

22. The Sinhalese chronicle *Culavamsa* (ch. 80, verses 68–70) uses the
word *jivita* (life) when it speaks of Tamils invading and destroying ceti-
yas and "allowing many of the bodily relics, their souls as it were [liter-
ally "their life," *jivitam*] to disappear" (Geiger 1953, 133).

23. One should note some scholars translate *paribhogacetiya* as "relics
of use" and *uddesikacetiya* as "commemorative relics."

24. Geary considers the Central Middle Ages to cover the period
from the ninth to the eleventh centuries. This period is also sometimes
referred to as "the later Carolingian and post-Carolingian period."

25. See, for example, Senake Bandaranayake, *Sinhalese Monastic Architecture: The Viharas of Anuradhapura* (1974).

26. See, for example, T. W. Rhys Davids, trans., *Buddhist Suttas* (1881),
vol. 11.

27. With the erection of funerary monuments is sanctioned the virtue of pilgrimage. The Buddha tells Ananda that there are four places
the believing person should visit "with feelings of reverence and awe"—
the Buddha's birthplace, the place where he attained supreme insight, the
place from which he preached his first sermon, and the place where he
passed away. Those who shall die while they with believing heart were
journeying on such a pilgrimage shall be reborn in the happy realms of
heaven.

28. See, for example, E. Conze, *Buddhist Thought in India* (1970), and
Frank E. Reynolds, "The Several Bodies of the Buddha" (1977).

29. See these texts: John S. Strong, *The Legend of King Asoka: A Study
and Translation of Asokavadana* (1983); Hermann Oldenberg, ed. and
trans., *The Dipavamsa: An Ancient Historical Record* (1982); Wilhelm Geiger, trans., *The Mahavamsa, or The Great Chronicle of Ceylon* (1986 [1950]);
and N. A. Jayawickrama, trans., *The Chronicle of the Thupa and Thupavamsa*
(1971).

30. The *Thupavamsa* is centrally concerned with the travels of the eighth relic deposit, originally located at Ramagama on the banks of the Ganges. It was subsequently washed away and taken in possession by the king of the Nagas, Mahakala. These relics were destined for their final deposition in Anradhapura (Sri Lanka) in the splendid stupa built by King Dutthagamani, the Ruvanmali Mahathupa (the Great Thupa of Golden Garlands).

31. The *Asokavadana* says *stupas*, while the *Dipavamsa* and *Mahavamsa* say *viharas*.

32. I am indebted to Benard, "The Living Among the Dead" (1988), for parts of this version. Other variant details of Constantine and Helena cited here are found in Helen C. Evans and William D. Wixom, eds., *The Glory of Byzantium* (1997); see, for example, descriptions of a Byzantine reliquary (81), and of the Stavelot Tryptych (461–62).

33. In *Butler's Lives of the Saints*, vol. 3, we learn that St. Helen, mother of Constantine the Great, went to Palestine "to venerate the places made sacred by the bodily presence of our Lord" after Constantine triumphed over Licinius in 324 and became master of the East. Stories about her playing a principal part in the recovery of the Holy Cross on Mount Calvary are mentioned. She is also described as taking charge of the execution of Constantine's decision that a church be built on the site of Golgotha and the holy sepulchre. St. Helen also built many churches and gave alms liberally (Butler 1957).

34. The history and religio-political significance of the Emerald Buddha has been richly documented. Some major references are Robert Lingat, "Le Culte du Bouddha d'Emeraude," (1934); Camille Notton, trans., *The Chronicle of the Emerald Buddha* (1933); Frank Reynolds, "The Holy Emerald Jewel" (1978); and S. J. Tambiah, *World Conqueror and World Renouncer* (1976), ch. 6.

35. Concerning the travels and significance of the Buddha's Tooth Relic in Sri Lanka, see B. C. Law, ed. and trans., *The Dathavamsa: A History of the Tooth Relic of the Buddha* (1925); E. S. Rajasekara, ed., *Dalada Sirita* (1920); A. M. Hocart, *The Temple of the Tooth in Kandy* (1931); and H. L. Seneviratne, *Rituals of the Kandyan State* (1978).

UNDERSTANDING SOCIAL TOTALITIES: STANLEY TAMBIAH'S EARLY
CONTRIBUTION TO SOCIOLOGY OF THAI BUDDHISM
James Taylor

A portion of this article (from the section "Paradigms in Theravada Buddhist Tradition: The Primitive Monks' Charter, Reform, and the Modern Kammaṭṭhāna Monks" to the end) is adapted from material taken from my recent book *Buddhism and Postmodern Imaginings in Thailand: The Religiosity of Urban Space* (2008).

1. The late Tom Kirsch (1977) has referred to this process as "upgrading."

2. In "A Performative Approach to Ritual" ([1979] 1981), Tambiah essentially sees rituals as having a duplex function, with both semantic and pragmatic interactive elements.

3. Information for this section on Tambiah is indebted to an interview conducted by Mariza Peirano (Tambiah 1996), an earlier interview by Alan MacFarlane (Tambiah 1983a), and also personal communication, Harvard University, December 1995.

4. In Collins's *Selfless Person: Imagery and Thought in Theravada Buddhism* (Cambridge: Cambridge University Press, 1990), Collins refers to Gombrich as his "*upajjhaya*" (p. ix).

5. See especially Gombrich's harsh critique "Knowledge of the Unknowable" (1985), and a response by linguist and Indologist Frits Staal (1986). In "At the Confluence of Anthropology, History, and Indology" (Tambiah 1987), Tambiah refers to Gombrich's remarks as the "tantrums" of a "grammarian pedant" (188). Space does not allow a full discussion of this debate, which was largely over issues of language, spelling, and history. See also Tambiah's own riposte to some of these critiques in his article "King Mahasammata" (1989b).

6. This prompted Staal to refer to Tambiah's approach as "Object Semantics" (Staal 1986, 193). Staal noted that to understand religion we would do better to look for the rules that govern practice, rather than look for "meanings" (217).

7. This research led to my book *Forest Monks and the Nation-state*, published in 1993.

8. Namely: Peripatetic, Settlement, Climacteric, and Terminal (Taylor 1993, 202).

9. In Thai, amulet-medallions are *Phra-khreung*. In my research I was more concerned with the relics of saints (*Phra-thaat*). The biographer of Phra Ajaan Man, Phra Ajaan Maha Bua, recounted how he lost invaluable relics of the Master through lay fervor. The relics, having by then seemingly miraculously transmogrified, suddenly appeared four years after the cremation of the Master in the hands of a prosperous businessman from Nakhorn Ratchasima. News spread rapidly thereafter as fervent relic-hunters, mostly women, sought them out. Because these sacra are valued for their *saksit* power among devotees, Maha Bua noted that many people do not admit to actually possessing them for fear of losing them. See Maha Bua, *Venerable Acariya Mun Bhuridatta Thera* (2005), 402–03.

10. See critique by Keyes (1987, 127ff.).

11. Although Tambiah often refers to Buddhism as a "single system," these days we often tend to think in terms of multiple Buddhisms, Buddhisms in the plural, influenced by the postmodern turn in the social/human sciences, the crisis of epistemology, and the politics of representation. A close reading of Tambiah's work, however, shows that by and large the difference is more a matter of semantics, as he considers Thai Buddhism an interactive, actor-oriented, contingent, permeable social field that is capable of various articulations (see Marcus and Fisher 1986, ch. 1; Keyes 1987, 128; and Taylor 1999 and 2007, on the varieties of postmodern Buddhist experiences). Tambiah's definition of "single system" may also be a reaction to Melford Spiro's Buddhist psychologism and method of disaggregating Buddhism into two distinct religious systems—"supernaturalism" and "Buddhism" (Spiro 1971).

12. See, for instance, Tambiah 1976, 5, and 1984, 7. I have not mentioned Malinowski or Weber, or various social linguists, who were obvious primary influences. Tambiah has also acknowledged the influence of Dumont and Sartre in his thinking.

13. National Archives of Thailand, *Seuksaathikaan* (Education Documents), Fifth Reign 12/8, 1:1–11.

14. This category may include rural monks who according to traditional calendrical rituals were expected first and foremost to chant extensively in traditional style from the suttas. This includes chanting sections not in favor with turn-of-the-century reformers, such as the *Mahaa Chaat* (literally "Great Birth" Sermon; *Vessantara Jataka*), ridiculed by Mongkut but considered to bring considerable merit to the listener (Taylor 1993, 64–65). For a discussion of the text's ritual relevance, see Tambiah 1970, 160ff.

15. Tambiah's original discussion of the *Aggañña Sutta* was in his *World Conqueror and World Renouncer* (1976), but he later elaborated on it in a 1989 article where he suggests, in response to a critique by Michael Carrithers, that the text has in fact a "persisting cosmological significance, acting as 'precedent,' 'point of reference,' and 'normative' account—that is, as a 'charter'" (Tambiah 1989b, 106). On the *Aggañña Sutta* see Maurice Walshe, trans., *The Long Discourses of the Buddha* (1996), 407–15.

16. Tambiah (1987) has noted that "the past as sanction embraces the Malinowskian 'charter' theory that the past is used as legitimator of the living present" (194).

17. Tambiah's means of working through texts/history and ethnography, whereby one analytical modality informs the other, constitutes in

part what Frank Reynolds called Tambiah's unique "holistic" contributions to Buddhist scholarship, unparalleled since the work of Paul Mus in the 1930s (see Reynolds 1987, 113–21).

18. In the forest monastery where I stayed as a monk for the rains' residence of 2007 it was common for local Thai-Lao rituals, such as Bun Khao Pradap Din (honoring the deceased relatives, held on the full moon, around mid-September), to be integrated into normative Buddhist calendrical rituals. Locals made no religious distinction between these.

19. Tambiah has called this a "pentadic" formulation (1984, 75–76).

20. In Thai, *Kammathaan* (and in Pali, *Kammaṭṭhāna*)—a term I prefer to "forest monks," as it is used by the monks themselves. The term literally means the bases or foundation of meditation practice, which are reckoned to be some forty subjects in total, though only a few are used by these monks in Thailand. The term is often preceded in Pali usage by the word *dhuṭanga*, meaning ascetic practices supposedly allowed by the Buddha himself for those with a preference for more rigor (see Taylor 1993, 22 n. 9).

21. In Pali, *Dhammayuttika Nikaya*, meaning literally "the sect that acts in accordance with the Dhamma." A *nikaya* here refers to both a state-sanctioned ordination lineage and a community of monks who share such affiliation. However, the community may also identity with segmented lines, or small face-to-face groups (as in monastic pupilages).

22. See Suksamran 1982, 36; Kangsadara 1989, 253; and *Acts on the Administration of the Buddhist Order* 1989.

23. See *Majjhima Nikaya* 119 (Kayagata-sati Sutta, or "Mindfulness of the Body"), and Robinson et al. 2005, 167.

24. Consisting of two hundred twenty-seven rules for monks, recited among monks of the same fraternity (Nikaya) each fortnight; the single most important sangha solidarity ritual.

25. A number of sources indicate that the Sri Lankan Ramañña Nikaya was first established in 186–64 when the then-*samanera* (novice) Ambagahawatte Sri Saranankara (1832–1886) returned to the island, having received the Upasampada (higher ordination) from the Ven. Gneiyadharma Sangharaja of Ratnapunna Vihara in Burma. Paññananda returned from Burma in 1863, shortly after Ambagahawatte returned (Carrithers 1983, 79–80). Both monks were originally from different nikayas in Sri Lanka.

Much as in Thailand, four factors account for the popular appeal of forest monks in Sri Lanka: their affinity and symbiotic relationship with nature and wild animals; the association between their isolated abodes and supernatural forces; their ascetic practices (in Pali/Sanskrit, *tapas* or *tapasa*, a term seemingly not used in Thailand as a designation for asceticism/ascetic practices) and use of *dhutangas* (austerities); and their acclaimed supernatural abilities (assumed to be derived largely from the above factors); for example, Paññananda is said to have had visitations from celestial beings right up until his death (Carrithers 1983, 88; also Coningham 1995, 232–33).

26. The similarities between the Thai and Sri Lankan reforms include improvement of vinaya practice; accurate calculation of the Uposatha days (that is, devotional full-moon and new-moon days; in Thai, Wan Phra, corresponding to the four weekly phases of the cycle of the moon); and emphasis on a return to a more primitive simplicity (see Khantipalo 1979).

27. Steven Kemper (1980, 28–29) has noted, from work in Sri Lanka during the 1970s, the salience and importance of the vinaya and how it was only then starting to become considered by anthropologists and textual scholars. He sees the vinaya as critical to the way the monks understand their relationship to the Buddha and his teachings. See also Carrithers 1983, 139–47.

28. Ajaan Man had fifty-seven years as a monk. His monastic career may be divided into four phases: 1892–1915; 1916–1928; 1929–1940; and 1941–49 (see Taylor 1993, 104–05).

29. Taylor 1993, 50–51; National Archives *Seuksaathikaan* (Education Documents), Fifth Reign 8/19, 1–19.

30. See also Paitoon 1995 on some local reactions in the northeast region to the turn-of-the-century reforms.

31. Vajirañāṇavarorasa, *Entrance to the Vinaya* (1992), Preface 1913, 1:x.

32. For relevant discussion, see also the recent work by Justin McDaniel, *Gathering Leaves and Lifting Words* (2008).

33. As Tambiah (1999) noted more recently: "As the first representative of a new dynasty, Rama I engaged in acts that bear the characteristic marks of an active king achieving legitimacy and stability within the orthodoxy of a Buddhist polity. These acts are the purification of the sangha, the enactment of new sangha laws, the sponsorship of a revised Buddhist canon, and a new version of the historic cosmological work, the *Traiphum*."

34. In his travels in the countryside in 1899, Wachirayan noted that monks did not use newly distributed printed texts, because they believed this form of communication was linked with Christian propagandizing (see Patrick Jory quoted in Veidlinger 2006, 116). The Pali *Tipitaka* was

first printed in Thailand in 1893 (Veidlinger 2006, 2), using a system of transcribing Pali to Thai, invented by Mongkut, called *kaanyut.*

35. Indeed, sponsoring the copying of religious manuscripts (usually involving forest monks in the reform Sinhalese lineage, who were most concerned with written culture and Pali scholarship) has early antecedents, as in fifteenth-sixteenth century Lanna-Thai; see Veidlinger 2006, 85, 96.

36. See Tambiah 1968 (following Leach 1966). In his early seminal work on ritual, Tambiah was seemingly influenced by Searle and Austin and the notion of ("paradoxically") *performative* utterances—in the idea that doing is a form of saying; and we should not forget his later interest in "indexicality" in Peircean semiotics. "Indexicality," Tambiah noted (1987, 196), "enables me to show how ritual and other dramatized events confer power and prestige on the participants and how the contexts of action are important to understand transformations of meaning." Rituals are not the static expression of normative or traditional values, but the consequence of a number of inferences involving doubt, disbelief, and uncertainty, though they demand a commitment from the actor, even, as can be the case with rituals involving Pali chants, when the actor does not really understand them. As Tambiah noted (1968, 179–80), in the village, Pali words used in sacred chants are meant to be heard but not necessarily understood. However, we also need to differentiate monks from laity, and recognize that there are different levels among monks, including levels at which this may not be the case. The comprehension of Pali also relates to literacy, which Tambiah studied at the beginning of the 1960s. For instance, kammathaan monks who have been ordained for some years are well versed in Pali and claim to comprehend the words meaningfully. They also use the rhythmic sounds as a meditation—especially in long mortuary or *paritta* chants. Tambiah (1968a, 100) has in fact noted that Buddhism is "aesthetically a musical religion, and that the memorizing of words is closely linked to musical rhythms." This musicality indicates the technique and the way of learning lengthy chants.

37. In a cross-cultural case study, Swain (1996) has looked at how, from the mid-first to mid-third century A.D., Hellenic aristocrats in Greek-speaking city-states under Roman rule used an elite language or dialect to distinguish themselves from commoners and show themselves as elaborately acculturated.

38. Tambiah (1968) also notes that in the character and role of sacred language multiple values are ascribed, which collectively contribute to its mystical power. These values are in "mutual tension." He gives as an

example the Triple Gem: the Buddha, as the source of sacred words; the Dhamma, as the (perceived) true words of the Buddha as inscribed or transmitted in written or oral form; and the Sangha, as the most appropriate agent for the recitation of these sacred words (1968, 183).

A MUSLIM KING AND HIS BUDDHIST SUBJECTS: RELIGION, POWER,
AND IDENTITY AT THE PERIPHERY OF THE THAI STATE
Irving Chan Johnson

1. In his dissertation, Roger Kershaw (1969) noted that Kelantanese Thais were already displaying pictures of the Thai royal family in their homes and temples in the 1960s. These images were either purchased in Thailand during trips across the border or via itinerant traders at temple fairs or during house-to-house visits. Some pictures were taken from colorful calendars printed by temples and commercial establishments such as banks and businesses. On the cult of the Thai kingly image see Peleggi (2002).

2. In the Kelantanese Thai dialect, young monks who have yet to become temple abbots (*than*) are addressed by the honorific *khun*.

3. Kelantan, like most of Malaysia, still maintains its historic Malay ruling house. The sultan, despite his ritually exalted position, does not hold obvious political clout and is not involved in the day-to-day administration of the state.

ECONOMIES OF GHOSTS, GODS, AND GOODS: THE HISTORY
AND ANTHROPOLOGY OF CHINESE TEMPLE NETWORKS
Michael Puett

1. The phrase comes from Hsu 1967. Otherwise-brilliant ethnographies of the self in contemporary China will occasionally fall into this paradigm as well when they contrast a modern self with a stereotypical, traditional vision of the self as residing under the ancestors' shadow. In fact, much of what we are discovering in ethnography resonates in very intriguing ways with earlier visions of the self.

2. For full discussions of the interplay of ghosts, ancestors, and gods in China, see Jordan 1972; A. Wolf 1974; Harrel 1974; Ahern 1973; J. Watson 1988; Weller 1987; Sangren 1987; Schipper 1993; Yu 1987; Seidel 1982, 1987; Brashier 1996; Keightley 2004; and von Glahn 2004. My summary here draws on the work of all of these scholars.

3. Schipper 1970, 1990; Goossaert 2000; Katz 1995; Guo 2003, 2005; Naquin 2000; Feuchtwang 1977; Faure and Siu 2003; and Skinner 1959, 1985.

4. For lineage construction in late imperial China, see Szonyi 2002, Faure 2007, and Brook 1989.

5. Unfortunately, tracing the history of these networks is no easy task. Their existence is certainly registered in the gazetteers and archives, but, since both of these materials are aimed at presentations of local phenomena, they do not trace out which temples were linked to which networks. To study this, the only approaches are tracing the networks through inscriptions and records in the temples, and tracing the icons of the gods and goddesses. But the task is made easier by the fact that the networks are very much in the process of being re-created right now.

6. Although such attempts to destroy the networks were made under the claim of modernization, it is worth noting that there is nothing modern about such attempts themselves. Although for space reasons I have avoided mention of the interplay of these networks with the state, suffice it to say that numerous attempts at dramatic state centralization at the expense of the networks and lineage structures have occurred in Chinese history. The dramatic growth of the networks in late imperial China was simply part and parcel of a concurrent loss in state power. The twentieth century saw an attempt to re-assert state power—a continuation of a very old battle.

7. A comparison of these theories with Tambiah's theory of ritual (see 1968b) would be very rewarding.

8. The theories also contain lengthy discussions of statecraft as well, in which vertical links are created by the state through the same techniques of transforming natural elements and humans into gods and ancestors. Thus Heaven is transformed into a deity, and the ruler is transformed into a Son of Heaven as well as a father and mother of the people. For a full discussion see Puett 2005 and 2008. For the ways such theories were employed in late imperial China, see Wilson 2002 and Zito 1997. A full comparison of this vision of statecraft with Tambiah's analysis of "galactic polities" in Southeast Asia is outside of the bounds of this essay, but it is a comparison I will undertake in another forum.

9. For a preliminary attempt to take early Chinese ritual theory seriously as theory, see Puett 2006 and Weller, Seligman, Puett, and Simon 2008, 17-42 and 179-82.

TRADE, RELIGION, AND CIVIC RELATIONS IN THE MANANGI LONG-DISTANCE TRADE COMMUNITY
Prista Ratanapruck

1. In his mention of "Ec 10," Tambiah was referring to "Social Analysis 10: Principles of Economics," a popular course that fulfilled a core course requirement at Harvard and was a requirement for economics majors.

2. For more detail about their trade history, see Cooke 1985, Ven Spengen 2000, and Ratanapruck 2007.

3. There is a small but growing body of literature on the continuity of transregional commercial networks of Asian merchants. See for example Bhattacharya et al. 2007. This work is a contribution to that body of literature.

4. I am using the 1984 translation by Lord: Aristotle, *The Politics*, trans. Carnes Lord (Chicago: University of Chicago Press, 1984).

5. Aristotle wrote in *The Politics*, "[M]an is by nature a political animal. Hence [men] strive to live together even when they have no need of assistance from one another, though it is also the case that the common advantage brings them together, to the extent that it falls to each to live finely. It is this above all, then, which is the end for all both in common and separately; but they also join together, and maintain the political partnership, for the sake of living itself" (*Politics* bk. 3, ch. 6; Bekker no. 1278b, 18–24).

COSMOLOGIES OF WELFARE: TWO CONCEPTIONS OF SOCIAL
ASSISTANCE IN CONTEMPORARY SOUTH AFRICA
James Ferguson

1. There is some anthropological work on welfare, of course, especially on welfare in the "global North" (see, e.g., Edgar and Russell 1998). The apparently low level of anthropological interest in the topic (especially in the topic of welfare in the "global South"), however, remains striking.

2. The discussion that follows is a condensed version of an argument that I have made at greater length elsewhere (see J. Ferguson 2007 and 2010).

3. See Fine 2000 for a useful critique of "social capital" theory.

"A RECURRENCE OF STRUCTURES" IN COLLAPSING NIGERIA
Victor Manfredi

In memory of two mentors. Anthropologist Michael Angulu Ọnwụejìọ̀gwụ̀ of Ìgboụ́zọ̀ ("Ibusa") was Professor in the University of Benin and eventually Vice-Chancellor of Tansian University. Historian Augustin Ẹ̀gwabọ́ Ìdúùwẹ was Òdíì of Ágbọ̀ (Agbor) and eventually Íregwài of Ògbe Ñmụ̀ Déin. The first draft of this paper was presented at the AAA panel "Violence and the Scope of Rationality," honoring Stanley Tambiah, on 30 November 2007. Thanks to the organizers of that day, to the editors of this book, and to H. Abíọ́lá, D. van den Bersselaar, P. Eke[h], J. Guyer, M. Ìghílẹ̀, B. Wuloo Ikari, S. Jell-Bahlsen, I. Miller,

S. Moore, L. Murphy, O. Ńdibé, the late I. Ǹzímìro, E. Ochonu, I. Òkóntà, 'D. Ọlọ́rúnyọ̀mí, Ọ. Ọ̀mọ́ruyì, O. Owen, and M. Vickers. Where possible, I replace "Western errorist" transcriptions of African words with more modern spellings. Tonemarks: [´] = high, [`] = low. Tone conventions: in Yorùbá and Kanà, no mark = mid; in Ìgbo, Ágbọ̀, and Ẹ̀dó, no mark = same as previous mark, and a sequence of two high marks = intervening downstep. In Ágbọ̀, the [+] sign indicates antidownstep.

1. Although I'm unaware of any published reference by Tambiah to Chomskyan syntax, he mentioned it often in class, and his [1979] 1981 essay cites the generative concept of "sequencing rules" from the formal pragmatics literature. Staal (1986, p. 190) explicitly contrasts Tambiah's "syntactic" approach to ritual with Geertz' behaviorist view. The quotation in the title of this paper is taken from the larger phrase "a recurrence of structures and their transformations in systemic terms" (Tambiah 1976, p. 5), in which a syntactic metaphor can also be inferred.

2. Informal description by anonymous People's Democratic Party lawyer at the Ẹ̀dó National Association meeting, 29 August 2008, in suburban Boston.

3. In Nigeria, "South-South" denotes the four states of the delta (Ẹ̀dó, Delta, Bayelsa, Rivers) plus Cross River and Akwa Ibom.

4. The four incinerated chiefs included Saro's brother-in-law Sam Orage and his prominent benefactor Edward Kobani.

5. President-elect Abíọ́lá resisted four years of torture in solitary confinement, during which his wife Kudirat was gunned down on Abacha's orders; then on 7 July 1998 Abíọ́lá expired under marathon hectoring by Tom Pickering and Susan Rice of the Clinton State Department (Eghagha and Oyèébámi 2008). Claims were pursued under the Alien Torts Act against General Abusalami for Abíọ́lá's persecution unto death, and against Shell for complicity in the murder of the Ogoni Nine (Ikari 2006, pp. 44–54). Abíọ́lá's autopsy gave no answers (http:// physiciansforhumanrights.org/library/report-1998-07-06.html) and Abacha's death, a month before Abíọ́lá's, was never publicly investigated. During a March 1998 trip to South Africa, Bill Clinton openly encouraged General Abacha to moult into a civilian dictator (Apple 1998), and such sympathy was probably not unrelated to the Clinton Foundation's admitted receipt of "between 1 and 5 million dollars" from Abacha's in-law, Gilbert R. Chagoury, via Dr. Susan Rice (Baker and Savage 2008). A published account of 1998 remarks by ex-ambassador Donald Easum at Foggy Bottom (Ògún 2009, pp. 131–35) shows U.S. government eagerness for Abacha and Abíọ́lá to be jointly liquidated ("Supposing the two of them were not there, who would you see as a successor?") in prepara-

tion for re-injecting General Ọbásanjọ́ into the contrived power vacuum (thanks to Dr. Ebe Ochonu, in the comments thread to his 2009 *Sahara Reporters* review, for this critical information).

6. See Íkòrò (1996, p.4f.) for the term *Ogoni*, and Rowell et al. (2005, p. 65) for the Shell inferno image in an Ogoni anthem: "The flames of Shell are flames of Hell/We bask below their light/Nought for us serve the blight/Of cursed neglect and cursed Shell" (2005, p. 65).

7. *Déin* has no clear etymology; one possibility is the univerbation of an Ágbọ̀ phrase meaning "our master" (< *dí* + *èyín*).

8. "Friend from outside" euphemizes Ẹ̀dó intervention, approximately along the rhetorical lines of the "Fraternal Soviet Liberation" of Hungary in November 1956. The Ẹ̀dó footprint is even more vivid: the term *ọ̀sị*, "friend," may be a quotidian word of Ágbọ̀, but it has no cognate in the rest of the Ìgbo cluster, and was almost certainly adopted from Ẹ̀dó *ọ̀se*, "friend, lover" (Melzian 1937, p. 169).

9. Prof. Àjàyí seems to accept the Ifẹ̀ foundation myth verbatim, and censured my use of the term *ethnohistory* in the course of a dinner table discussion in 1993. The Ọba's junior brother has pushed back against Àjàyí in literary form (Ákẹnzùa 2008).

10. Notes taken in 2006 by Dr. Dmitri v.d. Bersselaar, University of Liverpool (p.c.) from [Agbor Dist. I AG 219], Nigerian National Archives, Ìbàdàn branch.

11 *Ịká*, pronounced "Èká" in Ẹ̀dó (Egharevba 1934; Melzian 1937, p. 33), is an ambiguous, outsider's term that can denote all Ìgbo-speakers west of the Niger—including also the Ànịọ́cha, Ụ́kwụ̀ ̀àni, and Òshimili districts (Forde and Jones 1950; Ọ̀hadíké 1994, pp. 69-96). Ágbọ̀'s 1938 demotion was still resented by Òbíkà's son and successor Íkenchúku (1938-1979), who griped about it in 1976 while giving me a lift to Benin-City in the royal Peugeot 604. Ọ̀nwụejìọ́gwụ̀ told me of confronting Jones in his Cambridge University retirement about the (1956) reclassification of southern chiefs—a move which Jones admitted was designed to favor Zik at the expense of Awo, who was officially regarded as a dangerous communist.

12. The name *Ìdúùwẹ* itself transparently means "brought from Ẹ̀dó."

13. In 1981, an Ògbe Ńmù̀ Déin elder who had been an NCNC stalwart playfully asked me to remind Zik—by then a septuagenarian grandee who was my neighbor in the Ìgbo university town of Ñsú̀ká ("Nsukka")—of a thirty-year-old promise to supply a revolver!

14. An instructive precedent occurred in 1956 when the Western Region deposed the Aláàfin of Ọ̀yọ́ who was refusing to join the AG. Similarly in 1963, the Midwest exiled the "Olu of Warri" Erejuwa II due

to "his personal and institutional conflict with certain NCNC party stalwarts" (Otite 1975, p. 75). One effective lever on customary chiefs is the monthly stipend paid by the regional or state government; Àzíkàíwe recognized the practice as creating a conflict-of-interest "dilemma" (1976, p. 6).

15. Lawsuits aside, Ògbe Ńmù̀ Déin pressed a second complaint against Òbí Íkenchúku, that he was stubbornly monogamous and took too long to produce an heir. When one arrived, he was provocatively named Kíagbò̀ekúzi, "What can Ágbò̀ say now?" The boy's mother feared for the infant's safety and raised him in exile, permanently impairing his fluency in the language.

16. Only temporarily, because a new expropriation had already begun: before relinquishing power the first time, Ọbásanjọ́ had made the Land Use Decree of 1978 "abolishing the customary proprietary rights of families and individuals—and traditional rulers—over both developed and undeveloped land" (Vaughan 2000, p. 149). Ọbásanjọ́ was not the only generalissimo-turned-agroindustrialist who managed to profit from this self-administered windfall.

17. A brief clip of a dance Ìdúùwẹ arranged for me that day can be heard at http://people.bu.edu/manfredi/Orogodo.mov.

18. There's at least a *phonetic* match between the root syllables of Yorùbá *igbó* MH "forest" and western Ìgbo *úgbo* HH "farm"(2002, 2005a, p. 482), but the latter is a transparent loan into Ìgbo from Ẹ̀dó and the connection is tangential to his argument, notwithstanding the semantic mismatch noted above.

19. Áfììgbo demeans Ọ̀nwụejìọ́gwụ̀ for "the difficulty he usually has with the use of the English language" (2002, 2005a, p. 478), and repeated the slur near-verbatim in a footnote (p. 492). He also bemoans Ọ̀nwụejìọ́gwụ̀'s proofreading abilities: "Even his name, Michael, is wrongly spelt at least once" (p. 478), although Áfììgbo himself in the same paper twice misspells the Ìgbo verb *enweghi*—truncating it as *enwegh* (pp. 480f.)—not to mention the many OCR-typos in the multi-volume Africa World Press reprints of Áfììgbo's collected papers. Then there are the literary oddities in other recent works which can't be blamed on hourly workers in Trenton, New Jersey; e.g., "Ogrugru" (Áfììgbo 1997, p. 6 and passim)—a toponym which is spelled better as *Ogurugu* even on ordinary road signs in the university town of Ǹsụ́ká where Áfììgbo had lived for more than a decade before writing "Ogrugru." Áfììgbo also mocks Ọ̀nwụejìọ́gwụ̀ for producing a "self-edited, self published and self-distributed journal, *Ọ̀dịnanị*, the journal of his [sic] museum at Ǹri" (p. 481), without irony, only one page after defending Ọ̀nwụmèchili's

paean to "Biafra[n] ... self reliance and scant respect for authority" (p. 480f.). The historian also gets basic facts wrong about Ọ̀dịnanị Museum, which was founded in 1972 not by Ọ̀nwụejìọ́gwụ̀ but by the same University of Ìbàdàn (photo, Ọ̀nwụejìọ́gwụ̀ 1981, p. 58) where Áfììgbo had acquired his own terminal academic credential just nine years before.

PEOPLE AND IDEAS TRAVEL TOGETHER: TAMBIAH'S APPROACH TO RITUAL AND COSMOLOGY IN BRAZIL
Mariza Peirano

1. See Peirano 1998 and 2008 for a general guide to anthropology in Brazil.

2. For a re-analysis of Malinowskiś Trobriand ethnographic material, see "The Magical Power of Words" (Tambiah 1968b) and "On Flying Witches and Flying Canoes" (Tambiah 1983b); for the re-analysis of Evans-Pritchard's Zande material, see "Form and Meaning of Magical Acts" (Tambiah 1973). All three essays are reprinted in *Culture, Thought, and Social Action* (Tambiah 1985b). See Tambiah 2002 for the intellectual biography of Edmund Leach.

3. Tambiah's approach to ritual inspired a great part of the large research program "An Anthropology of Politics: Rituals, Representations, and Violence" sponsored by Núcleo de Antropologia da Politica (NuAP), which lasted from 1997 to 2005 and resulted in the publication of more than thirty books. See NuAP 1998, and www.ppgasmuseu.etc.br/museu/pages/nuap_publicacoes.html.

4. I am referring to Tambiah's trilogy on Thailand, *Buddhism and the Spirit Cults in North-east Thailand* (1970), *World Conqueror and World Renouncer* (1976), and *Buddhist Saints of the Forest and the Cult of Amulets* (1984).

5. See especially Tambiah's "A Performative Approach to Ritual" ([1979] 1981), later included in *Culture, Thought, and Social Action* (1985b).

6. *Leveling Crowds* received two reviews in Brazil (Comerford 1998 and Chaves 1999), and was the subject of a longer essay (Peirano 2000).

7. See Sahlins 2005 (a version of which appears as Sahlins's contribution to this book) for a pioneering use of these two notions.

PARADOXES OF ORDER IN THAI COMMUNITY POLITICS
Michael Herzfeld

1. I am indebted to Charles ("Biff") Keyes for pointing this out to me when he visited the community with me at an early point in my thinking about its problems.

2. That view reinforces the hierarchical implications of the wai, which is further marked by the relative height at which the parties hold their hands when making that gesture.

3. It is perhaps worth noting that when Thais speak of their country formally they call it *prathaet thai* (Thai-land); when speaking more informally, they usually call it *moeang thai*, a designation that preserves some of the sense of that original Siamese polity with its relativistic power structure.

STRUCTURAL WORK: HOW MICROHISTORIES BECOME MACROHISTORIES AND VICE VERSA
Marshall Sahlins

This article is a revised version of the Munro lecture delivered at Edinburgh University in April 2004. I am profoundly grateful to Janet Carstens and Jonathan Spencer for the opportunity and the hospitality. The final, definitive version of this paper has been published in *Anthropological Theory* 5(1), 2005 by SAGE Publications. All rights reserved. ©

1. Other examples of structural amplification can be found in M. Sahlins (1991), concerning the incidents that set off the great war of 1843–1855 in Fiji between the kingdoms of Bau and Rewa, and M. Sahlins (2004, ch. 3), concerning the assassination that changed the relations of the forces in that war.

2. Greater documentation of the Elián Gonzalez affair may also be found in M. Sahlins (2004).

3. Brunet (1986, 53f.) mentions this incident at Puigcerdá in 1825, along with several analogous disputes among communities of the Rousillon during the French Revolution in which the parties attempted to engage the opposition between the republican and royalist causes in their particular local interests. Brunet treats such engagement of a higher ideology and greater authority rather as a fantastic mask of peasant rivalries of longer standing. Still, he says, "the masks end up one day sticking to the skin" (1986, 58).

4. I am generally using the Crawley translation of Thucydides as adapted in Strassler, ed., *The Landmark Thucydides* (New York: Free Press, 1996).

5. For Manicas, "no doubt it was the special character of the Greek polis—its particularism, its fierce pride in autonomy, and, within its own boundaries, its open character—which permitted, and indeed fostered, *stasis*. The struggle between rich and poor, the struggle for citizenship and participation, were struggles not only endemic in the polis-world,

but in many ways were unique to that world" (1982, 680). But the same class dimensions are cited by those, notably de Ste Croix (1981), who find such struggles much more general.

6. Given James Madison's classical education, one could justly consider the following notice of structural amplification in *The Federalist Papers* an echo of Aristotle's *Politics*. Speaking in no. 10 of the "causes of faction," Madison wrote:

> an attachment to different leaders ambitiously contending for preeminence and power; or to persons of other descriptions whose fortunes have been interesting to the human passions, have, in turn, divided mankind into parties, inflamed them with mutual animosity, and rendered them much more disposed to vex and oppress each other than to co-operate for their common good. So strong is this propensity of mankind to fall into mutual animosities that where no substantial occasion presents itself, the most frivolous and fanciful distinctions have been sufficient to kindle their unfriendly passions and excite their most violent conflicts. But the most common and durable source of factions has been the various and unequal distribution of property. (Madison et al. 1987, 124)

7. The tendency for factions within Greek cities to call in outside aid against their fellow citizens did not begin within Corcyra. With regard to enlisting the Persians in such *staseis*, the practice is in evidence well back in the fifth century.

8. "Such ancient conceptions show that it is not the assimilation of Nature and Society which philosophy was called upon to establish, but rather their separation from one another" (Kahn 1960, 192).

9. Contemporary movements of ethnic cleansing offer too many tragic examples of the exacerbation of local rural differences by ferocious ethnonationalist forces. Tambiah's work (1996) has already been cited in this connection. Discussing Serb-Croat-Muslim conflicts in the former Yugoslavia, Mart Bax (2000) makes the special point that they cannot be analyzed simply from the top down but (as I have tried to do here) as a reciprocal interaction between local and greater causes.

PERSPECTIVES ON THE POLITICS
OF PEACE IN ACEH, INDONESIA
Mary-Jo DelVecchio Good and Byron J. Good

1. For a selection of new and critical references on contemporary Aceh, see Aspinall 2005 and 2009; Barron et al. 2005; Barron 2008; Daly, Feener, and Reid 2012; Danusiri 1999; Drexler 2008; Good, Good, Grayman, and Lakoma 2006 and 2007; Grayman, Good, and Good 2009; Kingsley and McCulloch 2006; Knight 2008; Nessen 2004; and Reid 2006.

2. Jayasinghe (2006) argues that GAM was destroyed in the tsunami and thus peace was more feasible than in Sri Lanka where fewer people died. This is not accurate. GAM was strong throughout Aceh and the rebels' refuge was most often in the mountains, far removed from the coastal areas devastated by the tsunami. However, the military and national police forces were located on the coast and suffered heavy losses.

3. Conflict-affected deaths from the past two decades have been estimated by various sources at 30,000 to 35,000.

4. For analysis of this original "trauma clinic," see also Good, Good, and Grayman 2010, Good 2011, and Good 2012.

5. One widely held view was that there was little left to extract from Aceh; its oil wealth, in particular, had been stripped.

6. See Drexler (2008) for a discussion of DOM-period (*daerah operasi militer*) and related human rights documents, and Martinkus (2004) for a powerful account of recent conflict.

7. See Begona Aretxaga's 2008 essay on the image of the traitor *cipayo* in Spain's Basque country. The Acehnese usage is oddly resonant with Aretxaga's analysis, suggesting a global discourse in the remainders of colonialism.

A TALE OF TWO AFFECTS: HUMANITARIANISM
AND PROFESSIONALISM IN RED CROSS AID WORK
Liisa Malkki

1. My interviews suggest, however, that the knitter doesn't just imagine a "world of suffering" (Didier Fassin; Luc Boltanski) or a generalized "humanity," but seeks to reach an imagined and manageable *specificity*, a specific recipient of the aid bunny, one specific child who metonymically stands for *universal* human suffering. This is akin to the child sponsorship programs we see on television; Bornstein (2003) shows how the usually Western sponsors want a relationship with a named child whom they can visualize and "feel for" through a photograph.

2. Sections of the discussion of FRC professionalism have been previously published in Malkki 2007.

3. The ever-more-brutal nature of contemporary conflicts and the accelerating breakdown in the distinction between civilians and combatants have done much to "disenchant" and weaken the efficacy of the protective symbols of the red cross, crescent, and diamond. This is a cause of concern for FRC aid workers on international missions.

4. Here, professionalism acts as a form of *de facto* neutrality. (Cf. Haskell 1998 on professionalism, and Michael Herzfeld and others on bureaucratic indifference.)

AT THE BASE OF LOCAL AND TRANSNATIONAL CONFLICTS:
THE POLITICAL USES OF INFERIORIZATION
Emiko Ohnuki-Tierney

1. There were a number of articles in the *New York Times* that juxtaposed the two. "It's the Same, but Not" (December 2, 2001) begins by
pointing out the differences: "recognizable enemies in the form of
nation-states (Japan, then Germany and Italy)" vs. "a faceless, borderless
fanaticism that extends from the Middle East to middle America." Nevertheless, the overall impression that the article seems intended to convey
to the reader, with photos of Ground Zero and the Pearl Harbor base
juxtaposed, is that the attack on Pearl Harbor and the events of 9/11 were
the same. Other media coverage included "Attack of Pearl Harbor Proportions? Greater?" by David Foster (*Wisconsin State Journal*, Sept. 13, 2001);
"America's Darkest Days" (*Wisconsin State Journal*, Dec. 7, 2001); photo
comparisons of the two attacks in the *New York Times*, Dec. 8, 2001; "Today,
as in 1941, Freedom is Not Free" (*Wisconsin State Journal*, Dec. 7, 2002); and
"Pearl Harbor Day, 2002" by Frank Rich (*New York Times*, Dec. 7, 2002).

AFTERWORD. GALACTIC POLITIES, RADICAL
EGALITARIANISM, AND THE PRACTICE OF ANTHROPOLOGY:
TAMBIAH ON LOGICAL PARADOXES, SOCIAL
CONTRADICTIONS, AND CULTURAL OSCILLATIONS
Michael M. J. Fischer

1. The anthropologists I have in mind are S. J. Tambiah (b. 1929),
Gananath Obeyesekere (b. 1930), H. L. Sereviratne (b. 1934), Chandra
Jayawardene (1929-1981), E. Valentine Daniel, and Sharika Thiranagama.
Reciprocally, Sri Lanka, in part due to these Sri Lankans, has attracted the
attention of other talented anthropologists: E. R. Leach (1910-1989), Nur
Yalman, Steven Kemper, and Dennis McGilvray.

2. The 1956 Act making Sinhala the official language of the country, and Sri Lanka the official name, was a critical event. Thereafter all
official government transactions had to be in Sinhala; non-Sinhala-
speaking civil servants were given a time period in which to learn the
language. Government-sponsored irrigation and colonization schemes
in the east, which encouraged Sinhala to settle there, stoked the discon-
tent of Tamils, who were concentrated in that part of the island. In 1958,
1977, and 1983 there were serious anti-Tamil riots. Tamil efforts at peaceful protest marches were met by organized violent thugs, often alleged
to be allied with the governing party. Tamil militancy began to form,
and resources were gathered by a string of bank robberies. The Sinhala
migrants to the colonization schemes in the east began to be attacked

by Tamils. As police and the army cracked down, they were targeted with landmines and attacks on police stations. Then came targeted assassinations and the use of suicide bombers, often targeting prominent politicians, including President Ranasinghe Premadasa, who was assassinated, and President Chandrika Bandaranaike, who was injured. Security forces went on reprisal attacks and used torture to try to extract confessions to use in court, and Tamils engaged in ethnic cleansing in the Tamil-dominated northern districts of Jaffna, Mannar, and Mullaitivu.

In 1978 the constitution was changed to make both Tamil and Sinhala national languages, and the new constitution specified that Tamil was to be used by the government in the north. But this and many other efforts to end the violence did not succeed for over three decades. In 1983 the Tamil Tigers (the Liberation Tigers of Tamil Eelam, or LTTE) began an armed insurgency to create a separate state. The ensuing civil war killed some 80,000–100,000 people. Only in May 2009 did the Tamil Tigers concede defeat.

3. Tambiah (1986, 1992), Obeysekere (1988), and Daniel (1996).

4. The linguistic slippage is one of the pleasures. *Tambi* is also, obviously, an affectionate short form of Tambiah. In a classificatory sense, a generation shift (mother's or father's younger brother) can be contained in the term, whereas in English *younger brother* is always in reference to the speaker and does not easily accommodate generation shifts without explanation or specification (*mother's younger brother*). I invoke the classificatory mother's brother here from Trobriand matrilineal cross-cousin marriage systems, for reasons that should become clear in the final section of this essay. In political usage, just as religious or civil rights movements in the United States may use the terms *brother* and *sister* for comrades as pure generational terms of address, so too members in the militant Tamil movements in the 1980s called one another *elder brother* (*anan*) or *younger brother* (*tambi*), or *elder* or *younger sister* (*akka, thambi*) as kinship terms outside normal family hierarchies.

5. Supreme Court Justice Henry Wijayakone Tambiah, the brother of Stanley J.'s father, was an important role model, particularly because he was not just an active lawyer and judge, but also wrote seven book-length treatises: on the laws and customs of the Tamils and of the Sinhalese, on the history of Sri Lanka's judicature, on landlord-tenant law, and, with Sir Ivor Jennings, the vice chancellor of the University of Ceylon, on the development of the laws and constitution of Ceylon, a contribution to a series on the development of laws in the British Commonwealth. Upon his retirement from the Supreme Court in Sri Lanka, H. W. Tambiah was invited to serve in West Africa.

Stanley J.'s father was also a practicing lawyer, but his interests ran rather toward developing coconut plantations (and one mango plantation) in the north around Jaffna—a less productive part of the island than the south, but his efforts still conferred on him the British-styled social position of the "planter" class. Both of Tambiah's parents inherited some property, and it was this that Tambiah's father began to develop into plantations. The Tambiahs were Vellala caste (the equivalent to the Sinhalese Goyagama caste), but converted to Christianity under the British. Tambiah's mother's father was a district chief who was persuaded by his superior, a British government agent, to convert, and his mother was sent to a boarding school where she was baptized into the (Anglican) Church of Ceylon. Tambiah's father was not interested in Christianity, but his mother was a churchgoer, as was the second of the family's four daughters, who became principal of a women's college and had a reputation for eloquence as a Christian preacher. Tambiah had four brothers: the eldest rose through the police ranks to become Inspector-General of Police (IGP); the next, R. T. Tambiah, became a surgeon, a Fellow of the Royal College of Surgeons (FRCS), and rose to become head of the Army Medical Corps; the third became a school teacher; and the fourth, H. D., became a lawyer and Supreme Court Justice.

Both S. J. and H. D. went to St. Thomas College in Columbo. The sisters were all university-educated, two of them becoming principals of girls' schools.

6. As Tambiah himself says, "One of the things (I think I mention in my introduction to *World Conqueror and World Renouncer*) that I realized, when I left Sri Lanka, was that as a minority member, I had to understand what Buddhism was all about, and Buddhist revival as a response to colonialism, and Buddhist nationalism in post-independence Sri Lanka. These are issues from which, in quotation marks, 'I was alienated' in Sri Lanka, but whose significance I recognized as important to grasp as an anthropologist. I felt that while I couldn't fully study Buddhism in Sri Lanka in its political expressions, I could do this in Thailand, a country which was more distant, and therefore with which I could empathize, and which I could study from inside" (Tambiah 1997a, 12).

Elsewhere he notes that after the passage of the Act making Sinhala the only official language, he understood that sooner or later if he remained at the university he would be required to teach in Sinhala. Educated in English and fluent in Tamil, he spoke colloquial Sinhala but was not fully literate in it and would have had to expend all his energy in translating texts and lectures into Sinhala. The opportunity to work in Thailand, offered by a colleague from his Cornell days, was a way out.

7. The significance of "tanks" (water reservoirs) in north central Sri Lanka has in part to do with debates over the ancient "hydraulic civilizations" of Anuradhapura and Polonnaruva (that is, over the degree to which irrigation systems require hierarchical modes of political authority for their expansion and maintenance over time). But primarily, Leach's *Pul Eliya: A Village in Ceylon* (1961) was a bravura demonstration of empirical method.

8. Tambiah taught at Cambridge for ten years before moving to the University of Chicago in 1973, where I first met him, and I vividly remember both his economic anthropology seminar, which began with Mandeville, and his engaged participation in my dissertation defense. In 1976 he moved to Harvard, where I also taught until 1981. We became colleagues again when I moved back to Cambridge in 1993.

9. Leach's account of an oscillation between *gumlao* (democratic egalitarian) and *gumsa* (ranked aristocratic) marriage patterns in the hills of the Burmese highlands, with a *shan* (more feudal, monarchical) pattern in the valleys, is, as Tambiah lucidly recaps, an "open system of many lineages linked in circles of [superior] wife-giver and [inferior] wife-taker communicating with one another diacritically through variations of dialect, dress, and other local differences, and capable of dynamically generating as well as contesting tendencies toward extra-local hierarchical political formations" (Tambiah 2002, 84). This account was exciting because it was not just a set of rules, as Levi-Strauss had argued, using the Kachin as a type case of generalized exchange in *The Elementary Forms of Kinship*. Instead it contained dynamic possibilities both of oscillation and of hierarchical accumulation, according to how players strategized and how economic production worked out (mainly shifting cultivation in the hills, and rice in the valleys). Cattle were the primary form of bridewealth, but cattle were not accumulated as capital. Instead they were used as meat for elaborate feasts (*manau*) and thus to build status in a redistribution back into the exchange system. Leach drew on a history of 150 years to establish his sense of oscillating *gumsa/gumlao*, adapting his terminology of equilibriating oscillation from Manfred Pareto's tale of alternating domination by lions and foxes to illustrate an economic "moving equilibrium" (ibid.). Matrilineal cross-cousin marriage "established a system of exchange of women that is directional in that wife-takers from one group must in turn be wife-givers to a third and so on ... [which] introduces the possibility of *speculation*, for groups may be able to hoard women if they are in an advantageous position politically and economically" (ibid.; emphasis added). Polygamy allows the possibility of accumulating women and affines and thereby the

possibility of developing hierarchical relations and feudal tendencies. As a minimal example: three chiefs can establish a matrilineal cross-cousin marriage circle in which lineage C takes wives from lineage B, which takes wives from lineage A, which takes wives from lineage C. And since families often have more than one daughter, headmen at the next stratum down can both take wives from these chiefs and daughters from their own status equals, reaffirming or contesting hierarchical relations. Although on the subject of myth Leach and Levi-Strauss had friendly relations, the debate between them over Kachin kinship went on acrimoniously for eighteen years. Tambiah's account of the dispute pays attention to the social drama of personal defensiveness and seeking acknowledgment over felt misreadings by the other, and to the first-hand ethnographic experience of Leach versus the more synthesizing effort of Levi-Strauss. But more importantly, Tambiah stresses the way in which Leach insisted that the relation between terms and reality is not one-to-one, but a matter of model reference patterns invoked by actors to account for manipulated realities.

10. Although the phrase *radical egalitarianism* is not one that Tambiah ever uses in his writing, nor does he (nor do I) recognize any provenance in his work (conversation with Tambiah 3 and 9 November 2010), it does serve well, and I so use it here, to show how egalitarian values, when turned into ideological absolutes, can turn into their opposites. In this sense it functions somewhat like Leach's argument about how *gumlao* (democratic egalitarian) marriage systems in highland Burma can transform into *gumsa* (ranked aristocratic) ones.

11. Leach was an active and financial supporter of the Labor Party, and it was through those connections that he would be knighted, becoming Sir Edmund Leach. The full 1976 quote cited by Tambiah, while a common anthropological stance of the time, is problematic, and Tambiah hastens to add his own corrective in a footnote. Leach: "In my own society I am a radical; where other societies are concerned I find myself in a double bind. I find it difficult to make judgments about other societies. Freedom and tolerance for me is the recognition and acceptance of difference between cultural systems, not within my own cultural system." Today this sounds as if it could only be said by someone who still thinks of himself as living in a nonglobalized world where other cultures are quite separate from his own. Leach goes on to say he is as interested in similarities as differences, and this should be understood as learning from the dilemmas of others that parallel our own dilemmas. Tambiah hastens to quickly say, "Leach was of course not saying that anything goes, such as mass murder, militant racism, genocide, and

other crimes against humanity." Such things, of course, are at the center of Tambiah's lived world experience and are either directly or indirectly at the center of his anthropological work, as they are for most of us who survived World War II (as did Leach) and the postcolonial conflicts since then. In later chapters of the Leach biography, Tambiah provides some of Leach's own contextualization of his ethnographies while noting how they were purified of some of these contexts in their academic setting. All these issues raise the ethical stakes of anthropology. In his chapter on Leach's "comparativist stance," Tambiah notes that Leach "did not approve of 'development anthropology' ... which he held to be a kind of neo-colonialism." Interesting then that Tambiah himself does not disavow but adopts *development anthropologist* as a label for himself (1985).

For a nice review of the changing political horizons of the ethical debates in anthropology as seen through the lens of Project Camelot, the Vietnam War and the Thai counterinsurgency debate, and aboriginal rights in Australia as viewed by Chandra Jayawardena acting within Australian anthropology, see Robinson 2004.

The debate over disruption of the regrowth of healthy local governance caused by the mobile sovereignty of transnational NGOs, development donors from the First World, global health funds for HIV/AIDS, and disaster relief have become central topics of anthropological work in the past few decades and are subjects of the contributions to this volume by Liisa Malkki and Mary Jo and Byron Good. The Goods particularly focus attention on the ways in which local Aceh cultural forms can be rewoven and local control can be allowed to regrow in nondysfunctional ways.

12. Tambiah has an interesting chapter on Leach's comparativist stance, in which the "radical" quote occurs, and which uses Leach's famous Virgin Birth essay as preface to his later structuralist readings of the Bible, which Leach undertook in an effort to repatriate the anthropological gaze back onto his own society. These are lively experiments by Leach, if lacking in the attention to the histories of interpretation with which Tambiah pursues historical materials.

13. Louis Dumont's *Homo Hierarchicus* (1966), most famously, crystallizes a thematic of Hindu thought, in which the householder withdraws from the world to work on his own reincarnating purity after fulfilling his worldly obligations, and individuals can detach themselves from the world into a *sadhu* status (albeit supported by merit-making donations from that world). *Sadhus*, however, have been powerfully involved in the recent Hinduvata fundamentalist movement and Bharatiya Janata Party politics in India, even serving in Parliament and state offices.

Buddhism ideologically separates itself from the hierarchies of the caste system, politically perhaps most dramatically in India under the effort by B. R. Ambedkar to have untouchables and dalits become Buddhist in an effort to assert egalitarian citizenship and reject the entire Hindu system.

14. *Juggernaut* comes from the Sanskrit *Jagannatha* (Lord of the Universe), one of the names of Krishna, and was associated by the British with the large wooden chariots used in ritual processions carrying the *murtis* (images) of Krishna and other gods; if one of these carts gathered speed and went out of control among the crowd it could crush anything in its way.

15. Ananda College plays a prominent role in Tambiah's account.

16. As a 27-year-old lecturer, Tambiah had brought a team of twenty-six Sinhalese and seven Tamil students to survey the recently settled peasant colonies. His report is reprinted in *Leveling Crowds*. Tambiah notes that the Gal Oya Valley Multipurpose Scheme was modeled on the TVA and the Darmodar Valley Corporation in India. It was one of a series of such global projects. Two more were the Helmand Valley project in Afghanistan and the Khuzistan Project in Iran.

17. I refer to this as *vulgar* Marxism, because Marx himself was quite aware of his nonrealistic schematizing at the two ends of his investigations of historical processes. At the beginnings of both cycles of the historical narratives that he tries to collate into an explanatory model there is violent "primitive accumulation": the seventeenth-century enclosure movement in Britain, with its production of a reserve labor force that enforces a brutal pressure on wages and on the freedom of capitalists to be more humane; and in the earlier "originary" stages of settlement, the appropriation of land around estates in Eastern Europe after the collapse of the Roman Empire, or the use of slavery in the ancient world, which constrained the return to free labor. The point of the "egalitarian" theme in Marx was trying to organize for a more just return to labor and for the dignity of every worker, whether involved in manual or mental labor, and to find a postindustrial mode of just organization rather than a return to a fantasized preindustrial pastoral past.

18. As a discriminated-against minority, the Tamils have argued for meritocratic access to civil service jobs, while the Sinhalese have argued for allocation of the jobs by a quota reflecting the proportion of Sinhalese to Tamils in the population, which they estimated at 6:1. The civil service system and its avenues of recruitment, of course, had been established by the British colonial state. The stakes intensified after independence.

19. Tambiah uses both terms. *Dialectic* echoes political economy accounts of accumulating social contradictions such as the use of capital-intensive irrigation and hydrology projects to produce a new peasantry using mainly traditional technologies, while the elites reproduce a different, privileged life style; or free education in local languages that produces vast pools of literate and semiliterate young men angry at the lack of the kinds of jobs to which they aspire. *Oscillation* echoes Leach's usage for unstable models of organization that can transform into one another, such as centralizing and decentralizing processes.

20. Levi-Strauss's analysis of the Oedipus myth is a key teaching text for the irresolvable tension between identity claims of being native and the reality that founders had to come from somewhere. Such aporias or irresolvable paradoxes, Levi-Strauss argues, are narrativized in myths as ways to play out their alternative and contradictory potentials. Hence, as Tambiah invokes Levi-Strauss, myths come in multiple variations, and it is by examining them as a set that one can recognize the mythic structure underwriting their various possible transformations.

21. Geertz also provides annalistic references in the footnotes to *Negar*, and argues in the text that the theater state was not mere theater, not mere still center, but also a politics of mobilizing men and material resources, involving militias, taxation, sharecropping, and tenure arrangements, not unlike Tambiah.

22. *Gumsa* is a model of ranked hierarchy; *gumlao* is an ideal of egalitarianism, in which all are of the same status.

23. I am indebted to conversations in Singapore with Kenneth Dean on his remarkable work (1993, 1998; Dean and Zhenman 2010) on spirit medium associations and temples in Putian and Singapore.

24. The stirring up of murderous rage against the author of the novel *Satanic Verses* was a major testbed of viral vectors traversing social membranes across the globe and acting parasitically within otherwise different social conflicts. The political arenas, social dramas, goals and stakes were different in Bradford (England), Pakistan, India, and Iran. While the Rushdie affair dramatized the transnational circuitry's power to transfer the frenzy of position-taking from one political arena to another, the more recent cartoon affairs suggest a new phase in the turbulence of the transnational circuitry, focusing attention on how such circulating controversies help and hinder the construction of global, national, and local public spheres. The construction of civil society is centrally on the agenda in both Iran (since President Khatami's call for open society, civil rights, and dialogue of civilizations) and Europe in a way that has not been the case since the French Revolution. The furor

stirred up by the Danish imams transnationally crystallized some of the stakes for many Europeans.

25. One is reminded of the Greek myth of the Ring of Gyges, a myth about kings seeing at a distance, about the transformations that occur through that distancing, and the media of both female beauty and money as effecting transformations.

Abramowitz, Sharon. 2005. "The Poor Have Become Rich, and the Rich Have Become Poor: Collective Trauma in the Guinean Languette." *Social Science and Medicine* 61:2106-18.

Acts on the Administration of the Buddhist Order of Sangha of Thailand. 1989. Bangkok: Mahamakuta Educational Council.

Adédìran, B. 1991. "Pleasant Imperialism: Conjectures on Benin Hegemony in Eastern Yorùbáland." *African Notes* (Ìbàdàn) 15:83-95.

Adénìran, T. 1974. "The Dynamics of Peasant Revolt: A Conceptual Analysis of the Àgbẹ̀kòyà Parapọ̀ Uprising in the Western State of Nigeria." *Journal of Black Studies* 4:363-75.

Áfìigbo [Afigbo], A. 1972. *The Warrant Chiefs: Indirect Rule in Southeastern Nigeria, 1891-1929.* London: Longman.

———. 1981. "The Age of Innocence: The Ìgbo and Their Neighbours in Pre-Colonial Times." Àhịajíọ kú. Lecture, Ministry of Information, Culture, Youth and Sports, Òweré [Owerri], Ímò State, Nigeria. Igbo-Net, http://ahiajoku.igbonet.com/1981.

———. 1996. "The Anthropology and Historiography of Central-South Nigeria Before and Since Ìgbo-Ukwu." *History in Africa* 23:1-15.

———. 1997. "Southeastern Nigeria, the Niger-Benue Confluence, and the Benue in the Precolonial Period: Some Issues of Historiography." *History in Africa* 24:1-8.

———. 2002. "*Ìgbo énwé ezè*: Beyond Ọnwụmèchili and Ọnwụejìọgwụ̀." Self-published. Ọkị́gwị́, Ábịa State. (See also Áfìigbo 2005a.)

———. 2003. "The Amalgamation: Myths, Howlers, and Heresies." In *The Amalgamation and Its Enemies: An Interpretive History of Modern Nigeria*, ed. R. Ọlániyàn, 45-57. Ilé-Ifẹ̀: Ọbáfẹ́mi Awólówọ̀ University Press.

———. 2005a. "*Ìgbo énwé ezè*: Beyond Ọnwụmèchili and Ọnwụejìọgwụ̀." In *Ìgbo History and Society: The Essays of Ádiéle Afìigbo*, ed. 'T. Fálọ́lá, 477-94. Trenton, N.J.: Africa World Press.

———. 2005b. "Local Government in Nigeria in the Era of Indirect Rule, 1900-1950." In *Nigerian History, Politics, and Affairs: The Collected Essays of Ádiéle Afìigbo*, ed. 'T. Fálọ́lá, 271-95. Trenton, N.J.: Africa World Press.

———. 2006. "The Spell of Oral History: A Case Study from Northern Ìgboland." *History in Africa* 33:39-52.

Agamben, G. 1998. *Homo Sacer: Sovereign Power and Bare Life*. Trans. Daniel Heller-Roazen. Stanford: Stanford University Press.

Ágbụ, O. 2004. *Ethnic Militias and the Threat to Democracy in Post-Transition Nigeria*. Uppsala, Sweden: Nordiska Afrikainstitutet (Nordic African Institute).

Ahern, Emily. 1973. *The Cult of the Dead in a Chinese Village*. Stanford: Stanford University Press.

Àjàyí, J. 2004. "Yorùbá Origin Controversy: You Can't Just Wake Up and Say Odùduwà was a Benin Prince." *The Punch*, 16 May 2004. http://groups.yahoo.com/group/AlukoArchives/message/316.

Ákẹnzùa, Ẹ. 2008. *Ekaladerhan*. Lagos: Inter Press.

Àlùkò, B. 2004. "Cultural Wars and National Identity: The Saga of the Yorùbá and the Biní-Ẹ̀dó." 19 May 2004. Dawodu.com, http://www.dawodu.com/aluko89.htm.

Ámadí, S. 1996. "Hangman's Court Is It." In *Ogoni: Trials and Travails*, ed. Civil Liberties Organisation, 121-245. Lagos: Civil Liberties Organisation.

Amarā Bhirakkhit (Amaro Koet). 1967 (2510 B.E. edition). *Pubbasikkhavaṇṇanā* (in Thai). Bangkok: Mahamakut Rajavidyalaya Press.

Anderson, Benedict. 1991. *Imagined Communities: Reflections on the Origin and Spread of Nationalism*. Revised ed. London and New York: Verso Books. Originally published 1983.

Anil Sakya, Phra. 2008. "King Mongkut and Dhammayut: A Modern Approach to Thai Buddhism." Paper presented at the 10th International Conference on Thai Studies, Thammasat University, Bangkok, 9-11 January 2008.

Aphichato Phikkhu. 1993. *Somdet Pra Buddhachahn (Pra Pimon Tam, Aht Aht Ahsopa Hama Thera)*. Bangkok: S. J. Reniker. Dhamma Spread, http://www.dhammaspread.org/Page407.htm.

Appadurai, Arjun. 2006. *Fear of Small Numbers: An Essay on the Geography of Anger*. Durham: Duke University Press.

Apple, R. W. 1998. "Clinton in Africa: The Policy; U.S. Stance toward Nigeria and Its Ruler Seems to Shift." *New York Times*, 28 March 1998. http://query.nytimes.com/gst/fullpage.html?res=9A01EFD8143BF93BA15750C0A96E958260.

Aquinas, Thomas. 1965. *Summa Theologiae*. Vol. 54 (3a., 46-52), *The Passion of Christ*. (Latin text and English translation). Ed. Richard T. A. Murphy. New York: Blackfriars in conjunction with McGraw Hill.

Aranha Filho, Jayme M. 2001. "Jakobson a bordo da sonda espacial Voyager." In *O dito e o feito: Ensaios de antropologia dos rituais*, ed. Mariza Peirano, 59-82. Rio de Janeiro: Relume Dumará.

Arendt, H. 1979. *The Origins of Totalitarianism*. New York: Harcourt Brace Jovanovich. Originally published 1951.

Aretxaga, Begona. 2008. "Madness and the Politically Real: Reflections on Violence in Postdictatorial Spain." In *Postcolonial Disorders*, ed. Mary-Jo DelVecchio Good, Sandra Teresa Hyde, Sarah Pinto, and Byron J. Good, 43-61. Berkeley and Los Angeles: University of California Press.

Aristotle. 1984. *The Politics*. Trans. Carnes Lord. Chicago: University of Chicago Press.

Aron, Raymond. 1957. *The Opium of the Intellectuals*. Trans. Terence Kilmartin. New York: Doubleday. Originally published as *L'Opium des intellectuels* (1955).

———. 1961. "Thucydide et le récit des événements." *History and Theory* 1:103-28.

Aspinall, Edward. 2005. *The Helsinki Agreement: A More Promising Basis for Peace in Aceh?* Policy Studies 20. Washington, D.C.: East-West Center Washington.

———. 2009. *Islam and Nation: Separatist Rebellion in Aceh, Indonesia*. Stanford: Stanford University Press.

Associated Press. 2008. "War Worsens as Sri Lanka Puts Pressure on Rebels." *New York Times*, 27 September 2008, World Asia Pacific section.

Ayọàdé, A. 2006. "Godfather Politics in Nigeria." In *Money, Politics and Corruption in Nigeria*, ed. International Federation for Electoral Systems (IFES). Proceedings of a seminar held at University of Ìbàdàn Conference Centre, in collaboration with Department for International Development (DFID), 1 June 2006. Arbuja: Garkida Press.

Àzíkàíwe [Azikiwe], N. 1976. *Ọ̀nịcha Market Crisis: An Example of Monocracy*. Àpapá, Nigeria: Times Press, for Zik Enterprises, Ǹsú̀ká.

Babb, L. A. 1993. "Monks and Miracles: Religious Symbols and Images of Origin among Osval Jains." *Journal of Asian Studies* 52 (1): 3-21.

Baker, P., and C. Savage. 2009. "In Clinton List, a Veil is Lifted on Foundation." *New York Times*, 19 December 2009. http://www.nytimes.com/2008/12/19/us/politics/w19clinton.html.

Bandaranayake, Senake. 1974. *Sinhalese Monastic Architecture: The Viharas of Anuradhapura*. Leiden: E. J. Brill.

Barron, Patrick. 2008. "Managing the Resources for Peace: Reconstruction and Peacebuilding in Aceh." In Aguswandi and Judith Large, eds., *Reconfiguring Politics: The Indonesia-Aceh Peace Process*. London: Conciliation Resources.

Barron, Patrick, Samuel Clark, and Muslahuddin Daud. 2005. *Conflict and Recovery in Aceh: An Assessment of Conflict Dynamics and Options for Supporting the Peace Process*. Jakarta: World Bank.

Bateson, Gregory. 1935. "Culture Contact and Schismogenesis." *Man* (n.s.) 35:178–83.

———. 1958. *Naven*. 2nd ed. Stanford: Stanford University Press. Originally published 1936.

Bax, Mart. 2000. "Warlords, Priests and the Politics of Ethnic Cleansing: A Case Study from Rural Bosnia-Hercegovina." *Ethnic and Rural Studies* 23:16–32.

BCP (British Consular Papers, 1825–1843). 1841. Letter of 8 February 1841, Richard Charlton to Governor Mataio Kekūanaō'a. Typescript of the original in Foreign Office and Executive file. Archives of Hawaii, Honolulu.

Beer, C. 1976. *The Politics of Peasant Groups in Western Nigeria*. Ìbàdàn: Ìbàdàn University Press.

Beier, U. 1957. "The Dancers of Ágbǫ̀." *Odù* 7:41. Includes 4 unnumbered pages of plates.

———. 1963. "Ọ̀sị̀ Ézi Festival in Ágbǫ̀." *Nigeria Magazine* 78, 184–95.

Benard, Elizabeth. 1988. "The Living Among the Dead: A Comparison of Buddhist and Christian Relics." *The Tibet Journal* 13, no. 3 (Autumn).

Berlin, Isaiah. 1992. *The Crooked Timber of Humanity*. New York: Random House. Originally published 1959.

Bhattacharya, Bhaswati, Gita Dharampul-Frick, and Jos Gommans, eds. 2007. "Spatial and Temporal Continuities of Merchant Networks in South Asia and the Indian Ocean." Special issue of *Journal of the Economic and Social History of the Orient* 50 (2–3).

Biehl, João. 2005. *Vita: Life in a Zone of Social Abandonment*. Berkeley and Los Angeles: University of California Press.

Billington, James H. 1999. *Fire in the Minds of Men: Origins of the Revolutionary Faith*. New Brunswick, N.J.: Transaction Publishers.

Bin Laden, Osama. 2005. *Messages to the World: The Statements of Osama Bin Laden*. Ed. Bruce Lawrence, trans. James Howarth. New York: Verso.

Bisson, T. 1994. "The 'Feudal Revolution.'" *Past and Present* 142:6–42.

Bloch, M. 1962. *Feudal Society*. Vol. 1, *The Growth of Ties of Dependence*. London: Routledge.

Boixadós, Roxana. 1994. "Fundaciones de ciudades como rituales: Análises de tres casos en el contexto de la conquista del Tucumán colonial." *Anuário Antropológico* 92:145–18.

Borges, Antonádia. 2004. *Tempo de Brasília: Etnografando lugares-eventos da política.* Rio de Janeiro: Relume Dumará.

———. 2007a. "Cobertos de vida: Os rituais funerários na África do Sul contemporânea e suas implicações teóricas para a antropologia." Paper presented at the annual meeting of the Associação Nacional de Programas de Pós-Graduação em Ciências Sociais (ANPOCS), October 22-26, 2007 in Caxambu, Brazil.

———. 2007b. "Mats, Blankets, Songs and Flags: Ethnography of the Politics of Funeral in Contemporary South Africa." Paper presented at Ethnografeast 3, 20-23 June 2007 in Lisbon, Portugal. http://ceas.iscte .pt/ethnografeast/papers/antonadia_borges.pdf.

Bornstein, Erica. 2003. *The Spirit of Development: Protestant NGOs, Morality, nd Economics in Zimbabwe.* New York and London: Routledge/ Taylor and Francis.

Borrero, Jose C., Costas E. Synolakis, and Hermann Fritz. 2006. "Northern Sumatra Field Survey after the December 2004 Sumatra Earthquake and Indian Ocean Tsunami." *Earthquake Spectra* 22: S93-S104.

Bradbury, R. 1956. "The Benin Village." Ph.D. dissertation, University of London.

———. 1967. "The Kingdom of Benin." In *West African Kingdoms in the Nineteenth Century,* ed. D. Forde and P. Kaberry, 1-35. New York: Oxford University Press.

———. 1968. "Continuities and Discontinuities in Pre-Colonial and Colonial Benin Politics (1897-1951)." In *History and Social Anthropology,* ed. I. Lewis, 193-252. London: Tavistock.

———. 1969. "Patrimonialism and Gerontocracy in Benin Political Culture." In *Man in Africa,* ed. M. Douglas and P. Kaberry, 17-36. London: Tavistock.

———. 1973. "The Benin Village." In *Benin Studies,* ed. P. Morton-Williams, 149-209. London: Oxford University Press. (Excerpt from author's dissertation, Bradbury 1956.)

Bradley, James. 2000. *Flags of Our Fathers.* New York: Bantam.

Brashier, K. E. 1996. "Han Thanatology and the Division of 'Souls.'" *Early China* 21:125-58.

Braudel, Fernand. 1979. *The Perspective of the World.* Vol. 3 of *Civilization and Capitalism, 15th-18th Century.* Trans. S. Reynolds. Berkeley and Los Angeles: University of California Press.

Breckenridge, Keith. 2005. "The Biometric State: The Promise and Peril of Digital Government in the New South Africa." *Journal of Southern African Studies* 31 (2): 267-82.

Brook, Timothy. 1989. "Funerary Ritual and the Building of Lineages in Late Imperial China." *Harvard Journal of Asiatic Studies* 49 (2): 465-99.

Brown, Clifford W. 1987. "Thucydides, Hobbes, and the Derivation of Anarchy." *History of Political Thought* 8:33-62.

Brown, Peter. 1971. "The Rise and Function of the Holy Man in Late Antiquity." *Journal of Roman Studies* 61:80-101.

———. 1981. *The Cult of the Saints: Its Rise and Function in Late Christianity.* Chicago: University of Chicago Press.

———. 1983. "The Saint as Exemplar in Late Antiquity." *Representations* 1.

Brunet, Michel. 1986. *Le Roussillon: Une societe contre l'Etat, 1780-1820.* Toulouse: Association des Publications de L'Université Toulouse-Mirail.

Burke, Edmund. 2001. *Reflections on the Revolution in France.* Edited by J. C. D. Clark. Stanford: Stanford University Press.

Buruma, Ian, and Avishai Margalit. 2004. *Occidentalism: The West in the Eyes of Its Enemies.* New York: Penguin Press.

Butler, Alban. 1957. *Butler's Lives of the Saints.* Edited, revised, and supplemented by Herbert Thurston and Donald Attwater. Vol. 3. New York: P. J. Kennedy and Sons.

Butler, Judith. 2005. *Giving an Account of Oneself.* New York: Fordham University Press.

Campbell, J. K. 1964. *Honour, Family, and Patronage: A Study of Institutions and Moral Values in a Greek Mountain Community.* Oxford: Clarendon Press.

Capitalism Magazine. 2000. "Elian Gonzalez: Why a Father's Rights Can Never Supersede Those of a Child." Interview with Edwin Locke. 25 March 2000. http://www.capitalismmagazine.com.

Carrithers, Michael. 1983. *The Forest Monks of Sri Lanka: An Anthropological and Historical Study.* Delhi: Oxford University Press.

Caryl, Christian. 2005. "Why They Do It." *New York Review of Books,* 22 September 2005, 28-32.

Chaa, Phra Ajahn. 2002. *Food for the Heart: The Collected Teachings of Ajahn Chaa.* Boston: Wisdom Publications.

Chaves, Christine A. 1999. "A face anônima da democracia moderna." *Anuário Antropológico* 97:249-57.

———. 2000. *A Marcha Nacional dos Sem-Terra: Um estudo sobre a fabricação do social.* Rio de Janeiro: Relume Dumará.

———. 2003. *Festas da política: Uma etnografia da modernidade no sertão (Buritis/MG).* Rio de Janeiro: Relume Dumará.

Cherki, Alice. 2000. *Frantz Fanon: A Portrait.* Ithaca: Cornell University Press.

Chicago Tribune. 2000a. "For Some Exiled Cubans, Elián Given Role of Modern-Day Moses." Article by Laurie Goering, 17 January 2000. http://www.chicagotribune.com.

———. 2000b. "Parental Authority: Elián Belongs with his Father." By Kathleen Parker, 19 January 2000. http://www.chicagotribune.com.

Chipman, Elana. 2007. "Our Beigang: Culture Work, Ritual, and Community in a Taiwanese Town." Ph.D. dissertation, Cornell University.

Clark, Gillian. 1999. "Victricius of Rouen, *Praising the Saints*: Introduction and Translation." *Journal of Early Christian Studies* 7, no. 3 (Fall): 365–99.

Clark, Hugh. 1991. *Community, Trade, and Networks: Southern Fujian from the Third to the Thirteenth Centuries.* Cambridge: Cambridge University Press.

Clark, Kenneth. 1969. *Civilization: A Personal View.* New York: Harper and Row.

CNN Crossfire. 2000. "Should Elián Gonzales' Father Be Allowed to Take His Son Home?" 4 January 2000. Transcript at http://www.cnn.com.

Cogan, Marc. 1981. *The Human Thing: The Speeches and Principles of Thucydides' History.* Chicago: University of Chicago Press.

Coleman, J. 1958. *Nigeria: Background to Nationalism.* Berkeley and Los Angeles: University of California Press.

Comerford, John. 1996. "Reunir e unir: As reuniões de trabalhadores rurais como forma de sociabilidade." M.A. dissertation, Universidade Federal do Rio de Janeiro.

———. 1998. "Ethnonationalist Conflicts and Collective Violence in South Asia: Review of *Leveling Crowds* by Stanley J. Tambiah." *Mana: Estudos de Antropologia Social* 4:180–183.

———. 1999. *Fazendo a luta: Sociabilidade, falas e rituais na construção de organizações camponesas.* Rio de Janeiro: Relume Dumará.

———. 2003. *Como uma família: Sociabilidade, territórios de parentesco e sindicalismo rural.* Rio de Janeiro: Relume Dumará.

Coningham, Robin A. E. 1995. "Monks, Caves and Kings: A Reassessment of the Nature of Early Buddhism in Sri Lanka." *World Archaeology* 27 (2): 222–42.

Connor, W. Robert. 1984. *Thucydides.* Princeton: Princeton University Press.

Conze, E. 1970. *Buddhist Thought in India.* Ann Arbor: University of Michigan Press.

Cooke, Merritt Todd. 1985. "The People of Nyishang: Identity, Tradition, and Change in the Nepal-Tibet Borderland." Ph.D. dissertation, University of California, Berkeley.

Coomaraswamy, Ananda. 1927. "The Origin of the Buddha Image." *Art Bulletin* 9 (4): 287–329.

Cooper, John. 2005. "Political Animals and Civic Friendship." In *Aristotle's Politics: Critical Essays*, ed. S. S. Richard Kraut, 65–90. Oxford: Rowman and Littlefield.

Couprie, Dirk L., Robert Hahn, and Gerald Naddaf. 2003. *Anaximander in Context: New Studies in the Origins of Greek Philosophy*. Albany: State University of New York Press.

Cowell, E. B., ed. 1901. *The Jataka*. Cambridge: Cambridge University Press.

Crapanzano, Vincent. 1973. *The Hamadsha: A Study in Moroccan Ethnopsychiatry*. Berkeley and Los Angeles: University of California Press.

———. 1980. *Tuhami: Portrait of a Moroccan*. Chicago: University of Chicago Press.

Crowder, M., and O. Ikime, eds. 1970. *West African Chiefs: Their Changing Status under Colonial Rule and Independence*. Ilé-Ifẹ̀: University of Ifẹ̀ Press, and New York: Africana Publishing Corporation.

Cummings, Bruce. 2001. "Point of View: Pearl Harbor a Bad Analogy for Sept. 11 Attacks." *Asahi Shimbun Asia Network*, 7 December 2001.

Daly, Patrick, Michael Feener, and Anthony Reid, eds. 2012. *From the Ground Up: Perspectives on Post-Tsunami and Post-Conflict Aceh*. Singapore: ISEAS Press.

Danusiri, Aryo. 1999. *The Village Goat Takes a Beating* (*Kameng Gampoeng Nyang Keunong Geulawa*). Documentary film produced by ELSAM (Lembaga Studi dan Advokasi Masyarakat). Official Selection of Amnesty Film Festival, Amsterdam, 2001.

Das, Veena, Arthur Kleinman, Mamphela Ramphele, and Pamela Reynolds, eds. 2000. *Violence and Subjectivity*. Berkeley and Los Angeles: University of California Press.

Davids, T. W. Rhys, trans. 1881. *Buddhist Suttas*. Vol. 11. Oxford: Sacred Books of the East.

de Ste Croix, G. E. M. 1972. *The Origins of the Peloponnesian War*. London: Duckworth.

Dean, Kenneth. 1993. *Taoist Ritual and Popular Cults in Southeast China*. Princeton: Princeton University Press.

———. 1995. "Multiplicity and Individuation: The Temple Network of the Three in One Religion in Putian and Xianyou." In *Proceedings of the Conference on Temples and Popular Culture*. Taipei: Center for Chinese Studies.

———. 1998. *Lord of the Three in One: The Spread of a Cult in Southeast China*. Princeton: Princeton University Press.

———. 2003. "Local Communal Religion in Contemporary South-east China." *China Quarterly* 174:338–58.

———. 2006. *Taoist Ritual and Popular Cults of Southeast China*. Princeton: Princeton University Press.

Dean, Kenneth, and Zheng Zhenman. 2010. *Ritual Alliances of the Putian Plain*. Boston: Brill.

Délánọ̀, I. 1966. *Òwe l'Ẹ̀sìnỌ̀rọ̀: Yorùbá Proverbs, Their Meaning and Usage*. Ìbàdàn: Oxford University Press.

Department of Social Development, Republic of South Africa. 2002. *Transforming the Present, Protecting the Future: Report of the Committee of Inquiry into a Comprehensive System of Social Security for South Africa*. Pretoria: Government Printer.

Derrida, Jacques. 2005. *Adieu to Emmanuel Levinas*. Stanford: Stanford University Press.

Détienne, Marcel, and Jean-Pierre Vernant. 1974. *Les ruses de l'intelligence: La mètis des grecs*. Paris: Flammarion.

Diamond, L., et al., eds. 1997. *Transition Without End: Nigerian Politics and Civil Society under Babangida*. Boulder, Colorado: Lynne Rienner Publishers.

Dower, John W. 2010. *Cultures of War: Pearl Harbor, Hiroshima, 9-11, Iraq*. New York: W. W. Norton.

Drexler, Elizabeth F. 2008. *Aceh, Indonesia: Securing the Insecure State*. Philadelphia: University of Pennsylvania Press.

Duara, Prasenjit. 1988. "Superscribing Symbols: The Myth of Guandi, Chinese God of War." *Journal of Asian Studies* 47 (4): 778–95.

Dudley, B. 1973. *Instability and Political Order: Politics and Crisis in Nigeria*. Ìbàdàn: Ìbàdàn University Press.

Duffield, Mark. 2001. *Global Governance and the New Wars: The Merging of Development and Security*. London and New York: Zed Books.

Dumezil, Georges. 1970a. *Archaic Roman Religion*. Chicago: University of Chicago Press.

———. 1970b. *The Destiny of the Warrior*. Chicago: University of Chicago Press.

———. 1973. *The Destiny of a King*. Chicago: University of Chicago Press.

———. 1986. *The Plight of a Sorcerer*. Berkeley: University of California Press.

———. 1988. *Mitra-Varuna: An Essay on Two Indo-European Representations of Sovereignty*. New York: Zone Books. Originally published 1948, as *Mitra-Varuna* (Paris: Gallimard).

Dumont, Louis. 1970. *Homo Hierarchicus: An Essay on the Caste System*. Trans. Mark Sainsbury. Chicago: University of Chicago Press.

Durkheim, E. 1957. *Professional Ethics and Civic Morals*. London: Routledge.

Edem, A., and A. Ekeng. 2008. *Memorandum of the Etubom Traditional Council on the Capping of His Majesty Edidem Bassey Ekpo Bassey II as Obong of Calabar*. Issued in Calabar on 18 April 2008. http://www .afrocubaweb.com/abakwa/etccapping.pdf.

Edevbie, O. 2004. "The Doctrine of Overlordship and the Warri Crisis." In *Warri City and British Colonial Rule in Western Niger Delta*, ed. P. Eke[h], 240–74. Buffalo, N.Y.: Urhobo Historical Society.

Edgar, Iain R., and Andrew Russell, eds. 1998. *The Anthropology of Welfare*. New York: Routledge.

Eghagha, B., and Y. Oyèébámi. 2008. "Abíọ́lá Was Beaten to Death, Says Al-Mustapha." *Guardian* (Lagos), 29 May 2008.

Egharevba, J. 1934. *Èkhérhe vb'Èbé Itan Ẹ̀dó*. Benin City: C.M.S.

———. 1960. *A Short History of Benin*. 3rd ed. Ìbàdàn: Ìbàdàn University Press.

Eickelman, Dale F. 1976. *Moroccan Islam: Tradition and Society in a Pilgrimage Center*. Austin: University of Texas Press.

Èjìọfọ́[r], L. 1982. *Ìgbo Kingdoms: Power and Control*. Énugwú: Fourth Dimension.

Eke[h], P. 1990. "Social Anthropology and Two Contrasting Uses of Tribalism in Africa." *Comparative Studies in Society and History* 32:660–700.

———. 2007. "Imperialism, Nigerian Historiography and the Nature and Outline of Ùrhobo History." In *History of the Ùrhobo People of the Niger Delta*, ed. P. Eke[h], 3–36. Buffalo, N.Y.: Ùrhobo Historical Society.

Èkére, C. 1961. Minutes of the meeting of the Ọ̀nwụ Committee on Ìgbo orthography held at the W.T.C. Énugwú on 13th September, 1961. Ms. 3 pp. Énugwú: Eastern Nigeria Ministry of Education.

Ẹ̀lá[h], F. 1983. *Nigeria and States Creation: Based on "The Unfinished Motion."* Port Harcourt: Haig-Betanova.

Elugbe, B. 1984. "Sound and Letter in Ẹdoid Orthographies." *Journal of the Linguistic Association of Nigeria* 2:91–97.

Embree, John F. 1950. "Thailand, A Loosely Structured Social System." *American Anthropologist* 52:181–93.

Éménanjọ, N. 1971. "Aspects of the Phonology and Morphophonemics of Ọ̀nịcha." B.A. thesis, University of Ìbàdàn.

Eoseewong, Nidhi. 1982. *Pen and Sail: Literature and History in Early Bangkok*. Chiangmai: Silkworm Books.

Èrédiaùwá. 2004. "For the Record: The Benin-Ifẹ̀ Connection." *Vanguard*, 9 May 2004. http://groups.yahoo.com/group/AlukoArchives/ message/297.

Evans, Helen C., and William D. Wixom, eds. 1997. *The Glory of Byzantium: Art and Culture of the Middle Byzantine Era, A.D. 843–1261*. New York: Metropolitan Museum of Art.

Evans-Pritchard, E. E. 1940. *The Nuer: A Description of the Modes of Livelihood and Political Institutions of a Nilotic People*. Oxford: Oxford University Press.

———. 1956. *Nuer Religion*. Oxford: Clarendon Press.

Fádìpè, N. A. 1940. "The Sociology of the Yorùbá." Ph.D. dissertation, University of London.

———. 1970. *The Sociology of the Yorùbá*. Ed. and with introduction by F. O. and O. O. Okediji. Ibàdàn: Ìbàdàn University Press.

Fairbanks, Arthur. 2001. "Anaximander Fragments and Commentary." In *The First Philosophers of Greece*, ed. and trans. Arthur Fairbanks. Reprint. Charleston, S.C.: Nabu Press. Originally published 1898 (London: K. Paul, Trench and Trubner). Reproduced in Hanover Historical Texts Project, http://history.hanover.edu/texts/presoc/ anaximan.htm.

Fálána, F. 2002. "Impeachment: A Letter to Ghali NaAbba." September 2002. Niger Delta Congress, http://www.nigerdeltacongress.com/ iarticles/impeachment_a_letter_to_ghali_na.htm.

Fálọlá, T., and A. Adébáyọ̀. 2000. *Culture, Politics, and Money among the Yorùbá*. New Brunswick, N.J.: Transaction Publishers.

Fassin, Didier. 2007a. "Humanitarianism as a Politics of Life." *Public Culture* 19:499–520.

———. 2007b. "Humanitarianism: A Non-Governmental Government." In *Nongovernmental Politics*, ed. M. Feher, G. Krikorian, and Y. McKee, 149–60. New York: Zone Books.

———. 2008. "The Humanitarian Politics of Testimony: Subjectification through Trauma in the Israeli-Palestinian Conflict." *Cultural Anthropology* 23 (3): 531–58.

Fassin, Didier, and Mariella Pandolfi, eds. 2010. *Contemporary States of Emergency: The Politics of Military and Humanitarian Interventions*. New York: Zone Books.

Fassin, Didier, and Richard Rechtman. 2007. *L'empire du traumatisme: Enquete sur la condition de victime*. Paris: Flammarion. Published in English as *The Empire of Trauma: An Inquiry into the Condition of Victimhood* (Princeton: Princeton University Press, 2009).

Fassin, Didier, and Paula Vasquez. 2005. "Humanitarian Exception as the Rule: The Political Theology of 1999 Tragedia in Venezuela." *American Ethnologist* 32:389–405.

Faure, David. 2006. *China and Capitalism: A History of Business Enterprise in Modern China*. Hong Kong: Hong Kong University Press.

———. 2007. *Emperor and Ancestor: State and Lineage in South China.* Stanford: Stanford University Press.

Faure, David, and Helen Siu. 2003. "The Original Translocal Society and Its Modern Fate: Historical and Post-Reform South China." *Provincial China* 8 (1): 40–59.

Fáwọlé, W. 2003. "Military Rule and the Unitarianization of Nigeria." In *The Amalgamation and Its Enemies: An Interpretive History of Modern Nigeria,* ed. R. Qláníyàn, 149–65. Ilé-Ifè: Qbáfémi Awólówò University Press.

Ferguson, James. 2007. "Formalities of Poverty: Thinking about Social Assistance in Neoliberal South Africa." *African Studies Review* 50 (2): 71–86.

———. 2010. "The Uses of Neoliberalism." In "The Point Is To Change It," ed. Noel Castree et al., 166–84. Special issue of *Antipode* 41 Supplement s1 (January).

Ferguson, Niall. 2001. "2011: Ten Years from Now, Historians Will Look Back and See the Events of Sept. 11 as Mere Tipples in a Tidal Wave of Terrorism and Political Fragmentation." *The New York Times Magazine,* 2 December 2001, 76–79.

Ferreira Neto, José. 1984. "A ciência dos mitos e o mito da ciência." M.A. dissertation, Universidade de Brasília.

Feuchtwang, Stephan. 1977. "School-Temple and City God." In *The City in Late Imperial China,* ed. G. W. Skinner, 581–608. Stanford: Stanford University Press.

Fine, Ben. 2000. *Social Capital Versus Social Theory: Political Economy and Social Science at the Turn of the Millennium.* New York: Routledge.

Fischer, Michael M. J. 1973. "Appendix I: Religious Riots." In "Zoroastrian Iran: Between Myth and Praxis." Ph.D. dissertation, University of Chicago.

———. 1989. "Legal Postulates in Flux: Justice, Wit and Hierarchy in Iran." In D. Dwyer, ed., *Law and Politics in the Middle East.* New York: J. F. Bergin.

———. 1990a. "Bombay Talkies, the Word and the World: Salman Rushdie's Satanic Verses." *Cultural Anthropology* 5(20): 107–59.

———. 1990b. "Social Change and the Mirrors of Tradition: The Bahais of Yazd." Ch. 5, *Debating Muslims: Cultural Dialogues between Postmodernity and Tradition.* Madison: University of Wisconsin Press.

———. 1990c. "Sacred Circles: Iranian (Zoroastrian and Shi'ite Muslim) Feasting and Pilgrimage Circuits." In J. S. Scott and P. Simpson-Housley, eds., *Sacred Spaces and Profane Places.* Westport, Conn.: Greenwood Press.

———. 2003. "Torn Religions" in "Autobiographical Voices (1, 2, 3) and Mosaic Memory: Ethnicity, Religion, Science." Ch. 6, *Emergent Forms of Life and the Anthropological Voice*. Durham: Duke University Press.

———. 2004. *Mute Dreams, Blind Owls, and Dispersed Knowledges: Persian Poesis in the Transnational Circuitry*. Durham: Duke University Press.

———. 2009. "Iran and the Boomeranging Cartoon Wars: Can Public Spheres at Risk Ally with Public Spheres Yet to Be Achieved?" *Cultural Politics* 5(1): 27-52.

Fleiss, Peter J. 1966. *Thucydides and the Politics of Bipolarity*. Baton Rouge: Louisiana State University Press.

Forde, D., and G. Jones. 1950. *The Ìbo and Ìbibio-Speaking Peoples of South-Eastern Nigeria*. Oxford: Oxford University Press.

Fortes, M., and E. Evans-Pritchard. 1940. *African Political Systems*. Oxford: Oxford University Press.

Frank, Georgia. 2000. *The Memory of the Eyes: Pilgrims to Living Saints in Christian Late Antiquity*. Berkeley and Los Angeles: University of California Press.

Fried, M. 1957. "The Classification of Corporate Unilinear Descent Groups." *Journal of the Royal Anthropological Institute* 87:1-29.

Friedman, J. 1975. "Tribes, States and Transformations." In *Marxist Analyses and Social Anthropology*, ed. Maurice Bloch, 161-202. London: Malaby Press.

Gailey, H. 1970. *The Road to Àbá: A Study of British Administrative Policy in Eastern Nigeria*. New York: New York University Press.

Galembo, P., ed. 1993. *Divine Inspiration: From Benin to Bahia*. Albuquerque: University of New Mexico Press.

García Márquez, Gabriel. 2000. "Shipwrecked on Dry Land." *Common Dreams*, 29 March 2000. http://www.Commondreams.org/views/032900-105.htm.

Geary, Patrick J. 1991. *Furta Sacra: Thefts of Relics in the Central Middle Ages*. Revised ed. Princeton: Princeton University Press. Originally published 1978.

Geertz, Clifford. 1968. *Islam Observed*. Chicago: University of Chicago Press.

———. 1977. "Centers, Kings, and Charisma: Reflections on the Symbolics of Power." In Joseph Ben-David and Terry Nichols Clarke, eds., *Culture and Its Creators: Essays in Honor of Edward Shils*, 150-171. Chicago: University of Chicago Press.

———. 1980. *Negara: The Theater State in Nineteenth-Century Bali*. Princeton: Princeton University Press.

Geertz, Hildred, and Clifford Geertz. 1975. *Kinship in Bali.* Chicago: University of Chicago Press.

Geiger, Wilhelm, trans. 1953. *Culavamsa, Part 2.* Colombo: Ceylon Government Information Department.

———. 1986. [1950]. *The Mahavamsa, or the Great Chronicle of Ceylon.* Colombo: Government Press. Originally published 1950, as *The Mahavamsa.*

Gellner, Ernest. 1969. *Saints of the Atlas.* London: Weidenfeld and Nicolson.

———. 1983. *Nations and Nationalism.* London: Basil Blackwell.

George, Kenneth M. 2004. "Violence, Culture, and the Indonesian Public Sphere: Reworking the Geertzian Legacy." In *Violence,* ed. Neal L. Whitehead, 25–54. Santa Fe: School of American Research Press.

Germano, David, and Kevin Trainor, eds. 2004. *Embodying the Dharma: Buddhist Relic Veneration in Asia.* Albany: State University of New York Press.

Ghazi, P. 1995. "Shell Refused to Help Saro-Wiwa Unless Protest Called Off." *The Observer,* 19 November 1995, p. 1.

Ghazvinian, J. 2007. *Untapped: The Scramble for Africa's Oil.* New York: Harcourt.

Gilsenan, Michael. 1973. *Saint and Sufi in Modern Egypt: An Essay in the Sociology of Religion.* Oxford: Clarendon Press.

———. 1982. *Recognizing Islam: Religion and Society in the Modern Arab World.* New York: Pantheon Books.

Góes Filho, Paulo de. 1999. "Construindo o internacional: Um enredo em três atos." *Cadernos do NuAP* [NuAP Working Papers] 4:80–92.

———. 2003. *O clube das nações: A missão do Brasil na ONU e o mundo da diplomacia parlamentar.* Rio de Janeiro: Relume Dumará.

Golomb, Jacob, and Robert Wistrich, eds. 2002. *Nietzsche, Godfather of Fascism? On the Uses and Abuses of a Philosophy.* Princeton: Princeton University Press.

Gombrich, Richard. 1971. *Precept and Practice: Traditional Buddhism in the Rural Highlands of Ceylon.* Oxford: Clarendon Press.

———. 1985. "Knowledge of the Unknowable." *Times Literary Supplement,* 4 (278): 359–60.

———. 1990. "How the Mahayana Began." In *The Buddhist Forum,* ed. Tadeusz Skorupski, 21–30. London: School of Oriental and African Studies.

Good, Byron J. 2012. "Theorizing the Subject of Medical and Psychiatric Anthropology." 2010 Marett Lecture. *Journal of the Royal Anthropological Institute.*

Good, Byron, Mary-Jo DelVecchio Good, Jesse Grayman, and Matthew

Lakoma. 2006. *Psychosocial Needs Assessment of Communities Affected by the Conflict in the Districts of Pidie, Bireuen, and Aceh Utara.* Jakarta: IOM.

Good, Mary-Jo DelVecchio. 2011. "Trauma in Post-conflict Aceh and Psychopharmaceuticals as a Medium of Exchange." In *Pharmaceutical Subjectivities: Psychopharmacology in a Globalizing World,* ed. Janis Jenkins. Santa Fe: School for American Research.

———. Forthcoming. "Acehnese Women's Narratives of Traumatic Experience, Resilience and Recovery." In *Legacies of Mass Violence,* eds. Devon Hinton and Alex Hinton. London: Palgrave.

Good, Mary-Jo DelVecchio, Byron J. Good, and Jesse Grayman. 2010. "Complex Engagements: Responding to Violence in Post-Conflict Aceh." In *Humanitarian Interventions,* ed. D. Fassin and M. Pandolfi. New York: Zone Books.

Good, Mary-Jo DelVecchio, Byron Good, Jesse Grayman, and Matthew Lakoma. 2007. *A Psychosocial Needs Assessment in 14 Conflict-Affected Districts in Aceh.* Jakarta: IOM.

Good, Mary-Jo DelVecchio, Sandra Teresa Hyde, Sarah Pinto, and Byron J. Good, eds. 2008. *Postcolonial Disorders.* Berkeley and Los Angeles: University of California Press.

Goody, Jack, and Stanley J. Tambiah. 1973. *Bridewealth and Dowry.* Cambridge: Cambridge University Press.

Goossaert, Vincent. 2000. *Dans les temples de la Chine: Rites populaires et religion savante.* Paris: Albin Michel.

Gray, John. 2003. *Al Qaeda and What It Means to Be Modern.* New York: New Press.

Grayman, Jesse Hession, Mary-Jo DelVecchio Good, and Byron J. Good. 2009. "Conflict Nightmares and Trauma in Aceh." *Culture, Medicine and Psychiatry* 33 (2): 290–312.

Griswold, A. B. 1968. *What Is a Buddha Image?* 2nd edition. Thai Culture, new series, no. 19. Bangkok: Fine Arts Department.

Guo, Qitao. 2003. *Exorcism and Money: The Symbolic World of the Five-Fury Spirits in Late Imperial China.* China Research Monographs no. 55. Berkeley: Institute of East Asian Studies, University of California.

———. 2005. *Ritual Opera and Mercantile Lineage: The Confucian Transformation of Popular Culture in Late Imperial Huizhou.* Stanford: Stanford University Press.

Hahn, Robert. 2001. *Anaximander and the Architects: The Contributions of Egyptian and Greek Architectural Technologies to the Origins of Greek Philosophy.* Albany: State University of New York Press.

Hallisey, Charles. n.d. "Relics as Memory Sites in the Buddhist Literature in Medieval Sri Lanka." Unpublished manuscript.

———. 1995. "Roads Taken and Not Taken in the Study of Theravada Buddhism." In *Curators of the Buddha: The Study of Buddhism under Colonialism*, ed. Donald S. Lopez. Chicago: University of Chicago Press.

Hanson, Victor Davis. 1996. "Introduction." In *The Landmark Thucydides*, by Thucydides, ed. Robert B. Strassler, ix–xxiii. New York: Free Press.

Harrel, C. Stevan. 1974. "When a God Becomes a Ghost." In *Religion and Ritual in Chinese Society*, ed. Arthur P. Wolf, 193–206. Stanford: Stanford University Press.

Haskell, Thomas L. 1998. *Objectivity Is Not Neutrality: Explanatory Schemes in History*. Baltimore: Johns Hopkins University Press.

Heesterman, J. C. 1985. *The Inner Conflict of Tradition: Essays in Indian Ritual, Kingship, and Society*. Chicago: University of Chicago Press.

Herzfeld, Michael. 2002. 'The Absent Presence: Discourses of Crypto-Colonialism." *South Atlantic Quarterly* 101:899–926.

———. 2004. *The Body Impolitic: Artisans and Artifice in the Global Hierarchy of Value*. Chicago: University of Chicago Press.

———. 2005. *Cultural Intimacy: Social Poetics in the Nation-State*. 2nd ed. New York: Routledge.

Hinton, Peter. 1992. "Meetings as Ritual: Thai Officials, Western Consultants and Development Planning in Northern Thailand." In *Patterns and Illusions: Thai Patterns of Thought*, ed. Gehan Wijewewardene and E. C. Chapman, 105–24. Singapore: Institute of Southeast Asian Studies.

Ho, Engseng. 2006. *The Graves of Tarim: Genealogy and Mobility across the Indian Ocean*. Berkeley and Los Angeles: University of California Press.

Hobbes, Thomas. 1962. *Leviathan*. New York: Collier Books.

Hocart, A. M. 1931. *The Temple of the Tooth in Kandy*. Memoirs of the Archaelogical Survey of Ceylon, vol. 4. London: Luzac.

Horton, R. 1979. "Ancient Ifẹ̀: A Reassessment." *Journal of the Historical Society of Nigeria* 9 (4): 69–149.

Hsu, Francis L. K. 1967. *Under the Ancestors' Shadow: Kinship, Personality, and Social Mobility in China*. Stanford: Stanford University Press.

Human Rights Watch. 2007. Human Rights Watch World Report 2007-Nigeria; Events of 2006. 11 January 2007. http://www.unhcr.org/refworld/docid/45aca2a316.html.

Hunter, David G. 1999. "Igilantius of Calagurris and Victricious of Rouen: Ascetics, Relics, and Clerics in Late Roman Gaul." *Journal of Early Christian Studies* 7, no. 3 (Fall): 401–30.

Hytonen, Yki. 2002. *Because We Are All Human: Finnish Red Cross, 1877–2002*. Helsinki: Finnish Red Cross.

Ìdúùwẹ, A. c. 1977–80. "History of Greater Ágbọ̀." Ms. in possession of V. Manfredi, posted at http://people.bu.edu/manfredi/Iduuwe .History.pdf.

Ìgè, I. 2008. "Odi Killings: Court Orders IG to Quiz Ọbásanjọ́." *Vanguard*, 16 May 2008. http://www.nigeriavillagesquare.com/forum/main-square/19143-odi-killings-court-orders-ig-quiz-obasanjo.html.

Ikari, B. 2006. *Ken Saro-Wiwa and MOSOP: The Story and Revelation*. Philadelphia: Xlibris.

Ikimẹ, O. 1969. *Niger Delta Rivalry: Iṣẹkiri-Ùrhobo Relations and the European Presence*. London: Longman.

Îkòrò, S. 1996. *The Kanà Language*. CNWS Publications, no. 40. Leiden: Research School of Asian, African, and Amerindian Studies, Leiden University.

Îlozùé, C. 1999. "*Îkeǹga, Ọ̀fọ́* Symbols in Owerri [Òweré] Removed." *Guardian* (Lagos), 26 April 1999.

Ìmáhìagbe, J. 1981. "An Account of the 'Ọ̀sịézi' Festival of the Ìká People." Term paper for Lit. 140, University of Nigeria, Ǹsụ́ká.

Imobighe, T., et al., eds. 2002. *Conflict and Instability in Nigeria: The Warri Case*. Ìbàdàn: Spectrum.

Inter-Agency Standing Committee (IASC). 2007. *IASC Guidelines on Mental Health and Psychosocial Support in Emergency Settings*. Geneva: IASC.

James, Erica C. 2008. "Haunting Ghosts: Madness, Gender, and Ensekirite in Haiti in the Democratic Era." In *Postcolonial Disorders*, ed. Mary-Jo DelVecchio Good, Sandra Teresa Hyde, Sarah Pinto, and Byron J. Good, 157–86. Berkeley and Los Angeles: University of California Press.

James, William. 1904. *The Varieties of Religious Experience*. London: Longmans, Green.

Jayasinghe, Namalie. 2006. "Post-tsunami Sri Lanka and Ethnic Conflict." M.Sc. thesis in Environment and Development, London School of Economics.

Jayawickrama, N. A., trans. 1971. *The Chronicle of the Thupa and Thupavamsa*. London: Luzac.

———. 1968. *The Sheaf of Garlands of the Epochs of the Conqueror: Being a Translation of Jinakalamalipakaranam of the Ratanapanna Thera of Thailand*. London: Pali Text Society.

Johnson, David. 1985. "The City-God Cults of T'ang and Sung China." *Harvard Journal of Asiatic Studies* 45 (2): 363–458.

Jones, G. 1956. *Report of the Position, Status and Influence of Chiefs and Natural Rulers in the Eastern Region of Nigeria*. Énugwú: Government Printer.

———. 1958. "Native and Trade Currencies in Southern Nigeria during the Eighteenth and Nineteenth Centuries." *Africa* 28:43–56.

Jordan, David. 1972. *Gods, Ghosts, and Ancestors: The Folk Religion of a Taiwanese Village*. Berkeley and Los Angeles: University of California Press.

Jordt, Ingrid. 2007a. *Burma's Mass Lay Meditation Movement: Buddhism and the Cultural Construction of Power.* Research in International Studies Series. Athens: University of Ohio Press.

———. 2007b. "What Is a 'True Buddhist': Meditation and the Formation of Knowledge Communities in Burma." *Ethnology* 45 (3): 193-208.

Joseph, R. 1987. *Democracy and Prebendal Politics in Nigeria: The Rise and Fall of the Second Republic.* Cambridge: Cambridge University Press.

Kahn, Charles H. 1960. *Anaximander and the Origins of Greek Cosmology.* New York: Columbia University Press.

Kangsadara, Niramol. 1989. "Prince Wachirayan's Reforms in the Buddhist Order (1898-1921)." In *Anuson Walter Vella* (In Memory of Professor Vella), ed. Ronald D. Renard, 249-63. Chiang Mai: Walter F. Vella Fund, Payap University.

Karp, Ivan. 1986. "Agency and Social Theory: A Review of Giddens." *American Ethnologist* 13:131-137.

Karp, Ivan, and Kent Maynard. 1983. "Reading *The Nuer.*" *Current Anthropology* 24:481-503.

Katz, Paul R. 1995. *Demon Hordes and Burning Boats: The Cult of Marshal Wen in Late Imperial Chekiang.* Albany: State University of New York Press.

———. 2007. "Orthopraxy and Heteropraxy beyond the State: Standardizing Ritual in Chinese Society." *Modern China* 33 (1): 72-90.

Kedourie, Elie. 1993 . *Nationalism.* Oxford: Blackwell Publishing. Originally published 1960.

Keightley, David N. 2004. "The Making of the Ancestors: Late Shang Religion and Its Legacy." In *Religion and Chinese Society,* ed. John Lagerwey, 1:3-63. Hong Kong: Chinese University of Hong Kong.

Kelly, John D. 1998. "Time and the Global: Against the Homogeneous, Empty Communities in Contemporary Social Theory." *Development and Change* 29 (4): 839-71.

———. 2003. "U.S. Power, After 9/11 and Before It: Not an Empire, Then What?" *Public Culture* 15 (2): 347-69.

Kelly, John D., and Martha Kaplan. 2001. *Represented Communities: Fiji and World Decolonization.* Chicago: University of Chicago Press.

Kemper, Steven. 1980. "Reform and Segmentation in Monastic Fraternities in Low Country Sri Lanka." *Journal of Asian Studies* 40(1): 27-41.

———. 1991. *The Presence of the Past: Chronicles, Politics and Culture in Sihala Life.* Ithaca: Cornell University Press.

Kermani, Navid. 2002. "A Dynamite of the Spirit: Why Nietzsche, Not the Koran, Is the Key to Understanding the Suicide Bombers." *Times Literary Supplement,* 29 March 2002, 13-15.

Kershaw, Roger. 1969. "The Thais of Kelantan: A Socio-Political Study of an Ethnic Outpost." Ph.D. dissertation, University of London.

Keyes, Charles F. 1987. "Theravada Buddhism and Its Worldly Transformation in Thailand: Reflections on the Work of S .J. Tambiah." *Contributions to Indian Sociology* 21 (1): 123-45.

Khantipalo Bhikkhu. 1979. *Banner of the Arahants: Buddhist Monks and Nuns from the Buddha's Time till Now.* Kandy, Sri Lanka: Buddhist Publication Society.

Khosrokhavar, Farhad. 2001. "Neo-Conservative Intellectuals in Iran." *Critique* 19:5-30.

Kingsley, Damien, and Lesley McCulloch. 2006. "Military Business in Aceh." In *Verandah of Violence: The Background to the Aceh Problem,* ed. Anthony Reid, 199-224. Singapore: Singapore University Press.

Kirch, Patrick, and Marshall Sahlins. 1992. *Anahulu: The Anthropology of History in the Kingdom of Hawaii.* Vol. 1, *Historical Ethnography.* Chicago: University of Chicago Press.

Kirk, G. S., J. E. Raven, and M. Schofield. 1983. *The Presocratic Philosophers: A Critical History with a Selection of Texts.* 2nd ed. Cambridge: Cambridge University Press.

Kirsch, A. Thomas. 1977. "Complexity in the Thai Religious System: An Interpretation." *Journal of Asian Studies* 36:241-266.

Knight, Mark. 2008. "Expanding the DDR Model: Politics and Organizations." *Journal of Security and Sector Management* 6:1-18.

Kristensen, William Brede. 1971. *The Meaning of Religion: Lectures in the Phenomenology of Religion.* Trans. J. B. Carman. The Hague: Nijhoff.

Kuhn, Philip. 2008. *Chinese Among Others: Emigration in Modern Times.* Lanham, Md.: Rowman and Littlefield Publishers.

Lackner, H. 1971. "Social Anthropology and Indirect Rule: The Colonial Administration and Anthropology in Eastern Nigeria, 1920-1940." Ph.D. dissertation, University of London.

———. 1973. "Social Anthropology and Indirect Rule: The Colonial Administration and Anthropology in Eastern Nigeria, 1920-1940." In *Anthropology and the Colonial Encounter,* ed. T. Asad, 123-51. London: Ithaca Press. (Excerpt from author's dissertation, Lackner 1971.)

Lagerwey, John. 2001. "Popular Ritual Specialists in West Central Fujian." In *Shehui, minzu yu wenhua zhanyan guoji yantaohui lunwenji,* ed. Wang Ch'iu-kui, Chuang Ying-chang, and Chen Chung-min, 435-507. Taipei: Hanxue Yanjiu Zhongxin.

Latour, Bruno. 2002. *War of the Worlds: What about Peace?* Trans. Charlotte Biggs. Chicago: Prickly Paradigm Press.

Law, B. C., ed. and trans. 1925. *The Dathavamsa: A History of the Tooth Relic of the Buddha.* Lahore: Punjab Sanskrit Book Depot.

Láwúyì, O. 2002. "Understanding the Nigerian State: Popular Culture and the Struggle for Meaning." In *The Transformation of Nigeria: Essays in Honor of 'Tóyin Fálọlá,* ed. A. Oyèébádé, 511–30. Trenton, N.J.: Africa World Press.

Leach, Edmund. 1954. *Political Systems of Highland Burma: A Study of Kachin Social Structure.* London School of Economics Monographs on Social Anthropology, no. 44. London: G. Bell and Son.

———. 1961. *Pul Eliya, a Village in Ceylon: A Study of Land Tenure and Kinship.* Cambridge: Cambridge University Press.

———. 1966a. "Ritualization in Man in Relation to Conceptual and Social Development." *Philosophical Transactions of the Royal Society of London* B, 251:403–8.

———. 1966b. "Virgin Birth." In *Proceedings of the Royal Anthropological Institute of Great Britain and Ireland for 1966.* London: Royal Anthropological Institute.

———. 1977. *Custom, Law, and Terrorist Violence.* Edinburgh: Edinburgh University Press.

Lean, G. 1995. "Shell 'Paid Nigerian Military.'" *Independent on Sunday,* 17 December 1995. http://archive.greenpeace.org/comms/ken/opay001.html.

Leaning, Jennifer, Susan M. Briggs, and Lincoln C. Chen, eds. 1999. *Humanitarian Crises: The Medical and Public Health Response.* Cambridge, Mass.: Harvard University Press.

Lévi-Strauss, Claude. 1945. "L'Analyse structurale en linguistique et en anthropologie." *Word* 1:33–53.

———. 1955. *Tristes Tropiques.* Paris: Plon.

———. 1966. *The Savage Mind.* Trans. George and Dorothy Weightman. Chicago: University of Chicago Press. Originally published as *La Pensée sauvage* (1962).

Lewis, Paul. 1996. "Blood and Oil: A Special Report; After Nigeria Represses, Shell Defends Its Record." *New York Times,* 13 April 1996. http://query.nytimes.com/gst/fullpage.html?res=9C05E2D81139F930 A25751C0A960958260.

Lifton, Robert Jay. 1999. *Destroying the World to Save It: Aum Shinrikyo, Apocalyptic Violence, and the New Global Terrorism.* New York: Henry Holt and Co.

Lilla, Mark. 2001. *The Reckless Mind: Intellectuals in Politics.* New York: New York Review of Books.

Lingat, Robert. 1934. "Le Culte du Bouddha d'Emeraude." *Journal of the Siam Society* 27 (1).

Linge, David E. 2000. "Leading the Life of Angels: Ascetic Practice and Reflection in the Writings of Evagrius of Pontus." *Journal of the American Academy of Religion* 68, no. 3 (September): 537–68.

Listopad, John. 2001. "The Mural Paintings of Wat Somanat Vihan in Bangkok." Paper presented at the AAS Annual Meeting, 22–25 March 2001, Chicago.

Little, Paul. 1995. "Ritual, Power and Ethnography at the Rio Earth Summit." *Critique of Anthropology* 15:297–320. Originally published online as "One Event, One Observer and Two Texts: Analyzing the Rio Earth Summit," at http://www.unb.br/ics/dan/Serie134empdf.pdf.

Lloyd, P. 1963. "The Iṣẹkiri in the Nineteenth Century: An Outline Social History." *Journal of African History* 4:207–231.

Loos, Tamara. 2006. *Subject Siam: Family, Law, and Colonial Modernity in Thailand.* Ithaca: Cornell University Press.

Lourie, Richard. 2002. *Sakharov: A Biography.* Hanover, N.H.: Brandeis University Press and University Press of New England.

Lovejoy, Arthur O., and George Boas. 1935. *Primitivism and Related Ideas in Antiquity.* Baltimore: Johns Hopkins University Press.

MacCulloch, J. A. 1961. "Relics." In *Encyclopedia of Religion and Ethics,* ed. James Hastings, vol. 10. New York: Charles Scribner's Sons.

Madison, James, Alexander Hamilton, and John Jay. 1987. *The Federalist Papers.* Edited by Isaac Kramnick. London: Penguin Books.

Maha Bua, Phra Ajaan. 2005. *Venerable Acariya Mun Bhuridatta Thera: A Spiritual Biography.* Trans. Ajaan Dick Silaratano. Udorn Thani, Baan Taad Forest Monastery: Forest Dhamma Books.

Maine, H. 1861. *Ancient Law: Its Connection with the Early History of Society and Its Relation to Modern Ideas.* London: Murray.

Malkki, Liisa. 2007. "Tradition and Improvisation in Ethnographic Field Research." In *Improvising Theory: Process and Temporality in Ethnographic Fieldwork,* ed. Allaine Cerwonka and Liisa Malkki. Chicago: University of Chicago Press.

Manfredi, V. 1991. "Ágbọ̀ and Ẹhụgbò: Ìgbo Linguistic Consciousness, Its Origins and Limits." Ph.D. dissertation, Harvard University. http://people.bu.edu/manfredi/dissertation.pdf.

———. 1993. "States of Insecurity: Some Nigerian Examples." Workshop on Personal Security in Africa, Committee on African Studies, Harvard University, 27 May 1993.

Manicas, Peter T. 1982. "War, Stasis, and Greek Political Thought." *Comparative Studies in Society and History* 29:673–88.

Marcus, George, and Michael Fischer. 1986. *Anthropology as Cultural Critique.* Chicago: University of Chicago Press.

Martinkus, John. 2004. *Indonesia's Secret War in Aceh.* Sydney: Random House Australia.

Marx, Emmanuel. 1977. "Communal and Individual Pilgrimage: The Region of Saints' Tombs in South Sinai." In *Regional Cults,* ed. R. P. Werbner, 29–51. London: Academic Press.

Mattisonn, Heidi, and Jeremy Seekings. 2003. "The Politics of a Basic Income Grant in South Africa, 1996–2002." In *A Basic Income Grant for South Africa,* ed. Guy Standing and Michael Samson. Cape Town: University of Cape Town Press.

McCulloh, John M. 1976. "The Cult of Relics in the Letters and Dialogues of Pope Gregory the Great: A Lexicographical Study." *Traditio* 32.

McDaniel, Justin 2008. *Gathering Leaves and Lifting Words: Intertextuality and Monastic Education in Laos and Thailand.* Seattle: University of Washington Press.

McGilvray, Dennis. 2008. *Crucible of Conflict: Tamil and Muslim Society on the East Coast of Sri Lanka.* Durham: Duke University Press.

McManners, John. 1986. Review of *Restless Bones: The Story of Relics* by James Bentley and *Relics and Shrines* by David Sox. *Times Literary Supplement,* 3 January 1986.

Meek, C. 1937. *Law and Authority in a Nigerian Tribe: A Study in Indirect Rule.* London: Oxford University Press.

Meillassoux, C. 1986. *Anthropologie de l'esclavage: Le ventre de fer et d'argent.* Paris: Presse Universitaires de France.

Melzian, H. 1937. *Concise Dictionary of the Bìní [Èdó] Language of Southern Nigeria.* London: Kegan Paul.

Miami Herald. 2000a. "Cubans Pay Homage to Marti, Elián." Article by Associated Press (Havana), 29 January 2000. http://www .miamiherald.com.

———. 2000b. "Family Members Moving Out of House where Elián Stayed." Article by Ana Acle, 25 May 2000. http://www .miamiherald.com.

Milosz, Czeslaw. 1953. *The Captive Mind.* New York: Knopf.

Missingham, Bruce. 2003. *The Assembly of the Poor in Thailand: From Local Struggles to National Protest Movement.* Chiang Mai: Silkworm Books.

Moore, William. 1936. *History of Itsẹkiri.* London: Stockwell.

———. 1970. *History of Itsẹkiri.* 2nd revised edition. Cass Library of African Studies: General Studies, no. 89. London: Frank Cass.

Moreira Santos, Ana Flávia. 2001. "Peirce e O Beijo no Asfalto." In *O dito e o feito: Ensaios de antropologia dos rituais,* ed. Mariza Peirano, 43–57. Rio de Janeiro: Relume Dumará.

Morris, Ian. 2000. *Archaeology as Cultural History: Words and Things in Iron Age Greece.* Madden, Mass.: Blackwell.

Morris, Rosalind. 2000. *In the Place of Origins: Modernity and Its Mediums in Northern Thailand.* Durham, N.C.: Duke University Press.

——. 2004. "Intimacy and Corruption in Thailand's Age of Transparency." In *Off Stage/On Display: Intimacy and Ethnography in the Age of Public Culture,* ed. Andrew Shryock, 225–43. Stanford: Stanford University Press.

Mykkänen, Juri. 2003. *Inventing Politics: A New Political Anthropology of the Hawaiian Kingdom.* Honolulu: University of Hawai'i Press.

Naquin, Susan. 2000. *Peking: Temples and City Life, 1400–1900.* Berkeley and Los Angeles: University of California Press.

National Archives of Thailand. *Seuksaathikaan.* Fifth Reign, 12/8, vol.1, 1–11; 8/19, 1–19, 12.

National Intelligence Council. 2005. *Mapping Sub-Saharan Africa's Future.* http://www.dni.gov/nic/PDF_GIF_confreports/africa_future.pdf.

Nessen, William. 2004. *The Black Road: On the Front Line of Aceh's War.* Documentary film written, filmed, and directed by William Nessen. Produced by Andrew Ogilvie, Electric Pictures, for SBS, Australia.

Newsweek. 2000. "Once More unto the Breach." Article by Jonathan Alter, 24 April 2000. http://www.thedailybeast.com/newsweek/2000/04/23/once-more-unto-the-breach.html.

Ñnànnà, O. 2004. "Alas! This Emperor Is Naked," part 2. Nigeria: People and Politics, *Vanguard* (Lagos), 23 December 2004. http://www.vanguardngr.com/.

Nordstrom, Carolyn. 2004. *Shadows of War: Violence, Power, and International Profiteering in the Twenty-First Century.* Berkeley and Los Angeles: University of California Press.

——. 1997. *A Different Kind of War Story.* Philadelphia: University of Pennsylvania Press.

Notton, Camille, trans. 1933a. *The Chronicle of the Emerald Buddha.* Bangkok: Bangkok Times Press.

——. 1933b. *P'ra Buddha Sihinga.* Bangkok: Bangkok Times Press.

NuAP (Núcleo de Antropologia da Politica). 1998. "An Anthropology of Politics: Rituals, Representations and Violence; A Research Project." *NuAP Working Papers* 1. Published simultaneously in Portuguese as "Uma antropologia da politíca: Rituais, representações e violência; Projeto de pesquisa." *Cadernos do NuAP* 1. Rio de Janeiro: NAU Editora.

Nzímìro, I. 1972. *Studies in Ìgbo Political Systems: Chieftancy and Politics in Four Niger States.* London: Frank Cass.

——. 1984. "Of What Relevance are Traditional Rulers?" *Guardian* (Lagos), 17–19 May 1984. Reprinted by Díké's Memorial Bookshop, Chọ̀bàá, Port Harcourt.

Ọbásanjọ́, O. 1980. *My Command: An Account of the Nigerian Civil War,*
1967-70. London: Heinemann.

Ọbáyẹmí, A. 1991. "Beyond the Legends: A Discussion of Ẹ̀dó-
Yorùbá Relations in Precolonial Times." In *Cultural Studies in Ifẹ̀,*
ed. B. Adédìran, 33–41. Ilé-Ifẹ̀: Institute of Cultural Studies, Ọbáfẹ́mi
Awólọ́ wọ̀ University.

Obeyesekere, Gananath. 1967. *Land Tenure in Village Ceylon: A Sociological*
and Historical Study. London: Cambridge University Press.

———. 1984. *The Cult of the Goddess Pattini.* Chicago: University of Chicago Press.

Òbí, C. 2001. *The Changing Forms of Identity Politics in Nigeria under Eco-*
nomic Adjustment: The Case of the Oil Minorities Movement of the Niger
Delta. Uppsala, Sweden: Nordiska Afrikainstitutet (Nordic African
Institute).

Ochonu, M. 2009. "The Lawful Migrant: Personal and Professional
Journeys of a Nigerian-Briton." Review of D. Ògún, *The Law, the Law-*
yers and the Lawless (2009). Sahara Reporters, posted August 15, 2009,
http://saharareporters.com/article/lawful-migrant-personal-and-
professional-journeys-nigerian-briton.

O'Connor, Richard A. 1978. "Urbanism and Religion: Community, Hierarchy, and Sanctity in Urban Thai Buddhist Temples." Ph.D. dissertation, Cornell University.

———. 1980. "Forest Monks and the History of Bangkok." *Visakha Puja*
(Bangkok), 32–37.

———. 1993. "Interpreting Thai Religious Change: Temples, Sangha
Reform and Social Change." *Journal of Southeast Asian Studies* 24 (2):
330–39.

Ọ́gbàlụ́, F. 1975. "Ìgbo Spelling." In *Ìgbo Language and Culture,* ed.
F. Ọ́gbàlụ́, and 'N. Émọ́nanjọ, 1:138–59. Ìbàdàn: Oxford University Press.

Oghuagha, P. 1992. "The Ìgbo and Their Neighbors." In *Groundwork of*
Ìgbo History, ed. A. Áfìigbo, 362–82. Lagos: Vista Books.

Ògún[etimojú], D. 2009. *The Law, the Lawyers and the Lawless.* London:
New European Publications.

Ọhadíkẹ́, D. 1991. *The Èkúmékú Movement: Western Ìgbo Resistance to the*
British Conquest of Nigeria, 1883-1914. Athens: Ohio State University
Press.

———. 1994. *Àníọ́ma: A Social History of the Western Ìgbo People.* Athens:
Ohio State University Press.

Ohnuki-Tierney, Emiko. 1999. "We Eat Each Other's Food to Nourish
Our Body: The Global and the Local as Mutually Constituent Forces."
In *Food in Global History,* ed. Robert Grew, 240–72. Boulder: Westview
Press.

———. 2002. *Kamikaze, Cherry Blossoms, and Nationalisms: The Militarization of Aesthetics in Japanese History.* Chicago: University of Chicago Press.

———. 2006. *Kamikaze Diaries: Reflection on Japanese Student Soldiers.* Chicago: University of Chicago Press.

Òjúkwu, O. 1969. *The Áhị̀ará Declaration: The Principles of the Biafran Revolution.* 1 June 1969. http://www.africaresource.com/war/vol2.2/biafra/ahiara.htm.

Òkóntà, I. 2007a. "Niger Delta: Behind the Mask; Ijaw Militia Fight the Oil Cartel." World War 4 Report, http://ww4report.com/node/2974.

———. 2007b. *When Citizens Revolt: Nigerian Elites, Big Oil, and the Ogoni Struggle for Self-Determination.* Trenton, N.J.: Africa World Press.

Òkóntà, I., and O. Douglas. 2001. *Where Vultures Feast: Shell, Human Rights, and Oil in the Niger Delta.* San Francisco: Sierra Club Books.

Okpehwo [Okpewho], I. 1998. *Once Upon a Kingdom: Myth, Hegemony, and Identity.* Bloomington: Indiana University Press.

Ọláníyàn, R., and A. Àlàó. 2003. "The Amalgamation, Colonial Politics and Nationalism, 1914-1960." In *The Amalgamation and Its Enemies: An Interpretive History of Modern Nigeria,* ed. R. Ọláníyàn, 1-22. Ilé-Ifẹ̀: Ọbáfẹ́mi Awólọ́wọ̀ University Press.

Oldenberg, Hermann, ed. and trans. 1982. *The Dipavamsa: An Ancient Historical Record.* Reprint. New Delhi: Asian Educational Services. Originally published 1879.

Ọlọ́rúnyọ̀mi, Ṣ. 1996. "Just before the Blackout: A Reconstruction of the Last Hours of Ken Saro-Wiwa and Eight Other MOSOP Activists." *Glendora Review* (Lagos) 1 (3): 21-24.

Òmọ́ruyì, Ọ. 1999. *The Tale of June 12: The Betrayal of the Democratic Rights of Nigerians (1993).* London: Press Alliance Network.

———. 2008. *Disillusioned Democrat: Reflections on My Public Life in Nigeria (1959-1999).* Ìbàdàn: Heinemann Educational Books (Nigeria) Ltd.

Ọnwụejìọ̀gwụ̀ [Onwuejeogwu], M. 1972. "Outline of the Dawn of Ìgbo Civilization in the Ìgbo Culture Area." *Ọ̀dịnanị* 1:15-56.

———. 1974. "An Outline of an Ìgbo Civilization: Ǹri Kingdom and Hegemony, A.D. 994 to Present." M.Phil. thesis, University College London.

———. 1981. *An Ìgbo Civilization: Ǹri Kingdom and Hegemony.* London: Ethnographica, Ltd.; Benin-City: Ethiope.

———. 2001. "*Ìgbo nwe ézè,* Ìgbo Have Kings: The Evolutionary Development of Complexities in the Ìgbo Political System." Lecture. Published as *Ị́gụ́arọ̀ Ìgbo Heritage: Inaugural Lecture 2001.* Anambra [?] Nigeria: Front for Defense of Igbo Heritage.

Ọnwụmèchili, C. 2000. "*Ìgbo énwé ezè:* The Ìgbo Have No Kings." Àhịajíọkụ́ Lecture, Ministry of Information, Culture, Youth and

Sports, Òweré ["Owerri"], Ímò State. http://ahiajoku.igbonet
.com/2000.

Ònyéchè, I. 2002. "Theịká People." Ikaworld.com, http://www.ikaworld
.com/index.php?mod=article&cat=IkaHistoryamp;Tradition&
article=207.

Orwin, Clifford. 1988. "Stasis and Plague: Thucydides and the Dissolu-
tion of Society." *Journal of Politics* 50:831–47.

Ostwald, Martin. 2000. *Oligarchia: The Development of a Constitutional
Form in Ancient Greece.* Historia: Zeitschrift für Alte Geschichte,
vol. 144. Stuttgart: Franz Steiner Verlag.

Otite, O. 1971. "History as a Process: A Study of the Ùrhobo of the Midwestern State of Nigeria." *African Historical Studies* 4:41–57.

———. 1975. "Encapsulated Political Systems." In *Colonialism and Change:
Essays Presented to Lucy Mair*, ed. M. Owusu, 67–84. The Hague:
Mouton.

Paine, Robert. 1989. "High-Wire Culture: Comparing Two Agonistic Systems of Self-Esteem." *Man* (n.s.) 24:328–39.

Paitoon, Mikusol. 1995. "Administrative Reforms and National Integration: The Case of the Northeast." In *Regions and National Integration in
Thailand, 1892–1992*, ed. Volker Grabowsky, 145–53. Wiesbaden: Harras-
sowitz Verlag.

Pandolfi, Mariella. 2008. "Laboratories of Intervention: The Humanitarian Governance of the Postcommunist Balkan Territories." In *Postcolonial Disorders*, ed. Mary-Jo DelVecchio Good, Sandra Teresa Hyde,
Sarah Pinto, and Byron J. Good, 157–86. Berkeley and Los Angeles:
University of California Press.

Parker, Kathleen. 2000. "Parental Authority: Elián Belongs with his
Father." *Chicago Tribune*, 19 January 2000. http://articles.chicago
tribune.com/2000-01-19/news/0001190319_1_child-on-american-
soil-childhood-riches-elian-gonzalez.

Patton, Kimberly C., and Benjamin C. Ray, eds. 2000. *A Magic Still Dwells.*
Berkeley and Los Angeles: University of California Press.

PBS Frontline. 2001. "Saving Elián: Interviews." February 2001. http://
www.pbs.org/wgbh/pages/frontline/shows/elian/.

Peirano, Mariza. 1998. "When Anthropology Is at Home." *Annual Review
of Anthropology* 27:105–28.

———. 2000a. "The Anthropological Analysis of Rituals." *Série Antropologia* 272:1–27. http://nrserver34.net/~danunb/doc/Serie272empdf.pdf.

———, ed. 2000b. "Análises de Rituais." *Série Antropologia* 283:1–119.
http://nrserver34.net/~danunb/doc/Serie283empdf.pdf.

———, ed. 2002. *O dito e o feito: Ensaios de antropologia dos rituais.* Rio de
Janeiro: Relume Dumará.

———. 2006. *A teoria vivida e outros ensaios de antropologia.* Rio de Janeiro: J. Zahar.

———. 2008. "Otherness in Context: A Guide to Anthropology in Brazil." In *A Companion to Latin American Anthropology,* ed. Deborah Poole. London: Blackwell.

———. 2009. "O paradoxo dos documentos de identidade: Relato de uma experiência nos Estados Unidos." *Horizontes Antropológicos* 15:53–80. Translated as "The Paradox of IDs: An Account of an Ethnographic Experience in the US," http://socialsciences.scielo.org/scielo .php?pid=S0104-71832008000100009&script=sci_arttext.

———. 2011. "Your ID, Please? The Henry Gates v. James Crowley Event from an Anthropological Perspective." *Vibrant* 8:39–67. http://www .vibrant.org.br/downloads/v8n2_peirano.pdf.

Peleggi, Marizio. 2002. *Lords of Things: The Fashioning of the Siamese Monarchy's Modern Image.* Honolulu: University of Hawaii Press.

Perera, Janaka. 2006. "UNP Urged to Study 1956 Buddhist Committee Report." *Asian Tribune,* 9 October 2006. http://www.dhammaweb.net/ dhamma_news/view.php?id=148.

Persico, Joseph. 2004. "Early Warnings: What Did He Know, and When?" *New York Times,* 18 April 2004.

Potter, Jack M. 1976. *Peasant Social Structure.* Chicago: University of Chicago Press.

Potter, Karl. 1963. *Presuppositions of India's Philosophy.* Englewood Cliffs, N.J.: Prentice Hall.

Potter, Sulamith Heins. 1977. *Family Life in a Northern Thai Village: A Study in the Structural Significance of Women.* Berkeley and Los Angeles: University of California Press.

Pratten, D. 2006. "The Politics of Vigilance in Southeastern Nigeria." *Development and Change* 37: 707–34.

———. 2007. *The Man-Leopard Murders: History and Society in Colonial Nigeria.* Edinburgh: Edinburgh University Press.

Price, David. 2002. "Lessons from Second World War Anthropology: Peripheral, Persuasive, and Ignored Contributions." *Anthropology Today* 18 (3): 14–20.

Puett, Michael. 2001. *The Ambivalence of Creation: Debates Concerning Innovation and Artifice in Early China.* Stanford: Stanford University Press

———. 2002. *To Become a God: Cosmology, Sacrifice, and Self-Divinization in Early China.* Cambridge, Mass.: Harvard University Asia Center.

———. 2005. "The Offering of Food and the Creation of Order: The Practice of Sacrifice in Early China." In *Of Tripod and Palate: Food, Politics, and Religion in Traditional China,* ed. Roel Sterckx, 75–95. New York: Palgrave MacMillan.

———. 2006. "Innovation as Ritualization: The Fractured Cosmology of Early China." *Cardozo Law Review* 28, no. 1 (October): 23-36.

———. 2008. "Human and Divine Kingship in Early China: Comparative Reflections." In *Religion and Power: Divine Kingship in the Ancient World and Beyond*, ed. Nicole Brisch, 199-212. Chicago: Oriental Institute of the University of Chicago.

Pugh, Michael. 1997. "Military Intervention and Humanitarian Action: Trends and Issues." *Disasters* 22:339-351.

Rajasekara, E. S., ed. 1920. *Dalada Sirita* [History of the Tooth Relic]. Colombo: Printed and published by L. D. Lewis.

Ratanapruck, Prista. 2007. "Kinship and Religious Practices as Institutionalization of Trade Networks: Manangi Trade Communities in South and Southeast Asia." *Journal of the Economic and Social History of the Orient* 50 (2-3): 325-46.

———. 2008. "Market and Monastery: Manangi Trade Diasporas in South Asia and Southeast Asia." Ph.D. dissertation, Harvard University.

Ray, Reginald. 1994. *Buddhist Saints in India: A Study in Buddhist Values and Orientations*. New York: Oxford University Press.

Reid, Anthony. 1995. *Witnesses to Sumatra: A Traveller's Anthology*. Kuala Lumpur and New York: Oxford University Press.

———, ed. 2006. *Verandah of Violence: The Background to the Aceh Problem*. Singapore: Singapore University Press.

Reuters. 2006. "Violence Left 3 Million Bereft in Past 7 Years, Nigeria Reports." *New York Times*, 14 March 2006. http://www.nytimes .com/2006/03/14/international/africa/14nigeria.html.

Reyna, S. 2007. "Developing Dystopia: The World Bank, Patrimonialism, Imperialism and Chadian Oil." Paper presented at Boston University African Studies Center, 3 December 2007.

Reynolds, Craig. 1976. "Buddhist Cosmography in Thai History, with Special Reference to Nineteenth-Century Culture Change." *Journal of Asian Studies* 35 (2): 203-220.

Reynolds, Frank. 1977. "The Several Bodies of the Buddha: Reflections on a Neglected Aspect of Theravada Tradition." *History of Religions* 16:374-89.

———. 1978. "The Holy Emerald Jewel." In *Religion and the Legitimation of Power in Thailand, Laos, and Burma*, ed. Bardwell Smith. Chambersburg, Penn.: Anima Books.

———. 1987. "Trajectories in Theravada Studies with Special Reference to the Work of Stanley Tambiah." *Contributions to Indian Sociology* 21 (1): 113-21.

Riding, Alan. 1989. "Vatican 'Saint Factory': Is It Working Too Hard?" Rome Journal, *New York Times*, April 15, 1989.

Robinson, Kathryn. 2004. "Chandra Jayawardena and the Ethical 'Turn' in Australian Anthropology." *Critique of Anthropology* 24 (4): 379-402.

Robinson, Richard H., Willard R. Johnson, and Thanissari Bhikkhu (Geoffrey DeGraf). 2005. *Buddhist Religions: A Historical Introduction.* 5th ed. Belmont, Ca.: Wadsworth/Thomson.

Rodney, Walter. 1969. "Gold and Slaves on the Gold Coast." *Transactions of the Historical Society of Ghana* 10:13-28.

———. 1970. *A History of the Upper Guinea Coast, 1545-1800.* Oxford: Clarendon Press.

Rowell, A. 2009. "Secret Papers 'Show How Shell Targeted Nigeria Oil Protests'; Documents Seen by *The IoS* Support Claims Energy Giant Enlisted Help of Country's Military Government." *The Independent,* 14 June 2009. http://www.independent.co.uk/news/world/americas/secret-papers-show-how-shell-targeted-nigeria-oil-protests-1704812.html.

Rowell, Anthony, James Marriott, and Lorne Stockman. 2005. *The Next Gulf: London, Washington and Oil Conflict in Nigeria.* London: Constable and Robinson.

Ryan, Greg. 2001. "It's the Same, But Not." *New York Times,* December 2, 2001, section 4.

Ryder, A. 1965. "A Reconsideration of the Ifẹ̀-Benin Relationship." *Journal of African History* 6:25-37.

Sagner, Andreas. 2000. "Ageing and Social Policy in South Africa: Historical Perspectives with Particular Reference to the Easter Cape." *Journal of Southern African Studies* 26 (3): 523-533.

Sahlins, Marshall. 1961. "The Segmentary Lineage: An Organization of Predatory Expansion." *American Anthropologist* 63:322-43.

———. 1963. "Poor Man, Rich Man, Big-Man, Chief: Political Types in Melanesia and Polynesia." *Comparative Studies in Society and History* 5:285-303.

———. 1985. *Islands of History.* Chicago: University of Chicago Press.

———. 1988. "Cosmologies of Capitalism: The Trans-Pacific Sector of 'The World System.'" *Proceedings of the British Academy* 74.

———. 1991. "The Return of the Event, Again: With Reflections on the Beginnings of the Great Fijian War of 1843 to 1845 between the Kingdoms of Bau and Rewa." In *Clio in Oceania,* ed. Aletta Biersack, 37-100. Washington, D.C.: Smithsonian Institution Press.

———. 1996. "The Sadness of Sweetness; or, The Native Anthropology of Western Cosmology." *Current Anthropology* 37 (3).

———. 2004. *Apologies to Thucydides: Understanding Culture as History and Vice Versa.* Chicago: University of Chicago Press.

——. 2005. "Structural Work: How Microhistories Become Macrohistories and Vice Versa." *Anthropological Theory* 5:5–30.

Sahlins, Peter. 1988. "The Nation in the Village: State-Building and Communal Struggles in the Catalan Borderland during the Eighteenth and Nineteenth Centuries." *Journal of Modern History* 60:234–63.

——. 1991. *Boundaries: The Making of France and Spain in the Pyrenees.* Berkeley and Los Angeles: University of California Press.

Sangren, Steven P. 1984. "Traditional Chinese Corporations: Beyond Kinship." *Journal of Asian Studies* 43 (3): 391–415.

——. 1987. *History and Magical Power in a Chinese Community.* Stanford: Stanford University Press.

Saro-Wiwa, K. 1989. *On a Darkling Plain: An Account of the Nigerian Civil War.* Port Harcourt: Saros International.

——. 1996. "My Story." In Civil Liberties Organisation, *Ogoni: Trials and Travails,* 40–100. Lagos: Civil Liberties Organisation.

Sartre, Jean-Paul. 1972. *Plaidoyer pour les intellectuels.* Paris: Gallimard.

Sasanasobhon, Phra, ed. 1968 (2511 B.E.). *His Majesty King Rama the Fourth (Mongkut).* Commemorative volume. Bangkok: Siva Phorn Limited Partnership.

Schimmel, Annemarie. 1975. *Mystical Dimensions of Islam.* Chapel Hill: University of North Carolina Press.

Schipper, Kristofer M. 1977. "Neighborhood Cult Associations in Traditional Taiwan." In *The City in Late Imperial China,* ed. G. W. Skinner. Stanford: Stanford University Press

——. 1990. "The Cult of Pao-sheng Ta-ti and Its Spreading to Taiwan: A Case Study of *Fen-hsiang.*" In *Development and Decline in Fukien Province in the Seventeenth and Eighteenth Centuries,* ed. E. B. Vermeer, 397–416. Leiden: Brill.

——. 1993. *The Taoist Body.* Trans. Karen C. Duval. Berkeley and Los Angeles: University of California Press.

Scott, James C. 1998. *Seeing Like a State: How Certain Schemes to Improve the Human Condition Have Failed.* New Haven: Yale University Press.

Scott, Michael W. 2007. *Severed Snake: Matrilineages, Making Place, and a Melanesian Christianity in the Southeast Solomons.* Durham: Carolina Academic Press.

Seidel, Anna. 1982. "Tokens of Immortality in Han Graves." *Numen* 29:79–114.

——. 1987. "Traces of Han Religion in Funeral Texts Found in Tombs." In *Dôkyô to shûkyô bunka,* ed. Akitsuki Kan'ei, 21–57. Tokyo: Hirikawa.

Seneviratne, H. L. 1978. *Rituals of the Kandyan State.* Cambridge: Cambridge University Press.

Sengupta, Somini. 2008a. "Army Bombs Headquarters of Rebels in Sri Lanka." *New York Times,* 3 October 2008, World Asia Pacific section.
——. 2008b. "Ethnic Divide Worsens as Sri Lanka Conflict Escalates." *New York Times,* 8 March 2008, World Asia Pacific section.
Siegel, James T. 2000. *The Rope of God.* Ann Arbor: University of Michigan Press.
Silva, José Maria da. 2007. *O Espetáculo do Boi-Bumbá.* Goiânia, Brazil: Editora da Universidade Católica de Goiás.
Silva, Kelly Cristiane. 2003. "A nação cordial: Uma análise dos rituais e das ideologias oficiais da comemoração dos 500 anos do Brasil." *Revista Brasileira de Ciências Sociais* 18:141–60.
——. 2004. "Paradoxos da autodeterminação: A construção do Estado-Nação e práticas da ONU em Timor-Leste." Ph.D. dissertation, Universidade de Brasília.
Silverstein, Michael. 2003. *Talking Politics: The Substance of Style from Abe to "W."* Chicago: Prickly Paradigm Press.
Skinner, G. William. 1959. "Overseas Chinese in Southeast Asia." *Annals of the American Academy of Political and Social Science* 321 (Jan.): 136–47.
——. 1985. "Presidential Address: The Structure of Chinese History." *Journal of Asian Studies* 44, no. 2 (Feb.): 271–92.
Sluka, Jeffrey. 2002. "What Anthropologists Should Know about the Concept of 'Terrorism.'" *Anthropology Today* 18 (2): 22–23.
Smith, D. 2001. "'The Arrow of God': Pentecostalism, Inequality, and the Supernatural in Southeastern Nigeria." *Africa* 71:587–613.
Snodgrass, Adrian. 1985. *The Symbolism of the Stupa.* Ithaca: Cornell University Southeast Asia Program.
Sontag, Susan. 2003. *Regarding the Pain of Others.* New York: Farrar, Straus and Giroux.
Soulet, Jean-François. 1974. *La vie quotidienne dans les Pyrénées sous l'Ancien Régime.* Paris: Hachette.
Southern, Richard. 1970. *Western Society and the Church in the Middle Ages.* London: Harmondsworth.
Sox, David. 1985. *Relics and Shrines.* London and Boston: Allen and Unwin.
Spiro, Melford E. 1971. *Buddhism and Society: A Great Tradition and Its Burmese Vicissitudes.* London: Allen and Unwin.
Staal, Frits. 1986. "The Sound of Religion." *Numen* 33 (2): 185–224.
Standing, Guy, and Michael Samson, eds. 2003. *A Basic Income Grant for South Africa.* Cape Town: University of Cape Town Press.
Statistics South Africa. 2005. *Labour Force Survey, September 2005.* Pretoria: Statistics South Africa.

Steil, Carlos. 1996. *O sertão das romarias. Um estudo antropológico sobre o Santuário de São Jesus da Lapa, Bahia*. Petrópolis, Brazil: Vozes.

———. 2001. "Política, etnia e ritual: O Rio das Rãs como remanescente de quilombos." In *O dito e o feito: Ensaios de antropologia dos rituais*, ed. Marizo Peirano, 197-210. Rio de Janeiro: Relume Dumará.

Stoler, Ann. 2004. "Affective States." In *A Companion to the Anthropology of Politics*, ed. David Nugent and Joan Vincent. Malden, Mass.: Blackwell Publishing.

Strong, John. 1983. *The Legend of King Asoka: A Study and Translation of Asokavadana*. Princeton: Princeton University Press.

———. 2004. *Relics of the Buddha*. Princeton: Princeton University Press.

Suksamran, Somboon. 1982. *Buddhism and Politics in Thailand*. Singapore: Institute of Southeast Asian Studies.

Swain, Simon. 1996. *Hellenism and Empire: Language, Classicism, and Power in the Greek World, AD 50-250*. Oxford: Clarendon Press.

Swearer, Donald. 1999. "Centre and Periphery: Buddhism and Politics in Modern Thailand." In *Buddhism and Politics in Twentieth-Century Asia*, ed. Ian Harrisp, 194-228. London: Pinter.

———. 2004. *Becoming the Buddha: The Ritual of Image Consecration in Thailand*. Princeton: Princeton University Press.

Szonyi, Michael. 1997. "The Illusion of Standardizing the Gods: The Cult of Five Emperors in Late Imperial China." *Journal of Asian Studies* 56 (1): 113-35.

———. 2002. *Practicing Kinship: Lineage and Descent in Late Imperial China*. Stanford: Stanford University Press.

Tambiah, Stanley J. 1968a. "Literacy in a Buddhist Village in North-East Thailand." In *Literacy in Traditional Societies*, ed. Jack Goody, 86-131. Cambridge: Cambridge University Press.

———. 1968b. "The Magical Power of Words." *Man* 3:175-208.

———. 1970. *Buddhism and the Spirit Cults in North-east Thailand*. Cambridge: Cambridge University Press.

———. 1973. "Form and Meaning of Magical Acts." In *Modes of Thought: Essays on Thinking in Western and Non-Western Societies*, ed. R. Horton and R. Finnegan, 199-229. London: Faber and Faber.

———. 1976. *World Conqueror and World Renouncer: A Study of Buddhism and Polity in Thailand against a Historical Background*. Cambridge: Cambridge University Press.

———. 1977. "The Galactic Polity: The Structure of Traditional Kingdoms in Southeast Asia." *Annals of the New York Academy of Sciences* 293:69-97.

———. [1979] 1981. "A Performative Approach to Ritual." *Proceedings of the British Academy* 65 (1979): 113-169.

———. 1982. "Famous Buddha Images and the Legitimation of Kings: The Case of the Sinhala Buddha (Phra Sihing) in Thailand." *Res* 4 (Autumn).

———. 1983a. Interview of S. J. Tambiah. Interviewed by Alan Mac-Farlane. Dspace@Cambridge. http://www.dspace.cam.ac.uk/handle/ 1810/433.

———. 1983b. "On Flying Witches and Flying Canoes: The Coding of Male and Female Values." In *The Kula: New Perspectives on Massim Exchange*, ed. Edmund R. Leach and Jerry Leach. Cambridge: Cambridge University Press.

———. 1984. *The Buddhist Saints of the Forest and the Cult of Amulets: A Study in Charisma, Hagiography, Sectarianism, and Millennial Buddhism.* Cambridge: Cambridge University Press.

———. 1985a. "An Anthropologist's Creed." In *Culture, Thought, and Social Action: An Anthropological Perspective*, 339-60 Cambridge, Mass.: Harvard University Press.

———. 1985b. *Culture, Thought, and Social Action: An Anthropological Perspective.* Cambridge, Mass.: Harvard University Press.

———. 1985c. "On Flying Witches and Flying Canoes: The Coding of Male and Female Values." In *Culture, Thought, and Social Action: An Anthropological Perspective*, 287-315. Cambridge, Mass.: Harvard University Press.

———. 1986. *Sri Lanka: Ethnic Fratricide and the Dismantling of Democracy.* Chicago: University of Chicago Press.

———. 1987. "At the Confluence of Anthropology, History, and Indology." *Contributions to Indian Sociology* 21 (1): 187-216.

———. 1989a. "Ethnic Conflict in the World Today." *American Ethnologist* 16:335-49.

———. 1989b. "King Mahasammata: The First King in the Buddhist Story of Creation, and His Persisting Relevance." *Journal of the Anthropological Society of Oxford* 20 (2): 101-22.

———. 1990. *Magic, Science, Religion, and the Scope of Rationality.* Cambridge: Cambridge University Press.

———. 1992. *Buddhism Betrayed? Religion, Politics, and Violence in Sri Lanka.* Chicago: University of Chicago Press.

———. 1996a. *Leveling Crowds: Ethnonationlist Conflicts and Collective Violence in South Asia.* Berkeley and Los Angeles: University of California Press.

———. 1996b. "The Nation-State in Crisis and the Rise of Ethnonationalism." In *The Politics of Difference*, ed. Edwin N. Wilmsen and Patrick McAllister, 124-43. Chicago: University of Chicago Press.

———. 1996c. "Relations of Analogy and Identity: Toward Multiple Orientations to the World." In *Modes of Thought: Explorations in Culture and Cognition,* ed. D. Olson and N. Torrance, 34–52. Cambridge: Cambridge University Press.

———. 1997a. "Continuity, Integration, and Expanding Horizons." Interview by Mariza Peirano. *Série Antropologia* 230:1–30. http://nrserver34 .net/~danunb/doc/Serie230empdf.pdf.

———. 1997b. "Participation In, and Objectification Of, the Charisma of Saints." In *India and Beyond: Aspects of Literature, Meaning, Ritual and Thought; Essays in Honour of Frits Staal,* ed. Dick Van der Meij. London: Kegan Paul.

———. 1999. "The Shaping of Thailand by the Chakri Dynasty." Special lecture to celebrate His Majesty King Bhumibol Adulyadej's seventy-second birthday. Bangkok: Thammasat University. http:// kanchanapisek.or.th/library/Tambiah-Thailand3.htm.

———. 2002. *Edmund Leach: An Anthropological Life.* Cambridge: Cambridge University Press.

Tambiah, Stanley J., and Jack Goody. 1973. *Bridewealth and Dowry.* Cambridge: Cambridge University Press.

Taminato, Marcel. 2007. "A poética das cores: Memórias passadas e histórias presentes; Uma etnografia na Embaixada Real da Tailândia." M.A. dissertation, Universidade de Brasília.

Taussig, Michael. 1992. *The Nervous System.* New York: Routledge.

Taylor, James L. 1993. *Forest Monks and the Nation-State.* Singapore: Institute of Southeast Asian Studies.

———. 1999. "Post-Modernity, Remaking Tradition and the Hybridisation of Thai Buddhism." *Anthropological Forum* 9 (2): 163–87.

———. 2001. "Embodiment, Nation, and Religio-Politics in Thailand." *South East Asia Research* 9 (2): 129–47.

———. 2007. "Buddhism, Copying, and the Art of the Imagination in Thailand." *Journal of Global Buddhism* 8:1–19.

———. 2008. *Buddhism and Postmodern Imaginings in Thailand: The Religiosity of Urban Space.* Farnham, U.K.: Ashgate Publishing.

Teixeira, Carla C. 1998. *A honra da política: Decoro parlamentar e cassação de mandato no Congresso Nacional.* Rio de Janeiro: Relume Dumará.

———. 1999. "O preço da honra." *Série Antropologia* 253:1–24. http:// nrserver34.net/~danunb/doc/Serie253empdf.pdf.

———. 2001. "Das bravatas: Mentira ritual e retórica da desculpa na cassação de Sérgio Naya." In *O dito e o feito: Ensaios de antropologia dos rituais,* ed. Mariza Peirano, 113–32. Rio de Janeiro: Relume Dumará.

Terray, E. 1975. "Classes and Class Consciousness in the Abron Kingdom of Gyaman." In *Marxist Analyses and Social Anthropology*, ed. M. Bloch, 85-137. London: Malaby Press.

Textor, Robert M. 1977. "The 'Loose Structure' of Thai Society: A Paradigm Under Pressure." *Pacific Affairs* 50 (3): 467-72.

Thanissaro Bhikkhu. 2005. "The Traditions of the Noble Ones: An Essay on the Thai Forest Tradition and Its Relationship with the Dhammayut Hierarchy." Paper presented at the Ninth International Thai Studies Conference, 3-6 April 2005, at Northern Illinois University, DeKalb, Ill.

———. 2007. *The Buddhist Monastic Code*. Vols. 1 and 2. 2nd revised ed. Ubon Ratchathani, Wat Pa Nanachat.

Theidon, Kimberly. 2007. "Transitional Subjects: The Disarmament, Demobilization and Reintegration of Former Combatants in Colombia." *International Journal of Transitional Justice* 1 (1): 66-90.

Thirayuth Boonmee (ธีรยุทธ บุญมี). 2003. *Kwaamkitwang Dawandtok* (*ความคิดหวังตะวันตก*). Bangkok: Winyuchon.

Thomas, N. W. 1910. *Anthropological Report on the Ẹ̀dó-speaking Peoples of Nigeria*. London: Harrison.

Thongchai Winichakul. 2000. "The Quest for '*Siwilai*': A Geographical Discourse of Civilizational Thinking in the Late Nineteenth-Century and Early Twentieth-Century Siam." *Journal of Asian Studies* 59:528-49.

Thucydides. 1996. *The Landmark Thucydides: A Comprehensive Guide to the Peloponnesian War*, ed. Robert B. Strassler. Revised edition of the Richard Crawley translation (1876). New York: Free Press.

Tilton, Doug. 2005. "BIG Fact Sheet #1: Overcoming Dependency with a BIG." Basic Income Grant Coalition website, http://www.big.org.za/index.php?option=articles&task=viewarticle&artid=5.

Todorov, Tzvetan. 2000. *Mémoire de mal, Tentation du bien: Enquête sur le siècle*. Paris: Robert Laffont.

Trainor, Kevin Michael. 1997. *Relics, Ritual, and Representations in Buddhism: Rematerializing the Sri Lanka Theravada Tradition*. Cambridge: Cambridge University Press.

Trajano Filho, Wilson. 1984. "Músicos e música na travessia." M.A. dissertation, Universidade de Brasília.

———. 1993. "Rumores: Uma narrativa da nação". *Série Antropologia* 143:1-35. http://nrserver34.net/~danunb/doc/Serie143empdf.pdf.

———. 1998. "Polymorphic Creoledom: The Creole Society of Guinea-Bissau." Ph.D. dissertation, University of Pennsylvania.

———. 2004. "Narratives on National Identity in the Web." *Vibrant* 1:22-44. Vibrant: Virtual Brazilian Anthropology, http://www.vibrant.org.br/downloads/a1v1_nniw.pdf.

Trimingham, J. Spencer. 1971. *The Sufi Orders in Islam.* London: Oxford
    University Press.

Troeltsch, Ernest. 1949. *The Social Teachings of the Christian Churches.*
    Trans. Olive Wyon. Vol. 1. New York: Free Press.

Úchèṅdù, V. 1977. "Patterns of Ìgbo Social Structure." Paper presented
    at the Institute of African Studies, University of Nigeria, Ṅsụ́ká,
    5-9 April 1977.

———. 1995. "Èzí nà ụ́lọ̀: The Extended Family in Ìgbo Civilization."
    Àhịajíọkú. Lecture, Ministry of Information, Culture, Youth and
    Sports, Òweré [Owerri], Ímò State. IgboNet, http://ahiajoku.igbonet
    .com/1995.

Vajirañāṇavarorasa, Somdet Phra Maha Samana Chao Krom Phraya.
    (Wachirayan). 1992. *The Entrance to the Vinaya: Vinayamukha.* Vol. 1.
    Bangkok: Mahamakut University.

Van der Waal, Kees, and John Sharp. 1988. "The Informal Sector: A New
    Resource." In *South African Keywords: The Uses and Abuses of Political
    Concepts,* ed. Emile Boonzaier and John Sharp. Cape Town: David
    Philip.

Van Spengen, Wim. 2000. *Tibetan Border Worlds: A Geohistoric Analysis of
    Trade and Traders.* London: Kegan Paul International.

Vaughan, F. 2000. *Nigerian Chiefs: Traditional Power in Modern Politics,
    1890s-1990s.* Rochester, N.Y.: University of Rochester Press.

Veidlinger, Daniel M. 2006. *Spreading the Dhamma: Writing, Orality, and
    Textual Transmission in Buddhist Northern Thailand.* Chiangmai: Silk-
    worm Books.

Vernant, Jean-Pierre. 1982. *The Origins of Greek Thought.* Ithaca: Cornell
    University Press.

———. 1983. *Myth and Thought among the Greeks.* London: Routledge and
    Kegan Paul.

Vickers, M. 2000. *Ethnicity and Sub-Nationalism in Nigeria: Movement for a
    Mid-West State.* Oxford: Worldview.

Vlastos, Gregory. 1953. "Isonomia." *American Journal of Philology*
    74:337-66.

Vlastos, Stephen. 2001. "Recalling Roosevelt's Day of Infamy." *Cedar Rap-
    ids Gazette,* 14 September 2001.

Von Glahn, Richard. 2004. *The Sinister Way: The Divine and the Demonic in
    Chinese Religious Culture.* Berkeley and London: University of Califor-
    nia Press.

Wall Street Journal. 2000. "Why Did They Do It?" Article by Peggy
    Noonan, 24 April 2000. http://online.wsj.com/article/SB95652673
    6138049046.html.

Walshe, Maurice, trans. 1996. *Aggañña Sutta*. In *The Long Discourses of the Buddha: A Translation of the Digha Nikaya*. Boston: Wisdom Publications. Originally published 1987, as *Thus Have I Heard: The Long Discourses of the Buddha*.

Walzer, Michael. 2002. "Five Questions about Terrorism." *Dissent* 49 (1): 1-6.

———. 2006. *Just and Unjust Wars: A Moral Argument with Historical Illustrations*. 3rd edition. New York: Basic Books. Originally published 1992.

Washington Post. 2000a. "Rare Act of Congress is Planned for Elián; GOP Leaders Back Citizenship Bills." Article by Karen DeYoung, 16 January 2000. http://www.cubanet.org/CNews/y00/jan00/17e22.htm.

———. 2000b. "A Modern Play of Passions." Article by Gene Weingarten, 6 April 2000. Available as "The Passion of Elian," 7 April 2000, at http://www.washingtonpost.com/wp-dyn/content/article/2008/06/03/AR2008060301281.html.

———. 2000c. "Seeing Mystery and Miracles in Miami." Article by April Witt, 21 April 2000. http://www.latinamericanstudies.org/elian/mystery.htm.

Waters, Tony. *Bureaucratizing the Good Samaritan: The Limitations of Humanitarian Relief Operations*. Boulder: Westview Press.

Watson, James L. 1985. "Standardizing the Gods: The Promotion of Tian Hou ('Empress of Heaven') along the South China Coast, 960-1960." In *Popular Culture in Late Imperial China*, ed. David Johnson, Andrew J. Nathan, and Evelyn S. Rawski, 292-324. Berkeley and Los Angeles: University of California Press.

———. 1988. "The Structure of Chinese Funerary Rites: Elementary Forms, Ritual Sequence, and the Primacy of Performance." In *Death Ritual in Late Imperial and Modern China*. ed. James L. Watson and Evelyn S. Rawski, 3-19. Berkeley and Los Angeles: University of California Press.

Watson, Ruth. 2003. '*Civil Disorder is the Disease of Ìbàdàn': Chieftaincy and Civic Culture in a Yorùbá City*. Oxford: James Currey.

Weber, Eugen. 1976. *Peasants into Frenchmen: The Modernization of Rural France, 1870-1914*. Stanford: Stanford University Press.

Weber, Max. 1970. *From Max Weber: Essays in Sociology*, ed. and trans. Hans H. Gerth and C. Wright Mills. London: Routledge and Kegan Paul.

Weissman, Fabrice. 2004. "Humanitarian Action and Military Intervention: Temptations and Possibilities." Trans. Roger Leverdier. *Disasters* 28:205-15.

Weller, Robert P. 1987. *Unities and Diversities in Chinese Religion*. Seattle: University of Washington Press.

Weller, Robert P., Adam B. Seligman, Michael J. Puett, and Bennett Simon. 2008. *Ritual and Its Consequences: An Essay on the Limits of Sincerity*. Oxford: Oxford University Press.

Westermarck, Edward. 1916. *The Moorish Conception of Holiness*. Helsingfors: Akademiska Bokhandeln.

Whitehead, Neil L., ed. 2004. *Violence*. Sante Fe: School of American Research Press.

Williamson, K. 1985. *Practical Orthography in Nigeria*. Ìbàdàn: Heinemann.

Wilson, Thomas. 2002. "Sacrifice and the Imperial Cult of Confucius." *History of Religions* 41 (3): 251-87.

Wiphaakphojanakhit, Toem. 1970 (2513 B.E.). *Prawatsaat Isaan* (History of the Northeast), vol. 2 (in Thai). Bangkok: Phim Khrangraek.

Wiwa, O. 1996. Testimony of Dr. Owens Wiwa before the Joint Briefing of the United States Congressional Human Rights Caucus and Congressional Black Caucus, 30 January 1996. Sierra Club of Canada, http://www.sierraclub.ca/national/nigeria/testimony-owens-wiwa.html.

Wolf, Arthur P. 1974. "Gods, Ghosts, and Ancestors." In *Religion and Ritual in Chinese Society*, ed. Arthur P. Wolf, 131-82. Stanford: Stanford University Press.

Wolf, Eric R. 1957. "Closed Corporate Peasant Communities in Mesoamerica and Central Java." *Southwestern Journal of Anthropology* 13:1-18.

Woodward, Susan L. 2001. "Humanitarian War: A New Consensus?" *Disasters* 25:331-44.

Yalman, Nur. 1967. *Under the Bo Tree: Studies in Caste, Kinship and Marriage in the Interior of Ceylon*. Berkeley: California University Press.

Yu Ying-Shih. 1987. "'O Soul, Come Back!': A Study in the Changing Conceptions of the Soul and Afterlife in Pre-Buddhist China." *Harvard Journal of Asiatic Studies* 47 (2): 363-95.

Yuan Bingling. 2000. *Chinese Democracies: A Study of the Kongsis of West Borneo (1770-1884)*. CNWS Publications, no. 79. Leiden: Research School of Asian, African, and Amerindian Studies, Leiden University.

Zachernuk, P. 1994. "Of Origins and Colonial Order: Southern Nigerian Historians and the 'Hamitic Hypothesis' c. 1870-1970." *Journal of African History* 35:427-55.

Zito, Angela. 1997. *Of Body and Brush: Grand Sacrifice as Text/Performance in Eighteenth-Century China*. Chicago: University of Chicago Press.

FELICITY AULINO is a medical anthropologist and ethnographic film-maker with primary area specialization in Thailand. She is currently a Mellon Postdoctoral Fellow in the Department of Anthropology at the University of Massachusetts Amherst and the Five College Consortium Program in Culture, Health, and Science.

JAMES FERGUSON is Professor of Anthropology at Stanford University and also holds honorary appointments at the Department of Social Anthropology at the University of Cape Town and the Department of Sociology and Social Anthropology at Stellenbosch University. He is the author or editor of several books, including *The Anti-Politics Machine: Development, Depoliticization, and Bureaucratic Power in Lesotho* (1990) and *Global Shadows: Africa in the Neoliberal World Order* (2006).

MICHAEL M. J. FISCHER is Andrew W. Mellon Professor in the Humanities and Professor of Anthropology and Science and Technology Studies at M.I.T. He is the author of *Zoroastrian Iran between Myth and Praxis* (PhD 1973), *Iran: From Religious Dispute to Revolution* (1980), *Anthropology as Cultural Critique* (with George Marcus, 1986; 2nd edition 1999), *Debating Muslims* (with Mehdi Abedi, 1990), *Emergent Forms of Life and the Anthropological Voice* (2003), *Mute Dreams, Blind Owls, and Dispersed Knowledges: Persian Poesis in the Transnational Circuitry* (2004), and *Anthropological Futures* (2009).

MIRIAM GOHEEN is Professor of Anthropology-Sociology and Black Studies at Amherst College and editor of the *African Studies Review*. She has spent long periods of time living in the Nso' Chiefdom of western Cameroon, where she has conducted extensive research over the past thirty years on political economy, gender, land tenure, and, more recently, youth and globalization. Her many publications include *Men Own the Fields, Women Own the Crops: Gender and Power in the Cameroon Highlands* (1996, 1999).

BYRON J. GOOD is Professor of Medical Anthropology, Department of Global Health and Social Medicine, Harvard Medical School, and Professor in the Department of Anthropology, Harvard University. He is the author of *Medicine, Rationality, and Experience: An Anthropological Perspective* (1994), and an editor of several books, including *Subjectivity: Ethnographic Investigations* (2007) and *Postcolonial Disorders* (2008).

MARY-JO DELVECCHIO GOOD, a comparative sociologist and medical anthropologist, is Professor of Social Medicine, Department of Global Health and Social Medicine, Harvard Medical School; an executive committee member of the Asia Center; and a faculty affiliate of the Weatherhead Center for International Affairs at Harvard University. She is the first editor of and a contributor to *Postcolonial Disorders* (2008) and *Pain as Human Experience* (1994) and the author of *American Medicine: The Quest for Competence* (1995). Her recent publications are devoted to political subjectivity in postcolonial Indonesia and include essays on the remainders of violence and the peace process in post-conflict Aceh.

MICHAEL HERZFELD is Ernest E. Monrad Professor of the Social Sciences at Harvard University. He has conducted extensive ethnographic research in Greece, Italy, and Thailand, focusing in part on nationalism and the competing histories of community and state. His many books include *Evicted from Eternity: The Restructuring of Modern Rome* (2009), *Cultural Intimacy: Social Poetics in the Nation-State* (2nd edition, 2005), *The Poetics of Manhood: Contest and Identity in a Cretan Mountain Village* (1988), and *Anthropology through the Looking-Glass: Critical Ethnography in the Margins of Europe* (1987).

IRVING CHAN JOHNSON is an Assistant Professor in the Southeast Asian Studies Programme at the National University of Singapore. He is currently working on a book on the Thai Buddhist community of Kelantan, Malaysia.

INGRID JORDT is an Associate Professor of Anthropology at the University of Wisconsin, Milwaukee. She is the author of *Burma's Mass Lay Meditation Movement: Buddhism and the Cultural Construction of Power* (2007).

LIISA MALKKI is an Associate Professor of Anthropology at Stanford University. Her published work includes *Purity and Exile: Violence, Memory, and National Cosmology among Hutu Refugees in Tanzania*

(1995) and *Improvising Theory: Process and Temporality in Ethnographic Fieldwork* (2007).

VICTOR MANFREDI has taught linguistics at a dozen universities in Nigeria, Europe, and North America, and since 1992 has been a research fellow in African Studies at Boston University as well as a part-time faculty member there in the fields of linguistics and African languages. He remains involved with Nigerian academic and human rights initiatives, while pursuing a long-term project in the comparative grammar of the Benue-Kwa group of the Niger-Congo language family and in the ideological history of Benue-Kwa speakers.

EMIKO OHNUKI-TIERNEY is William F. Vilas Professor of Anthropology at the University of Wisconsin, Madison. She is the author of numerous books and articles, including *Illness and Culture in Contemporary Japan* (1984) and *Kamikaze, Cherry Blossoms and Nationalisms: The Militarization of Aesthetics in Japanese History* (2002).

MARIZA PEIRANO is Professor of Anthropology at the Universidade de Brasilia (Brazil). She has written on ethnography, ritual, and how anthropology has been conceived in different national contexts. Her latest book is *A teoria vivida e outros ensaios de antropologia* (2006).

MICHAEL PUETT is Professor of Chinese History in the Department of East Asian Languages and Civilizations at Harvard University. He is the author of *The Ambivalence of Creation: Debates Concerning Innovation and Artifice in Early China* (2001) and *To Become a God: Cosmology, Sacrifice, and Self-Divinization in Early China* (2004), as well as co-author, with Adam Seligman, Robert Weller, and Bennett Simon, of *Ritual and Its Consequences: An Essay on the Limits of Sincerity* (2008).

PRISTA RATANAPRUCK is an Assistant Professor in the Department of Anthropology at the University of Virginia. She is currently working on her first book, *Market and Monastery: Manangi Trade Diasporas in South and Southeast Asia*.

MARSHALL SAHLINS is Charles F. Grey Distinguished Service Professor (Emeritus) of Anthropology and of Social Sciences at the University of Chicago.

STANLEY J. TAMBIAH is Esther and Sidney Rabb Professor (Emeritus) of Anthropology at Harvard University. He began field work in Sri Lanka (1956-1959), the island of his birth, and later worked in Thailand. He is the author of ten books, including *World Conqueror and World Renouncer: A Study of Religion and Polity in Thailand against a Historical Background* (1976), *The Buddhist Saints of the Forest and the Cult of Amulets: A Study in Charisma, Hagiography, Sectarianism, and Millennial Buddhism* (1984), *Magic, Science, Religion, and the Scope of Rationality* (1990), *Buddhism Betrayed? Religion, Politics, and Violence in Sri Lanka* (1992), and *Leveling Crowds: Ethnonationalist Conflicts and Collective Violence in South Asia* (1996).

JAMES L. TAYLOR is a Senior Lecturer in Anthropology at the School of Social Sciences, University of Adelaide, Australia. He is the author of *Forest Monks and the Nation-State: An Anthropological and Historical Study in Northeastern Thailand* (1993) and *Buddhism and Postmodern Imaginings in Thailand: The Religiosity of Urban Space* (2008).

www.ingramcontent.com/pod-product-compliance
Lightning Source LLC
Chambersburg PA
CBHW022136020426
42334CB00015B/926